Y0-ARB-556

# Youth Softball:

A Complete Handbook

# Youth Softball:

## A Complete Handbook

**Edited by:** Jill Elliott, M.S.
Martha Ewing, Ph.D.

*Youth Sports Institute*
*Michigan State University*
*Robert Malina, Ph.D., Director*

**COOPER**
Publishing
Group

Copyright © 1992, by Cooper Publishing Group, LLC

ALL RIGHTS RESERVED

No part of this publication may be reproduced, stored in a retrieval system, or transmitted, in any form or by any means, electronic, mechanical photocopying, recording, or otherwise, without the prior written permission of the publisher.

Library of Congress Cataloging in Publication Data:

Elliot, Jill

Youth Softball: A Complete Handbook

Cover Design: Gary Schmitt

Publisher: I. L. Cooper

Library of Congress Catalog Card Number: 88-43250

ISBN: 1-884125-46-8

Printed in the United States of America by Cooper Publishing Group LLC, P.O. Box 562, Carmel, IN 46032.

10 9 8 7 6 5 4 3 2

*The Publisher and Author disclaim responsibility for any adverse effects or consequences from the misapplication or injudicious use of the information contained within this text.*

# YOUTH COACHING SERIES

The Youth Coaching Series of books were written to provide comprehensive guides for coaches, parents, and players participating in youth soccer, baseball, football, softball, and basketball.

Developed by the Youth Sports Institute of Michigan State University, these books meet the guidelines established for youth coaches by the National Association for Sport and Physical Education.

**Books in the Series:**

*Youth Baseball: A Complete Handbook* (ISBN: 01-8)

*Youth Basketball: A Complete Handbook* (ISBN: 44-1)

*Youth Football: A Complete Handbook* (ISBN: 45-X)

*Youth Soccer: A Complete Handbook* (ISBN: 23-9)

*Youth Softball: A Complete Handbook* (ISBN: 46-8)

**For more information about these and other coaching books or to place an order:**

Call: _ 1-317-574-9338

Fax: 1-317-574-9456

Write: Cooper Publishing Group
P.O. Box 562
Carmel, IN 46032

# Contents

---

# Introduction

*Youth Softball* was written for the softball coach of youth ages 6 to 18. The book was designed for coaches who want to improve their teaching effectiveness. The guiding principle of the book was that teaching the skills of softball as well as the concepts of offensive and defensive play is fundamental to the development and enjoyment of each softball participant. In our minds coaching and teaching are synonymous. The goal we had in writing this book was to provide you with a comprehensive understanding of softball skills and the knowledge from sport science to be a more effective coach.

The scope of *Youth Softball* ranges from a description of the role of a softball coach to guidelines for rehabilitation of softball-related injuries. The book is divided into six sections to facilitate the finding of information about specific topics. Each chapter is written with ample illustrations to help the coach gain a clear understanding of the scientific concepts and the skills of softball. A comprehensive set of drills for teaching the skills and strategies of softball is also included in the Appendix. A matrix identifying the skills to be taught by each drill is also included for your convenience.

Youth coaches will find that this book provides many answers to the challenges faced in teaching softball skill techniques. Chapters 7 through 17 pertain to the technical instruction of each skill (including key elements and common errors). The remaining chapters address topics such as planning effective instruction, psychology of coaching youth, and working with parents. These topics are not typically found in coaching books. The 28 chapters contain information that meet the guidelines established for youth coaches as described in *Guidelines for Coaching Education: Youth Sports*, prepared by the National Association for Sport and Physical Education.

The authors of each chapter have had extensive experience coaching and teaching. This technical experience combined with the scientific study of sport becomes readily apparent by the practical suggestions that you will find in each chapter.

This book is written for the coach, but our ultimate goal is to provide youth with a positive and enjoyable experience in softball. It is our hope that all boys and girls will improve their softball skills, have fun playing and being part of a team, and have their self-esteem enhanced as a result of your coaching.

Jill Elliott
*Coach*
*Waverly High School*
*Lansing, Michigan*

Martha E. Ewing, Ph.D.
*Youth Sports Institute*
*Michigan State University*

Tom George
*Youth Sports Institute*
*Michigan State University*

# Acknowledgements

We wish to thank the following individuals for their assistance in the preparation of this book: Steve Eliott for photographing the action sequences; Eileen Northrup, editorial assistant, for her patience during the typing and revision of the manuscript, including the drawing of illustrations via computer; and Tom George and Glenna DeJong for providing the initial templates for the illustrations. Thanks to Tom Smith and Dianne Ulibarri for their comments and critique on the skills chapters. A very special thank you to the youth softball players listed below for their patience during the photo sessions:

Melissa Baldwin
Heather Bouck
Michelle Bryant
Corey Elliott
Ryan Elliott
Trish Franco
Katie Garrison
Justin Gullett
Ryan Gullett
Jason Hadley
Nick Harris

Jenny Lapka
Stephanie Logan
Megan Long
Eileen Malkewitz
Jamie Rutter
Teresa Spedoske
Jason Uslan
Amy Wilinski
Jim Zlomak
Rachael Zlomak

# Section I
# Organizing for the Season

# 1
# Role of the Coach

*Paul Vogel, Ph.D.*

---

QUESTIONS TO CONSIDER

- What are the primary roles of a youth softball coach?
- What benefits does softball offer participants?
- What potential detriments can occur in the presence of inadequate adult leadership?
- What principal goals should a coach seek to achieve?

---

## INTRODUCTION

For young people participating in a softball program, the quality and subsequent benefits of their experience is determined largely by their coach. Strong leadership during practices, games, and special events encourages each young person to nurture and develop individual strengths physically, psychologically, and socially. Poor or weak leadership not only inhibits such growth, it may actually undermine a youth's existing strengths in these areas.

While it is difficult to provide a totally beneficial experience, as a softball coach it is your responsibility to ensure that the benefits gained by each youth far outweigh the detriments. To accomplish this, you must know what these benefits and detriments are, and you must plan each practice and activity carefully to maximize the benefits for each child.

### Possible Benefits for Participants

The numerous benefits for youth include:

- developing appropriate skills
- developing physical fitness

- learning appropriate conditioning techniques that affect health and performance
- developing a realistic and positive self-image
- developing a lifetime pattern of regular physical activity
- developing a respect for rules as facilitators of safe and fair play
- obtaining enjoyment and recreation
- developing positive personal, social, and psychological skills (e.g., self-worth, self-discipline, team work, goal-setting, self-control)

Many players achieve significant benefits in at least some of these areas depending on the frequency, duration, and intensity of participation and the quality of coaching leadership.

*Many significant benefits can be gained in youth softball.*

### Possible Detriments for Participants

Players are likely to benefit from a softball program when the coach sets appropriate objectives in the areas of skill, knowledge, fitness, and personal/social development. If, however, the coach sets inappropriate goals or teaches poorly, detriments may result.

To fully understand the value of a good coach, contrast the benefits listed previously with these possible detriments for the participant:

- developing inappropriate physical skills
- sustaining injury, illness, or loss of physical fitness
- learning incorrect rules and strategies of play
- learning incorrect conditioning techniques
- developing a negative or unrealistic self-image
- avoiding future participation in activity for self and others
- learning to misuse rules to gain unfair or unsafe advantages
- developing a fear of failure
- developing anti-social behaviors
- wasting time that could have been made available for other activities

When incorrect techniques and negative behaviors are learned by young athletes, the next coach must perform the difficult and time-consuming task of extinguishing these behaviors.

To maximize the benefits and minimize the detriments, you must understand your role as a softball coach and provide quality leadership.

*The benefits of participation relate directly to the quality of leadership.*

## GOALS FOR THE COACH

As a coach, it is important to:

1. effectively teach the individual techniques, rules, and strategies of the game in an orderly and enjoyable environment
2. appropriately challenge the cardiovascular and muscular systems of your players through active practice sessions and games
3. teach and model desirable personal, social, and psychological skills

Winning is also an important goal for the coach and participants but it is one you have little control over because winning is often contingent on outside factors (e.g., the skills of the opposition, calls made by umpires). If you con-

centrate on the three areas mentioned and become an effective leader, winning becomes a natural by-product.

The degree of success you attain in achieving these goals is determined by the extent to which you make appropriate choices and take correct actions in organizing and administering, teaching and leading, and protecting and caring.

## Organization and Administration

Effective coaching relies heavily on good organization and administration. Organization involves clearly identifying the goals and objectives that must be attained if you are going to create a beneficial experience (with few detriments) for the participating youths. Steps necessary to organize the season so it can be efficiently administered include:

- identifying your primary purposes as a coach
- identifying goals for the season
- selecting and organizing the season's objectives
- selecting and implementing the activities in practices and games that lead to achievement of the objectives
- evaluating the effects of your actions

Specific information, procedures, criteria, and examples necessary to effectively complete these steps are included in Chapter 3, Chapter 4, and Chapter 23.

## Teaching and Leading

Teaching and leading are the core of coaching activity. Principles of effective instruction such as setting appropriate player expectations, using clear instructions, maintaining an orderly environment, maximizing the amount of practice time that is "on task," monitoring progress, and providing specific feedback are included in Chapter 4. This chapter gives you many insights into how you may effectively teach your players. Other important information for teaching and leading young athletes includes motivating your players, communicating effectively, maintaining discipline, and developing good personal and social skills. Coaching guidelines for each of these areas are included in Section 5.

*The only real control you have over winning and/or*

*losing is the manner in which you plan and conduct your practices and supervise your games.*

Because of the influence you have as "coach," your players will model the behaviors you exhibit. If you respond to competition (successes and failures), fair play, umpires' calls, and/or spectators' comments with a positive and constructive attitude, your players are likely to imitate that positive behavior. If, however, you lose your temper, yell at umpires, or bend and/or break rules to gain an unfair advantage, your players' actions are likely to become negative. When what you say differs from what you do, your players will be most strongly affected by what you do. Negative behavior by players can occur even if you tell them to "be good sports and to show respect to others" and then ignore this advice by acting in a contrary manner. In essence, "actions speak louder than words" and you must "practice what you preach" if you hope to positively influence your players' behavior.

## Protecting and Caring

Although coaches often eliminate the potential for injury from their minds, it is impor-tant for them to (a) plan for injury prevention, (b) effectively deal with injuries when they occur, and (c) meet their legal responsibilities to act prudently. The information on legal liabilities in Section 1, and conditioning youth softball players, nutrition for successful performance, and prevention, care, and rehabilitation of common softball injuries in Section 6, provides the basis for prudent and effective action in these areas.

## SUMMARY

Your primary purpose as a youth softball coach is to maximize the benefits of participation in softball while minimizing the detriments. To achieve this, you must organize, teach, model, and evaluate effectively. Your players learn not only from what you teach but from what you consciously or unconsciously do. You're a very significant person in the eyes of your players. They notice when you're organized and fair, are a good instructor, know the rules, are interested in them or in the win/loss record, know how to control your emotions, know how to present yourself, and treat others with respect. The choices you make and the actions you take determine how beneficial the experience is for the members of your team..

# 2
# Legal Liabilities

*Bernard Patrick Maloy, J.D., M.S.A.*
*Vern Seefeldt, Ph.D.*

---

### QUESTIONS TO CONSIDER

- In terms of legal liability, what are the coaching duties?
- Against which risks to their players are coaches responsible for taking reasonable precautions?
- Do children who participate in youth sports assume the risk of their own injuries?
- What influence does the age and maturity of the athletes have upon the coach?
- Do coaches' legal responsibilities to their players extend beyond the field of play?
- Are coaches responsible for informing players, parents, and guardians about the risks and hazards inherent in sports?
- What legal responsibilities do coaches have to their players when coaches delegate duties to assistants?

---

## INTRODUCTION

It is inevitable that the role of a coach is expanded beyond that of mere instructor or supervisor when it comes to working with youth sports. Because coaches are the most visible administrators to players, parents, and officials, they are expected to handle anything from correcting player rosters to picking up equipment on the field, from assuaging parents' feelings to arranging transportation for players. While these duties may tax the limits of a coach's patience, they remain very important areas of responsibility.

## LEGAL DUTIES

Coaches are subject to certain terms of legal responsibility. However, it would be wrong to assume these legal duties were created by the courts to be imposed on the coaching profession. They are time-honored, recognized obligations inherent in the coaching profession. Thus, they should be termed coaching responsibilities (see Chapter 1). These are responsibilities expected of a coach regardless of pay and regardless of whether the coaching is performed for a school, a religious organization, or a youth sports association.

## WHERE DOES COACHING RESPONSIBILITY BEGIN?

The primary responsibility of coaches is to know their players. In that regard it is always important to remember that young athletes are children first, athletes second. The degree of responsibility that coaches owe their teams is measured by the age and maturity of their players. The younger and more immature a player, the more responsibility a coach bears in regard to the instruction, supervision, and safety of that child (see Chapter 26). Additionally, the coach is expected to be aware of any physical or mental handicap that a player may have and must know how to recognize emergency symptoms requiring medical attention (see Chapter 27). A coach in youth sports must always bear in mind that:

- Nine-year-olds participating in organized sport activities for the first time require more instruction and attention than teenagers with playing experience.
- A 10-year-old child should not be expected to behave, on or off the playing court, differently than other 10-year-old children.
- All children with special needs or handicaps must be identified.
- A plan for the emergency treatment of children with special needs and those who sustain injuries should be devised.

As will be discussed, coaches do not have to guarantee the safety of their young players. However, coaches are responsible for taking reasonable precautions against all foreseeable risks that threaten their players. Coaches must realize that those precautions are not measured by what they thought was reasonable, but rather by what was reasonable according to the age and maturity of their players.

## Do You Know How to Coach?

The volunteer coach is the backbone of many organized youth activities. Nevertheless, despite good intentions, some degrees of qualifications and certification are necessary for responsible coaching. Therefore, in addition to personal athletic experience and background, coaches should attend programs and seminars on the development of athletic skills, youth motivation, and emergency medical treatment. A coach's responsibility begins with an understanding of current methods of conditioning (Chapter 24), skill development (Section 3), and injury prevention and care (Chapters 26 and 27).

*Coaches have certain responsibilities that they may not transfer to assistant coaches, parents, or league officials.*

In many cases, a youth sports league or association offers classes, materials, or advice on skill development and injury prevention and care. Generally, those associations require some certification or recommendation regarding coaching background, skills, and experience before an applicant is permitted to coach youth sports. Coaches must avail themselves of instructional programs or other information helpful for coaching youth sports. In other words, coaches are responsible for their own incompetencies. A youth sports coach should create a competency checklist:

- Does the youth sports association certify its coaches?
- Does the association require coaches to attend coaching clinics and emergency medical programs?
- Do you know how to identify the necessary individual athletic skills based on size, weight, and age?
- Do you know of any agencies that will help identify those skills?
- What steps should you take to become certified in first aid treatment?

*Knowledge of your coaching incompetencies is the first step toward seeking a corrective solution.*

Coaches must be able to recognize their limitations. Acknowledging that skills, youth motivation, and medical treatment may be different today than when you played is the first step toward becoming a responsible coach.

## Where Do Your Coaching Duties Lie?

As noted, youth sports coaches are many things to their teams, parents and guardians, and supporters. Coaching responsibilities extend to areas beyond the softball field. These responsibilities require the same effort and devotion as on-the-field duties and may include:

- league or team fund-raising activities
- assisting during registration periods
- talking to interested players and their par-

ents about the league and its athletic and social goals
- providing or planning team transportation to and from practices and games
- attending league or association meetings
- buying, selecting, or maintaining equipment
- maintaining locker rooms and field areas
- supervising players during pre-practice and post-practice periods

## What Misconceptions Do Many Coaches Have?

There are two common misconceptions regarding youth sports. The first is that children participating generally assume the risk of their own injury; the second, that the role of the coach is severely limited by legal liability.

The legal defense of assumption of risk as it applies to sports is very specific. An athlete assumes the risk of injury from dangers inherent to the sport itself. In other words, it is recognized that injuries occur, especially in sports such as softball (e.g., the collision of two players chasing a fly ball, the injury of a player on the field resulting from an errant pitch).

Many risks confronting athletes are not inherent to the sport; rather, they're the result of improper instruction, supervision, or equipment (e.g., protective equipment or gloves that are defective or have been poorly fit, lack of instruction in athletic skills).

The interpretation of *assumption of risk* is complicated when it is applied to youth sports because young athletes require careful supervision regarding their own welfare. The concept that young athletes must assume the responsibility for their injuries sustained in practices or games must be contrasted with whether or not the coach or other adult supervisors were negligent in their instruction and supervision of the activity. In such a comparison it is unlikely that responsibility for *assumption of risk* will serve as a viable excuse.

*When an injury occurs in youth sports, the coaches responsibility is considered a much greater factor than the assumption of risk by the player.*

Fortunately, most coaches inherently understand the limitations involved in *assumption of*

*risk*. The motivation for many youth coaches is the involvement of their own children in sports. And, like most parents, those coaches accept injury as a natural risk of the sport, but they will not tolerate an injury resulting from lack of proper skill development or poor equipment.

Youth sport coaches should concern themselves less with whether adhering to these responsibilities is good legal protection, and more with the thought that their actions represent the standards expected of youth sport coaches. Actually, the areas of expertise legally required of coaches can serve as measures of qualification and certification. Youth sport leagues and conferences realize that coaches must adhere to legal principles of liability not merely to protect the league and the coach from costly litigation but also to ensure that children continue to participate in athletics. It's very doubtful that parents would continue to support youth sports programs that were plagued by poor coaching, lack of supervision, or poor medical treatment procedures. In short, these imposed responsibilities are good business practices for youth sports.

## COACHING RESPONSIBILITIES

As a youth softball coach you have many responsibilities beyond teaching your players the skills and techniques of softball. Your coaching responsibilities are: providing proper instruction, providing reasonable supervision, warning of hazards and risks, providing competent personnel, preventing and caring for injuries, providing safe equipment, and selecting participants. Each of these responsibilities are discussed in subsequent sections.

### Providing Proper Instruction

A coach must teach the physical skills and mental discipline or attitude required to play softball (see Sections 3, 4, and 5). You must enhance the development of those skills while reducing the chance of injury. Specifically, volunteer coaches, who represent that they can teach the sport or activity, must be aware of the rules of safety and know how to teach the proper methods of conditioning. For example, when young players are injured, coaches should be prepared to competently assess whether:

- the conditioning or skill drills are realistic for players of young or immature years
- video, film, or written materials, in addition to on-field instruction, would improve instructional techniques
- the players are taught the correct way to wear equipment
- all the players, starters and substitutes, have been given the same amount of time, instruction, and practice on the correct methods of play, conditioning, and the rules
- conditioning techniques and skill drills are current
- coaching methods are accurately evaluated by the league
- parental comments and concerns have been integrated into the coaching instruction
- provision has been made in coaching instruction for learning-disabled and mentally or emotionally handicapped children who participate
- criticism or comments regarding coaching instruction are met with a positive response

The foregoing list consists of some expectations a parent or guardian has of a coach. While those expectations impact heavily on liability, they more accurately serve as guidelines by which youth sports coaches can evaluate their instruction. Again, a youth sports coach must remember that the age and immaturity of the players are key factors to instructional techniques. The coach must be sensitive to the outside environment in which a young player lives, as well as the sports environment created by the coach. Only then can you ensure a youngster the full benefit of your instruction (see Chapter 1).

## Providing Reasonable Supervision

A coach is responsible for the reasonable supervision of the players. There is little question that this responsibility starts on the field of play during all practices and games. Again, the scope of this responsibility depends on the age and maturity of the players. The younger the player, the greater the degree of responsibility a coach must take for the player's safe supervision.

In youth sports, a coach's supervisory responsibility may extend to times and places other than the field. In some instances, this may include managing parents or guardians and supporters as well as the players and assistant coaches. A coach's checklist of potential supervisory functions should question:

- Is there a supervisor available for a reasonable time before and after practice?
- Have parents or guardians advised who will pick up their children after practices and games?
- Who is assigned to remain with the players until all have been called for, according to instructions provided by parents or guardians?
- How are parents or guardians notified of practice and game times, dates, and places?
- Who is responsible for player transportation to and from games?
- Are substitute players supervised off the field during games?
- Are players allowed off the field during practice for bathroom or other personal comforts? If so, how are those players supervised?

Many youth sports leagues or associations have a rule that coaches are responsible for the behavior of team parents, guardians, and fans. Such a rule becomes very important in those instances where parents believe their child has been slighted on the field during play, or off the field from lack of play. Coaches should recognize that their conduct can incite parents, guardians, and supporters. A coach must ask:

- Have team and league rules regarding parental involvement, the rules of play, and rules regarding team participation been communicated to parents and guardians?
- Do parents and guardians know my coaching philosophy and team goals?
- Have the team and parents and guardians been notified that only the coach is permitted to discuss a decision with a referee?

The coach's role in supervision of the softball field can be made easier by holding a parents' orientation meeting at the start of the season (see Chapter 18). The parents have a right to know what to expect of the coach. Also, the meeting prepares parents to become actively involved with other parents in stopping any unruly conduct. Again, the supervisory responsibility starts with coaches who conduct themselves in the spirit of good sportsmanship. It also includes a coach's support of game officials in order to defuse angry parents, guardians, supporters, or players.

## Warning About Hazards and Risks

A coach is responsible for informing players, parents, and guardians about the risks and hazards inherent to softball. Obviously, it's not expected that coaches will dissuade parents and guardians from permitting their youngsters to participate. By the same token, a coach's experience and knowledge helps to assure parents and guardians that the greatest care possible will be taken for the well-being of their children.

The age and maturity of the players play a major role in the degree of risk from playing softball. Older, more experienced children may face a greater risk of injury from softball simply due to the more sophisticated style of play. However, those children and their parents or guardians already should be fairly well-versed in the risks of softball. Therefore, they don't need the same information and assurances as parents and guardians whose children are younger and have never participated.

*The coach must inform athletes and parents of the potential dangers inherent in playing youth softball.*

The youth league or association may provide information regarding sports hazards, but the responsibility to warn parents and athletes remains a very important coaching duty (see Chapter 26). Therefore, a coach would be well-served to provide parents, guardians, and players with as much information and materials as possible regarding softball at registration, as well as during the season. The coach must be prepared to instruct or advise:

- how many injuries his or her teams with similar age and experience have suffered, and what types of injuries occurred
- what types of equipment, clothing, or shoes are not recommended or permitted for play
- how equipment should properly fit
- what written, video, or audio materials are available that will instruct parents and guardians about the sport and its risks

- what style, conduct, or manner of play is to be avoided due to the likelihood of injury to the player or an opponent
- what conduct or manner of play is not permitted under the rules
- whether the field and facilities have been inspected for hazards and determined to be safe for play

*Hosting a parents' orientation meeting prior to the first game is an excellent way to describe your role in the prevention and care of their children's injuries.*

## Providing Competent Personnel

We've already examined the coach's responsibility to provide quality instruction. Also, we have examined many of the attendant roles and duties that coaches must provide with that instruction. In many cases, the sheer numbers of players and responsibilities demand that a coach have some assistance. It is not unusual for a coach to delegate some of those coaching or supervisory duties to assistant coaches or parents (see Supplement 18-8). However, the coach must ensure that the people who are assisting are competent. Obviously, having a responsible coach is of little value if the players are subject to the directions of incompetent assistants. Therefore, in a coach's absence, an assistant coach or aide must be able to provide the same responsible instruction and supervision as the players and parents expect from the head coach. It is wise, then, for a coach to learn:

- whether the league or association certifies assistant coaches
- what policies the league or association has regarding the use of parents for supervision, transportation, or instruction
- whether assistant coaches have any hidden past regarding child abuse or other conduct that constitutes a threat to children
- whether there is any reason to suspect an assistant's or aide's coaching competency
- whether teenagers may be qualified as assistants with coaching and supervisory duties

It is a coach's responsibility to determine whether assistant coaches and team aides are qualified to step into the coach's shoes.

## Preventing and Caring for Injuries

There are few areas that demand as much attention as the prevention and care of injuries (see Chapters 26 and 27). It is not uncommon to find youth sports programs conducting softball practices without qualified medical personnel or knowledgeable athletic trainers readily available. In those instances, the first attendant to an injured player is usually the coach or teammates. The coach's responsibility is to recognize when immediate medical treatment is required and to ensure that assistant coaches and teammates do not attempt to touch, move, or help the injured player. Obviously, the care of injuries can be a very confusing task.

Many problems in the initial care of athletic injuries might be solved if coaches were required to qualify as emergency medical technicians, or to have some type of comparable training in first aid and health care. In the absence of those qualifications, however, coaches must use their best discretion, based on experience. Obviously, those deficiencies are compounded in youth sports where most of the coaches are volunteers.

In addition to recognizing when emergency medical help is needed, a coach must be able to recognize symptoms of medical problems. If a player has a disease, diabetes for instance, the coach has the responsibility for checking with the player's parents about medication, learning how to recognize the symptoms of shock or deficiency, and what type of emergency treatment to request.

A coach must also be aware of the effects a conditioning program may have on players (see Chapter 24). For instance, if practices are conducted during hot weather, a coach should provide ample water (see Chapter 25), change the time of practice to early morning or late afternoon, learn the symptoms of heat stroke or exhaustion, and learn how to provide for immediate care (see Chapter 27).

It's impossible to categorize all the areas of concern for injuries that a coach may face. However, there are precautions that you can take to ensure that your responsibilities have been reasonably met:

- Attend league-sponsored programs dealing with athletic injuries.

- Check with local health authorities, local hospitals, and coaching associations to learn about the availability of emergency medical care at the field.
- Implement a plan for the immediate notification of parents or guardians in case their child is seriously injured.
- Do not attempt unfamiliar care without emergency medical competency or ability.
- Identify players with specific medical handicaps before the season and prepare reasonable emergency plans in case of sudden illness.
- Do not permit players who have suffered injuries requiring medical attention to play or participate until their return to practice and competition has been approved by a physician.
- Notify parents or guardians of any minor injuries occurring to, or complaints by, their children.

It is wise to document the circumstances of a serious injury (see Chapter 27). In many cases, a written report shows that coaches have reasonably met their responsibility. Such a report is also helpful to medical personnel in the subsequent treatment of an injury. The documentation should include:

- a record of all facts surrounding the injury including who, when, and where the injury occurred and the injured player's responses
- a list and description of the equipment involved, if any
- a list of those who witnessed the injury
- a record of actions taken in response to the injury prior to the arrival of medical personnel

When completed, provide copies of the injury report to the attending physician, the medical response personnel, and the league or association. Be sure to keep a copy for your own files.

## Providing Equipment

A coach must take reasonable care to provide the team with proper and safe equipment (see Supplement 18-6). You should know the various types and brands of equipment, master the proper maintenance procedures, and learn to outfit players properly and safely. Generally, you are not responsible for equipment defects unless you're directly involved in the manufacture of equipment. However, you are expected to know whether or not the proper equipment is being used, or if it is defective, and to ensure that defective equipment is not distributed to players. A coach must take reasonable care to:

- select or recommend the proper equipment for the sport
- select or recommend specific types of equipment for specific uses
- properly fit players
- verify that old equipment has been properly reconditioned or recertified for use
- disallow players who are not properly equipped and dressed to participate in practices or games
- have knowledge of league or association rules regarding proper dress and equipment
- instruct players and parents on the proper maintenance of sports equipment in their possession
- utilize a written inventory for reporting and tracking the repair of damaged equipment
- become aware of manufacturers' recommendations and warnings

### Selecting Participants

A softball coach is obligated to protect the health and safety of players during practices and games. The potential for injuries to occur in softball is reduced when players are matched according to size, age, and playing experience. Injuries that occur when players are mismatched in terms of body size and playing experience are more likely to be viewed as the result of irresponsible teaching and supervision rather than as an inherent risk of playing softball.

Coaches should protect players by following these guidelines:

- Never permit an injured athlete to compete in practices and games.
- Never allow athletes who are out of condition to compete.
- Never place players in drills in which there is the potential for mismatches in physical conditioning, chronological age, and/or skill level.

## SUMMARY

A youth sports coach cannot guarantee a child's safety. Legally, a coach is responsible for reasonably foreseeing risks and hazards to the players.

For example, if a youth sports group uses a field that has permanent fences or light poles near the foul lines, or if the field has holes in it from other activities, a coach should recognize the foreseeable risks to players and supervise, instruct, and/or warn of those dangers.

Some consider this foreseeability factor as a legal precept. However, it is predicated on knowledge and experience of softball. Therefore, its true application is not in legal theory but in the real world of sports.

The curricular objectives for youth sports coaches are defined in the following reference: *Guidelines for Coaching Education: Youth Sports*, National Association for Sport and Physical Education, 1986. The *Guidelines* identify the competencies that coaches of young athletes should possess or acquire. The competencies are listed under five categories of content within the general title of "Scientific Bases of Coaching." An outline of the content follows:

### Curricular Objectives for Youth Sport Coaches

#### Scientific Bases of Coaching

*A. Medical-Legal Aspects of Coaching*

Every young athlete should be provided a safe and healthful environment in which to participate. The coach should have basic knowledge and skills in the prevention of athletic injuries, and basic knowledge of first aid.

Every youth sports coach should:

1. Demonstrate knowledge and skill in the prevention and care of injuries generally associated with participation in athletics
2. Be able to plan and coordinate procedures for the emergency care of athletes
3. Be knowledgeable about the legal responsibilities of coaching, including insurance coverage for the coach and athlete
4. Recognize and insist on safe playing conditions and the proper use of protective equipment

5. Be able to provide young athletes with basic information about injury prevention, injury reporting, and sources of medical care

### B. Training and Conditioning of Young Athletes

Every youth sport athlete should receive appropriate physical conditioning for sports participation. The coach should use acceptable procedures in their training and conditioning programs.

Every youth sports coach should:

1. Be able to demonstrate the basic knowledges and techniques in the training and conditioning of athletes
2. Recognize the developmental capabilities of young athletes and adjust training and conditioning programs to meet these capabilities
3. Know the effects of the environmental conditions (e.g., heat, cold, humidity, air quality) on young athletes and adjust practice and games accordingly
4. Be able to recognize the various indications of over-training, which may result in injury and/or staleness in athletes, and be able to modify programs to overcome these consequences

### C. Psychological Aspects of Coaching

A positive social and emotional environment should be created for young athletes. The coach should recognize and understand the developmental nature of the young athlete's motivation for sport competition and adjust his/her expectations accordingly.

Every youth sports coach should:

1. Subscribe to a philosophy that emphasizes the personal growth of individuals by encouraging and rewarding achievement of personal goals and demonstration of effort, as opposed to overemphasis on winning
2. Demonstrate appropriate behavior of young athletes by maintaining emotional control and demonstrating respect to athletes, officials, and fellow coaches
3. Demonstrate effective communication skills such as those needed to provide appropriate feedback, use a positive approach, motivate athletes, and demonstrate proper listening skills
4. Emphasize and encourage discussion of matters concerning the display of sportsmanship in competitive and noncompetitive situations
5. Be sufficiently familiar with the principles of motivation, including goal setting and reinforcement, in order to apply them in constructive ways
6. Be able to structure practice and competitive situations to reduce undue stress, and/or to teach young athletes how to reduce any undue stress they experience related to performance

### D. Growth, Development, and Learning of Youth Athletes

Youth athletes should have positive learning experiences. The coach should have a knowledge of basic learning principles and consider the influence of developmental level on the athlete's performance.

Every youth sports coach should:

1. Recognize the physical and cognitive changes that occur as children develop and how these changes influence their ability to learn sports skills
2. Concentrate on the development of fundamental motor and cognitive skills that lead to improvement of specific sports skills
3. Understand the physical and cognitive differences manifested by early and late maturers

### E. Techniques of Coaching Young Athletes

Every young athlete should have the opportunity to participate regularly in a sport of his/her choosing. The coach should provide guidance for successful learning and performance of specific sport techniques, based on the maturity level or proficiency of the athlete.

Every youth sports coach should:

1. Know the key elements of sport principles and technical skills and the various teaching styles that can be used to introduce and refine them
2. Recognize that young athletes learn at different rates and accommodate these differences by flexibility in teaching styles
3. Be able to organize and conduct practices throughout the season in order to provide maximal learning

4. Be able to select appropriate skills and drills, and analyze errors in performance
5. Be able to provide challenging but safe and successful experiences for young athletes by making appropriate modifications during participation
6. Understand why rules and equipment should be modified for children's sports

## Implementation

These guidelines are considered the minimum levels toward which youth sport coaching education programs should strive. To cover the topics of Sections A-D requires at least three hours of clinic time plus additional home study. Another three hours should be devoted to the techniques of coaching session.

Presentations developed for the scientific bases of coaching (Sections A-D) should be as sport specific as possible. The frequent use of audiovisual aids such as videotapes, films, overheads, and slides is helpful. Presentations should be short, with numerous practical examples as well as opportunities for practical exercises and questions. Having materials (e.g., books, pamphlets, self study exams) available for the coaches to study either prior to or following the clinic is essential for adequate coverage of the topics.

For additional information about youth sport coaching education materials and organizations, write the Youth Sports Coalition Steering Committee, 1900 Association Drive, Reston, VA 22091.

**REFERENCES**

Berry, R., & Wong, G. (1986). *Law and business of the sports industries.* (Vol. II, pp. 227-302, 320-341). Dover, MA: Auburn House Publishing Co.

Clement, A. (1988). *Law in sport and physical activity.* (pp. 27-61). Indianapolis, IN: Benchmark Press.

Maloy, B. (1988). *Law in sports: Liability cases in management and administration.* Indianapolis, IN: Benchmark Press.

National Association for Sport and Physical Education. (1986) *Guidelines for Coaching Education.* Reston, VA: Youth Sports.

Responsibility is also Part of the Game. *Trial, 13,* 22-25, January, 1977.

Schubert, G., Smith, R., & Trentadue, J. (1986). *Sports law.* (pp. 220-231). St. Paul, MN: West Publishing Co.

Seefeldt, V. (1985). Legal liability. In P. Vogel & K. Blase (Eds.), *AHAUS associate coaches manual: Fundamentals of coaching youth ice hockey.* (pp. 167-174). East Lansing, MI: Institute for the Study of Youth Sports.

Wong, G. (1988). *Essentials of amateur sports law.* (pp. 336-350). Dover, MA: Auburn House Publishing Co.

# 3
# Planning for the Season

*Paul Vogel, Ph.D.*

QUESTIONS TO CONSIDER

- Why should planning for the entire season precede day-to-day planning?
- What steps should a coach follow when organizing for the season?
- What skills, knowledge, aspects of fitness, and personal/social skills should be included as objectives for the season?
- How should the season be organized to be most effective from a coaching–learning point of view?

## INTRODUCTION

Planning for the season involves two basic tasks. First, coaches must select the content that will be the focus of instruction during the season (objectives that involve physical skills, sport-related knowledge, fitness capacities, and personal/social skills). Second, these desired outcomes should be organized into a plan from which practices, games, and other events can be efficiently managed.

What follows provides reasons why season planning is useful and gives you steps necessary to develop a season's plan as well as examples of season objectives. Materials and examples are also provided at the end of this chapter for completing your season plan.

## WHY PLAN?

Coaches agree that teaching the skills, rules, and strategies of softball are among their primary responsibilities. Most coaches would also agree that improving the physical condition of the players, promoting enjoyment of the game, teaching good sportsmanship, and attempting to avoid physical and psychological injury are also outcomes they wish to achieve. Many coaches however, fail to recognize the importance of planning to accomplish these goals.

*Achievement of goals and objectives requires effective planning.*

Organized practices are vital to maximizing the benefits of softball. Disorganized practices often result in players failing to obtain desired skills, knowledge, fitness, and attitudes and often contribute to injuries. Organizing your season and planning your practices prior to going on the field can result in the following benefits:

- efficient use of limited practice time
- inclusion of season objectives that are most essential
- appropriate sequence of season objectives
- directing practice activities to the season's goals and objectives
- reduction of the time required for planning
- enhanced preparation of the team for competition
- improved ability to make day-to-day adjustments in practice objectives
- deterrent to lawsuits involving coaches' liability

## DEVELOPING A SEASON PLAN

Use these three steps to develop a season plan:

1. Identify the goals and objectives of the season
2. Sequence the season objectives into the pre, early, mid, and late portions of the season
3. Identify practice objectives

The relationship of these three steps to fulfilling your role as the coach and to evaluating the outcomes you desire for your players is illustrated in Figure 3-1.

### Identify Goals and Objectives for the Season

Your primary role as coach is to maximize the benefits for your players while minimizing the potential detrimental effects of participation. This alone provides the basis for identifying the specific goals and objectives for your coaching effort. You will affect your players either positively or negatively in each of the following areas:

- physical skills (hitting, throwing, catching, fielding, pitching, bunting, baserunning, offensive and defensive strategies)
- knowledge (rules, tactics, training techniques, terminology, nutrition, safety)
- fitness (muscular strength, endurance, flexibility, aerobic fitness)
- personal/social skills (enjoyment of softball, motivation, discipline, sportsmanship, other character traits)

By thinking of these four broad areas of player outcomes as goals, you are taking the initial step toward fulfilling your major role of "maximizing the benefits" of participation in softball and "minimizing the potential detrimental effects of participation" by clearly specifying the objectives for the season.

Although the identification of goals is an important first step, it is the selection of specific objectives within each goal area that provides the direction necessary to organize the season and plan effective practices.

### Selecting Skill Objectives

Supplement 3-1 provides you with a list of objectives for each physical skill area. By reviewing the individual techniques listed, you can select objectives that are best for your players. To help with this task, appropriate objectives for players at five levels of play (beginning, ages 6, 7-8, 9-10; intermediate, ages 11-13, and advanced, ages 14 and over) are suggested. A detailed description of each of these individual techniques, including key elements and common errors in their performance, as well as progressions for teaching, can be found in Section 3. The key elements of performance are the bases for assessing players and for focusing your coaching efforts. This information should be reviewed if you do not have a good understanding of these individual techniques.

### Selecting Knowledge Objectives

Cognitive outcomes (e.g., knowledge of rules, strategies, and information related to physical conditioning) are important for your players. Rules pertaining to softball, how to warm up and cool down, what to eat for a pregame meal, and exercises to avoid are all important objectives because they can influence a player's performance. Objectives that include cognitive skills are listed in Supplement 3-2. You may wish to add to, delete from, or alter the objectives on this list as you determine those that are most appropriate for your team. By identifying these objectives, it's more likely they'll be taught at specific times during the season and at an appropriate level of understanding.

### Selecting Fitness Objectives

Generally, your primary concern for athletes in the 6-13 age range should be to develop

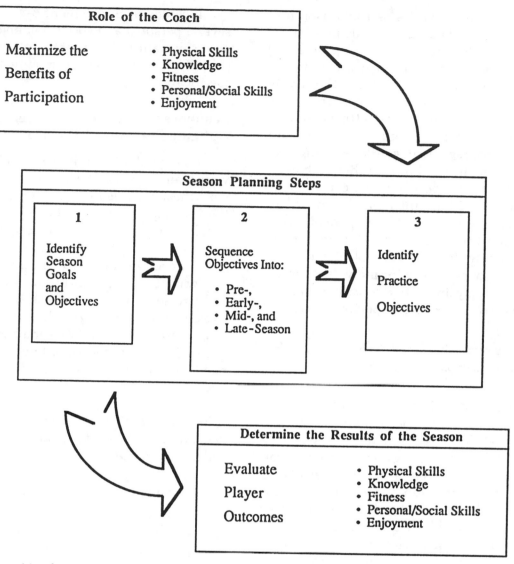

**Figure 3-1.** A coach's role as it relates to planning the season and evaluating the players.

physical skills, knowledge, and appropriate personal/social skills. This is not to suggest that conditioning is unimportant. It is, however, the studied opinion of many coaches and specialists in growth and development that the specific training designed to promote high levels of sport-related fitness should receive a lower priority at this age. For highly skilled softball players 14 years of age and older, a gradually increasing emphasis should be placed on conditioning the muscular and energy production systems. Part of the reason for this recommendation is that when young athletes train for skilled performance, they also obtain conditioning stimuli that are sufficient to cause the body to adapt to the fitness demands associated with learning

and performing softball skills. As players become highly skilled, conditioning becomes a more important factor for enabling more frequent, more intense, and more enduring application of their abilities. Supplement 3-3 includes an overview of fitness objectives you may wish to include in your season plan for older players who are also highly skilled.

*For younger players, fitness should be a by-product of learning the physical skills.*

### Selecting Personal and Social Skill Objectives

A primary objective in the season plan should be to have all players feel increasingly better about their abilities as the season progresses. This should occur not only in the areas of physical skills, knowledge, and fitness, but should also include qualities such as persistence, self-control, tolerance, respect for authority, encouragement of teammates, concentration on the task, commitment to best efforts, and cooperation. Athletes need guidance (modeling, direction, encouragement, gentle rebuking, etc.) to develop such attributes. When achieved, these personal and social qualities contribute to performance in both athletic and non-athletic situations. Moreover, unlike opponents, officials, and/or the "breaks of the game," these qualities are within the control of individual players. The opportunity for individual control has been strongly linked to motivation, and motivation is strongly linked to performance.

*Coaches are responsible for developing socially desirable skills in their players.*

As a coach, perhaps your most important and lasting contribution is helping your players improve their feelings of self-worth and socially desirable skills. By focusing on controllable qualities such as "effort" versus uncontrollable "outcomes," which are often dependent on others (e.g., an umpire's call, a "bad hop," the ability of another team), you have a unique opportunity to make a significant and lasting contribution to the personal character of your athletes.

Contributing to team membership is another worthy objective that coaches should set for every player. Athletes, especially those who engage in team sports such as softball, must learn to overcome the natural tendency to blame others for a loss or even a bad performance. Players must be taught that their role is to play as well as they can and to think, do, and say those things that can help their teammates do the same. The team will only be as good as its weakest link. Often, an otherwise excellent team performs at a mediocre level due to the dissension created by "putting others down," making excuses, or transferring blame to others.

*Coaches should reward effort when they review the accomplishments of the team.*

Included in Supplement 3-4 is a listing of several personal and social skill objectives that you may want to incorporate into your season plan. The listing may be modified and made specific to your players.

## Sequence Objectives Into Pre, Early, Mid, and Late Portions of the Season

Once you've identified season objectives for your team, they can be listed as shown on the worksheet provided in Supplement 3-5. While the list may need to be revised as the season unfolds, the objectives should become the basis of your planning for the season.

Categorize the listed objectives into goals you want to achieve in the pre-, early-, mid-, and late-season (see Figure 3-2). Some objectives may be emphasized throughout the season, whereas others may be emphasized in only one division of the season. Photocopy Supplement 3-6 and use it to complete this step of your season plan.

*Deciding what objectives should be achieved in the pre-, early-, mid-, and late-season is the basis for all subsequent planning.*

### Pre-season Objectives

If pre-season activity is possible, it can save you valuable practice time. Many of the objectives pertaining to knowledge of the rules and strategies and some of those involving conditioning can be all, or partially, achieved before formal practice even begins.

Objectives appropriate for the pre-season involve skills, knowledge, fitness capacities, or personal/social skills that can be achieved independently (all or in part) by the player in a safe and efficient manner before the initiation of formal practices. This could include learning the basic rules, violations and penalties, and strategies; obtaining appropriate equipment; and developing strength and aerobic fitness.

### Early-season Objectives

The early-season should be devoted to determining how well your players have mastered the fundamental and/or prerequisite objectives you have selected and to teaching, reteaching, or practicing those objectives. Objectives appropriate for the early-season should contain abilities that are prerequisite to attaining other identified objectives. For example, players must be able to make contact with the pitch before they can be expected to hit to the opposite field. This attention to the sequence of skills is particularly important for the inexperienced player, who should spend more time on learning skills typically placed in the early-season division. In addition to objectives associated with physical skills, early-season objectives should include logistical and organizational concerns, safety, strategy, discipline, fitness, socialization, rules of play, and team rules. These are all essential in preparing players for early-season games and to provide a foundation for the rest of the season.

| SEASON PLAN WORKSHEET | | | | | |
|---|---|---|---|---|---|
| Coach: _____ | | Season: _____ | | | |
| | | Season Division | | | |
| Goal Areas | Objectives | Pre | Early | Mid | Late |
| Physical Skills | Baserunning | | X | X | |
| | Hitting | | X | X | X |
| | Batting | | X | X | |
| | Bunt: Square around | | X | X | X |
| | Bunt: Drag | | X | X | X |
| | Throwing | | X | X | X |
| | Catching flys | | X | X | X |
| | Fielding grounders | | X | X | X |
| | Pitching | | X | X | X |
| | | | | | |
| Knowledge | Rules of the Game | | | | |
| | terms | X | X | X | |
| | scoring | X | X | X | |
| | substitution | X | X | X | |
| | Strategies | | | | |
| | offensive | | | X | X |
| | defensive | | | X | X |
| | | | | | |
| | | | | | |
| Fitness | Flexibility | | | | |
| | hip | X | X | X | X |
| | shoulder | X | X | X | X |
| | | | | | |
| | Cardiovascular | X | X | X | X |
| | | | | | |
| Personal/Social | Personal | | | | |
| | best effort | | X | X | X |
| | listening | | X | X | X |
| | Social | | | | |
| | cooperation | | X | X | X |
| | fair play | | X | X | X |
| | | | | | |
| | | | | | |

**Figure 3-2.** An abbreviated example of a season plan for young softball players.

## Mid-season Objectives

Mid-season objectives should continue to focus on teaching individual techniques. However, a large share of practice time should be devoted to refining these techniques within the context of game-like drills and controlled scrimmages. Time should be spent combining individual techniques (e.g., fielding the ball and throwing to the appropriate base), and integrating these techniques with game strategy. Many of the cognitive, fitness, and personal/social objectives established for the early-season should continue to be emphasized during the mid-season.

## Late-season Objectives

Late-season objectives should be focused on the maintenance and refinement of the team's offensive and defensive play. A greater portion of practice time should be spent on game-like drills and controlled scrimmages. Practices should be organized so fitness levels are maintained and emphasis continues on cognitive and personal and social skills.

Generally, you should focus on single skills in the early-season, skill combinations in the mid-season, and combinations of both within systems of play in the later portion of the season. There are no hard and fast divisions among these three phases of the season (in fact, they should blend or overlap through good transitions). However, you should have them clearly in mind as you view the entire season in terms of what you wish to accomplish and the time in which it must be done.

## Identify Practice Objectives

As you place objectives into season divisions and adjust the number of weeks assigned to each division, you will likely find that you have chosen to cover more than your available practice time allows. A good guide in such situations is to devote enough time to the cumulative instruction and practice of each objective so the majority of players are able to make significant improvements on most of the objectives included in the season plan. Merely exposing your team to the individual techniques of the game, without spending sufficient time for them to be learned, results in frustration for you and the players. Your players must receive sufficient instruction, practice, and feedback to master the objectives at an appropriate level for use in a game situation. Accordingly, select, teach, and practice only the objectives that are essential to the game at your team's level of play. You can always add objectives to your plan as it is implemented, but you cannot recover time wasted on objectives that are not achieved or that are inappropriate for your players' level of development.

*Select, teach, and practice the key objectives that are essential to your team.*

Generally, the allotment of time to physical skill objectives should be based upon the following instructional sequence and distributed across several practices. You should allow time:

1. to introduce the objective—tell the players what you want them to learn and why it is important
2. for the players to try the individual techniques and for you to determine their levels of performance
3. for you to teach the key elements of the individual techniques and for players to practice these elements
4. for skill refinement and automation such that an individual technique can be used in game situations

The time allotment to fitness, cognitive, and personal/social objectives may not be as structured as the allotment for physical skill objectives. Fitness goals may be achieved along with practice of individual techniques in drills and scrimmages. Similarly, some cognitive, and personal/social objectives may be concomitantly attained during the practice of physical skills. However, some of these objectives may need practice time specifically devoted to them.

Integrating your chosen objectives into a season calendar (see Figure 3-3) will give you a master plan of everything you need to manage your coaching activities. The season calendar converts your plans to practice outlines. The daily entries on the calendar provide a guide from which specific plans can be developed. Supplement 3-7 provides a blank reproducible worksheet that you can use to develop a master plan of practices.

The following list includes examples of entries that can be included on a calender:

- registration dates and deadlines
- date team roster is distributed
- sign-up date for practice time at available fields
- dates and times for coaches' education meetings
- equipment distribution dates and times
- date and time for parents' orientation meeting
- dates and times for league meetings
- sequential numbers designating practices (e.g., #1 designates first practice)
- practice objectives and time allocations
- game days and times
- tournament dates
- dates and times for special events

The most important part of developing a season calendar is the decision you make about what objectives to include and how much practice time you devote to each objective on a practice-by-practice basis. Using your season plan worksheet, select an appropriate number of objectives listed under the "pre- and early-season" that you wish to include in your first practice and enter them in the space labeled "practice #1" on your season calendar. This process should be repeated for your second, third, and subsequent practices through the early-, mid-, and late-season divisions.

*The two most important decisions in planning the season are deciding what objectives to teach and how much time you should spend teaching them.*

You will spend less total time planning for your season and practice if you use the approach suggested here than if the task is done practice-by-practice throughout the season. This process will also help you verify which skills you believe are most important as you run out of available practice time and are forced to either exclude objectives from your plan or find other ways to achieve them outside of the normal practice time. In addition to the good feeling and confidence that comes with completing a season calendar, you will have developed the base necessary to systematically change your plans as unexpected events develop. More importantly, you will know before the mid- to late-portions of the season whether in your initial plan you assigned too much or too little time to some of your early-season objectives. A completed plan that's been implemented and refined is also an invaluable resource for next year's coaching assignment or as a guide for new coaches coming into the program.

## SUMMARY

Your role as a coach can be best filled through the leadership and instruction you provide in practice and game situations. Clearly, those coaches who are most effective in helping their players acquire the necessary physical skills, knowledge, fitness, and personal/social skills are those who have clear objectives and who organize to achieve them. Organization of the season by selecting and then teaching objectives in a proper order, and for an appropriate amount of time, is a major step toward helping players acquire the benefits of softball.

## SEASON PLANNING CALENDAR

Coach ___Goodbody___ Team ___Falcons___ Month _____

| S | M | T | W | T | F | S |
|---|---|---|---|---|---|---|
| | Coaches' education meeting 7:00-9:00 (High School) | | Team rosters distributed, sign-up for practice times/gyms 7:00-8:00 (Rec Office) | | | |
| | | Parents' orientation meeting 7:00-8:30 (Elementary School Rm. 10) | | | | |
| | | Practice #1 | | Practice #2 | | Practice #3 |
| | | Practice #4 | | Practice #5 | | Practice #6 |
| | | Practice #7 | | Practice #8 | | |

**Figure 3-3.** An example of a season planning calendar.

### Practice #1

05 Overview of practice
10 Team rules and regulations
05 Warm-up

*Teach and evaluate:*

15 Catching/throwing
10 Fielding ground balls (gbs)
15 Pitching (everyone)
20 Hitting
05 Cool-down
05 Handouts: team rules,
     practice and game schedule,
     rules of play

### Practice #2

05 Overview of practice
10 Review rules of play
05 Warm-up (catching/throwing)*

*Teach and evaluate:*

10 Baserunning (1B, EBH)
15 Outfield fly balls (fbs)/gbs

*Practice:*

10 Infield gb drills
15 Hitting drills
05 Cool-down/team talk
05 Cool-down/team talk
05 Handouts: Coaching hints
     for individual skills

### Practice #3

05 Overview of practice
10 Review rules of play
10 Warm-up (catching/throwing)*

*Teach and evaluate:*

20 Position play: base
     coverage, position resp.

*Practice:*

15 Outfield fb/gb
20 Hitting*
05 Cool-down
10 Chalk talk: defensive
     strategies

### Practice #4

05 Overview of practice
10 Warm-up (catching/throwing)

*Teach and evaluate:*

10 Baserunning: leadoffs
15 Position play: back ups*

*Practice:*

15 Position specific fielding
     (gb/fb)
20 Hitting drills
10 Baserunning (1B, EBH)
05 Cool-down
05 Defensive strategy review

### Practice #5

05 Overview/questions
10 Warm-up (catching/throwing)*

*Teach and evaluate:*

15 Sliding
15 Bunting

*Practice:*

20 Hitting*
10 Infield/outfield gb drills
05 Cool-down
10 Chalk talk: offensive
     strategy

### Practice #6

05 Overview/questions
15 Warm-up (catching/throwing)*

*Teach and evaluate:*

10 Relays/cutoff

*Practice:*

15 Position play (situations)
10 Bunting
15 Hitting drills
10 Baserunning
05 Cool-down
05 Review offensive strategy

### Practice #7

05 Overview/questions
15 Warm-up (catching/throwing)*

*Teach and evaluate:*

10 Leads, stealing w/pitch*
10 Tag up, halfway w/fly ball

*Practice:*

10 Fielding gb drills
15 Fly balls w/relays
20 Hitting*
05 Cool-down

### Practice #8

05 Overview/questions
15 Warm-up w/throwing*

*Teach and evaluate:*

10 Position play – infield
     outfield priority

*Practice:*

15 Position play – situations
     (include inf/of priority)
10 Bunting
20 Hitting
10 Baserunning
05 Cool-down

*Pitchers practice pitching
(i.e., before/after their turn to
hit). The pitcher must also
understand that to become a
highly skilled pitcher he/she
must also practice pitching
outside of team practices!

**Figure 3-3 (continued)**

# Skills and Abilities of Softball

| FUNDAMENTAL MOTOR SKILL | SUGGESTED EMPHASIS | | | | |
|---|---|---|---|---|---|
| | 6 yrs. | 7-8 yrs. | 9-10 yrs. | 11-13 yrs. | 14 yrs. and up |
| **Defensive Skills** | | | | | |
| Catching | X | X | X | X | X |
| Throwing | X | X | X | X | X |
| Speed throwing | | | | X | X |
| Fielding | | | | | |
|    Direct ground balls | X | X | X | X | X |
|    Crow hop | | | X | X | X |
|    Charging ground balls | | | X | X | X |
|    Forehand/backhand | | | | | X |
|    Fly balls: direct | | | X | X | X |
|    Fly balls: overhead | | | | | X |
|    Pitching (non-game situation) | X | X | X | | |
|    Pitching (game situation) | | | | X | X |
| **Position Play** | | | | | |
| General (play/learn each position equally) | X | X | X | | |
| Specialization | | | | X | X |
| Base coverage | | | X | X | X |
| Back-ups | | | X | X | X |
| Position responsibilities | X | X | X | X | X |
| **Situations** | | | | | |
| General (easiest out) | X | X | | | |
| Specific (lead runner, bunt defense, etc.) | | | X | X | X |
| **Offensive Skills** | | | | | |
| Hitting | | | | | |
|    Tee ball | X | X | | | |
|    Coaches pitch/machine pitch | | | X | | |
|    Player pitch | | | | X | X |
| Bunting | | | | | |
|    Square around | | | | X | X |
|    Pivot | | | | | X |
|    Bunt for a hit | | | | | X |
|    Slap hit | | | | | X |

## SKILLS AND ABILITIES OF SOFTBALL

| FUNDAMENTAL MOTOR SKILL | \multicolumn{5}{c}{SUGGESTED EMPHASIS} |
|---|---|---|---|---|---|

| FUNDAMENTAL MOTOR SKILL | 6 yrs. | 7-8 yrs. | 9-10 yrs. | 11-13 yrs. | 14 yrs. and up |
|---|---|---|---|---|---|
| **Offensive Skills** (Cont.) | | | | | |
| Baserunning | | | | | |
| Through first | X | X | X | X | X |
| Extra bases | | X | X | X | X |
| Leading off | | | | | |
| Option 1 | | | X | X | |
| Option 2 | | | | | X |
| Tagging up (fly ball) | X | X | X | X | X |
| Halfway/tag (base specific) | | | | | X |
| Stealing | | | | | X |
| Sliding | | | | | |
| Bent leg | | X | X | X | X |
| Pop-up | | | | | X |
| Head first | | | | | X |
| | | | | | |
| **Offensive Strategy** | | | | | |
| Bunt | | | | X | X |
| Bunt/run | | | | X | X |
| Bunt for a hit | | | | | X |
| Slap hit | | | | | X |
| Steal | | | | | X |
| Hit and run | | | | X | X |
| Take | | | | | X |
| | | | | | |
| **Defensive Strategy** | | | | | |
| Cutoff | | | | | X |
| Relays | | | | X | X |
| Rundowns | | | | | X |
| First and third (double steal) | | | | | X |
| Pickoffs | | | | | X |

# Knowledge Objectives*

| LEVEL OF PLAYER<br>APPROXIMATE AGE | SUGGESTED EMPHASIS | | |
|---|---|---|---|
| | Elem. School<br>Beginner<br>6-10 yrs. | Middle School<br>Intermediate<br>11-13 yrs. | High School<br>Advanced<br>14 yrs. and up |
| **Rules of the Game** | | | |
| the playing field | X | X | |
| the start of play | X | | |
| method of scoring | X | | |
| unlimited substitutions | | X | X |
| pitching | X | X | |
| baserunning | X | X | X |
| fair balls/foul balls | X | X | |
| outs—lag, force | X | X | |
| out of play area | | | X |
| infield fly | | | X |
| **Prevention of Injuries** | | | |
| equipment and apparel | X | X | X |
| field conditions | X | X | X |
| structural hazards | X | X | X |
| environmental hazards | X | X | X |
| use of appropriate techniques | X | X | X |
| contraindicated exercises | X | X | X |
| overuse injuries | X | X | X |
| **Conditioning** | | | |
| energy production system | | | X |
| muscular system | | | X |
| principles of training | | | X |
| methods of conditioning | | | X |
| warm-up/cool-down procedures | X | X | X |
| **Nutrition** | | | |
| proper diet | X | X | X |
| vitamins and minerals | X | X | X |
| water intake | X | X | X |
| ergogenic aids | X | X | X |
| steroids | X | X | X |
| meal patterns | X | X | X |
| weight control | X | X | X |
| **Softball Terminology** | X | X | X |

**Other Knowledge Objectives**

*Note that these knowledge objectives must be taught. It should not be assumed that young athletes will have learned these just by playing softball.

# Fitness Objectives*

|  | SUGGESTED EMPHASIS | | |
|---|---|---|---|
|  | Elem. School | Middle School | High School |
| **LEVEL OF PLAYER** | Beginner | Intermediate | Advanced |
| **APPROXIMATE AGE** | 6-10 yrs. | 11-13 yrs. | 14 yrs. and up |

**Energy Production**

| | | | |
|---|---|---|---|
| aerobic capacity | | | X |
| anaerobic capacity | | | X |
| aerobic/anaerobic capacity | | | X |

**Muscular Fitness (strength, endurance, and power)**

| | | | |
|---|---|---|---|
| neck | | | X |
| shoulder | | | X |
| upper arm | | | X |
| lower arm | | | X |
| wrist | | | X |
| abdominal | | | X |
| hip/spine | | | X |
| low back | | | X |
| groin | | | X |
| upper leg | | | X |
| lower leg | | | X |
| ankle | | | X |

**Muscular Flexibility**

| | | | |
|---|---|---|---|
| neck | | | X |
| shoulder | | | X |
| trunk | | | X |
| hip | | | X |
| ankle | | | X |

**Other Fitness Objectives**

*Note that progress is made in many of these objectives at the beginning and intermediate levels of play. This development should occur concomitantly through carefully planned practice sessions designed to enhance physical skills. The "Xs" in this chart suggest that coaches should not plan "fitness only" drills for their team until the players have reached approximately 14 years of age and are at the advanced level of play.

# Personal and Social Objectives

| LEVEL OF PLAYER<br>APPROXIMATE AGE | SUGGESTED EMPHASIS | | |
| --- | --- | --- | --- |
| | Elem. School<br>Beginner<br>6-10 yrs. | Middle School<br>Intermediate<br>11-13 yrs. | High School<br>Advanced<br>14 yrs. and up |
| **Personal** | | | |
| best effort | X | X | X |
| initiative | X | X | X |
| persistence | X | X | X |
| responsibility | X | X | X |
| self-discipline | X | X | X |
| following directions | X | X | X |
| listening | X | X | X |
| **Social** | | | |
| respect for authority | X | X | X |
| leadership | X | X | X |
| respect for others | X | X | X |
| fair play | X | X | X |
| cooperation | X | X | X |
| appropriate winning behavior | X | X | X |
| appropriate losing behavior | X | X | X |
| tact | X | X | X |
| encouragement of teammates | X | X | X |
| respect for rules | X | X | X |
| sport-related etiquette | X | X | X |
| respect for property | X | X | X |

**Other Objectives**

**Supplement 3-5.**

| SEASON PLAN WORKSHEET | | | | |
|---|---|---|---|---|
| **Coach:** _____ | | **Season:** _____ | | |

| Goal Areas | Objectives | Season Division | | | |
|---|---|---|---|---|---|
| | | **Pre** | **Early** | **Mid** | **Late** |
| Physical Skills | Catching fundamentals | | | | |
| | Throwing fundamentals | | | | |
| | Speed throwing | | | | |
| | Fielding | | | | |
| | ground balls/fly balls | | | | |
| | position techniques | | | | |
| | Pitching | | | | |
| | Hitting | | | | |
| | Bunting | | | | |
| | Baserunning | | | | |
| Knowledge | Rules of the game | | | | |
| | baserunning/scoring | | | | |
| | tagging up (ground balls/fly balls | | | | |
| | force outs/tag outs | | | | |
| | foul ball/out of play ball | | | | |
| | Strategies | | | | |
| | offensive | | | | |
| | defensive | | | | |
| | | | | | |
| Fitness | Flexibility | | | | |
| | leg, hip, shoulder, etc. | | | | |
| | Strength | | | | |
| | leg, shoulder, abdominal, arm | | | | |
| | Cardiovascular: general | | | | |
| | Speed: sprint work | | | | |
| Personal/Social | Personal | | | | |
| | effort | | | | |
| | listening | | | | |
| | Social | | | | |
| | cooperation | | | | |
| | fair play | | | | |
| | positive communication | | | | |
| | (inter-player) | | | | |

| SEASON PLAN WORKSHEET | | | | | |
|---|---|---|---|---|---|
| Coach: _____ | | | Season: _____ | | |
| | | Season Division | | | |
| Goal Areas | Objectives | Pre | Early | Mid | Late |
| | | | | | |
| | | | | | |
| | | | | | |
| | | | | | |
| | | | | | |
| | | | | | |
| | | | | | |
| | | | | | |
| | | | | | |
| | | | | | |
| | | | | | |
| | | | | | |
| | | | | | |
| | | | | | |
| | | | | | |
| | | | | | |
| | | | | | |
| | | | | | |
| | | | | | |
| | | | | | |
| | | | | | |
| | | | | | |
| | | | | | |
| | | | | | |
| | | | | | |
| | | | | | |
| | | | | | |
| | | | | | |
| | | | | | |
| | | | | | |

Supplement 3-7.

## SEASON PLANNING CALENDAR

Coach _____ Team _____ Month _____

| S | M | T | W | T | F | S |
|---|---|---|---|---|---|---|
|   |   |   |   |   |   |   |
|   |   |   |   |   |   |   |
|   |   |   |   |   |   |   |
|   |   |   |   |   |   |   |
|   |   |   |   |   |   |   |

# 4
# Planning Effective Instruction

*Paul Vogel, Ph.D.*
*Eugene W. Brown, Ph.D.*

QUESTIONS TO CONSIDER

• What four steps can coaches use to systematically instruct their players?
• What guidelines for instruction should be applied to ensure effective instruction?
• What are the features of an effective practice plan?
• What are the characteristics of a good drill?

## INTRODUCTION

Effective instruction is the foundation of successful coaching. This is particularly true when you are coaching players in the six- to 16-year-old age range. Successful results in competition are directly related to the quality of instruction that players have received during practices. Effective instruction requires:

• clear communication of "what" is to be learned (objectives which represent skills, rules, strategies, and/or personal/social skills)
• continual evaluation of players' performance status on the objectives selected
• use of a systematic method of instruction
• application of guidelines for effective instruction
• evaluation and alteration of instruction in accordance with the degree to which players obtain the desired objectives

## CLEARLY COMMUNICATING THE CONTENT TO BE LEARNED

The results (or outcomes) of effective instruction can be grouped into three areas.

1. Physical—individual techniques and conditioning
2. Mental—rules, strategies, positional responsibilities
3. Social—personal and social skills

*Clearly stated objectives are a prerequisite to effective instruction.*

To provide effective instruction, you must identify the teaching objectives for each of these three areas. Players do not learn skills merely through exposure and practice. Rather, they must have specific feedback revealing what they are doing correctly and, equally as important, what they are doing incorrectly. Specific feedback cannot be communicated to your players unless the skill to be learned and its key elements of performance are clearly specified and understood by the coach. By using the suggestions and procedures outlined in Chapter 3, you can be confident that the objectives you include are appropriate for your players. Application of the steps explained in Chapter 3 also results in a systematic plan (pre-season to late-season) for covering the objectives you select. This type of season plan provides a solid base from which effective instruction can occur.

## CONTINUALLY EVALUATING THE PERFORMANCE OF PLAYERS

As a coach, it's important to evaluate your players' ability based on the objectives you have selected. Their current status on these objectives determines the instructional needs of the team. The evaluation should include physical, mental, and social content because deficiencies in any one of these areas may preclude successful participation in the sport. For example, the highly skilled softball player who lacks motivation may be a liability rather than an asset to the team because of the poor example set for teammates. Also, knowledgeable players who understand the rules and strategies of offense and defense but who lack the skills and fitness to perform as team members must also be evaluated and taught to improve their deficiencies.

*To conduct effective practices, you must continually assess players' needs.*

The physical, mental, and attitudinal abilities of players who are new to the program or team are usually unknown. Even when accurate records are available from the previous season, considerable changes normally occur in the abilities of returning players. The result is you know very little about many of your players. Accordingly, you may have to spend more time evaluating players' abilities at the beginning of the season. However, evaluations must also occur, skill by skill, practice by practice, throughout the entire season. As your players' needs change, so should your instructional emphasis.

### Assessment of Physical Needs

#### Performance Assessment

Assess physical skills by carefully observing your players while they participate in individual and small group drills, scrimmages, and/or games. Descriptions of individual techniques, their key elements, and common errors of performance are found in Section 3. You must have this information to properly evaluate your players.

In addition to knowledge about how individual techniques of softball are performed, the following visual evaluation guidelines help you make accurate observations and assessments regarding physical performance.

- Select a proper observational distance
- Observe the performance from different angles
- Observe activities in a setting that is not distracting
- Select an observational setting that has a vertical and/or horizontal reference line
- Observe a skilled reference model
- Observe slower moving body parts first
- Observe separate key elements of complicated skills
- Observe the timing of performance components
- Look for unnecessary movements
- Observe the full range of motion

#### Fitness Assessment

Evaluating the fitness of your players requires two levels of assessment; namely, the aerobic and anaerobic energy systems. Precise physiological abilities are difficult to determine because they often require sophisticated measurement apparatus, take a lot of time, and the results are often confounded by players' skills and experience. Due to these complexities, your assessment of fitness should be at a more practical level. For the most part, you should compare individual players with their teammates on the characteristics of energy and muscular system fitness that are explained in Chapter 24. When skill, size, and maturity levels are judged to be similar between players and one is more (or less) fit than the others on a given attribute, you can assume a differential on that attribute. You can then instruct the underdeveloped player on how to make changes. Similarly, when a player cannot keep up with teammates on a series of drills that require either maximum effort or longer, sustained effort, it is prudent to assume that one or both of the energy systems is inadequately trained.

### Assessment of Cognitive Needs

Knowledge of strategy, rules, positional responsibilities, and set plays can be evaluated during drills, scrimmages, and games by noting the response of your players to situations that require a decision prior to action. By clearly communicating what you want the players to know in certain circumstances, and then asking questions and observing how they react, you can learn what they know and what skills and knowledge they can appropriately apply.

## Assessment of Personal/Social Needs

An assessment of social needs, though subjective, is not difficult. Informally converse with your players and observe their interactions with other team members during practices, games, and informal gatherings to determine what needs exist. Strengthening the personal/social weaknesses of your players, however, may be more difficult than enhancing their performance of individual physical techniques and their knowledge about the game.

As skilled performance is contingent on learning the key elements of each skill, the modification of a negative or interfering attitude requires you to correctly analyze the underlying problem. Ask yourself, the parents, or the player why the behavior in question is occurring. This may require some probing. Often the problem is not related to softball. The fact that you care enough about the individual player to invest some time and energy may be all that is needed to reverse or eliminate a negative quality that could become a burden for the individual and the team. Based upon the information obtained, generate a specific strategy for modifying the behavior. The information in Chapters 19 through 22 will help you identify strategies for dealing with important personal/ social skills.

Evaluating the status of players in the physical, mental, and attitudinal areas of performance is necessary in order to obtain insight about how to conduct practices that match your players' needs. Whether your players are performing at low, moderate, or high levels, they can all improve with good instruction.

## USING A SYSTEMATIC MODEL FOR INSTRUCTION

Although there are many ways to instruct young softball players, the following approach has proven both easy to use and effective in teaching and/or refining skills.

1. Get the attention of the players by establishing credibility
2. Communicate precisely what needs to be learned
3. Provide for practice and feedback
4. Evaluate results and take appropriate action

## Step 1: Establish Credibility

Players must direct their attention to the coach before instruction can occur. To encourage this, arrange the players so that each one can clearly see your actions and hear your instructions. Choose where you stand in relation to the players so that you avoid competing with other distractions. Often it's a good strategy to have the players seated or kneeling in front of you as you begin.

Immediately establish the precedent that when you speak, important information is being communicated. Point out that the team cannot maximize its practice opportunity when several people are talking at once.

*Establish and maintain the precedent that when you speak, important information is being communicated.*

As you begin your instruction, establish the need for competence on a particular physical skill or ability by relating it to some phase of successful team and/or individual play. An excellent way to gain your players' attention and motivate them to want to learn individual techniques is to mention how a local, regional, or national level player or team has mastered the skill and has used it to great advantage. The objective of your introductory comments is to establish the idea that mastery of this skill is very important to individual and team play and that the key elements of its execution are achievable.

The next, and perhaps even more important, task is to clearly establish in the minds of the players that they need to improve their abilities on this skill. This can be accomplished with the following steps:

1. Briefly describe the new skill and then let them try it several times in a quick paced drill

2. Carefully observe their performance and identify their strengths and weaknesses (use the key elements of the skill as a basis for your observations)
3. Call them back together and report your observations

This approach allows you to point out weaknesses in performance on one or more key elements that are common to many, if not all, of the players. Using this approach enhances your credibility and motivates the players to listen to and follow your instructions. Also, your subsequent teaching can be specifically matched to the needs (weaknesses) you observed. Of course, if in observing you determine that your players have already achieved the desired skill level, then you should shift your focus to another skill. This might mean moving on to the next phase of your practice plan.

## Step 2: Communicate Precisely What Needs To Be Learned

When you and your players know their status (strengths and weaknesses of their performance) on a particular skill, you have created an environment for teaching and learning. Because individuals learn most efficiently when they focus on one aspect of a skill at a time, it's important to precisely communicate the one key element on which you want an individual, pair, group, or team to concentrate. Demonstrate the key element, and explain it, so that all players know exactly what they're trying to achieve.

*Individuals learn most effectively by focusing their practice efforts on one clearly understood element of skilled performance.*

When your players are at two or three different levels of ability, you may want to establish two or three instructional groups. This can be accomplished using the following three divisions:

1. Early Learning—focus on learning the key elements of the skill in a controlled situation
2. Intermediate Learning—focus on coordination of all key elements in common situations
3. Later Learning—automatic use of the skill in game-like conditions

## Step 3: Provide for Practice and Feedback

Organize your practice time and activities to provide players with:

1. as many repetitions (trials) as possible within the allotted time (minimize standing in lines)
2. specific, immediate, and positive feedback on what they did correctly and then on what they can do to improve. Follow this instruction with some form of encouragement to continue the learning effort.

Repetitions and feedback are essential to players' achievement and are therefore fundamental to effective coaching. You can expect a direct relationship between the gains in players' performances and the degree to which you find ways to maximize these two dimensions of instruction. John Wooden, UCLA basketball coach of fame, was found to provide over 2,000 acts of teaching during 30 total hours of practice, of which 75 percent pertained directly to skill instruction. This converts to more than one incidence of feedback for every minute of coaching activity!

*Repeated trials and specific feedback on what was right, followed by what can be improved and an encouraging "try again," produces results.*

Feedback can be dramatically increased by using volunteers and/or the players themselves as instructional aids. When instruction is focused on one key element of performance and the important aspects of performing the skill have been effectively communicated to the players, they are often as good, and sometimes better, at seeing discrepancies in a partner's performance as some adults. Thus, working in pairs or small groups can be very effective in increasing both the number of trials and the amount of feedback that individuals get within a given amount of practice time. Also, by providing feedback, players are improving their mental understanding of how the skill should be performed.

## Step 4: Evaluate Results and Take Appropriate Action

Evaluation of players' performances must occur on a continuing basis during practices and games. This is the only valid means to answer the question, "Are the players achieving the skills?" If they are, you have two appropriate actions to take:

1. Enjoy it. You're making an important contribution to your players.
2. Consider how you can be even more efficient. How can you get the same results in less time or how can more be achieved within the same time allotment?

If the players are not achieving the instructional objectives, it's important to ask why. Although it is possible that you have players who are very inept at learning, this is seldom the case. First assume that you are using inappropriate instructional techniques or that you simply did not provide enough instructional time. Go through the instructional factors related to effective planning, motivating, communicating, and discipline in Section 5, and conditioning in Section 6, to determine which of the guidelines or steps were missed and/or inappropriately implemented. Then alter your subsequent practices accordingly. Steps for how to complete this type of evaluation are described in more detail in Chapter 23. Continuous trial, error, and revisions usually result in improved coaching effectiveness, which then translates into increased achievement by the players. In those instances where you cannot determine what to alter, seek help from a fellow coach whose teams are consistently strong in the physical skills that are causing difficulty for your players. This is an excellent way to obtain some good ideas for altering your approach.

## APPLYING GUIDELINES FOR EFFECTIVE INSTRUCTION

As you provide for practice and feedback to your players (see Step 3), you may wish to use some of the guidelines for instruction that have been found by recent research to be effective in improving student learning. Nine guidelines for effective instruction are named below and described in more detail in Supplement 4-1.

1. Set realistic expectations
2. Structure instruction
3. Establish an orderly environment
4. Group your players according to ability
5. Maximize on-task time
6. Maximize the success rate
7. Monitor progress
8. Ask questions
9. Promote a sense of control

## PLANNING EFFECTIVE PRACTICES

If practices are to be effective, they must be directed at helping players meet the objectives defined in the season plan. Objectives are best achieved by using appropriate instructional methods. Instruction is both formal (planned) and informal (not planned) and can occur during practices, games, and special events. Virtually any time players are in your presence, there is potential for teaching and learning.

All coaches, even those who are highly knowledgeable and experienced, are more effective teachers when they organize and plan their instruction. This does not mean that unplanned instruction should not be used to assist your players in learning more about softball. In fact, unplanned events that occur often present ideal opportunities to teach important skills. By capitalizing on temporary but intense player interest and motivation, a skilled coach can turn an unplanned event into an excellent learning opportunity. For example, an opponent's offense may prove so effective during a game that your defensive players become highly motivated to learn the tactics necessary to stop such an attack. Often these "teachable moments" are unused by all but the most perceptive coaches.

### Features of an Effective Practice

Scheduled practice sessions usually constitute the largest portion of contact between you and your players. Each practice session requires that you select both the content of instruction and its method of presentation. To do this effectively and efficiently, each of your practice plans should:

- be based upon previous planning and seasonal organization (see Chapter 3)
- list the objectives that will be the focus of instruction for that practice
- show the amount of time allotted to each objective during the practice
- identify the activities (instructional, drill, or

scrimmage) that will be used to teach or practice the objectives

- identify equipment and/or special organizational needs
- apply the guidelines for effective instruction (included in Supplement 4-1)

An effective practice combines the seasonal plan, assessment of your players' abilities, instruction, and an evaluation of practice results. The evaluation portion should be retained even if it means changing future practices to meet the needs of players that may have been unanticipated. The features of an effective practice plan are outlined in Table 4-1. Not all of the features are appropriate for every practice you conduct. There should be a good reason, however, before you decide not to include each feature.

## Format and Inclusions in a Practice Plan

Several ingredients that should be included in a practice plan are: the date and/or practice number; the objectives and key points, drills and/or activities; amount of practice time devoted to each objective; equipment needs; and a place for evaluation. The date and/or practice number are helpful to maintain organizational

**Table 4-1.** Features of an effective practice.

| Features | Coaching Activity |
| --- | --- |
| Practice overview | Inform the team about the contents and objectives of the practices (e.g. important new skills, positional play, new drills) to motivate and mentally prepare them for the upcoming activity. |
| Warm-up | Physically prepare the team for each practice by having them engage in light to moderate aerobic activity sufficient to produce slight sweating. Follow this by specific stretching activities. |
| Individual skills and drills | Review and practice objectives previously covered. |
| Small group skills and drills | Introduce and teach new objectives. |
| Team skills and drills | Incorporate the individual and small group drills into drills involving the entire team. |
| Cool-down | At the end of each practice, use activities of moderate to light intensity followed by stretching to reduce potential soreness and maintain flexibility. |
| Team talk | Review key points of the practice, listen to player communications, make announcements, and distribute handouts. |

efficiency. The objectives are the reason for conducting the practice and, therefore, must be clearly in mind prior to selecting the activities, drills, games, or scrimmage situations you believe will develop player competence. The key points of each objective you desire to have your players achieve must be clearly in mind. It also helps to have the key points written prominently on your plan or notes. Supplement 4-2 provides an example plan written to cover the objectives of Practice 5 listed on the season calendar in Chapter 3. In order to communicate the essential features of a practice plan to many readers, this example contains far more narrative than is necessary for most coaches. You need to record only information that will be needed at some later date. Accordingly, phrases, symbols, key words, and other personalized communications will substitute for the more extensive narrative included in the example. A full-sized copy of the practice plan form that you may reproduce is included in Supplement 4-3.

### Practice Time

Allotting time for each objective during practices is a difficult but important task for the coach. Sufficient practice time results in the majority of your players making significant improvement on each objective. Although these changes may not be noticeable in a single session, they must occur when considered across all practice sessions devoted to each objective. Assigning too little time may result in players' exposure to individual techniques but often results in little change in performance. Keep in mind, however, that practice time must be distributed across several objectives (and/or drills or activities within the practice of a single objective) to keep players' interests high. This is particularly true for younger players who tend to have short attention spans and thus need frequent changes in drills or activities.

### Instructional Activities

The selection and implementation of instructional activities, drills, or games should constitute most of each practice session. Players' achievements are directly related to your choices and actions in these important areas. Instructional activities should be conducted in accordance with the guidelines presented in

Supplement 4-1. Because most practices are composed largely of drills, you should follow the same guidelines in Supplement 4-1 and develop your drills to include these important features:

- have a meaningful name
- require a relatively short explanation
- provide an excellent context for mastering an objective
- match skill, knowledge, or fitness requirements of softball players
- keep the players' "on-task time" high
- are easily modified to accommodate skilled and unskilled players
- provide opportunity for skill analysis and feedback to players

Drills should be written on file cards or paper. It's also helpful to organize drills according to objective, group size (individual, small group, team), possession (offensive and defensive), and position (infielders, outfielders or pitchers). When you find a good drill, classify it and add it to your collection. A format for collecting drill information is provided in reproducible form in Supplement 4-4.

### Equipment Needs

The equipment needed to conduct a drill or activity should be recorded on the practice plan. It's frustrating and ineffective to discover after you've explained and set up an activity or drill that the necessary equipment is missing. Therefore, after you've planned all the activities for your practice, review them and list the essential equipment needed.

### Evaluation

The evaluation/comment portion of the practice plan can be used to highlight ways to alter the practice to accommodate players at unexpected skill levels, or to note changes to be made to improve the plan. It also provides a place for announcements or other information that needs to be communicated to your players.

## SUMMARY

Effective instruction is the foundation of successful coaching. It requires practices that include clear communication of what is to be learned, a continuous evaluation of players' performance on the objectives of the practices, a systematic method of instruction, and the use of guidelines for instruction that have been associated with player achievement.

Systematic instruction includes: (a) establishing credibility; (b) providing precise communication of what needs to be learned; (c) providing many practice trials and specific, immediate, and positive feedback; and (d) evaluating the achievement of your players. Use of the guidelines for effective instruction (realistic expectations, structured instruction, order, grouping, maximizing time, success, monitoring, and providing a sense of control) in combination with systematic instruction maximizes the results of your coaching effort.

# Guidelines for Effective Instruction

---

**QUESTIONS TO CONSIDER**

- What are the nine guidelines for effective instruction?
- How can setting realistic expectations for your players influence their achievement?
- How can you coach players of different ability levels on the same team?
- When players are attempting to learn new things, what success rate motivates them to want to continue to achieve?

---

## Introduction

This supplement provides an overview of nine guidelines for effective instruction. As you plan your practices, this list should be reviewed to help maximize your coaching effectiveness. The nine guidelines are:

1. Set realistic expectations
2. Structure instruction
3. Establish an orderly environment
4. Group your players according to ability
5. Maximize on-task time
6. Maximize the success rate
7. Monitor progress
8. Ask questions
9. Promote a sense of self-control

### 1. Set Realistic Expectations

The expectations coaches communicate to their players can create a climate for learning that will positively influence player achievement (Rutter et al. 1979). Clear, but attainable, objectives for performance and expenditure of effort for all players on your team will facilitate achievement. As stated in a recent review (Fisher et al. 1980), the reasons associated with this occurrence may be related to the following ideas.

In comparison to athletes for whom coaches hold high expectations for performance, the athletes perceived to be low performers are:

- more often positioned farther away from the coach
- treated as groups, not individuals
- smiled at less
- receive less eye contact from the coach
- called on less to answer questions
- have their answers responded to less frequently
- praised more often for marginal and inadequate responses
- praised less frequently for successful responses
- interrupted more often

*Players tend to achieve in accordance with the coaches' expectations.*

Coaches and former athletes will be able to understand how even a few of the above responses could reduce motivation and achievement. It is saddening that many capable children are inappropriately labeled as non-achievers on the basis of delayed maturity, poor prior experience, inadequate body size, body composition, and/or many other factors which mask their true ability. Yet, if expectations are low, achievement is likely to be low.

There are at least two important messages in this guideline:

- Expect that, as the coach, you're going to significantly improve the skills, fitness, knowledge of rules and strategies, and attitude of every one of your players during the course of the season.

- Set realistic goals for your players. Make a commitment to help each player achieve those individual goals, and expect improvement.

## 2. Structure Instruction

Your players' achievements are strongly linked to clear communication of the intended outcomes of instruction (objectives), why the goals and objectives are important (essential or prerequisite skills), and what to do to achieve outcomes (instructional directions) (Bruner 1981 and Fisher et al. 1980). Effective instruction is based upon the systematic organization of the content to be taught. The critical steps to take are as follows:

- Select the essential skills, fitness capacities, knowledge of rules and strategies, and personal/social skills from the many options available
- Clearly identify the elements of acceptable performance for each objective that you include in your plans
- Organize and conduct your practices to maximize the opportunity your players have to acquire the objectives by using the effective teaching practices contained in this chapter

## 3. Establish an Orderly Environment

High achievement is related to the following elements (Fisher 1978):

- an orderly, safe, business-like environment with clear expectations
- player accountability for effort and achievement
- rewards for achievement of expectations

Where such conditions are missing, achievement is low.

The following coaching actions will lessen behavioral problems that interfere with learning and, at the same time, promote pride and responsibility in team membership.

- Maintain orderly and disciplined practices
- Maintain clear and reasonable rules that are fairly and consistently enforced

*Caution: strong, over-controlling actions can backfire.* Over-control causes frustration and anxiety while under-control leads to lack of achievement. The best of circumstances is a relaxed, enjoyable but business-like environment. The ability to balance these two opposing forces to maximize achievement and enjoyment by keeping both in perspective may be one of your most difficult tasks.

## 4. Group Your Players

Decisions about the size and composition of groups for various learning tasks are complex, but nonetheless related to achievement (Webb 1980). Typically, in groups of mixed ability, the player with average ability suffers a loss in achievement, while the player with low ability does slightly better. The critical condition for grouping to be effective is to have players practicing at the skill levels needed to advance their playing ability. Typically, this involves groups of similar ability being appropriately challenged. Although this can be difficult to achieve, most effective coaches design practices that maximize a type of individualized instruction.

Your team will have individuals at many levels of ability. While this situation presents a seemingly impossible grouping task, there are some good solutions to this problem:

- When a skill, rule, or strategy is being taught that all your athletes need to know, use a single group for instruction
- As you identify differences in your players' abilities, divide the team and place players of similar ability in small groups when working on these tasks
- When a skill, rule, or strategy is being practiced where individual athletes are at several levels of ability (initial, intermediate, or later learning levels), establish learning stations that focus on specific outcomes to meet each groups' needs

The placement of players into smaller learning groups must be independently decided for each skill, rule, or strategy. A player who is placed at a high level group for practicing individual techniques for dribbling and passing the ball should not necessarily be placed in a high level group for shooting or defensive techniques. It is important that the following occur at each learning station:

- order is established and maintained (an assistant may be necessary)
- tasks that are to be mastered at each station must be clearly understood
- many opportunities must be provided at each station
- a means for giving immediate, specific, and positive feedback must be established.

### 5. *Maximize On-Task Time*

Research on the amount of time that athletes are active in the learning process, rather than standing in lines or watching others perform, reveals that actual "engaged" learning time during practices is regularly less than 50 percent of the total practice time, and often falls to five or 10 percent for individual athletes. There are several actions you can take to maximize the use of available time.

- Reduce the number of athletes who are waiting in line by using more subgroups in your drills
- Secure sufficient supplies and equipment so that players do not have lengthy waits for their turn
- Reduce the transition time between drills by preplanning practices to minimize reformulation of groups and equipment set-up time
- Use instructional grouping practices that have players practicing skills at their appropriate performance level
- Clearly outline and/or diagram each portion of practice and communicate as much of that information as possible before going on the court
- Complete as many pre and post warm-up/cool-down activities as possible outside of the time scheduled on the court
- Recruit assistants (parents or older players) to help you with instructional stations under your supervision

*Remember: Saving ten minutes a day across 14 weeks of two practices per week equals 280 minutes of in-* *structional time for each player.* Time gained by effective organization is available for practicing other skills of the game.

### 6. *Maximize the Success Rate*

The relationship among successful experiences, achievement, and motivation to learn is very strong (Fisher 1978 and Rosenshine 1983.) The basic message in this research is to ask players to attempt new learning that yields 70% to 90% successful experiences. This level of success motivates them to want to continue to achieve. There are two major implications of the finding:

- Reduce each technique, rule, or strategy into achievable sub-skills and focus instruction on those sub-skills
- Provide feedback to the players such that, on most occasions, something that they did is rewarded, followed by specific instructions about what needs more work, and ending with an encouraging "Try again!"

### 7. *Monitor Progress*

If you organize your practice to allow athletes to work at several stations in accordance with their current abilities and needs, it follows that players often will work independently or in small groups. When players are left to work on their own, they typically spend less time engaged in the activities for which they are responsible. When coaches are actively moving about, monitoring progress, and providing individual and small group instructional feedback, players make greater gains (Fisher 1978). Within this context, you can provide much corrective feedback, contingent praise, and emotionally neutral criticism (not personal attacks or sarcasm) for inappropriate behavior. These actions have a positive influence on both achievement and attitude.

### 8. *Ask Questions*

Asking questions also relates to player achievement (Brophy 1976). Questions must, however, promote participation or establish, reinforce, and reveal factual data associated with physical skills, rules, or strategies. Use of this teaching technique seems to work best when there is a pause of three or more seconds before you ask for a response, at which time the players are cued to think about the answer (Rowe 1974).

### 9. Promote a Sense of Control

Your players should feel that they have some control over their own destiny if they are to reach their potential as basketball players. This sense of control can be developed by:

- organizing your instruction to result in many successful experiences (i.e., opportunities to provide positive feedback)
- teaching your players that everyone learns at different rates and to use effort and their own continuous progress as their primary guides (avoid comparing their skill levels with those of other players)
- encouraging individual players to put forth their best effort (reward best efforts with positive comments, pats on the back, thumbs up signs, or encouraging signals)

In these ways, players quickly learn that the harder they work and the more they try, the more skillful they will become. At the same time, you'll be eliminating the natural feeling of inferiority or inability that grows in the presence of feedback which is limited to pointing out errors. Although some players develop in almost any practice situation, many potentially excellent players will not continue in an environment where they feel there is no possibility of gaining the coach's approval.

## Summary

The information in this supplement provides a base from which effective practices can be developed and implemented. Not all coaches can claim that they use all of these guidelines throughout all of their practice sessions. All coaches should, however, seek to use more of these techniques more frequently as they plan and implement their practices.

### REFERENCES

Brophy, J.E., & Evertson, C. (1976). *Learning from teaching: A developmental perspective.* Boston, MA: Allyn and Bacon.

Bruner, J. (1981, August). On instructability. Paper presented at the meeting of the American Psychological Association, Los Angeles, CA.

Fisher, C.W. Filby, N.N., Marliave, R.S., Caher, L.S., Dishaw, M.M., Moore, J.E., & Berliner, D.C. (1978). *Teaching behaviors, academic learning time and student achievement.* Final report of Phase III-B, *Beginning teacher evaluation study, technical report.* San Francisco, CA: Far West Laboratory for Educational Research and Development.

Fisher, C.W., Berliner, D.C., Filby, N.N., Marliave, R.S., Caher, L.S., & Dishaw, M.M. (1980). Teaching behaviors, academic learning time and student achievement: An overview. In C. Denham and A. Lieberman (Eds.), *Time to learn.* Washington, D.C.: U.S. Department of Education, National Institute of Education.

Rosenshine, B.V. (1983). Teaching functions in instructional programs. *The Elementary School Journal, 83,* 335-352.

Rowe, M.B. (1974). Wait time and rewards as instructional variables: Their influence on language, logic, and fate control. Part one, Wait time. *Journal of Research in Science Teaching, 11,* 81-94.

Rutter, M., Maugham, B., Mortmore, P., & Ousten, J. (1979). *Fifteen thousand hours.* Cambridge, MA: Harvard University Press.

Webb, N.M. (1980). A process-outcome analysis of learning in group and individual settings. *Educational Psychologist, 15,* 69-83.

# Sample Practice Plan
*Eugene W. Brown*

---

## QUESTIONS TO CONSIDER

- How should coaches determine the amount of detail to be included in their practice plans?
- How is a practice plan related to a season planning calendar?
- What are the features of an effective practice?
- How can practice plans help a coach to achieve objectives previously listed for the team?

---

## Introduction

This supplement contains a sample practice plan and an overview of the organization and content of the plan. This plan is presented as an example of what might be included in a well-organized practice of intermediate level youth players (10 to 13 years of age) conducted by a highly organized coach. This plan illustrates the fifth of eight practices before the first game. Its outline is derived from the procedures outline in the season planning calendar presented in Section 1, Chapter 3.

## Organization and Content of the Sample Practice Plan

Note that a considerable amount of detail is included in the sample plan. This is provided to make it easier to understand the nature of the activities included in the practice. When you prepare a plan for your own use, the level of detail can be substantially reduced. If you're a seasoned coach, you may only need the names of the drills, key coaching points, and a few diagrams. However, most inexperienced coaches will need more detail.

Note that this sample practice plan contains all of the features of an effective practice that are presented in Table 4-1 of this chapter. These features have also been checked at the bottom of the first page of the sample practice plan.

## Objectives

The objectives of the sample practice plan should be taken directly from the objectives previously listed by the coach in a season planning calendar in Chapter 3. These objectives may need to be modified slightly because of what the coach was able to cover in previous practices and what the coach has learned from assessing the abilities of the players in previous practices.

## Overview of Practice Activities

The overview of practice activities should last only a minute or less. The coach only needs to simply state what is planned for the practice. This helps to mentally prepare and organize the players for the practice. The overview gets the players to "think softball" again. Therefore, a good time to respond to players' questions is immediately after the overview.

## Warm-up & Stretching

The softball-specific warm-ups included in this sample practice plan consist of two light aerobic activities. These activities are used to increase the breathing rate, heart rate, and muscle temperature to exercise levels. They also help to reacquaint the athletes to their practice

**Supplement 4-2.**

```
┌─────────────────────────────────────────────────────────────────────┐
│                        ┌─────────────────────┐                       │
│                        │    PRACTICE PLAN    │                       │
│                        └─────────────────────┘                       │
│  ┌───────────────────────────────────────────────────────────────┐   │
│  │ OBJECTIVES: Review & practice sliding and bunting; practice    │   │
│  │ hitting, fielding ground balls by infielders and outfielders;  │   │
│  │ discuss offensive strategy        DATE: June 18                │   │
│  │                                   #:    5                      │   │
│  └───────────────────────────────────────────────────────────────┘   │
└─────────────────────────────────────────────────────────────────────┘
```

OBJECTIVES: *Review & practice sliding and bunting; practice hitting, fielding ground balls by infielders and outfielders; discuss offensive strategy*

DATE: *June 18*

#: *5*

| TIME | COACHING ACTIVITIES (name, description, diagram, key points) |
|------|-------------------------------------------------------------|
| 5 min. | **Overview of Practice Activities:**<br><br>(1) teach sliding and bunting techniques<br>(2) individual hitting and fielding ground balls<br>(3) offensive strategy |
| 10 min. | **Warm-up:**<br><br>(1) Jog 2 times around the bases<br>(2) Throwing and catching; including pitching<br><br>**Stretching:**<br><br>(1) calf-stretch<br>(2) seated straddle<br>(3) kneeling quad stretch stretch<br>(4) trunk and hip stretch<br>(5) arm circles<br>(6) shoulder stretch |

EQUIPMENT: *One softball per 2 players, bats, bases, portable chalk board, chalk, eraser, whistle, clipboard, and batting helmets.*

NOTE: Features of an effective practice include: √ practice overview; √ warm-up; √ individual skills and drills; √ small group skills and drills; √ team skills and drills; √ cool-down; √ team talk. (Check the features included in this practice plan.)

EVALUATION: _____

(additional space on back)

## PRACTICE PLAN CONTINUED

| TIME | COACHING ACTIVITIES (name, description, diagram, key points) |
|------|-------------------------------------------------------------|
| 15 min. | **Teach Sliding** <br><br> (Key points: bent left leg; hands in air; chin on chest; shoulders parallel to ground) <br><br> **Finding Your Sliding Leg Drill** <br><br> (a) Move to grassy area <br> (b) "Inverted" crab position <br><br> **Sliding Progression Drill** <br><br> (a) Learn "Figure 4" straight-in slide <br> (b) Wet grass – start with 3 steps and slide <br> (c) Add more steps prior to take-off |
| 15 min. | **Teach Bunting** <br><br> (Key points: Square around; grip; catch ball on bat) <br><br> **Practice Bunting Position** <br><br> (a) Correct position – square around bunt <br> (b) Bat height <br> (c) Bend knees for pitches of various heights <br> (d) Bat movement |

## PRACTICE PLAN CONTINUED

| TIME | COACHING ACTIVITIES (name, description, diagram, key points) |
|------|---|
| | *Soft Toss Bunting Drill* <br><br> (a) Feeder tosses ball to bunters <br> (b) Bunter focuses on giving with the pitch with both arms |
| 20 min. | *Hitting Stations* <br><br> (a) Practice hitting off tee into backstop (tennis balls) from behind backstop <br> (b) Shadow swings (on-deck circle) <br> (c) Pitching machine (live balls) or coach pitching <br> (d) Hip Rotation Drill <br><br> (Key points: Weight transfer – hit against front foot; eyes on ball; arm and wrist action (bent to straight)) |
| 10 min. | *Infield/Outfield Ground Ball Drills* <br><br> (a) Diamond Drill (straight to fielder) <br> (b) Glove side; throwing side (3rd and 4th lines) <br><br> (Key points: correct technique; ball hit / rolled to specific location) |

## PRACTICE PLAN CONTINUED

| TIME | COACHING ACTIVITIES (name, description, diagram, key points) |
|------|-------------------------------------------------------------|
| 5 min. | *Cool-down*<br><br>(a) General Baserunning Drill – Jogging<br>　(1) Single<br>　(2) Triple<br><br>(b) Stretching<br>　(1) Shoulder stretch<br>　(2) Calf stretch<br>　(3) Trunk and hip stretch |
| 10 min. | *Chalk Talk: Offensive Strategy*<br><br>(Have players put on warm-up jacket or sweatshirt)<br><br>(a) Sacrifice bunt<br>(b) Characteristics of No.1 hitter<br>(c) Hitting in relation to the count |

environments and prepare the muscles and joints for stretching activities which follow.

The six stretching activities were selected to maintain flexibility in several muscle groups and joints of the body. On average, approximately 45 seconds can be spent on each of the eight activities included in this phase of the practice. Thus, it is assumed that the players are familiar with each of the eight activities and can quickly change from one to the next. If any of these stretches needs to be taught to the players, more time will be needed for the warm-up session or some activities will need to be excluded.

## Teaching Two Skills

The coach must be highly organized to teach two skills in the 30 minutes allotted. One way to facilitate this process would be to provide the players with handouts covering the key points at a previous practice and to have the players read the information before the current practice. Players should be encouraged to create a "Softball Playbook" to organize the handouts on skills, strategies, conditioning, and team rules.

Note that the majority of the 15 minutes allotted should be devoted to practice and not to a detailed discussion of the skill. All players can practice sliding at one time while coaches observe each player and give corrective feedback. Partners are used for the bunting drills. Tell players that they have 15 minutes for each skill to get as many quality repetitions completed as possible.

## Individual Skill Techniques

The drills selected and the manner in which they are conducted should challenge the players to achieve higher levels of performance of individual skills. Selection and conduct should be based upon what the coach has learned from observing the players in previous practices and an understanding of the direction players must proceed to achieve future goals.

In this sample practice plan, 30 minutes are provided for six drills. While the players are engaged in the practice of individual techniques, the coach(s) should be active in observing per-

formances, providing individual and immediate feedback to the players, and developing ideas about what to include in future practices to improve their level of performance.

If the drills run at a brisk pace, the players may concomitantly enhance their fitness level. The potential for simultaneous enhancement of individual techniques and fitness of players within the same practice activities is an example of economical training.

## Cool-Down

In this sample practice plan the same activities are used in the cool-down as were planned for the warm-up and stretching for the beginning of the practice. The cool-down activities could differ from the warm-up activities. The important aspect of the cool-down activities, however, is that they involve the body parts exercised during the practice. This helps clear out waste products built up in the muscle, reduce the pooling of blood in the extremities, reduce the potential for soreness in the muscles, and prevent the loss of flexibility that may accompany intense muscular exercise.

Note that, in an attempt to save time, simple information can be given to the players while they're engaged in their cool-down activities.

## Equipment

After coaches plan their practice, they should review each activity to determine what equipment will be needed to carry out the practice. A written list, included on the practice plan, is helpful when coaches are in a hurry to get to practice on time.

## Evaluation

The evaluation of the practice should be completed after the practice and before planning the next practice. This evaluation should address: (a) the appropriateness of the organization and content of the practice, (b) the success of the coaching methods used, and (c) the degree to which planned objectives (physical skills, tactics, personal and social skills, and fitness) were achieved. This type of evaluation is helpful in improving your coaching methods and in directing future practices to meet the needs of your players.

## Summary

The sample practice plan and overview of its organization and content are presented in this supplement to provide guidance and insight to coaches for making their own practice plans. It is not presented to be directly used by coaches because each team is unique in its needs at any point in time during the season. Therefore, coaches should plan each practice session to meet the specific needs of their players.

**Supplement 4-3.**

## PRACTICE PLAN

OBJECTIVES: _____ DATE: _____
_____ #: _____
_____
_____
_____

| TIME | COACHING ACTIVITIES (name, description, diagram, key points) |
|------|-------------------------------------------------------------|
|      |                                                             |

EQUIPMENT: _____
_____

NOTE:  Features of an effective practice include:  ___ practice overview;  ___ warm-up;
    ___ individual skills and drills;  ___ small group skills and drills;  ___ team skills and
    drills;  ___ cool-down;  ___ team talk.  (Check the features included in this practice plan.)
EVALUATION: _____
_____

## PRACTICE PLAN CONTINUED

| TIME | COACHING ACTIVITIES  (name, description, diagram, key points) |
|------|-------------------------------------------------------------|
|      |                                                             |

**Supplement 4-4.**

DRILL NAME: _____ CLASSIFICATION(S): _____

SOURCE: _____ _____

OBJECTIVES: _____

FACILITIES AND EQUIPMENT: _____ _____

DIAGRAM:                                    DIRECTIONS:

COMMENTS: _____
_____
_____

# Section II
# Rules of Play

# 5
# Basic Softball Rules With Modifications for Youth Players

*Bonni L. Kinne, M.S.*

---

### QUESTIONS TO CONSIDER

- What modifications could be made to the rules of softball to meet the developmental needs of youth players?
- How should the rules of softball be applied in order to promote safety, enjoyment, and fairness?

---

## INTRODUCTION

Softball is a sport that is currently enjoyed by males and females of all different ages, ability levels, and cultures. In the United States, there are individuals participating in fast pitch, slow pitch, and modified softball competition; men's, women's, and co-ed leagues; and adult and youth divisions. There is also the weekend athlete who plays the game more for recreation than for competition. This chapter will focus upon one small, but very important, segment of the softball population: boys and girls, ages 7 to 18 years.

The softball rules described in this chapter represent a portion of the playing rules established by the Amateur Softball Association of America (ASA). Although the ASA revises its rule book (ASA 1991) each year, most of the basic rules have remained the same since soft-ball began. Throughout the content of this chapter, several rule modifications for youth competition are recommended. While these modifications do alter the game slightly, all of them are a necessary part of youth softball because:

1. they assist young players with the development of both defensive and offensive skills
2. they enable a greater number of young players to actively participate in each game
3. they reduce the risk of injuries
4. they help each game progress at an appropriate pace

The most important rule modifications presented include:

1. the dimensions of the field
2. the size of the softball

3. the number of players allowed on defense and offense
4. the length of the game

All of the modifications are described in detail, and most are illustrated in tabular form as well.

## RULE 1—DEFINITIONS

For a complete glossary of softball terms, see Chapter 6.

## RULE 2—THE PLAYING FIELD

Minimum fence distance—the distance from home plate to the outfield fence is a minimum of 225 ft. in men's fast pitch softball and a minimum of 200 ft. in women's fast pitch. This distance is measured from the back corner of home plate to the front edge of the outfield fence (see Figure 5-1).

Distance between bases—the distance between the bases in both men's and women's fast pitch softball is 60 ft. This distance is measured from the back corner of home plate to the outside corner of first base, from the outside corner of first base to the center of second base, from the center of second base to the outside corner of third base, and from the outside corner of third base to the back corner of home plate (see Figure 5-1).

Pitching distance—the distance from home plate to the pitcher's plate is 46 ft. in men's fast pitch softball and 40 ft. in women's fast pitch. This distance is measured from the back corner of home plate to the front edge of the pitcher's plate (see Figure 5-1).

### Modifications for Youth Competition

The dimensions of the field for young players should be smaller than those of a regulation softball field (see Table 5-1).

Other field dimensions—the other dimensions of a softball field (see Figure 5-2) include:

1. the 3-ft. line
2. the on-deck circle
3. the batter's box
4. the catcher's box
5. the coach's box
6. the pitcher's circle

**Table 5-1.** Recommended field dimensions for youth competition.

| AGE GROUP (Years) | MINIMUM FENCE DISTANCE (Feet) | DISTANCE BETWEEN BASES (Feet) | PITCHING DISTANCE (Feet) |
|---|---|---|---|
| 7-10 | 150 | 55 | 35 |
| 11-12 | 175 | 60 | 35 |
| 13-14 | 175 | 60 | 40 |
| 15-18 | 200 | 60 | 40 |

Because these dimensions do not have to be modified for youth competition, they are not described in detail.

## RULE 3—EQUIPMENT

### The Official Bat

The official softball bat, which must be stamped "Official Softball" by its manufacturer, is made of wood, metal, or any other material approved by the ASA. It measures no more than 34 in. in length and weighs 38 oz. or less. If the bat is round, it may not have a diameter greater than 2¼ in.; and if it is three-sided, it may not have a hitting surface larger than 2¼ in. All official bats have a 10-15 in. safety grip normally made of cork or tape and a safety knob that protrudes from the end of the handle at a 90-degree angle.

### Modifications for Youth Competition

Great care should go into the selection of a softball bat. A shorter, lighter bat is recommended for young players because it is more easily handled and controlled, it enables the batter to use better mechanics, and it helps the batter generate a greater amount of bat speed (see Table 5-2).

**Table 5-2.** Recommended bat size for youth competition.

| AGE GROUP (Years) | MAXIMUM LENGTH (Inches) | MAXIMUM WEIGHT (Ounces) |
|---|---|---|
| 7-10 | 28 | 26 |
| 11-14 | 30 | 30 |
| 15-18 | 32 | 34 |

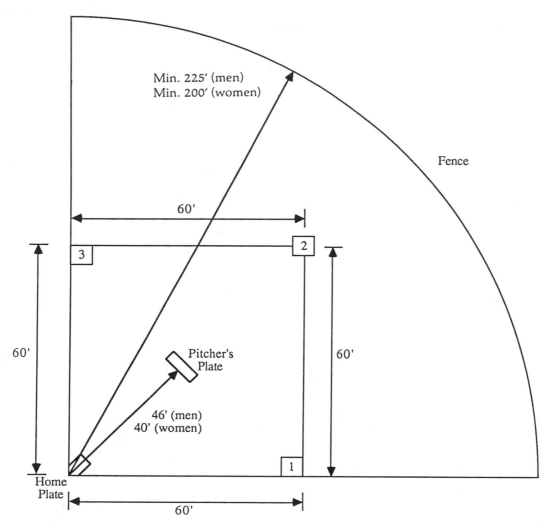

Min. 225' (men)
Min. 200' (women)

Fence

60'

3

2

60'

60'

Pitcher's
Plate

46' (men)
40' (women)

1

Home
Plate

60'

**Figure 5-1.** Official dimensions of a softball field.

## The Warm-Up Bat

The official warm-up bat must be stamped "WB" or "Warm-Up Bat Only" by its manufacturer. It weighs 48 oz. or more and has a diameter of at least 2½ in.

## The Official Ball

The official softball used in both men's and women's fast pitch is known as the white-stitch 12-in. ball. Its circumference measures between 11⅞ and 12⅛ in. and its weight is between 6¼ and 7 oz. All softballs have a cover normally made of horsehide or cowhide and a core that is usually composed of kapok or cork and rubber.

In order to be considered official, the softball must be marked with the ASA logo.

*Modifications for Youth Competition*

The size of the softball for young players should be smaller than that of a regulation softball (see Table 5-3).

**Table 5-3.** Recommended softball size for youth competition.

| AGE GROUP (Years) | TYPE OF SOFTBALL | CIRCUMFERENCE (Inches) | WEIGHT (Ounces) |
|---|---|---|---|
| 7-10 | White-Stitch 11-In. Ball | 10⅞—11⅛ | 5⅞—6⅛ |
| 11-18 | White Stitch 12-In. Ball | 11⅞—12⅛ | 6¼—7 |

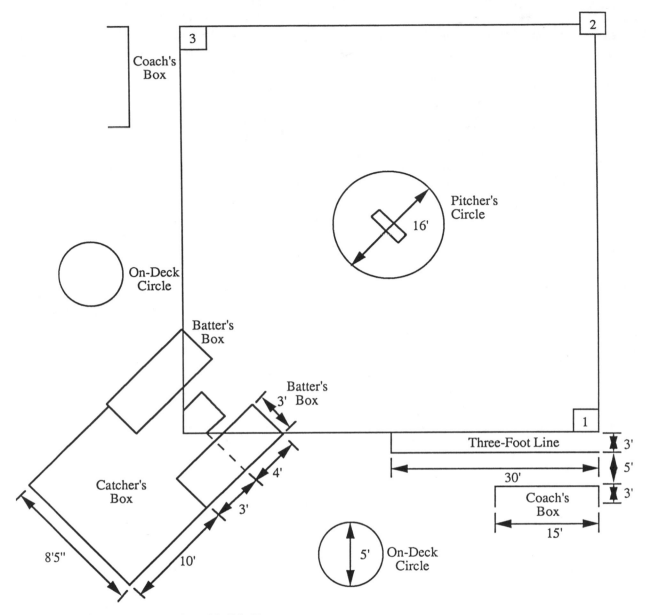

**Figure 5-2.** Other dimensions of a softball field.

## Home Plate

Home plate is a five-sided figure normally made of rubber. The front edge is 17 in. wide, the two sides parallel to the length of the batter's box are each 8½ in. long, and the two sides that meet to form the back corner are each 12 in. long (see Figure 5-3).

## The Pitcher's Plate

The pitcher's plate is a four-sided figure made of rubber or wood. It measures 24 in. in length and 6 in. in width (see Figure 5-4).

## The Bases

First, second, and third bases are usually made of canvas. Each base is 15 in. long, 15 in. wide, and no more than 5 in. thick (see Figure 5-5).

### Modifications for Youth Competition

The use of a double base at first base has been approved by the ASA and is recommended for all youth competition. The double base, which is usually made of canvas, measures 15 by 30 in. on the top and is no more than 5 in.

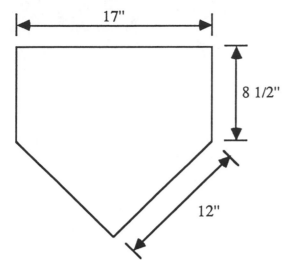

**Figure 5-3.** Official dimensions of home plate.

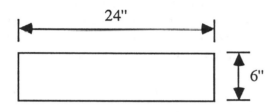

**Figure 5-4.** Official dimensions of the pitcher's plate.

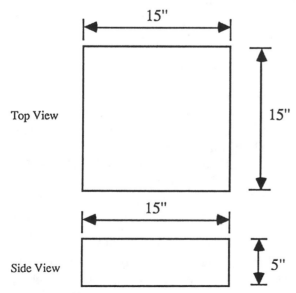

**Figure 5-5.** Official dimensions of the bases.

thick (see Figure 5-6). One half of the base, positioned in fair territory, is colored white while the other half, positioned in foul territory, is colored orange (see Figure 5-7). The purpose of the double base is to reduce the number of injuries that often occur during close plays at first base. This is accomplished by teaching each offensive player to touch the orange portion of the base when running out base hits and each defensive player to touch the white portion when forcing out a batter-runner. Any batted ball that strikes the white portion of the base is considered to be a fair ball while any batted ball striking the orange portion is considered to be foul.

Although they are not mentioned in the ASA rule book, it is also recommended that breakaway bases be used at second base and third base. The purpose of breakaway bases is to reduce the number of injuries that often occur when players slide head-first or feet-first into these bases.

## Gloves/Mitts

The official softball glove/mitt has a maximum size specification for each part. The webbing, for example, may not exceed 5 in. in width. Although any defensive player may use a glove, mitts may only be worn by the first baseman and the catcher. The pitcher is required to use a one-color glove that is neither white nor gray. Multicolored gloves may be worn by any other defensive player, but gloves having white or

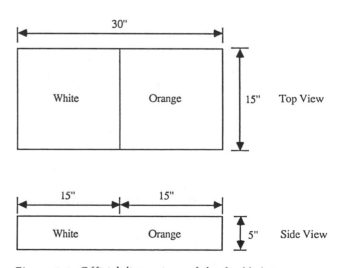

**Figure 5-6.** Official dimensions of the double base.

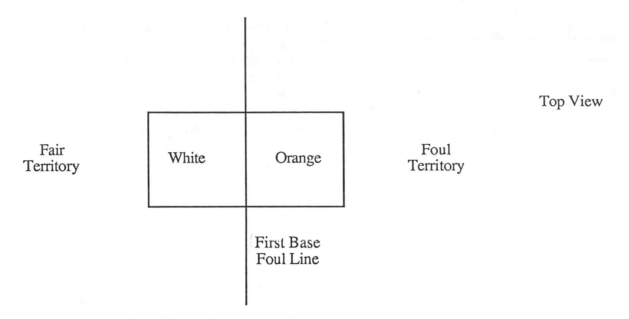

Top View

Fair
Territory

White

Orange

Foul
Territory

First Base
Foul Line

**Figure 5-7.** Positioning of the double base.

gray circles on them are prohibited for all fielders.

### Modifications for Youth Competition

Great care should go into the purchase of a softball glove/mitt. A smaller glove is recommended for young players because it is more comfortable to wear, and it enables the fielder to use better mechanics (see Table 5-4).

## Shoes

The official softball shoe is usually made of canvas or leather uppers. The sole of the shoe may either be smooth or have spikes attached. Metal spikes are legal provided the spikes are not rounded or greater than 3/4 in. in length.

### Modifications for Youth Competition

Metal spikes should not be allowed in any youth competition because they have been implicated in a couple of different types of injur-

**Table 5-4.** Recommended glove/mitt size for youth competition.

| AGE GROUP (Years) | MAXIMUM LENGTH (Inches)— Top of Second Finger Bottom Edge | MAXIMUM WIDTH (Inches)— Width of Palm |
|---|---|---|
| 7-10 | 9½ | 5¾ |
| 11-14 | 10¾ | 6½ |
| 15-18 | 12 | 7¼ |

ies. The person wearing the spikes is at risk for a serious ankle or knee injury if he/she gets the spikes caught in the ground while sliding, running, or pivoting; and all of the players run the risk of being badly cut by someone's spikes.

## Catching Equipment

All catchers must wear a mask with a throat protector.

### Modifications for Youth Competition

A catching helmet, body protector, and shin guards should also be required in all youth competition. In addition, it is recommended that a mask with a throat protector be worn by any player who warms up a pitcher.

## Batting Helmet

All hitters, baserunners, and on-deck batters must wear a batting helmet. The official softball helmet has two earflaps and is approved by the National Operating Committee on Standards for Athletic Equipment (NOCSAE). Although batting helmets are also legal for use by the pitcher and catcher, no other defensive player may wear one unless it is medically warranted.

### Modifications for Youth Competition

It is also recommended that a batting helmet be worn by any player positioned in a coach's box.

## Rule 3: Summary

The following is a list of the recommended youth modifications associated with Rule 3:

1. The maximum bat size for age groups 10 years and under should be 28 in. long and 26 oz. in weight; for 11-14-year-olds, the maximum size should be 30 in. in length and 30 oz.; and for 15-18-year-olds, the bat should be no more than 32 in. long and 34 oz. in weight.
2. An 11-in. softball should be used for age groups 10 years and under while the official 12-in. softball should be used for 11-18-year-olds.
3. The double base should be used at first base, and breakaway bases should be used at second and third.
4. The maximum glove/mitt size for age groups 10 years and under should be 9½ in. long and 5¾ in. in width; for 11-14-year-olds, the maximum size should be 10¾ in. in length and 6½ in. wide; and for 15-18-year-olds, the glove/mitt should be no more than 12 in. long and 7¼ in. in width.
5. Metal spikes should not be allowed.
6. All catchers should wear a mask with a throat protector, a catching helmet, a body protector, and shin guards; and a mask with a throat protector should be worn by any player who warms up a pitcher.
7. Batting helmets should be worn by all hitters, baserunners, and on-deck batters as well as any player positioned in a coach's box.

# RULE 4—PLAYERS AND SUBSTITUTES

## Number of Players

In order to start and/or continue a game, each team must consist of nine players (a pitcher, catcher, first baseperson, second baseperson, third baseperson, shortstop, left fielder, center fielder, and right fielder). If a team has less than nine players at the beginning of or at any time during the course of the game, that team must forfeit.

### Modifications for Youth Competition

It is recommended that each team's lineup consists of 10 defensive players for age groups 10 years and under. The tenth player, designated as the short fielder, is used as an extra outfielder. It is also suggested that each team's offensive lineup be composed of the entire roster.

## Designated Player

If a team wishes to use a designated player (DP), the DP's name must be listed in the batting order as one of the nine hitters in the team's starting lineup. The starting player for whom the DP is used is known as the DEFO for "defense only," and the DEFO is listed tenth on the lineup card. At any time during the game, the DP may be replaced by a pinch hitter, a pinch runner, or the DEFO. The DP may also enter the game at any one of the nine defensive positions provided this change does not alter the batting order.

### Modifications for Youth Competition

It is recommended that a designated player not be used for age groups 14 years and under. Because the DP concentrates mainly on batting and the DEFO works mostly on fielding, this rule tends to limit a young player's ability to develop both defensive and offensive skills.

## Re-Entry

Each starting player, including the designated player, may be removed from the game and then re-entered one time provided the player returns to the same position in the batting order.

### Modifications for Youth Competition

It is recommended that each player be given the opportunity to actively participate in at least two complete innings per game for age groups 14 years and under. The re-entry rule assists teams in complying with this modification.

## Substitutions

A substitute may be used to replace any player who is presently in the lineup. In order to be considered a legal substitute, the home plate umpire must immediately be notified of the player's entry into the game. The umpire, in turn, is responsible for informing the official scorer of the change. If a pitch is delivered before the umpire is made aware of the substitution, the substitute is considered to be illegal; and if this violation is discovered and reported to the umpire by the opposing team, the illegal substitute is declared ineligible.

## Rule 4: Summary

The modifications for youth competition associated with Rule 4 include:

1. the number of defensive players in each team's lineup
2. the number of offensive players in each team's lineup
3. the use of a designated player
4. the minimum number of innings per game in which each player should actively participate (see Table 5-5)

## RULE 5—THE GAME

### Last at Bat

The home team is given the privilege of batting last during each inning unless league or tournament rules state otherwise. If a game is played at a neutral site, a coin toss usually determines which team bats last.

### Number of Innings

A regulation softball game consists of seven innings unless the team batting last scores a greater number of runs in 6½ innings or takes the lead before three outs have occurred in its half of the seventh inning. If a game is tied at the conclusion of seven innings, additional innings are played. These extra innings continue until one team is ahead at the end of a complete inning or the team batting last scores the go-ahead run before three outs have been recorded in its half of the inning. In the event a game must be terminated before seven innings are complete, it is considered a regulation game if a minimum of five complete innings have been

played or the team batting last has scored a greater number of runs in a minimum of 4½ innings. A regulation tie is declared if the game is stopped when the score is even at the end of at least five complete innings or the team batting last ties the score during an incomplete inning provided a minimum of 4½ innings have been played. Games that must be terminated prior to being considered regulation are resumed in progress at a later date.

### Modifications for Youth Competition

It is recommended that a regulation game consist of five innings for age groups 10 years and under. It is also suggested that a 1½ hour time limit be placed on all games for age groups 14 years and under. This time limit means that once 1½ hours have expired, the inning in progress is completed in its entirety and then the game is declared official. For 15-18-year-olds, it is recommended that a 10-run rule be in effect. This 10-run rule states that a game is terminated and declared official if one team leads by 10 or more runs at the end of at least five complete innings or the team batting last is ahead by 10 or more runs after a minimum of 4½ innings have been played.

### The Winning Team

The team that scores the greatest number of runs during an official game is declared the winner.

### Scoring Runs

A run is scored each time an offensive player properly touches first base, second base, third base, and home plate before the defensive team completes the third out of an inning. If a batter-runner makes the third out before safely reaching first base or if a baserunner makes the third out during a force play, any runs that scored prior to the completion of the third out are not

**Table 5-5.** Recommended youth modifications for Rule 4.

| AGE GROUP (Years) | NUMBER OF DEFENSIVE PLAYERS/TEAM | NUMBER OF OFFENSIVE PLAYERS/TEAM | DESIGNATED PLAYER | NUMBER OF INNINGS/PLAYER |
|---|---|---|---|---|
| 7-10 | 10 | Entire Roster | No | 2 or More |
| 11-14 | 9 | 9 | No | 2 or More |
| 15-18 | 9 | 9 | Yes | No Restrictions |

counted. In addition, a baserunner is not credited with a run if a preceding runner makes the third out of an inning.

### Modifications for Youth Competition

It is recommended that a maximum of 10 players per team be given the opportunity to bat during each inning for age groups 10 years and under. This modification assists those teams that may experience some difficulty recording the third out of an inning.

## Offensive Conferences

Each team is allowed one charged conference between the coach and an offensive player during every inning.

## Rule 5: Summary

The modifications for youth competition associated with Rule 5 include:

1. the number of innings in a regulation game
2. the use of a 1½ hour time limit
3. the use of a 10-run rule
4. the maximum number of players per team that may bat during each inning (see Table 5-6)

## RULE 6—PITCHING REGULATIONS

### Preliminary Steps

Before beginning the windup, a pitcher must stand with:

1. the pivot foot touching the pitcher's plate
2. the non-pivot foot in contact with or in back of the pitcher's plate
3. both feet positioned between one end of the pitcher's plate and the other
4. the shoulders lined up with first and third bases
5. the hands apart

6. the softball positioned in either the pitching hand or the glove

Only after completing these steps is he/she allowed to receive a signal from the catcher. Once the signal has been taken, the pitcher must bring the hands together and grasp the softball firmly in both hands for 1 to 10 seconds before beginning the delivery.

### The Delivery

During the delivery, a pitcher must:

1. release the pitch simultaneously with one forward step towards the batter
2. push off the pitcher's plate with the pivot foot
3. keep the pivot foot in contact with the pitcher's plate and/or the ground as the forward step is taken
4. release the pitch using an underhanded motion

### The Windup

During the windup, a pitcher is not allowed to:

1. begin the pitching motion and then stop
2. separate the hands, swing the ball back and forth, and then bring the hands together again
3. stop or reverse any forward motion of the ball
4. execute more than one arm revolution during a windmill pitch
5. continue the windup after completing the forward step

### Illegal Pitching Actions

A pitcher is not allowed to:

1. release the pitch before the catcher is positioned in the catcher's box

**Table 5-6.** Recommended youth modifications for Rule 5.

| AGE GROUP (Years) | NUMBER OF INNINGS/GAME | 1½-HOUR TIME LIMIT | 10-RUN RULE | NUMBER OF BATTERS/INNING |
|---|---|---|---|---|
| 7-10 | 5 | Yes | No | 10 or Less |
| 11-14 | 7 | Yes | No | No Restrictions |
| 15-18 | 7 | No | Yes | No Restrictions |

2. be on or near the pitcher's plate without having possession of the ball
3. take longer than 20 seconds to release the next pitch once the catcher has returned the ball
4. deliberately pitch the ball on the ground in an effort to prevent the batter from hitting it
5. apply any foreign substance, except powdered resin, to the ball, the pitching hand, or the fingers
6. wear anything on the pitching hand, fingers, wrist, or forearm
7. release the pitch before all of the defensive players, with exception of the catcher, are positioned in fair territory
8. take longer than 1 minute to warm up at the beginning of an inning or when relieving another pitcher
9. throw more than five warm-up pitches at the beginning of an inning or when relieving another pitcher
10. make a throw to any one of the bases while in position to pitch
11. step forward off the pitcher's plate without releasing the pitch
12. step sideways off the pitcher's plate while in position to pitch
13. release the pitch before the hitter is positioned in the batter's box
14. deliver the next pitch before all of the baserunners have returned to their respective bases following a foul ball

## Defensive Conferences

Each team is allowed one charged conference between the coach and a defensive player with every pitcher per inning.

## Rule 6: Summary

Although there are not any specific modifications for youth competition associated with Rule 6, it is highly recommended that young players not be allowed to pitch to their peers until they reach the age of 11 years. Instead, tee-ball, pitching machine ball, and/or coach's pitch should be used (see Table 5-7). These softball variations enable young players to better develop both their pitching and hitting skills. A complete set of rule modifications for each of

**Table 5-7.** Recommended softball variations for youth competition.

| AGE GROUP (Years) | TYPE OF SOFTBALL VARIATION |
|---|---|
| 7-8 | Tee-Ball Only |
| 9-10 | 1. Tee-Ball or 2. Pitching Machine Ball or 3. Coach's Pitch |
| 11-12 | 1. Pitching Machine Ball or 2. Coach's Pitch or 3. Regulation Softball |
| 13-18 | Regulation Softball Only |

these variations is found at the end of this chapter.

## RULE 7—BATTING

### Preliminary Steps

Prior to the pitch, a batter must stand with both feet completely inside the batter's box and assume this stance within 10 seconds of the umpire's signal to do so.

### Batting Order

Each player bats in the position in which his/her name appears in the batting order. When a substitute enters the game, he/she hits in the same batting position as the player who is replaced. The privilege of batting first in an inning is given to the player whose name follows that of the final batter in the previous inning. If an inning ends before a batter completes a turn at bat, that player becomes the first batter of the next inning and begins with a count of no balls and no strikes.

### Strikes

A strike is declared when:

1. a pitch enters the strike zone without first hitting the ground
2. a pitch is swung at and completely missed
3. a foul tip is caught by the catcher
4. a foul fly ball is not caught, and the batter has less than two strikes
5. a batted ball hits the batter while he/she is still positioned in the batter's box and has less than two strikes

## Balls

A ball is declared when:

1. a pitch is outside the strike zone or hits the ground in front of home plate, and the batter does not swing at it
2. an illegal pitch is thrown, and the batter does not swing at it
3. the ball is not thrown directly back to the pitcher following a pitch, and the bases are empty
4. an extra warm-up pitch is thrown by the pitcher

## Fair Ball

A batted ball is ruled fair if it:

1. settles in fair territory between home plate and first base or between home plate and third base
2. bounces past first or third while it is in fair territory
3. is first touched in fair territory
4. strikes first, second, or third base
5. lands in fair territory beyond first, second, or third
6. goes beyond the outfield fence while it is in fair territory

## Foul Ball

A batted ball is ruled foul if it:

1. settles in foul territory between home plate and first base or between home plate and third base
2. bounces past first or third while it is in foul territory
3. is first touched in foul territory
4. lands in foul territory beyond first or third base
5. hits the batter or the bat while both are still in the batter's box

## Outs

A batter is called out when he/she:

1. steps across home plate into the other batter's box while the pitcher is in position to pitch
2. fails to take a proper turn at bat, and the opposing team reports the violation to the home plate umpire immediately after the incorrect hitter has batted
3. interferes with the catcher by stepping out of the batter's box
4. intentionally interferes with the catcher while standing in the batter's box
5. hits a fly ball into foul territory, and an offensive player interferes with a defensive player's attempt to catch it
6. intentionally hits a batted ball twice while it is in fair territory
7. swings at and completely misses a third strike and then is hit by the ball
8. uses an altered bat
9. uses an illegal bat
10. hits the ball while one foot is touching the ground completely outside the batter's box
11. hits the ball while one foot is touching home plate
12. hits a fly ball that is caught by a defensive player
13. hits a fly ball that is ruled an infield fly by one of the umpires
14. hits a line drive or a bunt that an infielder intentionally drops while at least first base is occupied, and there are less than two outs
15. reaches first base safely as a result of a baserunner intentionally interfering with a defensive player's attempt to throw the ball
16. reaches first base safely as a result of a baserunner intentionally interfering with a defensive player's attempt to catch a thrown ball
17. receives a third strike that is caught by the catcher
18. receives a third strike while first base is occupied, and there are less than two outs
19. bunts the ball foul after there are two strikes

A batter-runner or baserunner is not called out if a defensive player makes a play while wearing an illegal glove.

### Modifications for Youth Competition

It is recommended that the infield fly rule not be used for age groups 10 years and under. In other words, a batter should not be declared automatically out if, with less than two outs, he/she hits a fly ball into the infield while first and second or first, second, and third are occupied. It is also suggested that the third strike rule not be used for age groups 14 years and under. Instead, a batter should be declared automatically out after receiving a third strike even if the catcher mishandles the pitch. For all age groups, it is recommended that a batter be called out if he/she intentionally throws the bat after being warned by the home plate umpire not to do so.

## On-Deck Batter

The on-deck batter is the offensive player who hits after the batter has completed a turn at bat. While waiting to hit, he/she must stand with both feet completely inside the on-deck circle nearest the offensive team's bench. Only two bats may be used to warm up. These bats may include two official softball bats, one approved warm-up bat, or a softball bat coupled with a warm-up bat. The on-deck batter must remain in the on-deck circle until becoming the batter or being called upon to give directions to a baserunner who is attempting to score.

## Rule 7: Summary

The modifications for youth competition associated with Rule 7 include:

1. the use of the infield fly rule
2. the use of the third strike rule
3. the option of calling a batter out for intentionally throwing the bat (see Table 5-8)

## RULE 8—BASERUNNING

### The Basics

In order to score a run, a baserunner must make contact with each base in its proper order although he/she does not have to run out of the way to touch a dislodged base. If a baserunner needs to return to a preceding base, he/she must touch the bases in reverse order. Baserunners who are declared safe at one of the bases may remain at that base until forced off by a succeeding runner. No more than one baserunner may occupy a given base at the same time.

**Table 5-8.** Recommended youth modifications for Rule 7.

| AGE GROUP (Years) | INFIELD FLY RULE | THIRD STRIKE RULE | DECLARED OUT FOR THROWING A BAT |
|---|---|---|---|
| 7-10 | No | No | Yes |
| 11-14 | Yes | No | Yes |
| 15-18 | Yes | Yes | Yes |

## Becoming a Batter-Runner

A batter becomes known as a batter-runner when he/she:

1. hits the ball into fair territory
2. receives a third strike that is mishandled by the catcher while first base is unoccupied or there are two outs
3. receives a base on balls
4. swings at a pitch, and the catcher interferes with the attempt to hit the ball
5. doesn't swing at a pitch that is outside the strike zone and then is hit by the ball

## Running the Basses With the Liability to be Put Out

A baserunner may attempt to advance to a succeeding base with the risk of being put out when:

1. the pitcher releases a pitch
2. a defensive player throws the ball, and it lands somewhere in the field of play
3. the batter hits the ball into fair territory
4. a defensive player catches a fly ball

### Modifications for Youth Competition

It is recommended that baserunners not be allowed to lead off until after the pitch crosses home plate or the batter hits the ball for age groups 14 years and under. It is also suggested that baserunners not be permitted to steal bases or advance on wild pitches and passed balls for age groups 12 years and under. These modifications help take some of the pressure off young catchers and enable them to focus more fully upon developing proper catching skills.

## Running the Bases Without the Liability to be Put Out

A baserunner may advance to a succeeding base without the risk of being put out when:

1. a defensive player not directly involved in the play interferes with the attempt to run the bases
2. the pitcher throws a pitch that travels out of play
3. he/she is forced to make room on the bases for a batter who has been awarded first base
4. the pitcher throws an illegal pitch
5. a defensive player touches a batted or thrown ball with some type of detached equipment
6. a defensive player throws the ball out of play
7. the batter hits a fair ball that goes over, under, or through the outfield fence
8. a defensive player carries the ball out of play

## Returning to a Base

A baserunner must go back to the original base when:

1. the batter, the batter-runner, or another baserunner interferes with a defensive player's attempt to field a batted ball
2. the batter, the batter-runner, or another baserunner interferes with a defensive player's attempt to throw the ball
3. the home plate umpire interferes with the catcher's throw
4. the pitcher hits the batter with a pitch, and the preceding base is unoccupied
5. a defensive player fails to catch a foul fly ball
6. an infielder intentionally drops a line drive or a bunt while at least first base is occupied, and there are less than two outs

## Putting the Batter-Runner Out

A batter-runner is declared out when he/she:

1. receives a third strike that is mishandled by the catcher but is tagged with the ball before safely reaching first base
2. receives a third strike that is mishandled by the catcher, but a defensive player in possession of the ball touches first base before he/she does
3. hits a fair ball but is tagged with the ball before safely reaching first base
4. hits a fair ball, but a defensive player in possession of the ball touches first base before he/she does
5. hits a fly ball that is caught by a defensive player
6. leaves the field of play instead of running to first base after hitting a fair ball or having been awarded first
7. interferes with a defensive player's attempt to catch a thrown ball by running inside the baseline on the way to first base
8. interferes with a defensive player's attempt to field a batted ball
9. interferes with a defensive player's attempt to throw the ball
10. interferes with a mishandled third strike
11. interferes with the catcher's attempt to put out a baserunner at home plate
12. runs backwards towards home plate in an effort to avoid being tagged with the ball
13. uses an altered bat
14. uses an illegal bat

## Putting the Baserunner Out

A baserunner is declared out when he/she:

1. runs outside the basepath in an effort to avoid being tagged with the ball
2. is tagged with the ball while not in contact with a base
3. is forced to leave a base as a result of the batter hitting a fair ball, and a defensive player in possession of the ball touches the next base before he/she does
4. runs past a preceding baserunner before the runner has scored or been declared out
5. leaves a base before a fly ball has been caught, and the defensive team properly appeals the violation
6. fails to touch one of the bases, and the defensive team properly appeals the violation
7. makes a motion towards second base after legally overrunning first and is tagged with the ball
8. interferes with a defensive player's attempt to field a batted ball
9. interferes with a defensive player's attempt to throw the ball
10. is not in contact with one of the bases and

is hit by a fair ball that has not yet traveled past an infielder

11. intentionally comes into contact with the ball after it has been mishandled by an infielder
12. is physically assisted by a coach while the ball is in play
13. is physically assisted by an offensive player, with exception of another baserunner, while the ball is in play
14. runs around the bases in the reverse direction in an effort to cause a defensive error
15. reaches a base safely as a result of a coach intentionally interfering with a defensive player's attempt to make the out
16. reaches a base safely as a result of an offensive player intentionally interfering with a defensive player's attempt to make the out
17. interferes with a defensive player's attempt to make a play after scoring or having been declared out
18. refuses to slide and maliciously runs into a defensive player who is in possession of the ball
19. leaves a base before the pitcher releases a pitch
20. fails to make an immediate attempt to advance or return to a base while the pitcher is in possession of the ball and is standing within the pitcher's circle
21. walks off a base and leaves the field of play

*Modifications for Youth Competition*

It is recommended that the appeal play not be used for age groups 14 years and under. Instead, a baserunner should be declared automatically out if he/she leaves a base before a fly ball has been caught or if he/she fails to touch one of the bases.

## Rule 8: Summary

The modifications for youth competition associated with Rule 8 include:

1. the option of leading off when the pitcher releases a pitch
2. the option of stealing bases or advancing on wild pitches and passed balls
3. the use of the appeal play (see Table 5-9).

**Table 5-9.** Recommended youth modifications for Rule 8.

| AGE GROUP (Years) | LEADOFF WITH THE PITCH | STEAL OR ADVANCE ON WILD PITCHES/ PASSED BALLS | APPEAL PLAY |
|---|---|---|---|
| 7-12 | No | No | No |
| 13-14 | No | Yes | No |
| 15-18 | Yes | Yes | Yes |

## SOFTBALL VARIATIONS FOR YOUTH COMPETITION

### Tee-Ball

The following is a list of the specific rules associated with tee-ball:

1. The pitcher must be in contact with the pitcher's plate when the batter hits the ball.
2. The home plate umpire stands directly behind the batter.
3. The catcher stands to the home plate umpire's right when a right-handed batter is hitting and to the home plate umpire's left when a left-handed batter is hitting.
4. The home plate umpire is responsible for placing the softball on the tee.
5. The tee is positioned on home plate while the batter is hitting.
6. The home plate umpire is responsible for removing the tee from home plate when the batter hits the ball and for returning the tee to home plate when the next batter steps into the batter's box.
7. Bunting is not allowed.
8. If a batted ball fails to travel at least 10 ft. into fair territory, it is declared a foul ball.
9. Each batter is allowed three swings.
10. If the batter hits a foul ball on the third swing, he/she continues to bat until hitting the ball fair or swinging and missing.
11. Official tee ball bats may be used.
12. The batting tee must be adjustable and must have at least 6 in. of rubber tubing at the top.

### Pitching Machine Ball

The following is a list of the specific rules associated with pitching machine ball:

1. The pitching machine is positioned on the pitcher's plate.
2. The coach of the offensive team is responsible for operating the pitching machine.
3. The pitcher on the defensive team must be positioned even with or behind the pitching machine when the batter hits the ball.
4. Bunting is not allowed.
5. If a batted ball strikes the pitching machine and deflects into foul territory without first being touched by a defensive player, it is declared a foul ball.
6. If a batted ball strikes the pitching machine and remains in fair territory or is touched by a defensive player before traveling into foul territory, it is declared a fair ball.
7. If a batted ball lodges under the pitching machine, the pitch is replayed.
8. Each batter is allowed five pitches.
9. If the batter hits a foul ball on the fifth pitch, he/she continues to bat until hitting the ball fair or swinging and missing.
10. Bases on balls and/or hit batsmen are not allowed.

## Coach's Pitch

The following is a list of the specific rules associated with coach's pitch:

1. The coach of the offensive team is known as the coach-pitcher, and the pitcher on the defensive team is known as the player-pitcher.
2. The coach-pitcher is responsible for pitching from the pitcher's plate.
3. The player-pitcher must be positioned even with or behind the coach-pitcher when the batter hits the ball.

4. Bunting is not allowed.
5. If the coach-pitcher intentionally interferes with a batted ball, the batter is out and the baserunners must return to their bases.
6. If the coach-pitcher accidentally interferes with a batted ball, the pitch is replayed.
7. Each batter is allowed five pitches.
8. If the batter hits a foul ball on the fifth pitch, he/she continues to bat until hitting the ball fair or swinging and missing.
9. Bases on balls and/or hit batsmen are not allowed.

## SUMMARY

This chapter describes the eight major rules associated with the game of softball. Throughout the chapter, several rule modifications for youth competition were suggested. The purpose of these modifications is to promote skill development, participation, safety, and enjoyment. Most of the youth modifications are presented in tabular form at the end of each rule in order to provide the reader with a quick and easy referencing system.

### REFERENCES

Amateur Softball Association of America. (1991). *Official Guide and Rule Book.* Oklahoma City, OK.

### SUGGESTED READINGS

Amateur Softball Association of America. (1992). *Official Guide and Rule Book.* Oklahoma City, OK.
Dixie Softball, Inc. (1992). *Official Rule Guide.* Birmingham, AL.
National Federation of State High School Associations. (1992). *Official High School Softball Rules.* Kansas City, MO.
Pony Baseball, Inc. (1992). *Rules and Regulations: Softball for Girls.* Washington, PA.

# 6
# Glossary of Softball Terms

*Jill Elliott, M.S.*

## INTRODUCTION

This glossary contains a listing of terms and definitions that are common to the game of softball. It is intended to familiarize coaches, players, and parents with the vocabulary that is used in relation to youth softball so that they may gain a greater understanding of the game and may communicate better with others about softball. The terms are listed alphabetically and are often accompanied by common variations of the defined term when appropriate.

*AB (at bats)* Usually indicates an official turn at bat in the scoring summary. An official at bat is anytime a player bats and does not sacrifice, walk, or get hit by a pitch. Only official at bats are considered in the player's batting average.

*Ahead in the count* The batter is ahead in the count when there are more balls than strikes and the count is not full (e.g., 1-0, 3-1). The pitcher is ahead in the count when there are more strikes than balls (e.g., 0-1, 1-2).

*Altered bat* An official softball bat that has been changed in some manner.

*Appeal play* An event in which an umpire may not make a ruling about an offensive violation until it has been properly reported by the defensive team.

*Assist* An assist is credited to a player who helps another player make a putout. For example, if a pitcher fields a ground ball and throws to the first baseperson in time to get the runner out, the pitcher gets the assist and the first baseperson gets the putout.

*Back-up* Player assumes a position behind a play such that an overthrow or loose ball will be recovered more efficiently.

*Bad hop* When the ball bounces in a direction other than what is expected. A bad hop is usually caused by uneven ground, a stone, or excessive spin on the ball.

*Ball* A pitch that does not move through the strike zone and is not swung at by the batter.

*Basepath* An area that encompasses 3 ft. on both sides of the baseline.

*Baserunner* An offensive player who has reached first base safely and has not been declared out.

*Batted ball* A ball that is intentionally or accidentally struck with the bat and travels into either fair or foul territory.

*Batter-runner* An offensive player who has completed a turn at bat but has neither reached first base safely nor been declared out.

*Batter's box* A designated area in which the batter must be positioned as the pitch is delivered; the batter must be in the batter's box when the ball is contacted.

*Battery* The pitcher–catcher combination.

*Batting average* The average number of times a

player reaches first base as a result of a hit. A player's batting average is equal to the total number of hits divided by the total official at bats.

**Batting order**   The order in which the offensive players take their turns at bat.

**BB (base on balls)**   Also referred to as a walk; when the pitcher has pitched four balls to the batter during a turn at bat, the batter is awarded first base.

**Behind in the count**   The batter is behind in the count when there are more strikes than balls. The pitcher is behind in the count when there are more balls than strikes and the count is not full.

**BF (batters faced)**   Indicates the number of batters faced by the pitcher in a pitching summary. A pitcher must throw one pitch to have faced a batter.

**Blooper**   A short fly ball that drops between the infielders and outfielders; usually unintentional.

**Bobble**   When the ball is not fielded cleanly but there is still a chance it can be recovered for a putout.

**Bunt**   A batted ball that is struck softly with the bat and travels a short distance into the infield.

**Call for the ball**   When a fielder communicates to other fielders that she/he is prepared to field the ball.

**Catch**   An event in which a defensive player secures a batted or thrown ball in either the glove or bare hand.

**Catcher's box**   The area in which a catcher must be positioned as the pitch is delivered.

**Charged conference**   An event in which play is interrupted to enable a coach to meet with either a defensive or offensive player.

**Check the runner**   If a runner is on base and does not have to advance on a batted ball, the fielder must check the runner's actions before finally deciding on the play to be made.

**Coach**   A team representative who is positioned in a coach's box while his/her team is on offense.

**Contralateral throw**   The most advanced stage of motor development in which the thrower strides with the foot on the side opposite that of the throwing hand (e.g., a right-handed thrower striding with the left foot).

**Corners**   Players positioned at first and third base are considered to be "at the corners" of the infield.

**Corners of the plate**   The inside or outside portions of home plate.

**Count**   The number of balls and strikes on the batter—stated as balls first, strikes second (e.g., a 2-1 count means 2 balls, 1 strike).

**Cover the base**   When a defensive player is at a base and ready for a play.

**Defensive team**   The team whose members are positioned in the field.

**Dislodged base**   A base that has been moved out of its normal position.

**Double play**   Any play where two outs are made in succession before the next batter has a turn at bat.

**E (error)**   Anytime the batter is allowed to remain at bat and/or a baserunner is allowed to stay on a base or advance to the next base(s) as a result of a defensive misplay.

**ER (earned run)**   A run scored without benefit of an error. If at anytime a runner advanced a base as a result of an error, the run scored by the runner is an unearned run.

**ERA (earned run average)**   The average number of earned runs allowed by a pitcher in a game. The earned run average equals the pitcher's total number of earned runs divided by the total number of innings pitched, multiplied by the innings per game. In softball, ERA = $ER/IP \times 7$.

**Extra base hit**   Any hit where the batter safely reaches a base beyond first base without benefit of an error.

**Fair ball**   Any legally batted ball on or within the foul lines. A ball that is initially foul, then without being touched rolls fair prior to first or third base is a fair ball. A ball that is initially fair, then rolls foul beyond first or third base is a fair ball.

**Fair territory**   That portion of the field which lies within and includes the first-base line, third-base line, back corner of home plate, and the outfield fence.

**Fielder**   A member of the defensive team.

**Fielder's choice**   A play in which the fielder chooses to put out a lead baserunner rather than the batter running to first base. The batter/runner safe at first base does not get credit for a hit.

**Fielding average**  A defensive player's average number of successful plays. Fielding average is equal to the total number of putouts and assists divided by the total number of putouts, assists, and errors.

**Fly ball**  A batted ball that travels up into the air.

**Force out**  When a baserunner is forced to advance on a batted ball because all of the previous base(s) are occupied. A fielder can put out the runner by touching the base only.

**Foul ball**  Any batted ball that is touched outside the foul lines prior to first or third base or initially lands outside the foul lines beyond first or third base.

**Foul line**  The line that extends from home plate to the outside edge of first base to the end of right field, and the line that extends from home plate to the outside edge of third base to the end of left field. The foul lines help designate fair ground and are part of fair ground.

**Foul tip**  A batted ball that travels straight back to the catcher and is secured by the catcher without first touching the ground.

**Full count**  When the count on the batter is 3 balls, 2 strikes.

**Fungo hitting**  When a coach (or player) tosses the ball up and hits it as desired to give players practice fielding various types of batted balls.

**Gap**  The area between the center fielder and right fielder and between the center fielder and left fielder. A ball hit through the gap is usually an extra base hit.

**Glove-side: Foot, knee, shoulder, elbow**  On the same side of the body as the glove hand.

**Go with the pitch**  To hit the ball in relation to the location of the pitch around the strike zone. A right-handed batter would hit the inside pitch to the left side of the field, the center pitch to the center of the field, and the outside pitch to the right side of the field.

**H (hit)**  A batted ball that allows the batter to reach first base safely without the benefit of an error.

**Halfway**  Refers to the lead a runner on first or second base might take on a fly ball hit to the outfield. If the ball is hit fairly close to the runner's base, the runner actually goes less than halfway (e.g., runner on first, fly ball to shallow right field). If the ball is hit a good distance from the base, the runner would go more than halfway (e.g., runner on first, fly ball to deep left field). Going halfway allows the runner a greater chance to safely advance to the next base if the ball is dropped or safely return to the initial base if the ball is caught.

**Helmet**  A type of protective head gear that must be worn by the catcher as well as members of the offensive team.

**Hole (in the hole)**  An area of the field not easily covered by the defense. For example, a shortstop who fields a ball many steps to her/his right is said to have gone "in the hole."

**Home run**  A legally batted ball that allows the batter to safely touch all four bases without the benefit of an error.

**Home team**  The team that hosts the softball game.

**HP (hit by a pitch)**  If the batter is in the batter's box and is hit by a pitch, the batter is awarded first base.

**Illegal bat**  A bat that fails to meet the specifications of an official softball bat.

**Illegal player**  A player who has entered the game without first notifying the home plate umpire.

**Ineligible player**  A player who is not allowed to continue participating in the game.

**Infield**  That portion of fair territory which is normally covered by the pitcher, catcher, first baseperson, second baseperson, third baseperson, and shortstop.

**Infield fly rule**  If there are runners on first and second OR first, second, and third, and the batter hits a fly ball on the infield, the batter is declared out—even if the ball is misplayed. The runner should react as if the ball is caught. The runner must tag up but can choose to advance with the fielder's touch of the ball. If the fly ball rolls foul prior to first and third base and remains untouched, the infield fly rule is no longer in effect.

**Inning: Top/bottom**  That portion of the game in which both teams are given the opportunity to participate for three outs on offense and three outs on defense. The top of the inning is the first half of the inning in which the visiting team bats. The bottom of the inning is the second half of the inning in which the home team bats.

**Interference**   Any act by an offensive player which hinders a defensive player's attempt to execute a play. Also, catcher interference is called if the catcher's mitt is contacted by the bat as the batter executes a swing.

**IP (innings pitched)**   The number of innings or partial innings pitched by a pitcher.

**Ipsilateral throw**   A less advanced stage of motor development in which a thrower strides with the foot on the same side of the body as the throwing hand (e.g., a right-handed thrower striding with the right foot).

**K**   The symbol for a strike out which occurs by swinging and missing the third strike.

**ꓘ**   Symbol for a strikeout which occurs without a swing but instead with a called strike by the umpire (commonly known as a "called third").

**Left on base**   When an offensive player reaches base safely but does not score before the half inning is over. If the bases are loaded and the batter strikes out for the third out, three runners are left on base.

**Line drive**   A fly ball that is struck solidly and travels in a relatively straight line.

**Look the runner back/check the runner**   To determine a runner's intent who is not forced to advance to a base by checking the action of the runner. The intent of the runner determines whether the play is made on the runner or the batter–baserunner.

**Obstruction**   When a defensive player who is not attempting to field a ball or does not have possession of the ball interferes with the progress of a baserunner.

**Offensive Team**   The team whose members are taking their turns at bat.

**On-base average**   The average number of times a batter reaches first base safely. A batter's on-base average is equal to the total number of times first base is safely reached divided by the total times at bat (including unofficial at bats).

**On deck**   The batter to hit after the current batter is the on-deck batter. The on-deck batter generally warms up in a designated on-deck circle.

**Opposite field**   When a right-handed batter hits the ball to the right side of the field, the batter is said to have hit to the opposite field. The same is true for a left-handed batter who hits the ball to left field.

**Outfield**   That portion of fair territory which is normally covered by the left fielder, center fielder, and right fielder.

**Out of play area**   The area beyond the boundaries of the playing area. When a softball field is not enclosed by a fence, the out of play area is usually indicated by a marked or imaginary line extending from the backstop to the end of the outfield and parallel to the foul lines.

**Overrun**   To run beyond a base. Runners can (and should) overrun first base but can be tagged out if they overrun second or third base. A player that overruns first base then turns toward the field cannot be tagged out unless the umpire judges the runner has made a clear move to go on to second base.

**Passed ball**   A pitch that is mishandled by the catcher and, as a result, allows a baserunner to advance.

**Perfect game**   A complete game in which the pitcher has not allowed a baserunner. There are no hits, no walks, and no errors.

**Pick off**   To tag out a runner who is leading off the base.

**Pinch hitter**   A substitute hitter; a player who has not yet been in the game who takes a turn hitting for a player who has been in the game.

**Pitch out**   To intentionally pitch the ball out of the strike zone. The pitchout is such that the catcher can easily catch the pitch, then throw to a base, yet the batter cannot hit the pitch.

**Pivot foot**   The foot used by a pitcher to push off the pitcher's plate; i.e., the right foot for a right-handed pitcher and the left foot for a left-handed pitcher.

**Plant the foot**   To firmly place the foot on the ground such that a forceful push off the ground can occur.

**PO (putout)**   A player who catches a fly ball, tags the base, or the baserunner, is credited with a putout. Also, if the pitcher strikes out the batter, the catcher is credited with a putout.

**Pronation**   In relation to throwing, when the

lower arm rotates such that the palm of the hand faces down.

*Pull hitter*   A hitter who consistently "pulls the ball."

*Pull the ball*   When a right-handed hitter hits the ball to the left side of the field, the hitter has pulled the ball. The same is true for a left-handed hitter who hits the ball to the right side of the field.

*Range*   The amount of ground a fielder can successfully cover. The greater the fielder's range, the more effective the fielder.

*RBI (runs batted in)*   The batter is credited with an RBI if a baserunner scores as a result of the batter's hit, walk, sacrifice, or putout.

*RS (runs scored)*   The number of runs scored by a player.

*Runner*   Another term used for a batter-runner or baserunner.

*Sacrifice*   (1) When a batter bunts the ball and is put out but the baserunner advances; (2) when a batter hits a long fly ball that is caught but gives the baserunner time to tag up and advance home.

*SB (stolen base)*   To safely advance to the next base without benefit of a hit, walk, etc.

*Shutout*   A game in which one of the teams is not allowed to score a run.

*Slugging average*   A batter's average number of bases reached safely by hits. Slugging average equals the total bases reached safely by hits divided by the total official times at bat.

*Soft hands*   Refers to giving with the force of the ball as it is being caught. A good fielder must have soft hands.

*Squeeze play*   A play in which the runner on third base leaves for home with the release of the pitch and the batter bunts the ball to allow the runner to safely score. Generally, if the batter does not successfully execute the bunt, the runner can be tagged out easily.

*Stealing*   An event in which a baserunner attempts to advance to the next base during a pitch.

*Strawberry*   Another word for a burn acquired through excessive friction between the ground and the skin.

*Strike*   A pitch that travels through the strike zone or a pitch that travels outside the strike

zone and is swung at and missed by the batter.

*Strike zone*   An area over the plate that extends from a batter's armpits to the knees.

*Supination*   In relation to throwing, when the lower arm rotates such that the palm of the hand faces up. Forearm supination during the follow-through is an indication of an incorrect throwing arm motion.

*Tag out*   To get the runner out by touching a runner who is off a base with the ball while the ball is secured in the hand(s). If the runner is tagged with the glove hand but the ball is in the bare hand, the runner is not out.

*Tag up*   When a line drive or fly ball has been caught, the baserunner must again touch the base before she/he can advance to the next base. The action of retouching the base is known as tagging up. If the ball is returned to the base or the runner is tagged out before the base is retouched, the runner is out. Once the runner has tagged up, she/he can advance to the next base as soon as the batted ball is touched by a fielder.

*Tandem relay*   A relay in which the throw to the relay person is backed up by another player.

*Throw down*   Generally refers to the catcher's throw to a player covering a base.

*Throwing-side: Foot, knee, hip*   On the same side of the body as the throwing arm.

*Turn at bat*   That period of time which starts when a batter first becomes positioned in the batter's box and ends when he/she is declared out or becomes a batter-runner.

*Unassisted*   When the same person that fields the ball makes the putout. A shortstop that fields a line drive then immediately tags out a runner is said to have an unassisted double play.

*Waste pitch*   A pitch that is intentionally pitched outside the strike zone such that the batter is tempted to swing. Because of the location of the pitch, if the batter does hit the pitch it is usually not a solid hit.

*Wild pitch*   A pitch thrown so poorly that the catcher cannot control it and, as a result, allows a baserunner to advance.

# Section III
# Individual Softball Techniques

# 7
# Fundamentals of Catching

*Jill Elliott, M.S.*

---

### QUESTIONS TO CONSIDER

- What are three fundamental rules of catching?
- When the eyes follow the ball to the glove, what part of the ball should be focused upon?
- What are two advantages of catching with two hands?
- Why do the arms give with the ball?
- How many rules can a beginner focus on at one time?

---

## INTRODUCTION

Every time a ball is pitched in softball, at least one player on the defensive team must catch it. Often, several players must catch the ball to make the play successful. If one player does not catch the ball, the play cannot be successful. Without the opportunity for defensive success through proper catching fundamentals, the game becomes very frustrating.

In general, there are three fundamental rules of catching: (1) the rule of the eyes, (2) the rule of the hands, and (3) the rule of the glove. Whether it is a thrown ball, a batted ball, a ground ball, or a fly ball, these rules always apply.

## THE RULE OF THE EYES

The eyes must follow the center of the ball directly into the glove. If the ball to be caught is high, the eyes look up. If the ball to be caught is low, the eyes look down. If the ball to be caught is to the right, the eyes go right, etc. (see Figures 7-1 and 7-2). The action of the eyes must occur with all catches; it must become a habit! Often a player will discontinue watching the ball before it enters the glove with what is perceived to be a "simple" catch. If neglecting to follow the ball with the eyes during a simple catch becomes a habit, the eyes will not follow the ball into the glove during a more difficult catch. When the eyes do not follow the ball into the glove, the catch is left to chance and chance is not a desirable part of defensive play.

## THE RULE OF THE HANDS

The ball should be caught with "two hands," in front and near the center of the body whenever possible. Both arms are slightly extended as the ball approaches, the throwing hand immediately covers the ball as it enters the glove, and both arms "give" to absorb the force of the ball (see Figure 7-3). Catching the ball with two hands minimizes "bobbles," and, equally important, reduces the time needed to transfer the ball to the throwing hand. Giving with the force

**Figure 7-1.** The rule of the eyes: Ball is low, eyes are low.

**Figure 7-2.** The rule of the eyes: Ball is to left, eyes following ball.

of the ball is especially important as the speed of the ball increases.

When the ball cannot be caught near the center of the body, two options are available. The first option is to move the feet so that the ball lines up with the center of the body. If there is not enough time to move the feet, a second option is to extend the glove to the ball and keep the throwing hand as close to the glove as possible (see Figure 7-4). Here, the throwing hand is not in a position to help secure the ball. However, it is in a position to (1) help recover a bobble, and (2) permit an efficient transfer of the ball from the glove to the throwing hand.

## THE RULE OF THE GLOVE

The rule of the glove dictates the direction the fingers should point when making a catch. In general, the fingers point in the direction the glove has to move to make the catch (see Figure 7-5). If the glove starts at the waist, a ball

**Figure 7-3.** The rule of the hands: Arms extended to ball, ready to "give."

**Figure 7-4.** The rule of the hands: Glove extended to ball, throwing hand close.

caught above the waist would require the glove to move up, in which case the fingers of the glove would point up. Using two hands, all fingers point up with the thumbs together. A ball below the waist requires the fingers to point down with the little fingers together.

A ball at the waist can be caught by: (1) catching the ball with the glove fingers in an upward direction and bending the knees (i.e., catching a thrown ball for a force out), or (2) catching the ball with the glove fingers in a downward direction and elevating the shoulders (i.e., fielding a batted ball). In all cases, the eyes follow the ball into the glove, and the throwing hand is as close to the glove hand as possible.

### Key Elements:

1. The eyes follow the center of the ball into the glove.
2. Both hands are involved in every catch.
3. The arms give to absorb the force of the ball.

(a)

(b)

**Figure 7-5.** The rule of the glove: Glove fingers point to the ball.

4. The fingers of the glove point in the appropriate direction in relation to the ball being caught.

*Common Errors:*

1. The eyes lose sight of the ball before it enters the glove.
2. The eyes look down when the ball is high or look up when the ball is low (see Figure 7-6).
3. The throwing hand is down at the side or behind the body which: (1) reduces the chance of recovering a bobble, and (2) makes the transfer of the ball to the throwing hand more time consuming.
4. The arms move toward the ball as it is being caught rather than giving with the ball. This increases the probability of: (1) the ball popping out of the glove, and (2) the player experiencing pain in the catching hand.
5. The fingers of the glove are down with a throw above the waist. In this situation the ball can go off the heel of the glove and into the face.

**Figure 7-6.** ERROR: Eyes lose contact with the ball before it enters the glove.

## DEVELOPMENTAL PROGRESSIONS

Learning how to catch a ball with a glove can be a very difficult task for beginning players. Therefore, it is important for the coach to understand that the beginner cannot work on all three rules of catching at one time. The rules of catching must be prioritized and emphasized one at a time.

### Eye Contact

Because the ball cannot be caught consistently if it is not seen, the rule of the eyes should be the first priority. At this stage, the success of the player is determined by the action of the eyes, rather than catching the ball. Once the eyes have been trained to follow the ball into the glove consistently, the rule of the hands becomes the second priority.

### Two Hands

Most beginners will instinctively want to keep the glove fingers down when catching the ball. Therefore, the rule of the hands is more easily emphasized when balls are rolled, bounced, or thrown waist high or below. The player watching the ball into the glove concentrates on: (1) extending the arms to the ball, (2) immediately covering the ball with the throwing hand, and (3) giving with the force of the ball.

### Glove Control

When the first two rules become a habit, the rule of the glove becomes the third priority. Balls are thrown to a variety of locations and the player concentrates on pointing the fingers of the glove in the correct direction. As the fingers of the glove automatically move in the correct direction, the player can concentrate on incorporating all three rules of catching.

Although only one rule of catching is emphasized at a time, skilled demonstrations throughout the learning process provide players with a model to imitate. In many cases, the other rules of catching can be learned and reinforced through imitation—without a conscious focus. Also, it is important to provide enough practice so that the rules of catching occur with every catch and the glove becomes no more than an extension of the hand.

Alternatives for softballs, such as the baseball-size Incrediball, can also be used for younger players because the smaller ball is easier to catch with a smaller glove. The smaller size ball will also be easier to grip when working on throwing mechanics.

## CATCHING LEAD-UP PROGRESSIONS

1. The player practices catching a large, soft ball without a glove.

2. The player progresses to a smaller, soft ball (Incrediball) without a glove.
3. The player practices catching the smaller ball (softball- or baseball-size Incrediball) with a mitten on the glove hand.
4. The player progresses to catching the smaller ball with a 6 in. × 6 in. pillow glued or sewn into a regular fielder's glove.
5. The player advances to a regular glove and practices catching:
   a. a Ping-Pong ball or a plastic golf ball
   b. a baseball-size Incrediball or tennis ball
   c. a regular game ball

# 8
# Fundamentals of Throwing

*Jill Elliott, M.S.*

---

QUESTIONS TO CONSIDER

- What are the four phases of throwing?
- Throwing accuracy is determined by what factors?
- What is the significance of the follow-through?
- What is indicated by an ipsilateral throwing pattern?
- Most mechanical errors occur in what phase of throwing?

---

## INTRODUCTION

The purpose of throwing in softball is to get the ball from one point to another as efficiently as possible. Although an easy "toss" is sometimes effective, the majority of throws require force and accuracy. Throwing a softball with force and accuracy can be reduced to four basic components or phases: (1) the preparatory phase, (2) the propulsive phase, (3) the release phase, and (4) the follow-through.

Slight variations of the throw may occur depending on the distance and speed requirements. Throwing variations include: (1) the snap throw, (2) the side arm throw, and (3) the underhand toss.

This chapter focuses on gaining an understanding of the basic components of throwing in order to teach throwing efficiency. Following the description of the basic throw is a description of throwing variations for specific game situations.

## PREPARATORY PHASE

### The Grip

The preparatory phase starts with gripping the softball. The grip involves spreading two, three, or four fingers across the seams with the thumb in opposition around the ball (see Figure 8-1). The softball should be thrown with two or three fingers and the thumb in contact with the ball. However, players with smaller hands may have to use four fingers to control the ball when force is applied in the throwing motion. When gripping the softball, it is important to use the fingers and thumb only. The ball should not contact the palm of the hand (see Figure 8-2).

### The Pivot

An important part of the preparatory phase involves getting the body into a position to pro-

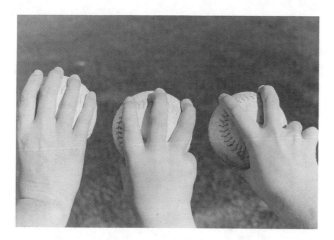

**Figure 8-1.** Gripping the ball with 4, 3, or 2 fingers.

**Figure 8-2.** Gripping the ball with the fingers and thumb only.

pel the ball efficiently. The body is placed in the correct position by pivoting (or stepping) on the throwing-side foot until the foot is perpendicular to the intended path of the ball (see Figure 8-3). The pivot turns the body sideways with the glove side toward the intended target. The purpose of the pivot and perpendicular body position is to: (1) place the body in a position to use the muscles involved in hip and trunk rotation effectively, and (2) create more distance through which the arm can move, which generates greater force on the ball.

### The Throwing Arm

As the pivot is completed, the throwing arm action begins. Initially, the throwing arm moves in a downward and backward direction until it is almost fully extended behind the body (see Figure 8-4). The hand remains on top of the ball throughout this extension movement. The throwing arm then moves in an upward direction until the elbow is behind and above the shoulder. The upper arm is near horizontal, the lower arm is near vertical, and the hand is now to the "inside" of the ball (see Figure 8-5). Here, the position of the ball is held relatively constant until the propulsive action of the shoulder is initiated.

### The Glove Side

As the ball is taken out of the glove and the throwing arm is extending back, the glove

arm extends toward the target. As the glove arm extends, the glove-side foot strides toward the target. Throwing with the glove-side foot striding toward the target is also known as throwing contralaterally. When the glove-side foot contacts the ground, the fingers of the

**Figure 8-3.** The throwing-side foot is perpendicular to the path of the ball.

**Figure 8-4.** Downward and backward movement of the throwing arm.

**Figure 8-5.** The upper arm near horizontal, the lower arm near vertical.

glove and the toes of the foot point toward the target and the glove-side knee bends to absorb the impact of the stride. As the glove-side foot fully contacts the ground, the propulsive phase begins.

## PROPULSIVE PHASE

The propulsive phase begins as the glove-side foot fully contacts the ground and ends as the ball is released from the hand. The glove-side foot contact initiates a series of force-producing joint actions which begin with the larger joints and move sequentially to the smaller joints. Although this joint sequence is more detailed than the action described here, it is important to understand the general concept as it relates to throwing forcefully.

### Hip and Trunk Rotation

The first action to occur is hip rotation. The hips rotate to bring the throwing-side hip toward the target. As hip rotation reaches its greatest velocity, the trunk, which until now has been riding along with the hips, begins to contribute to the force production. The trunk begins its rotational contribution at a greater velocity than the velocity of the hips.

### Shoulder Action

As the hips and trunk rotate, a relaxed shoulder allows the throwing arm to lag behind

until its turn to make a contribution to the force production. The arm lag enables the lower arm to incline backward from its previous near vertical position (see Figure 8-6). This backward incline is a position not possible to duplicate slowly or manually. The arm lag stretches the shoulder muscles, which enables a more forceful contraction of these muscles to bring the arm through at the greatest velocity. The forceful contraction of the shoulder muscles brings the upper arm forward and rotates it slightly inward. This action of the shoulder is known as *medial rotation* or rotation *to the middle*.

### Glove Side

Because all of the action thus far has been of a rotating nature, opposite actions of the glove side of the body will also contribute to the total rotational velocity. These actions are: (1) pulling the previously extended glove to the glove-side shoulder as the throwing side rotates forward, and (2) forcefully extending the previously bent knee of the glove-side leg as the ball is released (see Figure 8-7). Both of these actions create an equal-but-opposite forward movement on the throwing side.

### Arm and Wrist Action

The final contributors to the joint sequence are elbow extension and wrist flexion (see Figure 8-7). Neither, however, is completely ex-

**Figure 8-6.** Throwing arm "lag."

**Figure 8-7.** Actions of the glove side. The glove is pulled to the body and out of view. NOTE: The glove-side knee is more extended than in Figure 8-6.

tended or flexed until just after the ball has been released. When all of the joint actions are complete, the ball is released at an initial velocity equal to the velocity of the hand. Therefore, the greater the velocity of the hand, created by the joint sequence, the greater the velocity of the ball. The entire propulsive phase takes less than .16 seconds for a skilled thrower to complete (Atwater 1968).

In summary, the force producing joint sequence occurs as follows: hip rotation, trunk rotation, shoulder medial rotation, elbow extension, and wrist flexion. Facilitating the opposite actions are the *glove pull* and the *glove-side knee extension*.

## RELEASE PHASE

If the force production phase is consistent, the path of the ball or throwing accuracy is determined by: (1) the path of the ball prior to release, and (2) the exact point of release. If the path of the ball goes from right to left prior to release, the ball will go to the left of the target. Likewise, if the path of the ball goes from left to right prior to release, the ball will go to the right of the target. Therefore, if an individual is consistently missing to the right or left of the target, it would be wise to check the path of the arm prior to release.

If the path of the ball prior to release is directly in line with the target, and the force production phase is consistent, the height of the throw is determined by the release point. A high throw will result from an early release, whereas a low throw will result from a late release. Either one of these trajectories may be desirable depending on the game situation. A low throw, for example, increases the chance of tagging a sliding baserunner. A shoulder-high throw allows a baseperson to stretch for the ball increasing the chance of *forcing out* a baserunner.

## FOLLOW-THROUGH PHASE

The follow-through occurs immediately after releasing the ball. The purpose of the follow-through is to: (1) prevent any interruption of the joint sequence prior to release, and (2) avoid injury by safely reducing the force produced in the propulsive phase. The follow-through is a direct result of the propulsive action phase. In general, the wrist continues to flex, the lower arm faces down, or pronates, the upper arm continues to rotate inward, the shoulder brings the path of the arm downward to the non-throwing side of the body, and the throwing-side leg comes forward to help maintain balance (see Figure 8-8).

Although the follow-through does not have any direct effect on the ball, it is important to note because it may provide insight into possible errors in the throwing pattern. For example, a follow-through in which the inside of the forearm faces up, or supinates, may be an indication of future elbow injury. Forearm supination is in direct opposition to the inward rotation of the upper arm and usually results in undue strain on the elbow joint. Forearm supination is common and is detectable by observing the position of the forearm in the follow-through (see Figure 8-9).

*Key Elements:*

1. The eyes focus on the target.
2. Pivot on the throwing foot to turn the body sideways to the target, glove side to the target.

**Figure 8-8.** The follow-through.

**Figure 8-9.** Correct forearm pronation immediately following the release of the ball.

3. A backward and downward extension, then upward preparatory action of the throwing arm.
4. A contralateral stride with the glove-side foot, the toes pointing to the target.
5. Summation of forces through proper joint sequence—hip, trunk, shoulder, elbow, wrist.
6. Release.
7. Follow through.

*Common Errors:*

1. Early stages of throwing, i.e., ipsilateral (throwing-side foot strides to the target).
2. Inconsistent release point. This problem improves with correct practice and feedback from the coach.
3. Forearm supination vs. pronation—results in elbow injury due to conflict with inward rotation of the upper arm.
4. Improper joint sequence which reduces the total force production. Errors include: (1) only the shoulders turn sideways to the target while the hips stay square to the target, (2) the elbow stays below the shoulder at release of the ball and the wrist flexes without the elbow extending (tucked elbow), or (3) elbow extension without inward medial rotation ("pushing" the ball).
5. Little or no follow-through which (1) minimizes the force applied to the ball prior to release, or (2) increases the chance for injury by abruptly stopping the body parts.

## PROGRESSIONS FOR TEACHING THROWING

The contralateral throwing pattern (see Figure 8-6) is the most advanced throwing pattern. Most individuals will progress through several specific throwing patterns before acquiring a contralateral pattern. A group of beginning players may exhibit a variety of throwing patterns. As a coach, it is important to understand that the throwing pattern executed by an individual is not an indication of throwing potential; rather, it is an indication of past experience. For example, it is likely that an individual who strides toward the target with the glove-side foot, or contralaterally, has had more experience throwing than an individual who strides with the throwing-side foot, or ipsilaterally. An ipsilateral throwing pattern does not indicate that the thrower is uncoordinated; it indicates that he/she has had less previous throwing experience. Understanding this can reduce frustration and anxiety for both the coach and the player.

When teaching an individual to throw correctly, learning priorities should be established and an emphasis should be placed on one phase of the skill at a time. The following progressions are suggested for teaching the various components of throwing.

### Preparatory Phase

#### Contralateral Stride

Learning any skill first requires an understanding of what is involved in performing that skill. Footprints in the dirt of the infield or tape on the floor of a gym can be used to help the individual gain an understanding of the footwork involved in throwing correctly (see Figure 8-10). Initially, the player stands sideways to the target, glove side in front; then the player steps toward the target, placing the glove-side foot into a footprint already on the ground.

#### The Pivot

Once the player understands how the contralateral step feels, the pivot can be introduced. Without a ball, the player: (1) faces the target, (2) pivots (or steps) on a footprint with the throwing-side foot, (3) strides to a footprint with the glove-side foot, and (4) completes the

**Figure 8-10.** Footprints in the dirt—contralateral stride.

throwing motion. When the player can execute the pattern without looking at the footprints, it is time to add a ball and a target. The player focuses the eyes on the target, pivots on the throwing-side foot, strides with the glove-side foot, and throws to the target.

Once the contralateral pattern has been established, the players must repeat the motion until the pattern becomes a habit. Anytime a breakdown in the pattern occurs, simply go back to the footprints.

### Propulsive Phase

The proper joint sequence can occur only with a contralateral stride. With this in mind, a focus on force production should be delayed until the correct stride has become a habit. If the player has to stop and think before striding correctly, an internalization of the correct stride has yet to take place. Players cannot successfully produce force without an automatic contralateral stride. Also, players cannot successfully internalize the contralateral stride if they focus on accuracy and force production while they are learning the movement pattern.

### Throwing Arm Motion

Correct execution of the throwing motion is the key to force production and injury prevention. To focus exclusively on the throwing motion, the player begins on one knee. Although the player does not stride, the contralateral feeling is reinforced with the throwing-side knee down and the glove-side knee up and in front of the body. In this position, the ball is held just above the ear with the elbow above and in front of the shoulder and the wrist extended (see Figure 8-11). From this position the

**Figure 8-11.** On one knee, the player focuses on elbow extension and wrist flexion.

**Figure 8-12.** On one knee, the player executes the throwing motion from the "propulsive position."

player simply executes elbow extension, wrist flexion, and release to a target several feet away.

When the pattern from elbow extension to release is understood, the throwing arm is then placed in its initial propulsive position. Still on one knee, the player begins with the elbow behind and above the shoulder and the glove extended to the target (see Figure 8-12). From here, the player executes shoulder rotation, elbow extension, wrist flexion, and follow-through. The glove is pulled to the glove side simultaneously with the propulsive throwing action. While executing the throwing motion in this position, the player must be aware of the elbow position in relation to the shoulder and the elbow leading the wrist to the target. Progressing further, the player, still on one knee, executes the entire throwing motion: the arm moves down and back, then up, forward, and finishes with the follow-through (see Figure 8-13).

**Figure 8-13.** On one knee, the player executes the entire throwing motion.

### Rotation

Although the sequential rotation of the hips, trunk, and shoulders play a significant role in force production, the force of throwing usually occurs quite naturally if the stride, rotation, and release are done properly. Telling a player to "throw as hard as you can" to a specific but large target (i.e., an area of the backstop) is usually effective in developing proper joint sequence. Also, throwing back and forth in groups of two and gradually increasing the

distance requirements will help develop throwing strength and efficiency.

Coaches should be aware that most errors in throwing occur in the propulsive phase. A player who looks uncoordinated when throwing usually is erring in the joint sequence. As a coach, understanding this sequence is extremely important for error correction.

### Release Phase

Getting the feel of various release points can be accomplished by attempting to hit various targets (i.e., high, low). The targets provide the individual with immediate feedback. The focus should be on the feel of each release in relation to each target. Players should not sacrifice force production for accuracy as the release points change with the force produced. It is also helpful to be aware of varying amounts of force in relation to the release points. Sometimes a softer toss is necessary in softball. A consistently accurate throw takes constant correct repetition, often over a period of years, and a lot of PATIENCE.

## Safety Considerations

When executing a forceful throw, a 7-oz. softball may create as much as 30 lb./ft. of stressful force on the shoulder muscle. Therefore, to prevent injury, there should be a gradual emphasis on velocity and distance. Early practices should involve easy throwing only.

To avoid injuries to other players, all throwing paths should be kept clear. Observers must stand behind and away from the throwers and keep their eyes on the balls in flight. Throwing practice should NOT take place near crowds or spectators. If there is any concern that someone may be hit with a thrown ball, the concern should be vocalized immediately (i.e., look out, cover up!).

## THROWING VARIATIONS

Several situations in softball require a throw other than the overhand throw. If a potential play on a baserunner is close to the fielder but cannot be made unassisted, other types of throws may be used to quickly release the ball. The following is a description of three other types of throws and possible situations for their use. The throws are: (1) the snap throw, (2) the side arm throw, and (3) the underhand toss.

## The Snap Throw

The snap throw uses only the shoulder rotation, elbow extension, and wrist flexion portion of the overhand throw. The ball is initially held above the shoulder approximately even with the ear. The elbow is to the side at a 90-degree angle, and the upper arm is parallel to the ground (see Figure 8-14). In this position, the ball is clearly visible to the receiver! A quick rotation of the shoulder, extension of the elbow, and flexion of the wrist combine to snap

**Figure 8-14.** The initial snap throw position.

**Figure 8-15.** The snap throw follow-through.

the ball forward. The arm finishes approximately parallel to the ground following the release of the ball (see Figure 8-15).

The snap throw is used in situations where a quick, short, direct throw is necessary. For example, the snap throw is used in a *rundown* (see Chapter 17). The ball is held in the initial snap throw position, is in clear view of the receiver, and is quickly released as dictated by the action of the runner. Similarly, a catcher retrieving a wild pitch with a runner coming home may also use a snap throw to return the ball to the pitcher covering the plate.

## The Side Arm Throw

The side arm throw is used by infielders who need to throw quickly to a base after fielding a batted ball. The shortstop, for example, may use the side arm throw to get the ball quickly to second base to force out the runner coming from first base. The side arm throw is quicker than the overhand throw because the throwing arm travels less distance prior to releasing the ball. Less distance traveled by the throwing arm prior to release also means less force produced behind the ball, which makes the side arm throw less effective over longer distances. The side arm throw is useful as a middle distance throw.

A right-handed infielder throwing to the left (e.g., shortstop to second base) fields the ground ball and in a continuous motion brings the ball to the throwing side. The hands separate, the throwing elbow leads the throwing arm back a short distance more, then leads the throwing arm forward and extends the arm out to the side. As the hands separate, the fielder takes a short step toward the target with the left foot. The ball is released so that it will hit the receiver about chest high and the arm follows through to the target (see Figure 8-16). This is also the technique used for the left-handed fielder throwing to the right (e.g., left-handed second baseperson throwing to shortstop).

A right-handed fielder throwing to the right (e.g., second baseperson to second base) anticipates the sidearm throw and fields the ball with the throwing foot further behind the glove foot than normal. With the hips now more open to the target, the fielder: (1) fields the ground ball,

(a)

(b)

**Figure 8-16.** The side arm throw.

(c)

**Figure 8-17.** The underhand toss pendulum motion.

(d)

**Figure 8-18.** The underhand toss follow-through.

(2) in a continuous motion brings the ball to the throwing side, and (3) simultaneously pivots on the throwing foot. The hands separate, the throwing elbow continues back, and then leads the throwing arm forward and extends the arm to the side. Depending on the distance the ball has to be thrown and the strength of the fielder's arm, a short step with the left foot prior to the forward motion of the arm may be desirable. The ball is released so that it will hit the receiver about chest high and the arm follows through to the target. This is also the technique used by the left-handed fielder throwing to the left.

## The Underhand Toss

The underhand toss is used when the ball is fielded close to the base and the fielder must throw to another player for the out. For example, the first baseperson may toss the ball underhand to the second baseperson when the first baseperson fields the ball close to first base and the second baseperson covers the base.

The player fields the ball and then steps to the target with the glove foot. As the glove foot steps to the target, the hands separate and the throwing arm drops back, then moves forward (see Figure 8-17). Throughout the arm motion, the elbow is extended and the wrist is stiff to create a pendulum motion of the tossing arm. The ball is released so that it will hit the receiver about chest high and the arm follows through to the target. Also, the throwing leg comes through with the throwing arm to ensure a smooth continuous motion (see Figure 8-18).

---

### REFERENCES

Atwater, A.E. (1968). *DGWS Softball Guide, 1968-1970*. Reston, VA: AAHPERD.

# 9
# Catching and Throwing as Combined Skills

*Jill Elliott, M.S.*

---

### QUESTIONS TO CONSIDER

- What is the importance of teaching catching and throwing as a combined skill?
- What are the four steps involved in speed throwing?
- What are three game situations where the speed throw can be used specifically?
- How can goals be set for everyone to have an equal opportunity to experience success?
- What are safety considerations of speed throwing?

---

## INTRODUCTION

Very rarely does a softball player have the luxury of throwing the ball without having to catch it first. For this reason it is important to consider throwing and catching together—or, as is commonly stated, "all in one motion." Whether fielding a ground ball, line drive, or fly ball, there is often an opportunity to make a play at another base. The efficiency with which a ball can be received and delivered is directly related to the success of making these plays. The purpose of this combined skill, which we call *speed throwing,* is to teach players to make the transition quickly from catching to throwing.

## FUNDAMENTALS OF SPEED THROWING

All of the fundamentals of catching and throwing are involved in speed throwing. Therefore, the learner should be able to catch and throw proficiently before speed throwing is introduced.

The key to speed throwing is to begin to throw the ball as it is being caught. Speed throwing can be broken down into the following four steps:

### Step 1

The ball is caught with two hands in front of the body as the glove-side foot steps TO the ball (see Figure 9-1).

### Step 2

The ball is transferred immediately to the throwing hand and cradled with the glove hand as both hands are brought to the throwing shoulder. Simultaneously, the throwing-side foot steps in a FORWARD direction but behind the glove-side foot and perpendicular to the intended path of the ball (see Figure 9-2).

**Figure 9-1.** Speed throwing Step 1.

**Figure 9-2.** Speed throwing Step 2.

## Step 3

The weight completely transfers onto the throwing-side foot and the hands separate. As the hands separate, the glove (or glove-side elbow for short, quick throws) points to the target, and the throwing arm begins to move back to the throwing position.

NOTE: The movement of the throwing arm depends on the requirements of the throw. A shorter, quicker throw requires the throwing arm to go directly to the throwing position. A long throw requires a full preparatory motion.

## Step 4

The glove-side foot strides to the target, the throwing arm begins to propel the ball forward, and the glove-side elbow pulls to the glove side (see Figure 9-3).

The speed throw can also be executed when the target is not in the same direction as that of the ball being received. If the glove-side foot steps to the ball and the throwing-side foot steps perpendicular to the target, the body will always be in a position to make a forceful throw. For example, if the second baseperson has to catch a throw coming from the third-base area and then has to quickly throw the ball to first base, the second baseperson: (1) steps to the throw from third base with the glove-side foot, (2) steps forward (behind the glove foot in relation to first base) and perpendicular to first base with the throwing-side foot, then (3) steps to first base with the glove-side foot and completes the throw (see Figures 9-4 and 9-5). (See also Chapter 11, "Second Base—Turning the Double Play.")

NOTE: Catching and then throwing the

**Figure 9-3.** Speed throwing Step 4.

**Figure 9-4.** Step to the ball with the glove-side foot.

ball in this manner also allows the ball to be kept in full view of the next receiver. Whether fielding a ball off the bat, running the ball in from the outfield, chasing a runner in a rundown or attempting to turn a double play, the ball should always be in a position to be seen by the receiver!

*Key Elements:*

1. The glove-side foot steps TO the ball as the ball is caught with two hands in front of the body.
2. The ball is transferred to the throwing hand and cradled with the glove hand as both hands are brought to the throwing shoulder.
3. Simultaneous with the transfer of the ball to the throwing hand, the throwing-side foot steps forward but behind the glove-side foot and perpendicular to the target.

4. The throwing arm begins to move to the throwing position.
5. Simultaneous with the action of the throwing arm, the glove-side foot steps to the target and the throw is completed.

As skill improves and the movement is understood, players should develop a rhythm of: (1) step, catch; (2) step behind; and (3) step and throw.

*Common Errors:*

1. The initial step to the ball with the glove-side foot occurs before the ball is caught, which reduces the ability to adjust to the ball's path when necessary.
2. The initial step to the ball with the glove-side foot occurs after the ball is caught, which eliminates the effect of momentum into the

**Figure 9-5.** Step perpendicular to the target with the throwing-side foot.

**Figure 9-6.** ERROR: The throwing-side foot steps parallel to the target.

ball and increases the time required to throw the ball following the catch.

3. The throwing hand does not stay as close as possible to the glove hand as the ball is caught, resulting in an inefficient transfer of the ball from the glove hand to the throwing hand. The total time prior to release is increased.

4. After the initial step with the glove-side foot, the throwing-side foot steps parallel to the target rather than perpendicular. As a result, the hips stay square to the target and cannot contribute to the force production (see Figure 9-6).

5. The throwing-side foot's step behind the front foot moves in a backward direction which carries the body's momentum in the opposite direction of the throw.

## PROGRESSIONS FOR TEACHING SPEED THROWING

Because catching and throwing proficiency are prerequisites of the speed throw, the success of this skill lies first in the footwork. The footwork can be practiced in a small amount of space without a ball. It can be practiced individually or as a group. By understanding the verbal cues "step as you catch," "step behind," and

"step and throw," this skill can also be practiced at home.

### Foot Movement Without the Ball

Initially, the footwork is practiced without a ball. Footprints are placed in the dirt or on the floor, and individuals simply follow the footprints (see Figure 9-7). When the correct steps become automatic, the individual is ready to practice with a ball.

### Foot Movement With the Ball

The ball is thrown to the individual who steps TO the ball as the ball is caught. The ball is returned to the thrower and the process is repeated. When practicing the step to the ball, the goal is to catch the ball as the glove-side foot contacts the ground. Accurate throws are essential to correctly practice the step to the ball.

Once the individual has successfully timed the step TO the ball several times in a row, the step forward and behind with the throwing foot, commonly called a *crow hop*, is added. The individual steps to the ball with the glove-side foot and steps behind with the throwing-side foot, then stops and repeats the process.

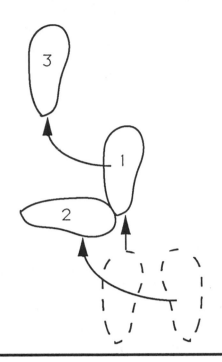

1 = Step to the ball with the glove-side foot

2 = Step "forward and behind" the glove-side foot with the throwing-side foot

3 = Step to the target with the glove-side foot and throw

— — — — = Player standing

──────── = Footprints to follow

**Figure 9-7.** Footprints in the dirt—speed throwing.

When the individual is successful at stepping to the ball with the glove-side foot and then stepping behind the glove-side foot with the throwing-side foot, the final stride to the target with the glove-side foot is added. With the weight of the body on the throwing-side foot as a result of the crow hop, the final stride to the target with the glove foot comes quite naturally. At this point, the individual practices: (1) stepping to the ball with the glove-side foot as the ball is caught, (2) transferring the ball to the throwing hand and cradling the ball with the glove hand during the "crow hop," and (3) stepping to the target with the glove-side foot as the ball is thrown.

## Speed Throwing With a Partner

When the steps of the speed throw are clearly understood and can be repeated automatically, the players begin to focus on decreasing the time it takes to execute the steps. Dividing into groups of two and forming two parallel lines, the players play catch incorporating the speed throw. The sequence is: (1) Player A throws the ball, (2) Player B receives the ball executing the speed throw and throws the ball back to Player A, (3) Player A receives the ball executing the speed throw and throws the ball back to Player B, etc.

*NOTE: As Player A receives the ball and executes the speed throw (Step 3 above), Player B, who has moved forward as a result of the speed throw, must take a step back to the original location—then prepare to step to the returning throw.*

Success is now dependent upon: (1) an accurate throw, (2) a clean catch and a quick transfer of the ball to the throwing hand, and (3) the correct footwork to result in a forceful return throw. Counting the number of successful catches and throws in a given amount of time pro-

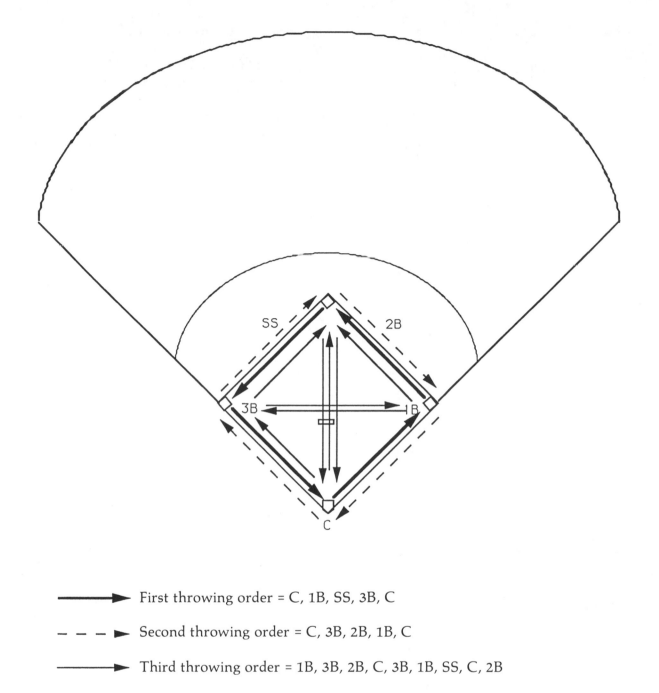

First throwing order = C, 1B, SS, 3B, C

Second throwing order = C, 3B, 2B, 1B, C

Third throwing order = 1B, 3B, 2B, C, 3B, 1B, SS, C, 2B

**Figure 9-8.** Speed throwing around the bases.

vides feedback on the player's speed throwing efficiency. When counting the number of catches and throws in a given amount of time, daily goals can be set relative to the skill level. Each group can have a different goal, and the goals can change as the skills of the groups change. Each group's goal should be to equal or exceed a specific number of catches per time interval rather than to surpass another group's number of catches. Setting goals in such a manner is es-

sential for each player to have an opportunity to experience success.

EXAMPLE: Group 1 consists of two highly skilled players. Group 1 may try to execute the speed throw 40 times in 60 seconds. Group 2 consists of two players of lower skill and 40 catches in 60 seconds is not possible. Group 2's goal may be to execute the speed throw 30 times in 60 seconds. If Group 1 executes 40 and Group 2 executes 30, both have been successful in reaching their goal and are rewarded equally! The next goal is 41 speed throws in 60 seconds for Group 1 and 31 speed throws in 60 seconds for Group 2. If, on the next day, the players from Group 1 and Group 2 exchange partners, the goal for both new groups may be to execute the speed throw 35 times in 60 seconds.

## Speed Throwing to Targets in Various Directions

For speed throwing to be totally specific to softball, players must be able to receive a ball from one direction and then throw it to a target in another direction. This can be practiced by placing a player at each base. The player at home plate throws to the player at first base who throws to the player at second base who throws to the player at third base who throws to the player at home plate. The ball goes "around the bases" several times, with each player concentrating on stepping to the ball with the catch and then correctly stepping behind and throwing the ball to the next base.

Next, the direction of the ball is reversed. The ball goes from home to third to second to first to home. Finally, the ball can be thrown diagonally across the infield. For example, the ball goes from first to third to second to home to third to first to second to home to second to first, etc. Speed throwing around the bases can

also be timed with goals set to equal or beat a specific number of catches per time interval. Goals should be flexible and specific to the skill level of the players. Efficiency in catching and throwing to targets in various directions will help prepare a player for the many diverse situations that may occur in a softball game (see Figure 9-8).

## SAFETY CONSIDERATIONS

When speed throwing is practiced for a specific time interval, the initial interval must be small and gradually increased over a period of weeks. This drill places great demand on the entire body. As the legs get tired, the demand on the arm increases. The increased demand on the arm can result in long term injury if proper precautions are not taken. A gradual increase of the time interval, however, can provide specific conditioning; for example, Week 1, 15 seconds, three times/day; Week 2, 30 seconds, two times/day; and Week 3, 60 seconds, one time/day.

Remember that all throwing paths should be kept clear. Individual groups of two should be well spaced, and observers should keep their eyes on the balls at all times. Players should be instructed to NEVER turn their back on a thrown ball or cross in front of another player who is receiving a ball.

# 10
# Fundamentals of Fielding

*Jill Elliott, M.S.*

---

### QUESTIONS TO CONSIDER

- What are four basic components common to most fielding techniques?
- Why should the fielder field the short hop as close to the ground as possible?
- What safety factors should be considered when practicing fielding?
- How should an infielder field a ball that has to be charged?
- What should the fielder do if he/she is not confident a fly ball can be caught successfully?

---

## INTRODUCTION

The purpose of fielding is to catch a batted ball and quickly and efficiently throw the ball to prevent the opposition's advancement on the bases. To complicate matters, the batted ball is usually hit with the intention of getting it by the fielder. On any given pitch, the ball could be hit on the ground or in the air, "easy" or "hard," or to the infield or to the outfield. The fielder is not in control of the batted ball. Because of this uncontrollable factor, the fielder must be in the proper position and ready for anything.

It is essential to have a systematic approach to efficiently fielding the ball. The following is a description of such an approach for the various types of batted balls that may have to be fielded. As with catching and throwing, there are four basic components common to most fielding techniques that should be understood before attempting to learn about specific techniques. These components are: (1) the fielder's ready position, (2) the approach to the ball, (3) the catch of the ball, and (4) the throw to complete the play.

## FOUR COMPONENTS OF FIELDING

### Ready Position

To allow quick and efficient movement to the ball, each fielder must assume the ready position prior to the release of the pitch. In the ready position, the feet are approximately shoulder-width apart, the glove-side foot is even with or slightly in front of the throwing-side foot, and the weight is evenly distributed over the balls of the feet. The knees are bent and the backside is down to keep the center of gravity fairly low to the ground and centered over the base of support. The shoulders are square to the batter with the trunk forward of vertical. The arms are relaxed and in front of the body with both hands low and facing the batter. The elbows are slightly bent. The head is up and the

**Figure 10-1.** Fielding ready position.

**Figure 10-2.** The catch.

eyes are focused on the hitter's strike zone. Most importantly, the fielder is balanced and ready (see Figure 10-1).

When the ready position is assumed is usually a matter of individual preference. In general, however, the longer the ready position is held, the more likely it is that the weight will shift back over the heels and inhibit movement to the ball. A long ready position also increases the chance of a fielder being distracted prior to the pitch. Therefore, it is recommended that the ready position be assumed sometime between the pitcher's step on the pitching plate and the start of the pitching delivery.

## Approach

The fielder's movement to the ball is called the approach. The approach is dependent upon the path of the ball in relation to the ready position of the fielder. A more detailed discussion of the approach will be presented later in this chapter. In general the ball should be approached so that it can be fielded on the centerline of

the body whenever possible. The movement of the body should be toward the ball. Efficient movement to the ball requires the weight to be shifted from one foot to another in such a way that balance is always maintained.

## The Catch

After successfully completing the approach, the subsequent catch and throw is identical to speed throwing. The glove is open to the ball with the fingers pointing in the appropriate direction and the eyes are focused on the center of the ball until the ball has been secured. The approach is timed so that the glove-side foot steps to the ball as it is being fielded. If the ball is fielded along the centerline of the body, the throwing hand immediately covers the ball as it enters the glove and both arms give to absorb the force of the ball (see Figure 10-2).

As the arms give, the ball is transferred to the throwing hand and cradled with the glove hand, and both hands continue to the throwing side of the body. If the ball cannot be fielded in the center of the body, the throwing hand must remain as close to the glove hand as possible so that a quick transfer of the ball can still be achieved.

When fielding a short hop, the fielder should catch the ball as close to the ground as possible (see Figure 10-3). This will reduce the various angles the ball might take coming off the ground and help avoid possible injuries (e.g., ball hitting the chin). The head must stay down in order to: (1) allow the eyes to continue to follow the ball until it is secured, and (2) keep the glove from pulling up too early.

### The Throw

As the ball is brought to the throwing side of the body, the weight completely transfers onto the glove-side foot. The throwing-side foot then steps in a FORWARD direction (crow hop), behind the glove-side foot and perpendicular to the target (see Figure 10-4). The weight completely transfers onto the throwing foot, the hands separate, and the throwing arm begins its preparatory motion. The glove-side foot strides to the target and the throw is completed (see Figure 10-5).

## GROUND BALLS—INFIELD

The infielder must be prepared to field any of four basic ground ball possibilities: (1) the ball that has been hit directly to the fielder, (2) the ball that has to be charged by the fielder, (3) the ball that has been hit to the glove side of the fielder or forehand, and (4) the ball that has been hit to the throwing side of the fielder or backhand. The ready position, the body movement once the ball has been caught, and all of the basic fundamentals of catching and throwing remain the same for each ground ball possibility. The approach, however, is dependent on the location of the ground ball and therefore varies with each possibility. The remainder of this section will focus on the different approaches to the four ground ball situations.

## Ground Balls—Direct

Any ground ball that can be fielded along the centerline of the body will be considered a direct ground ball. The ball should be fielded along the centerline whenever possible. From the ready position, one or more steps are taken toward the ball. The steps are alternated and timed so the glove-side foot steps in the direction of the ball as the ball is about to enter the glove. This step causes the body to momentarily re-assume the ready position. Re-assuming the ready position will maximize balance by providing a larger base of support and will allow the ball to be fielded along the centerline of the body. If the ball is hit hard and there is no time for a step in the direction of the ball, the body weight simply shifts over the glove-side foot as

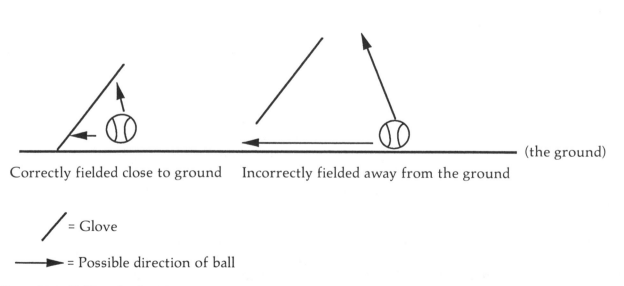

Correctly fielded close to ground      Incorrectly fielded away from the ground

/ = Glove

———► = Possible direction of ball

**Figure 10-3.** Fielding the short hop.

**Figure 10-4.** The crow hop.

**Figure 10-5.** The throw.

the ball is fielded. The step in the direction of the ball OR the weight shift over the glove foot will quickly free the throwing-side foot for the subsequent crow hop.

Similar to catching, the glove fingers point down with a ground ball below the waist, the eyes are focused on the center of the ball until the ball is secured, the ball is caught with two hands in front of the body, and the arms give to absorb the force of the ball. As with speed throwing, once the ball is secured: (1) the hands then bring the ball to the body, (2) the throwing-side foot steps forward yet behind the glove foot (crow hop), (3) the glove-side foot strides to the target, and (4) the throw is completed.

*Key Elements:*

- Ready position.
- The eyes focus on the center of the ball until it is secured with the throwing hand.

- The body weight shifts over the glove-side foot as the ball is being fielded.
- The ball is fielded with TWO hands in front of the body and the arms give to absorb the force of the ball.
- Crow hop: (1) the throwing foot steps or hops behind the glove foot; (2) the glove foot strides to the target; and (3) the throw is completed.

*Common Errors:*

- The eyes focus 2-3 ft. in front of the reception leaving the catch to chance.
- The head raises up. This not only causes the eyes to lose sight of the ball, but it also pulls the shoulders and glove up and gives the ball a chance to get under the glove.
- The throwing-side foot steps as the ball enters the glove which prevents an efficient crow hop.

- The throwing hand is away from the glove or is behind the body as the ball enters the glove.

## Progressions for Teaching Beginners

The direct ground ball is the simplest type of ground ball to be fielded in a softball game. Therefore, an individual must acquire the fundamentals for fielding the direct ground ball before other, more complicated, fielding skills can be successfully learned.

### Relation to Speed Throwing

The first goal of the coach is to get the player to understand what is required to properly field a direct ground ball. If the player is skilled enough to have already learned the speed throw, simply suggest "step (or shift) as you field the ball, crow hop, and throw." Because the footwork has previously been learned, the focus can be on the eyes following the ball into the glove and the hands out in front and working together. If this is done effectively, the player will go from a somewhat choppy execution to a smoother, automatic execution.

### Footprints/Invisible Ball

For lower-skilled players who lack the requisites for the speed throw, the footwork for the ground ball can provide a base for future learning of the speed throw. Using footprints in the dirt or on the floor, the player starts in a ready position and, without having to field a ball, follows a laid-out pattern of footprints. Because the beginner may not be able to coordinate the initial step to the ball with the glove-side foot, that step can be temporarily eliminated. Verbal cues such as "field the ball, step behind, step and throw" may aid the fielder. Following the footprints without a ball should be repeated several times initially, and again each day at the beginning of fielding practice.

### Stationary Ball

Once the fielders can duplicate the steps without following footprints, a stationary ball is used. The ball is placed directly in front of the fielder's body and the fielder is instructed to "field the ball, step behind, step and throw." Check to be sure the ball is picked up with two hands and the eyes are on the ball until the ball is secured.

### Rolling the Ball

The ball is now rolled slowly to the player from about 10 ft. away. The steps should be very slow and deliberate at first. The coach can help the process with verbal cues such as "two hands out in front, eyes on the ball, field the ball, step behind, step and throw" as the player executes the skill. The speed and the distance of the rolled ball can be gradually increased.

### Moving to the Ball

Next, the players need to understand that they have to move to the ball. Now the ball is rolled to various locations so the player has to move to get in front of the ball. At this point, the coach can begin to fungo hit, starting with slow ground balls and gradually increasing to faster ground balls. A variety of games and drills may be used to reinforce these fundamentals. Eventually the timed step to the ball as it's fielded can be introduced, although many times it begins to show up naturally.

## Safety Considerations

The individuals should be spaced well apart and throwing paths should be kept clear. The ground condition should be checked prior to fielding practice and potential bad-hop areas should be avoided. Also, the skill level of the individual should be considered when determining the speed of the ground balls to be fielded. Individuals should not be expected to learn at the same rate. When fungo hitting, the player catching for the batter should be placed well away from the bat and be instructed to let the ball go if it is missed and deflected near the batter! Close supervision is necessary if the players are fungo hitting to each other.

## Ground Balls—Charging (bunts, slow rollers)

Many steps are needed to charge a bunt or slow rolling ground ball. Because of the time used moving to the ball, a clean catch and a quick throw is essential. To ensure fielding efficiency when charging a ground ball, a two-handed pick-up is desirable. Using two hands: (1) makes it easier to pick up a ball with excessive spin, (2) puts the body in a more balanced position to make a forceful and accurate throw, and (3) reduces the temptation to lift the head before the ball is secured.

## Basic Technique

From the ready position, the infielder runs as hard as possible to the ball. As the fielder runs to the ball, the body and the hands stay low to the ground (see Figure 10-6). Just prior to fielding the ball, the feet momentarily reset into the ready position. The feet can be quickly reset with a jump[1] into the ready position (see Figure 10-7). The ball is fielded along the centerline of the body with the throwing hand picking up the ball and the glove hand wrapping around the ball to secure it in the throwing hand. Though both hands are used, their roles are reversed. Both hands take the ball to the throwing side of the body as the crow hop is executed, and the throw is completed.

The right-handed first baseperson charging the ball and making a throw to first base must remember that the most efficient way to crow hop is to open the hips to the first-base foul line (throw with the hips facing the first-base foul line). The opposite is true for the left-handed first baseperson. The right-handed third baseperson throwing to third base should open the hips toward the infield.

## Advanced Technique

Advanced infielders with strong throwing arms can further reduce the time needed to charge and throw a ball. As the ball is approached, the feet are set in a position around the ball so that an efficient weight TRANSFER can take place toward the target. The feet may be set such that the throwing-side foot is perpendicular to the target and the glove-side foot points toward the target.[2] With the ball secured, the body weight simply transfers to the throwing-side foot as the ball is taken to the throwing position, then transfers to the glove-side foot

---

[1] As skill and timing increase, the jump into the ready position will have the throwing-side foot contact the ground first and the glove-side foot contact the ground as the ball is being fielded. The weight is smoothly transferred to the glove-side foot in order to free the throwing-side foot for the crow hop and throw.

[2] A short step to the target with the glove foot may be necessary if it is not initially possible to point it toward the target (see Chapter 8, "Side Arm Throw").

**Figure 10-6.** The fielder stays low when charging the ball.

**Figure 10-7.** The fielder resets the feet as the ball is fielded.

**Figure 10-8.** Foot placement around the ball.

**Figure 10-9.** Weight transfer to the throwing-side foot.

as the ball is thrown (see Figures 10-8 and 10-9). A ¾ arm or side-arm throw may be used to decrease throwing time.

The first baseperson or third baseperson charging a ball and throwing to a base behind them should position the feet around the ball so that: (1) the throwing-side foot is in front of the ball and perpendicular to the base, and (2) the glove-side foot is behind the ball and pointing toward the base. After the ball is fielded, the weight is transferred to the throwing-side foot as the ball is taken to the throwing position. The weight is then transferred to the glove-side foot and the ball is thrown. A short step with the glove-side foot prior to the weight shift may be necessary to completely open the hips to the base.

*Key Elements:*
- Ready position.
- Charge the ball hard, body position low.
- The feet are momentarily placed in the ready position stance as the pickup point is approached.
- The head is down and the eyes are focused on the moving ball.
- The throwing hand fields the ball and the glove hand wraps around the ball.
- The ball is quickly taken to the throwing position.
- Crow hop (or weight shift) and throw.

*Common Errors:*
- The eyes lose focus early, often resulting in the ball being bobbled or missed.

- The pickup is attempted with only one hand—the throwing hand or the glove hand. This technique is unreliable even among highly skilled individuals.
- The charge and pickup occur off-balance, resulting in rushed, erratic throws.
- The fielder takes the long way around to throw to a target behind them (i.e., right-handed first baseperson turns toward the infield to throw to first base). This action may: (1) increase the time necessary to field and throw the ball, (2) impair the accuracy of the throw because the target is not immediately visible, and (3) hide the ball from the receiver to make a more difficult catch.

## Suggestions for Teaching

### Stationary Ball/Slowly Rolled Ball

Charging the ball correctly can be learned by placing a stationary ball 15-20 ft. in front of the player. The player then has to: (1) charge the ball hard, (2) quickly reset the feet in the ready position, (3) correctly field the ball with the throwing hand, secure the ball in the throwing hand with the glove hand, (4) keep the head down with the eyes following the ball into the hands, and (5) crow hop and throw. Once the technique is achieved using a stationary ball, the ball may then be hit or rolled slowly, requiring the player to charge and adjust to the moving ball.

### With Baserunners

Many times charging the ball can be performed correctly in a practice situation. Problems often occur in a game situation, when the need for speed is emphasized. Therefore, to fully prepare an infielder, it is necessary to practice charging the ball in simulated game situations prior to actual game conditions. This can easily be accomplished in practice by using baserunners when rolling or hitting slow ground balls.

Initially, there is a runner at home plate only (the batter) and the play is to be made at first base. From there, runners can be placed at first base, first and second base, second and third base, etc. Sufficient practice will help reduce the panic that sometimes occurs during game situations.

## Ground Balls—Forehand

There are basically two types of ground balls which require a forehand catch: (1) those that are hit hard and close to the glove side leaving no time to get in front of the ball, and (2) those hit a bit slower and several feet away. The close, hard-hit ball will be addressed first.

### Pivot

From the ready position, the feet pivot so that the hips and shoulders are square to the path of the ball. If necessary, the glove-side foot may take a short step as the throwing-side foot pivots to slightly extend the fielder's reach. The glove remains low to the ground as it is moved to the location of the ball. The throwing hand stays as close to the glove hand as possible and the eyes follow the ball into the glove.

The weight is placed on the glove-side foot as the ball is fielded. The throwing-side foot steps (or hops) perpendicular to the target as the ball is transferred to the throwing hand. Then the ball is taken to the throwing position, the glove-side foot strides toward the target, and the throw is completed (see Figures 10-10 to 10-12).

### Crossover

The ground ball hit several feet away requires that the initial step be taken with the

**Figure 10-10.** Forehand pivot to the ball.

**Figure 10-11.** Crow hop.

**Figure 10-12.** Stride and throw.

throwing-side foot. From the ready position, the throwing-side foot crosses in front of the glove-side foot and the glove-side foot pivots so that the hips and shoulders are square with the path of the ball. The crossover step allows a large and more powerful initial step to be taken toward the ball (see Figure 10-13). If the ball is hit fairly hard, fielding range can be increased by angling the crossover step about 45 degrees back from the original position.

The body maintains a low position throughout the approach and the arms are used to gain needed velocity. The steps to the ball are coordinated so the ball is fielded as the weight moves over the glove-side foot. In this position, the throwing-side foot steps or hops perpendicular to the target and the throw is completed.

*Key Elements:*
- Ready position.
- Glove-side foot pivot or short step, throwing-side foot pivot; OR crossover step with the throwing-side foot, to square the body with the intended point of pickup.
- The eyes follow the ball into the glove.
- The throwing hand is as close to the glove as possible.
- The weight shifts to the glove-side foot as the ball is fielded.
- The throwing-side foot steps behind the glove foot (crow hop) and throw is completed.

*Common Errors:*
- The body does not square to the ball which results in: (1) the eyes losing sight of the

**Figure 10-13.** Forehand crossover step to the path of the ball.

**Figure 10-14.** Backhand pivot to the ball.

ball, (2) the ball being fielded off-balance, and (3) an inefficient throw.

- The throwing hand is behind the body rather than as close to the glove as possible. This increases the time needed to transfer and throw the ball.
- The glove is held high when moving to the ball and results in a less efficient downward motion to catch the low ball.

## Ground Balls—Backhand

Similar to the forehand, there are two types of ground balls which require a backhand catch: (1) balls that are hit hard and close to the throwing side; and (2) balls that are hit slow and several feet away. The close, hard-hit ball will be addressed first.

### Pivot

From the ready position the feet pivot to square the hips and shoulders with the path of the ball. If necessary, the throwing-side foot may take a short step as the glove-side foot pivots to slightly extend the fielder's reach. The weight shifts to the throwing-side foot and the glove slides (staying low) to the location of the ball. The throwing hand remains as close to the glove as possible and the eyes follow the ball into the glove (see Figure 10-14). The ball is efficiently transferred to the throwing hand with the glove wrist remaining stiff and the glove arm moving upward and turning inward to meet the throwing hand.

Often, when the ball is hit hard enough to allow only a pivot on the throwing-side foot, there is plenty of time to transfer the weight to the glove-side foot, then complete crow hop and throw. If there is no time for a weight transfer and crow hop, the body pivots on the throwing-side foot until the foot is perpendicular to the target. The glove-side foot strides toward the target and the throw is completed.

### Crossover

Ground balls requiring a longer reach are fielded with an initial crossover step with the glove-side foot. The throwing-side foot pivots as the glove-side foot crosses over so that the hips and shoulders are square with the path of the ball (see Figure 10-15). If the ball is hit

**Figure 10-15.** Backhand crossover step to the ball.

fairly hard, the crossover step is angled back about 45 degrees from the original position in order to increase fielding range. The body position remains low throughout the approach and the arms are used to gain velocity. The glove moves to the ball along the ground and remains open with the thumb down. The throwing hand remains as close to the glove as possible, and the eyes are focused on the center of the ball.

The steps to the ball are coordinated so weight is moving over the glove-side foot as the ball is fielded. The throwing-side foot then continues through the catch and plants behind the glove-side foot (in relation to the target.) With the weight on the throwing-side foot, the glove-side foot strides toward the target and the throw is completed (see Figure 10-16). If

**Figure 10-16.** The throwing-side foot continues through the catch.

the throw is long, and a crow hop following the plant of the throwing foot is required, the fielder must carefully evaluate the situation. It may be best to just hold the ball in a critical game situation.

*Key Elements:*
- Ready position.
- Throwing-side foot pivot or short step, glove-side foot pivot; OR crossover step with the glove-side foot—to square the body with the ball.
- The body and glove stay low during the approach.
- The eyes follow the ball into the glove.
- Weight moves over the glove-side foot as the ball is fielded.
- The throwing hand is as close to the glove as possible—the glove wrist remains stiff, the glove arm moves upward and turns inward to meet the throwing hand.
- The throwing-side foot continues through the catch and pivots perpendicular to the target.
- The glove-side foot strides toward the target to complete the throw.

*Common Errors:*
- During the approach, the glove is placed at or above waist level before moving downward resulting in: (1) lost time getting to the ball, and (2) the glove moving in the wrong direction in the event of a high bounce.
- Swatting at the ball vs. giving with the ball.
- The wrist of the glove arm circles around to transfer the ball to the throwing hand resulting in: (1) lost time, and (2) the ball circling around and out of the glove.

**Suggestions for Teaching**

The forehand and backhand techniques are advanced techniques and should be introduced only when the player has become proficient at approaching ground balls and fielding them along the midline of the body. The first priority of learning to field with the forehand or backhand technique is to develop proper judgment of balls hit to the side of the body. A very efficient way for all players to develop judgment is through the use of a ball and a wall. Each player starts out 2-3 ft. away in a side orientation to the wall. To practice the forehand, the throwing side is closest to the wall; for the backhand, the glove side is closest to the wall. Without a glove, the player tosses the ball to the wall just above the ground and attempts to catch it with the glove hand only. The player should focus on giving with the ball as the ball is caught and then quickly transferring the ball to the throwing hand, and again tossing the ball to the wall. As skill increases, the speed of the ball and the distance from the wall can be increased. Counting the number of tosses and catches in 30 seconds can provide feedback on backhand/forehand efficiency. This exercise is initially quite difficult, but improvement usually occurs rapidly!

A variation of this drill using a glove requires the player to face the wall, 5-15 ft. away and throw the ball to either side. The player focuses on: (1) footwork, (2) reception, and (3) efficiency of transferring the ball to the throwing hand. These drills can be done during practice (i.e., instead of waiting in line to bat) or at home and can be used throughout a career to keep forehand and backhand skills sharp!

# GROUND BALLS—OUTFIELD

Fielding a ground ball in the outfield differs slightly from fielding a ball in the infield. One reason for this difference is time. The forehand and backhand are used sparingly in the outfield because there is more time to get in front of the ball. A second reason is a successfully fielded ground ball does not always require an immediate throw. The ball can be run into the infield. However, it often requires a quick and long throw, in which case efficiency and accuracy are essential. A third reason is the outfield is the last line of defense. A ball that gets past the outfielder can be disastrous. The outfielder must take extra precautions to keep the ball in front of him/her.

The following is a description of various outfield fielding techniques. Included are: (1) ground balls, direct; (2) ground balls, charging; and (3) balls hit to forehand/backhand.

## Ground Balls—Direct

### Movement to the Ball

The outfielder picks up the flight of the ball as it comes off of the bat. Once determined, the outfielder quickly moves to field the ball. If the ball is hit directly to the outfielder, he/she moves straight to the ball. If the ball is hit slightly to the right or left of the outfielder, the outfielder uses a drop step to begin movement to the ball. A drop step is a short step with the ball-side foot that puts the outfielder in a position to arc to the ball. The arc should place the outfielder directly in line with the ball (see Figure 10-17). With the shoulders square to the path of the ball, the fielder now moves straight to the ball.

### Fielding the Ball

As the ball nears, the throwing-side knee drops to the ground and the glove-side knee bends to 90 degrees with the foot perpendicular to the path of the ball. The glove is open and both hands are in front covering the space between the legs (see Figure 10-18). The head and eyes follow the ball into the glove and the throwing hand immediately covers the ball.

### Returning the Ball to the Infield

The ball is transferred to the throwing hand as the fielder either: (1) crow hops into the throw, or (2) runs the ball to the infield. If a long throw is required, the outfielder should reach near complete extension of the throwing arm during the backswing and near complete extension at release. Also, the glove-side shoulder should drop to increase the length of the throwing arm lever and help increase the distance of the throw (see Figure 10-19).

If the outfielder chooses to run the ball to the infield, the ball is carried in a position near

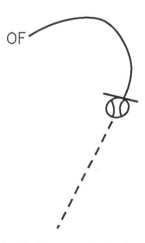

**Figure 10-17.** Outfield arc to the path of the ball (drop step, arc).

**Figure 10-18.** Fielding a ground ball in the outfield.

**Figure 10-19.** Adjustments for long outfield throw.

the ear, ready to throw if necessary. If a throw does become necessary, the outfielder executes a crow hop and completes the throw.

### Key Elements:

- Ready position—glove can be about waist level.
- Move toward the ball with the shoulders square to the path of the ball; right foot drop step with a ball hit to the right of the fielder, left foot drop step with a ball hit to the left of the fielder.
- The throwing-side knee drops as the ball nears, the glove-side knee bends, and the foot is perpendicular to the path of the ball.
- Both hands are in front, covering the space between the legs.
- The head is down and the eyes follow the ball into the glove.
- The ball is fielded and thrown or run into the infield.

### Common Errors:

- Running directly to the ball hit to either side of the outfielder requiring a less reliable forehand or backhand catch rather than using a drop step and arcing to the ball.
- Incorrectly timing the drop of the glove-side

knee—adjusting to the speed of the ground ball comes through practice.

- The outfielder drops to the glove-side knee rather than the throwing-side knee which interferes with a smooth transition into the throwing motion.
- Attempting to throw the ball from the outfield using the shorter infield throwing motion puts undue strain on the throwing arm and/or produces less force to apply to the ball.
- Running the ball to the infield and, if necessary, throwing with the weight moving over the throwing-side foot rather than the glove-side foot. This results in a less than forceful and often inaccurate throw.

### Suggestions for Teaching

#### Stationary Ball

To learn correct fielding technique, the outfielder initially works with a stationary ball. The ball is placed in the outfield grass, with the player one step behind. A step is taken to the ball with the glove-side foot and the throwing-side knee drops to the ground. The glove-side knee is bent, both hands are in front, and the head is down with the eyes on the ball. The pickup is made, the outfielder quickly comes up with the weight over the glove-side foot, executes a crow hop, and completes the throw. When one step to the ball becomes comfortable, the fielder starts progressively further back from the stationary ball. The drop step and arc can be practiced by starting behind and to one side of the stationary ball. A drop step is taken and the arc is made so that the fielder is in a position to drop to one knee and field the ball in the center of the body.

### Moving ball

Once the technique is learned, the outfielder must work on timing his/her approach to various speeds of ground balls. Timing can be learned by first rolling the ball to the outfielder from only a few feet away. As the outfielder becomes comfortable with fielding a moving ball, the distance over which the ball is rolled and the speed at which the ball is rolled is gradually increased. As the fielder becomes consistently successful with the rolled ball, the ball may then be hit to the outfielder, with the hitter starting fairly close to the fielder and gradually working back to home plate. At this stage, repetition, variety in speed and direction, and constructive feedback are essential for continued improvement.

## Ground Balls—Charging

Charging a ground ball is differentiated from fielding a direct ground ball because it requires a quick and strong throw to a specific base. Charging a ball is an advanced skill and is used conservatively (i.e., winning run on second base, ground ball to right field). An outfielder has a greater chance of missing a charge ball because there is little room for adjustments to bad hops or misjudgments.

From the ready position, the fielder runs hard to the ball. The approach is coordinated so that the weight is on the glove-side foot as the ball is fielded. The back of the glove fingers are on the ground, just outside of the glove-side foot. The head is down, the eyes are focused on the center of the ball, and the throwing hand is as close to the catch as possible (see Figure 10-20). Once the catch has been made, the throwing-side foot continues to step forward and

plants perpendicular to the target (see Figure 10-21). If the momentum of the fielder does not allow the foot to plant perpendicular to the target on the step forward, the fielder follows the forward step with a skip on the throwing foot to plant the foot perpendicular to the target. The skip can help the fielder regain body control and add momentum to the throw, especially if the throw is a long throw. The glove-side foot then strides to the target and the throw is completed.

### Key Elements:

- The fielder must charge the ball hard.
- The eyes are focused on the center of the ball all the way into the glove.
- The ball is fielded with the back of the glove fingers on the ground just outside the glove-side foot and the throwing hand is as close to the catch as possible.
- The weight is on the glove-side foot as the ball is caught.

**Figure 10-20.** Fielding the ball to prevent a game winning run.

**Figure 10-21.** Forward step into the throw home.

- Using this technique when it's not absolutely necessary.

### Forehand and Backhand

In the outfield, balls that are hit to the extreme right or left of the fielder are the only balls that require a forehand or backhand catch. Anytime an outfielder moves laterally to field a ball, he/she should employ a crossover step in order to quickly and efficiently begin movement to the ball (see Figure 10-22). The crossover step is taken to properly align the outfielder's pursuit with the path of the ball. Many times outfielders instinctively run directly to the ball. If the ball is hit hard or is a good distance away from the fielder, he/she will not be able to field it.

Taking the proper pursuit angle to the ball will allow the outfielder to reach the path of the ball before it passes by (see Figure 10-23). The angle of pursuit taken depends on the speed of the ball, the speed of the outfielder, and the distance between the outfielder's starting position and the ball's path. Understanding these angles is attained by practicing the fielding of ground balls at various speeds and distances from the fielder. Keep in mind that ground balls in the outfield should be approached at full speed with the ball being fielded in the center of the body whenever possible.

- The throwing-side foot continues forward to plant perpendicular to the target or skips to plant perpendicular to the target to place the body in an efficient throwing position.
- The glove-side foot strides to the target and the throw is completed.

*Common Errors:*

- Attempting to field the ball in the center of the body: (1) takes more time to field and throw the ball, or (2) creates an unbalanced position because the fielder is charging hard.
- The eyes move up to check the runner before the ball has been caught.
- The ball is fielded with the fingertips of the glove and falls out on the way to the throwing hand.
- Inefficient transfer of weight after the pickup; i.e., too many steps.

**Figure 10-22.** Outfielder's crossover step.

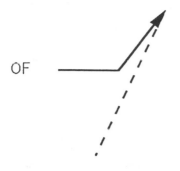

Time-consuming incorrect
angle of pursuit

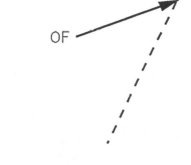

More efficient correct
angle of pursuit

**Figure 10-23.** Correct, incorrect angle of pursuit.

*Key Elements:*

- Movement to the ball is initiated with a cross-over step.
- The outfielder's path to the ball is dictated by the speed of the ball, the speed of the outfielder, and the distance of the ball from the outfielder.
- The eyes are focused on the center of the ball until it enters the glove.
- The glove-side foot plants as the ball is fielded.
- The outfielder takes as few steps as possible in order to maintain momentum, and crow hops and throws to the appropriate location, or runs the ball into the infield.

*Common Errors:*

- The outfielder uses a forehand or backhand catch when there is plenty of time to get in front of the ball.
- The outfielder does not take the appropriate angle to the ball which results in an inefficient pursuit.
- The outfielder does not plant the feet hard enough to quickly change the body's momentum into the throw. Too many steps are taken after the catch is made.

## FLY BALLS—POP-UPS

Catching a fly ball is basically the same for the infielder and the outfielder; the only difference is the distance the ball travels before it is caught and the distance the ball has to be thrown after it is caught. Therefore, this discussion will address all types of fly balls, regardless of posi-

tion. The types of fly balls included are those hit: (1) in front of or slightly behind the fielder, (2) over a fielder's head, (3) in the sun, and (4) near a fence.

## Fly Balls—In Front of or Slightly Behind the Fielder

Similar to fielding ground balls, the flight of the fly ball is picked up immediately off of the bat, and the initial step takes place as soon as the flight of the ball is determined. From the ready position, the player quickly moves to the expected spot of the catch and waits for the ball. If the ball carries to the fielder or is directly in front of the fielder, a stationary or straight-in approach is used. If the ball is slightly behind, or to either side of the fielder, a drop step is used so that the fielder can move to be directly in line with the ball. The fielder should run to the spot of the catch on his/her toes in order to keep the eyes level and clearly focused on the ball. With the body positioned under the ball, the hands move up and in front of the head. The arms extend to the ball and give as the ball is caught slightly on the throwing side of the body (see Figure 10-24).

### Moving Into the Catch

When a throw will be required following a catch, the outfielder moves to a position behind the expected point of the catch. As the ball approaches, several quick steps are taken into the catch. The steps are alternated and timed so the weight is moving to the glove-side foot as

**Figure 10-24.** Arms extended to the ball, ready to give.

**Figure 10-25.** Weight moving to the glove-side foot.

the ball is caught. The hands move up and in front of the head, the arms extend slightly to the ball, and the ball is caught on the throwing side of the body (see Figure 10-25).

With the weight on the glove-side foot and the ball secured, the eyes move to the target and the ball transfers to the throwing hand as the throwing-side foot steps AHEAD of the glove foot (see Figures 10-26a, b). The step ahead of the glove foot is also known as a *travel step*. The travel step will create more momentum into the throw than the crow hop, as long as the throwing-side foot is planted perpendicular to the target. If the throwing-side foot plants parallel rather than perpendicular to the target, the subsequent loss of hip rotation will negate the added momentum. Following the travel step, the glove-side foot strides to the

target and the throw is completed (see Figure 10-26c).

*Key Elements:*
- Ready position.
- Initial movement to the ball as soon as its flight is determined via straight-in or drop-step approach.
- The movement to the ball is hard and players should run on the toes to keep the eyes level.
- Move to a position at or behind the expected spot of the catch and wait for the ball.
- Both arms extend to the ball as it approaches and give with the ball as it is caught slightly on the throwing side of the body.
- When an immediate throw is required following the catch, the fielder moves into the catch: (1) the weight moves to the glove-side foot as the ball is caught, (2) the throwing-side foot steps ahead of the glove-side foot, perpendicular to the target, and (3) the glove-side foot strides to the target and the throw is completed.

| (a) | (b) | (c) |

**Figure 10-26.** The travel step, stride, and throw.

*Common Errors:*
- Running to the ball flat-footed which causes one's vision of the ball to be "blurred."
- The fielder drifts with the ball rather than running hard and waiting for the ball.
- The arms extend too early and directly in front of the eyes, blocking the fielder's vision.
- The arms extend too late, causing the glove to move in the opposite direction of the ball at the time of the catch. The arms must give with the catch!
- The eyes remain straight ahead or look down with the glove high—this is a poor and dangerous technique.
- The throwing hand is not involved in the catch resulting in a less reliable catch and wasted transfer time on the throw.
- No room is left to step into the ball when a throw is to follow.
- The throwing-side foot plants parallel to the target on the travel step, eliminating hip rotation during the throw.

## Progressions for Teaching

### Fly ball Judgment

Before focusing on movement to the fly ball, the fielder must learn to judge the ball's flight. The flight of the ball should start small and increase gradually according to the fielder's success at catching. This can be done by initially throwing short, low fly balls and progressing to throwing longer and higher fly balls. Each fielder should be evaluated individually, and thrown or tossed fly balls in accordance with their ability. Low, short fly balls for higher skilled fielders are not challenging. Long, high fly balls for lower skilled players will not facilitate success.

### Movement to the Ball

As the fielders become proficient at judging fly balls, correct footwork must be learned for efficient movement to the ball. Correct footwork can be learned by temporarily eliminating the ball. Through the use of imagery, the player sets up a situation in his/her mind and physically and verbally goes through the correct execution. For example: "Fly ball slightly back and to the left, glove-side foot drop step, run hard to the spot of the catch, catch the ball." When the player feels comfortable with the proper footwork, a ball may be used. Fly balls may be thrown to the right, left or center; short or long; or high or low. The objective is to combine quick, correct judgment with proper footwork. The next progression requires the player to set up behind the ball, and move into the catch to make a throw.

### Game Simulated Fly Balls

As skill allows, fungo hitting becomes the next step. Again, fly balls should start short and low and gradually increase to higher and longer fly balls, hit to the player's right or left. Eventually, the coach can fungo hit from home plate with fielders at all positions in order to simulate specific game situations.

## Fly Balls—Over a Fielder's Head

Once the flight of the ball has been determined to be over the fielder's head, the fielder has to get to the end of the ball's flight as quickly as possible. To initiate movement to the ball, the fielder drops the ball-side foot back while pivoting on the opposite foot (see Figure 10-27). The opposite foot then crosses over the ball-side foot so that the fielder is directly in line with the ball. Because the ball commonly "tails" to the foul line, the fielder usually drops the foot closest to the foul line when the ball is hit *directly* overhead. The drop step would occur with the left foot for fielders on the right side of the field and with the right foot for fielders on the left side of the field.

If the initial steps are determined to be in the wrong direction, the fielder has two options to correct the direction:

*Option 1:* Plant the foot on the side of the desired direction and pivot and drop back with the other foot (see Figure 10-28). The eyes stay focused on the ball at all times.

*Option 2:* Continue running back and, at the moment a necessary change in direction becomes obvious, quickly turn the head to the

**Figure 10-27.** Drop step to begin movement to the ball.

side of the ball and change the direction of the run. The eyes lose sight of the ball for an instant but immediately regain focus with the completion of the head turn.

With practice, Option 2 becomes more efficient.

If possible, the fielder should begin to turn toward the infield as the point of catch nears and wait for the ball. If this is not possible, while the player is still running, the arms and hands fully extend to the ball just prior to the catch. The eyes follow the ball over the shoulder and into the glove (see Figure 10-29). When a quick throw is required following a catch, the throwing-side foot continues through the catch and plants perpendicular to the target as quickly as possible. It may be necessary to take more than one step to change one's momentum. Once

(a)      (b)

**Figure 10-28.** Change of direction, Option 1.

the throwing-side foot has been planted, the glove-side foot strides toward the target and the throw is completed. If the play requires a long throw, an extra crow hop may also be necessary.

*Key Elements:*

- Drop step to the side of the ball.
- The opposite foot crosses over so the player is in a direct line to the ball.
- The arms extend to the ball just prior to the catch.
- The eyes follow the ball into the glove.
- The throwing-side foot is planted as soon as possible.
- An extra crow hop is taken for a long throw.
- The glove-side foot strides to the target to complete the throw.

**Figure 10-29.** The arms extend to the ball.

*Common Errors:*

- The arms extend to the ball too soon, which slows the fielder's movement to the ball.
- The arms never extend to the ball or they lower too soon when the fielder assumes the ball cannot be caught in the air.
- Turning the wrong direction and not immediately correcting the movement.
- Backpedaling, which is significantly slower and often results in a loss of balance.

## Fly Balls—In the Sun

The fielder should always be aware of the position of the sun in relation to his/her position on the field. When a player is looking toward the sun while pursuing a fly ball, he/she raises the glove to a position that will shade the eyes (see Figure 10-30). The ball can then be followed through the sun area by viewing it on one side of the glove. As the ball nears the fielder, both hands move to catch the ball. For safety reasons, when a fielder loses sight of a ball and cannot relocate it, it is best to cover up rather than attempt a chance catch.

## Fly Balls—Near a Fence

If the fielder is in a position to attempt to catch a ball hit high and near a fence, the fielder must first be aware of the initial distance away from the fence. With the hit, the fielder moves immediately to the fence and extends the throwing arm to locate the fence. Once the fence is located, the fielder moves from the fence to catch the ball. If there is not enough time to get to the fence first, the fielder uses the extended throwing arm to help cushion any contact with the fence (see Figure 10-31). If the fielder has to jump to catch the ball, the throwing arm is used to facilitate the jump. When the fence is on the glove-side of the fielder, the glove arm extends to locate the fence, then moves up to catch the ball.

**Figure 10-30.** Shading the eyes with the glove.

**Figure 10-31.** Extending the arm to the fence.

# 11
# Position Play

*Jill Elliott, M.S.*

## QUESTIONS TO CONSIDER

- What is the correct position of the back-up fielder in relation to the play being backed up?
- What is the significance of letting the ball come to the glove versus reaching for the ball when attempting to tag a runner?
- How is a force play related to speed throwing?
- When a fly ball is hit between an outfielder and an infielder, which fielder has priority to make the catch?
- Why is communication among fielders important?

## INTRODUCTION

In addition to being proficient at the basic skills of fielding, throwing, and catching, each defensive player must also know the techniques and responsibilities unique to a specific position. Defensive success is achieved through a combination of the correct execution of basic skills and the correct execution of techniques and responsibilities specific to position play.

Basic techniques and responsibilities for each position are described below. The positions are discussed in the following order: (1) pitcher, (2) catcher, (3) first base, (4) second base, (5) third base, (6) shortstop, (7) left field, (8) center field, and (9) right field.

## PITCHER

### Fielding

The primary responsibility of the pitcher is to effectively pitch the ball. For defensive and safety reasons, however, the pitcher must also be prepared to field the ball. Immediately after the follow-through of a pitch, the pitcher should assume the fielding ready position (see Figure 11-1). Pitchers must be prepared to react quickly to a hard-hit ball up the middle of the field. The slower-hit ball requires the pitcher to be knowledgeable of the area to be covered and of communication with the other infielders. Generally, the pitcher fields only those balls within the width of the pitching circle to an area fairly close to home plate (see Figure 11-2). As the pitcher approaches home plate, the fielding area overlaps with the fielding area of the other infielders making communication essential.

If the ball is hit in the air, the pitcher should attempt to catch only those balls landing within or near the pitching circle. Infielders have priority over the pitcher on pop-ups. Therefore, any time an infielder calls for a ball, the pitcher must step out of the way. Again, knowledge of the area to be covered and communication with

(a)             (b)

**Figure 11-1.** Entering the fielding ready position.

the other infielders is essential and must be practiced.

### Between Pitches

Upon the return throw from the catcher, the pitcher must check the action of any base-runners. If a runner has taken a big lead and is slow in getting back to the base, a quick throw may get the runner out. If the runner attempts to advance to the next base on the return throw from the catcher (i.e., delayed steal), the pitcher must react quickly and throw the ball to that base. In any event, a runner that is being closely monitored tends to take a smaller lead. The smaller the lead, the longer it takes to run to the next base, regardless of what happens with the pitch. Checking a runner between each pitch should become a habit so that it does not detract from the role of pitching.

### Backing Up

The pitcher is responsible for backing up center-field throws to second base and left field,

center-field throws to third base, and all out-field throws to home plate. (The left fielder generally backs up throws to third base from right field.) When it is uncertain as to whether the throw is to be made to third base or home plate, the pitcher should immediately position him/herself outside the center of the third-base foul line and react to the play from there.

### Covering Home Plate

The pitcher must cover the plate anytime runners are in scoring position and the catcher leaves home plate in order to play a ball. Generally, the catcher only leaves home plate with runners in scoring position in order to retrieve a wild pitch or a passed ball. The pitcher must immediately react to a wild pitch/passed ball and move quickly to home plate, with the hands up so that the catcher has a clear target (see Figure 11-3). Upon reaching home plate, the glove-side foot is planted on the front edge of the first-base side of the plate and the throwing-side foot is slightly behind the glove foot, creat-

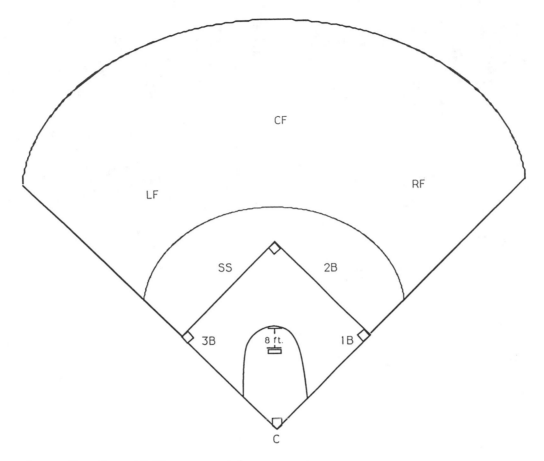

**Figure 11-2.** Position Play: General fielding areas—pitcher.

ing a balanced waiting position. The ball is received from the catcher and secured in the glove. The glove is then placed on the third-base side of home plate, with the backside of the glove toward the runner (see Figure 11-4). As the runner slides into the glove, the pitcher immediately retreats to the infield. Collisions between the pitcher and the runner must be avoided!

## CATCHER

### Receiving the Pitch

The first responsibility of a catcher is to receive the pitch from the pitcher. A catcher's stance varies with the game situation. When the bases are empty, the catcher uses a crouched or down position. With runners on base, the catcher uses a semi-crouched position or up position.

### Crouched Position

In the crouched position, the catcher squats down with the feet approximately shoulder

**Figure 11-3.** The pitcher's approach to home plate.

**Figure 11-4.** The pitcher prepares to tag and retreat.

**Figure 11-5.** The crouched receiving position.

width apart, the glove-side foot even with or slightly in front of the throwing-side foot, and the weight distributed on the balls of the feet. The glove-side arm is extended in front of the body and slightly flexed, with the glove open wide, producing a large target. The throwing arm is positioned behind the back or behind the leg in order to protect it from a foul tip or a wild pitch (see Figure 11-5). The target is positioned along the centerline of the catcher so that the stance location changes slightly with the desired pitch location. For example, on an inside pitch, the catcher's midline should be lined up with the inside edge of the plate (see Figure 11-6). Similarly, on an outside pitch, the catcher's midline should be lined up with the outside edge of the plate.

### Semi-Crouched Position

With runners on base, the catcher must be prepared to make a throw following each pitch. The semi-crouched position allows the catcher to quickly execute a throw. The catcher starts in the down position. As the pitcher prepares to deliver the pitch, the catcher widens his/her stance by moving the glove-side foot out and raising the hips. In the semi-crouched position, the glove-side foot is slightly in front of the throwing foot, the hips are up, and the back is approximately parallel to the ground (see Figure 11-7). The throwing hand is loosely clenched and placed behind the glove so that the hand is

protected, yet in position to quickly transfer the ball (see Figure 11-8).

**Figure 11-6.** Receiving an inside pitch.

**Figure 11-7.** The semi-crouched receiving position.

## The Throw

If the situation requires a throw to a base, upon receiving the pitch the catcher shifts the weight over the glove-side foot and simultaneously leans forward in order to rise to a standing position. In a continuous motion, the catcher executes a crow hop to plant the throwing-side foot perpendicular to the target. If the throw is to be made to first base or third base and the batter is on the side of the throw, the crow hop must place the catcher in front of the batter. During the crow hop, the ball is transferred to the throwing hand as both hands move toward the throwing shoulder. The throwing elbow is placed shoulder high and leads the throwing hand back in order to place the shoulder muscles on stretch. The glove-side foot strides toward the target, and the elbow leads the throwing hand forward in order to quickly complete the joint sequence and release the ball (see Figure 11-9).

If the catcher has a strong throwing arm, he/she may execute a quick jump pivot upon receiving the pitch. The jump pivot consists of placing the throwing-side foot perpendicular to the target and the glove-side foot toward the target. The pivot must be executed as the catcher is standing up to complete the throw. Otherwise, valuable time is lost. With the jump pivot, the body weight lands on the throwing-side

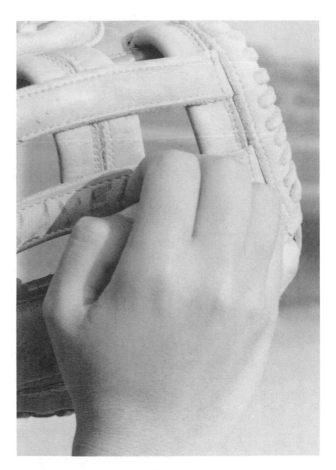

**Figure 11-8.** Position of the throwing hand.

foot and quickly transfers to the glove-side foot during the throw. The throwing action of the arm is the same as with the crow hop, but quicker (see Figure 11-10).

## Blocking Pitches

Occasionally, pitches hit the ground before they get to the catcher. With runners on base, the catcher must be prepared to block a pitch and keep the ball in front of the body. Assuming the catching stance as close to home plate as possible will allow the catcher to block a pitch closer to the ground and reduce the effect of a bad bounce.

### Blocking Pitches—Center

On low pitches directly in front of the catcher, he/she drops down to the knees and then slides into the pitch. The head is down

**Figure 11-9.** The crow hop and throw.

(a)

(b)

**Figure 11-10.** The jump pivot and throw.

**Figure 11-11.** The center block.

and the eyes focus on the ball, while the shoulders remain square to the pitcher. The back is slightly curved forward in order to deflect the ball downward, and the glove is placed between the knees and open (see Figure 11-11). After the ball has been blocked, the catcher immediately moves to recover the ball. The catcher positions his/her feet around the ball such that

a crow hop can be easily executed into a potential throw. The catcher fields the ball and immediately looks for a play.

**Blocking Pitches—Left**

When a pitch is pitched to the ground on the left side of the catcher, he/she takes a quick step with the left foot and moves the body to the left by pushing off with the right foot. The right knee is placed on the ground, followed by the left knee. The hands fill the space between the knees, with the glove open to the ball and contacting the ground. As the catcher moves toward the ball, the left shoulder is turned inward in order to deflect the ball forward. The head is down and the eyes focused upon the ball, with the arms tight to the sides of the body (see Figure 11-12). The initial step must place the catcher in such a position that the ball may be blocked along the centerline of the body. A pitch slightly to the left of the catcher requires a less forceful step than a pitch further to the left. After the ball has been blocked, the catcher jumps to his/her feet, quickly recovers the ball, and prepares to throw. When recovering the ball, the feet are positioned around the ball in such a way that the crow hop can be easily executed into a potential throw (see Figure 11-13).

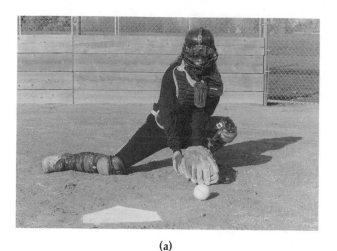

(a)

(b)

**Figure 11-12.** Blocking pitches to the left.

**Figure 11-13.** Recovering the ball.

## Blocking Pitches—Right

When the ball is pitched to the ground on the right of the catcher, he/she takes a quick step with the right foot and pushes off with the left foot. The catcher then drops to his/her left knee, followed by the right knee. The hands fill the space between the knees, with the glove open to the ball and in contact with the ground. The right shoulder turns inward in order to deflect the ball forward, and the head is positioned downward with the eyes focused upon the ball (see Figure 11-14). As with the ball to the left, the initial step must place the catcher in a position to block the ball along the midline of the body. After the ball has been blocked, the catcher jumps to his/her feet, quickly picks the ball up, and prepares to throw.

## Retrieving Wild Pitches and Passed Balls

If a pitch gets by the catcher and there are runners on base, the catcher must get to the ball quickly and efficiently. The moment the ball has passed the catcher, he/she executes a drop step to the side the ball passed and uses the ball-side arm to help keep the umpire clear of the path to the ball. A passed ball on the left requires a drop step with the left foot and a clearing motion with the left arm. A passed ball on the right requires a drop step with the right foot and a clearing motion with the right arm (see Figure 11-15).

Following the initial drop step, the catcher stays low and moves directly to the ball. As the catcher prepares to field the ball, his/her feet are positioned so that the throwing-side foot is planted just beyond the ball and perpendicular to home plate (see Figure 11-16). The ball is picked up with the throwing hand and is secured with the glove. As soon as the ball is secured, the catcher shows the ball to the pitcher,

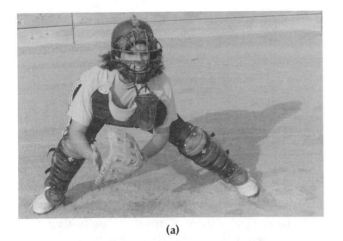

(a)

**Figure 11-15.** Drop step to the side of the ball.

(b)

**Figure 11-16.** Foot placement beyond the ball.

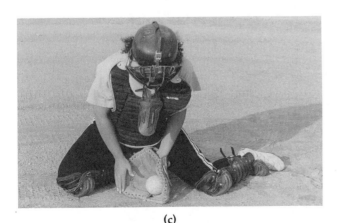

(c)

**Figure 11-14.** Blocking pitches to the right.

and then shifts the weight to the glove-side foot and snaps (see Chapter 8 "Snap Throwing") the ball to the pitcher (see Figure 11-17). The throw must be controlled and not rushed.

## Fielding

The catcher's basic fielding responsibilities include: (1) fielding bunts or weakly hit ground balls in the area around home plate, (2) calling the position of a throw when a bunt is fielded by another infielder, (3) catching any pop-ups in the home plate area (see Figure 11-18), (4) forcing or tagging out runners attempting to score, and (5) backing up first base when no other runners are on base. A description of each

**Figure 11-17.** The ball is in full view of the pitcher.

of these responsibilities and techniques for execution is provided below.

### Fielding the Bunt

On a bunt, the catcher moves to the ball and positions the feet around the ball (throwing-side foot perpendicular to the target) so that the ball is fielded with two hands near the midline of the body (see Figure 11-19). The catcher then: (1) executes a crow hop to help gain momentum into the throw, or (2) executes a weight shift from the throwing-side foot to the glove-side foot. The option chosen usually depends on the strength of the throwing arm and the skill of the catcher (see Figures 11-20 and 11-21). It is extremely important that the catcher communicate with the other infielders. Imme-

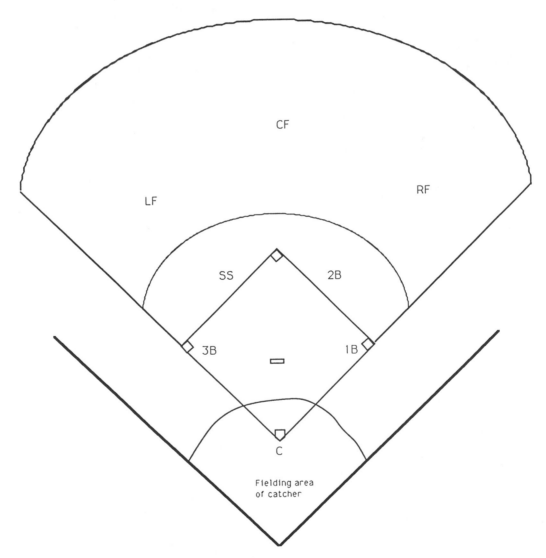

**Figure 11-18.** Position Play: General fielding area—catcher.

**Figure 11-19.** Fielding the bunt.

**Figure 11-20.** The crow hop prior to the throw.

diately calling for the ball will eliminate uncertainty and possible collisions.

### Calling the Throw

In a bunt situation, the catcher is the only player involved that can see the entire playing area. Therefore, if another infielder has a better opportunity to field a ball, the catcher is responsible for letting the other players know. As soon as the catcher knows that another player will field the ball, the catcher must focus on the action of the runners. If, for example, the runner on first base did not get a good jump on the bunt, the catcher must see this and yell "2!" The player fielding the ball may then respond and throw to second base.

### Catching Pop-ups

Because the catcher is positioned close to the batter, it is not always possible to immediately pick up the flight of a pop-up hit around the home plate area. Other fielders can help the catcher by yelling "Up!" or "Back!" or any other helpful word and simultaneously point to the location of the ball. When the ball is popped up, the catcher removes the mask with the

**Figure 11-21.** The weight shift prior to the throw.

throwing hand and focuses on the flight of the ball. When the flight of the ball is determined, the mask is thrown in the opposite direction (see Figure 11-22). Waiting to throw the mask will eliminate the possibility of tripping over the mask while attempting to catch the ball. The spin of a ball that has been popped up near or behind home plate usually causes the ball to carry toward the infield. If the catcher turns his/her back to the infield to make the catch,

**Figure 11-22.** The mask is thrown in the opposite direction of the ball.

the ball will carry toward the catcher. The ball is caught with two hands, above the head. Immediately following the catch, the catcher looks to hold any baserunners.

If the pop-up is hit so that the catcher and an infielder call for the catch simultaneously, the infielder has priority (again, because of the spin the ball will carry toward the infield, thus making it easier for the infielder to catch).

### Tag Plays at Home Plate

Unless the runner is forced to go home, the catcher must tag the runner with the ball in order to get the runner out. To do this safely and efficiently, the catcher initially moves to the front edge of home plate and gives a target for the throw (see Figure 11-23). As the ball approaches home plate, the catcher must determine whether it will arrive on time to tag the runner. If the ball will not arrive on time to tag the runner, the catcher must remain out of the runner's way. If the ball will arrive on time to tag the runner, the catcher moves to block the plate.

As the ball arrives, the catcher takes a short step with the left foot to line it up with the third-base foul line (see Figure 11-24). If the position of the left foot is anything but parallel to the path of the runner (the third-base foul line), contact between the catcher and the runner may result in injury to the knee. As the throw is caught, the shoulders square to the runner. The ball is held with the throwing hand and protected with the glove, and is placed on the ground in front of the foot in order to tag

**Figure 11-23.** Target for the throw.

**Figure 11-24.** The catcher prepares to tag the runner.

the sliding runner. If the runner attempts to slide around the tag, the catcher slides the ball and glove along the ground toward the runner. With other runners on base, the catcher must make the tag, then immediately check the runners and prepare to throw.

## Force Plays at Home Plate

A force play at home plate occurs when runners are on all three bases or when the bases are loaded. When the ball is hit, the catcher immediately moves to the front of the plate. The weight is evenly distributed over both feet and the shoulders are square to the fielder making the throw. A shoulder-high target is provided for the fielder. As soon as the path of the throw is known, the catcher quickly adjusts the throwing-side foot to the front edge of home plate and steps toward the ball with the glove-side foot (see Figure 11-25). If the throw is off target, the catcher must move away from the plate and catch the ball so that the other base-runners may not advance further.

If there are less than two outs, the catcher: (1) steps toward the ball with the glove-side foot in order to make the catch, (2) immediately executes a crow hop, and (3) throws to first base in an attempt to complete a double play (as in the speed throw) (see Figures 11-25 to 11-27). Although the double play throw can go to any base, the throw to first base is generally more successful. The runner moving toward first base has to wait for the pitch, hit the ball, and follow through with the swing before initiating the run. The runners moving toward second base or third base may initiate the run on the release of the pitch.

## Backing Up

When no runners are on base, the catcher plays an important role in backing up first base. When a throw is made from the second-base position or the second-base side of the short-

**Figure 11-26.** The crow hop.

**Figure 11-25.** Step to the ball with the glove-side foot.

**Figure 11-27.** The stride and throw to first base.

stop, the catcher runs to a point behind first base, directly in line with the fielder (see Chapter 17). When the throw is made from the third base or shortstop position, the right fielder is the primary back up. The catcher, however, should be in a position to field any balls that deflect off of the first baseperson's glove or off of the runner toward the home-plate side of first base.

## FIRST BASE

### Ready Position Location

#### Fast Pitch

In fast pitch softball, the first baseperson is responsible for fielding any bunt to the first-base side of the infield. Generally, as the skill of the pitcher increases, the possibility of a bunt increases. Therefore, as the level of play increases, the general ready position location becomes closer to home plate. At the beginning levels of fast pitch softball, the first baseperson starts even with, or a few steps in front of, first base. As the level of play advances, the first baseperson is positioned about 8-10 ft. in front of the base.

In a probable bunt situation (e.g., runner on first base, no outs, low score), the ready position is assumed about halfway between home plate and first base. The first baseperson must be ready to quickly charge a soft bunt, yet ensure that the ball does not get by on a push bunt. Once the batter has two strikes, the possibility of a bunt is greatly reduced and the first baseperson moves back to his/her regular position.

The first baseperson assumes the ready position about 3-4 ft. from the first-base foul line. Adjustments are made relative to the individual's ability to field balls hit on the left side of the fielder and the game situation (i.e., left-handed pull hitter). The first baseperson should guard against ground balls hit down the first-base line (see Figure 11-28).

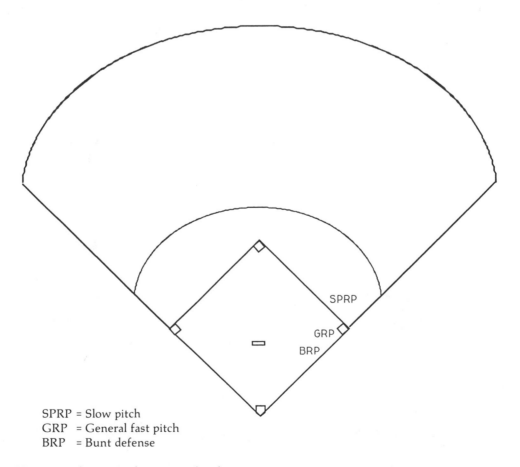

SPRP = Slow pitch
GRP  = General fast pitch
BRP  = Bunt defense

**Figure 11-28.** Various ready position locations—first base.

## Slow Pitch

The possibility of a bunt is non-existent in the game of slow pitch. Therefore, the first baseperson generally assumes the ready position several steps behind first base. Because there is more time to move to the ball when playing behind the base, the distance of the ready position from the foul line can also be increased (see Figure 11-28).

## Fielding Responsibilities

The first baseperson's basic fielding responsibilities include: (1) fielding bunts, ground balls, and fly balls hit to the first-base area, (2) receiving throws to first base for force plays and tag plays, (3) backing up, and (4) acting as a cutoff person for throws from the outfield to home plate. Each of these responsibilities and techniques for execution are described below.

## Fielding Batted Balls

The first baseperson is responsible for fielding all bunts, ground balls, and fly balls hit to the first-base area (see Figure 11-29). This area, however, does not have exact boundaries. Therefore, communication with other fielders is essential. When a ground ball is hit or bunted toward the first-base area, fielding the ball is the primary responsibility of the first baseperson. Once the ball has been fielded, the first baseperson must decide whether to make the play unassisted or rely on the second baseperson to take the throw. When the play can be made with either option, it is best to touch the base or tag the runner. A slow ground ball hit to the right side (fielder's right) of first base is best fielded by the first baseperson, with the second baseperson covering first base. The first baseperson can get to this ball quicker and, therefore, make the play more easily.

The first baseperson has priority on fly balls hit in front of first base, extending to the pitching circle. The second baseperson, however, has priority on fly balls behind first base and on fly balls that are called for simultaneously. If called off, the first baseperson must cover first base.

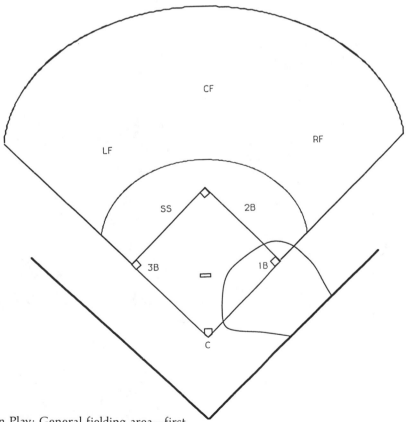

**Figure 11-29.** Position Play: General fielding area—first base.

### Receiving Throws at First Base

*Force plays*

When the ball is hit to another infielder, the first baseperson immediately turns toward the infield, quickly finds first base, and looks to receive the throw. The receiving ready position at the base consists of the heels of both feet placed on the front edge of the base, and the shoulders square to the throw. The feet are about shoulder width apart and the weight is evenly distributed over both feet (see Figure 11-30).

AFTER the flight of the throw has been determined, the throwing-side foot is placed on the front edge of the base and the glove-side foot stretches toward the ball (see Figure 11-31). If the ball is thrown to the right of the base, the throwing-side foot adjusts to the right side of the base. If the ball is thrown to the left of the base, the throwing-side foot adjusts to the left side of the base. If the first baseperson stretches with the glove-side foot before the flight of the throw has been determined, adjustments to poor throws will be difficult. Also, contacting the base with the throwing-side foot

sideways, ankle toward the ground, will reduce the potential of losing contact with the base when a long stretch is required.

If the ball is thrown too low, the first baseperson must decide whether: (1) to stretch in order to catch the ball on the short hop, or (2) to widen the feet in order to field the throw as if it were a ground ball. If the ball cannot be caught while maintaining contact with the base, the first baseperson must leave the base and catch the ball. If the throw is toward the home plate side of first base, the first baseperson may tag the runner by sweeping the ball across the baseline as it is caught.

### Tag plays—From the catcher

If a runner on first base takes a big lead with every pitch and/or is slow in returning to the base, the catcher may throw to first base in order to tag the runner out. This play, commonly known as the pickoff play, is not a force play because the runner may choose to run to second base. Therefore, the first baseperson must move efficiently to catch the throw and tag the runner.

The play begins with a sign from the catcher. Following the sign, the first baseperson adjusts the ready position so that the base is no more than 2-3 steps away. As the ball crosses the strike zone, the first baseperson turns to-

**Figure 11-30.** Receiving ready position.

**Figure 11-31.** Foot adjustment and stretch.

ward the glove-side foul line, looks toward the catcher for the throw, and listens for the runner. The ball is caught[1] and taken to the ground directly in front of the base using a sweeping motion (see Figure 11-32). If the runner cannot be heard or seen, the first baseperson must listen for directions from other fielders and immediately prepare to throw the ball to second base.

### Backing Up

Although the pitcher traditionally backs up home plate, sometimes it is best for the first baseperson to assume this role. Many times beginning pitchers are not ready to assume multiple responsibilities. Therefore, when it is determined that there will not be a play at first base and a runner has a chance to score, the first baseperson may back up home plate. The first baseperson must also be aware of potential problems at other bases and back up those plays whenever necessary.

### Cutoffs

On an outfield throw to home plate with more than one runner on base, the first base-

[1]When making a tag at any base, it is important to let the ball come to the glove. The ball will travel at a greater speed than the fielder can move the ball. This also emphasizes the significance of forceful, accurate throws!

person (or pitcher) moves to a cutoff position. The cutoff position is assumed directly between the origin of the throw and home plate and generally even with the front of the pitching circle (see Figure 11-33). Adjustments are made in relation to the origin and strength of the throw. A throw from deep in the outfield or a weak throw will require the cutoff person to be further from home plate. A common error is to be positioned too close to home plate, which blocks the catcher's view of the throw and limits the catcher's ability to react to the play.

In the cutoff position, the arms are raised overhead in order to give a clear target for the throw. The cutoff person listens for directions from the catcher. In general, the only time the ball is cut off is when the catcher yells "Cut!" or if the throw is off target. Otherwise, the ball goes through to the catcher (see Chapter 17).

## SECOND BASE

### Ready Position Location

The ready position for the second baseperson is generally located halfway between first and second base, 5-10 ft. behind the basepath (see Figure 11-34). This general location varies, however, depending upon the hitting tendencies of the batter, the game situation, and the

**Figure 11-32.** Preparing to tag the runner returning to first base.

**Figure 11-33.** Assuming the cutoff position.

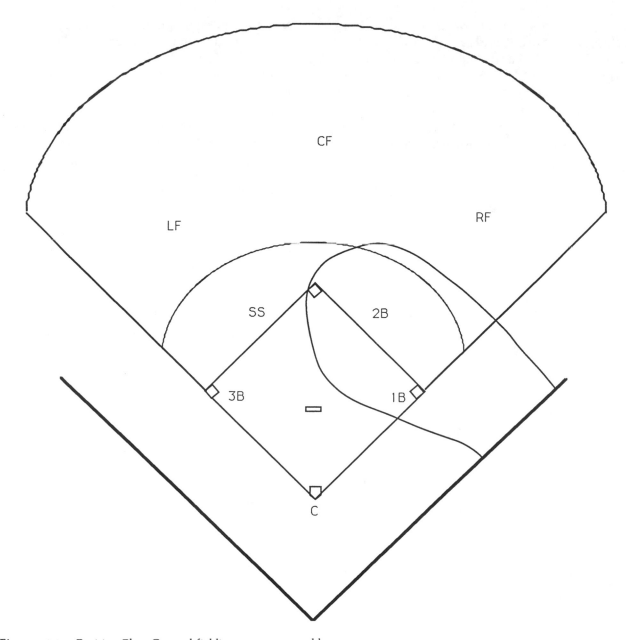

**Figure 11-34.** Position Play: General fielding areas—second base.

ability of the second baseperson. For example, a right-handed second baseperson with strong forehand fielding ability but weak backhand fielding ability would be more effective playing slightly closer to second base, especially if the batter tends to hit the ball up the middle. However, in a bunt situation the fielder would move slightly closer to first base. A runner on third base might require the second baseperson to position him/herself in front of the basepath in order to allow time to make a throw to home plate.

## Fielding Responsibilities

The second baseperson's basic fielding responsibilities include: (1) fielding all ground balls and fly balls hit in the second base area, (2) covering first and second base, (3) force plays at second base, including the double play, (4) tag plays at second base, (5) tag plays at first base, and (6) relaying the ball from right field and right-center field to the infield. A description of the techniques for executing these responsibilities follows.

## Fielding Batted Balls

The second baseperson is responsible for fielding all ground balls and fly balls hit to the second base area (see Figure 11-34). As with all positions, this area has no definite boundaries; therefore, communication with other fielders is essential. On fly balls, the second baseperson has priority over the pitcher and first baseperson. If all three call for the ball, the pitcher and first baseperson must allow the second baseperson to make the catch. Outfielders, however, have priority over the second baseperson. If the right fielder and the second baseperson both call for the ball, the second baseperson must allow the right fielder to make the catch. The second baseperson must also be prepared to back up any ground ball or line-drive hit to the pitcher or the first baseperson.

## Base Coverage

Generally, if the ball is hit to the right side of the field, the second baseperson covers first base. Similarly, if the ball is hit to the left side of the field, the second baseperson covers second base. More specifically, the second baseperson covers first base any time the first baseperson attempts to field a ball. For example, a bunt situation may require the first baseperson to charge the ball even if it is fielded by the pitcher. Therefore, the second baseperson must cover first base and receive the throw (see "Position Play—First Base").

The second baseperson covers second base on any ball hit to third base, shortstop, left field or to the left side of center field. For example, on a ball hit to left field, the shortstop moves into position for a possible relay, and the second baseperson covers second base. In a situation where a baserunner is on first base and there are less than two outs, the second baseperson must be prepared to cover either first or second base. If the ball is bunted, the second baseperson covers first base. If the ball is hit to the left side of the field, the second baseperson covers second base for the force out.

## Force Plays at Second Base

### Turning the Double Play

There are several methods used to turn a double play at second base. Each has its advantages and disadvantages. The simplest method for teaching youth softball players is to speed throw across the base (see Chapter 9). Speed throwing across the base allows the player two options.

### Option 1:

The player's first option is to: (1) step on the base with the glove-side foot as the ball is caught, (2) step across the base with the throwing foot perpendicular to the target, and (3) step toward the target with the glove-side foot in order to complete the throw (see Figure 11-35)

### Option 2:

The player's second option is to: (1) step across the base with the glove-side foot as the ball is caught, (2) drag the throwing-side foot across the base and plant it perpendicular to the target, and (3) step toward the target with the glove-side foot and complete the throw (see Figure 11-36).

With either option, it is essential to plant the throwing-side foot away from the base in order to keep the fielder clear of the runner's path. A player who is proficient at speed throwing will quickly learn how to turn a double play. If a double play attempt is not realistic for the skill of the second baseperson or if the force out at second base is the only play to be made, the second baseperson receives the throw using the same techniques as that described for the first baseperson (see "Receiving Throws at First Base").

## Tag Plays at Second Base

When making a tag at second base, the second baseperson must position the body so that the shoulders are square to the throw and the ball is caught in the center of the body. Body position varies with the origin of the throw. When positioning for the throw, it is important to leave the first-base side of second base open (see Figure 11-37). A sliding runner may injure a player's foot if it is positioned on the first-base side of second base. The ball is caught with two hands, and the glove is placed on the first-base side of second base. Adjustments are made in relation to the path of the runner. The glove should give as the runner is tagged in order to reduce the force of impact.

**Figure 11-35.** Speed throwing across the base, Option 1.

**Figure 11-36.** Speed throwing across the base, Option 2.

### Tag Plays at First Base

Occasionally it may be desirable to have the second baseperson take the throw from the catcher when attempting a pickoff play at first base. In this situation, a pitchout is called and the second baseperson sprints to cover first base as the pitch is thrown. The second baseperson should attempt to move discretely behind the runner. The player should position him/herself so that the feet straddle the base, toward the infield, and the shoulders are square to the catcher (see Figure 11-38). The ball is caught and placed on the ground in front of the base. Adjustments are made in relation to the path of the runner.

### Relays

Generally, when the ball is hit deep to right field or to right-center field, the second baseperson positions him/herself in the outfield in order to receive the throw and relay the ball to the infield. The location of the relay position depends upon the outfielder's throwing ability, the location of the ball, and the intended target (base) of the relay. A weak throwing arm and a long hit would require the relay location to be

**Figure 11-38.** Tag play at first base.

fairly deep into the outfield. A potential play at third base would require the relay person to be positioned in line with the outfielder and third base.

Once in the appropriate location, the relay person faces the outfielder with the arms overhead in order to give a clear target (see Figure 11-39). As the ball approaches, the glove-side foot begins to step toward the intended target, while the shoulders remain square to the ball (see Figure 11-40). As the ball is caught the relay person executes a crow hop and rotates the shoulders parallel to the intended target. Simultaneously, the ball is taken to the throwing position. The glove-side foot strides toward the target and the ball is thrown.

If the intended target is a reasonable distance away and the relay person has a strong throwing arm, the outfielder's throw is received as the weight moves over the throwing-side foot. As the ball is caught, the throwing-side foot quickly pivots perpendicular to the target and the glove-side foot strides forward in order to complete the throw. Eliminating the crow hop will save time but will reduce momentum into the throw. Therefore, it is essential for the relay person to have a strong throwing arm when using this method!

**Figure 11-37.** Tag play at second base with a throw from left field.

**Figure 11-39.** Giving a clear target in the relay position.

**Figure 11-40.** Preparing to turn the ball to the infield.

## THIRD BASE

### Ready Position Location

#### Fast Pitch

Similar to the first-base ready position location, the third-base ready position is dependent upon the game situation. The more likely a batter is to bunt the ball, the closer the general ready position is to home plate. When the situation does not require a bunt, the third baseperson plays even with or slightly in front of third base. When each batter is a potential bunter, the third baseperson plays 8-10 ft. in front of third base (see Figure 11-41). In a probable bunt situation, the third baseperson moves to a position halfway between home plate and third base. This position allows the third baseperson to field a bunt efficiently and not allow the batter to easily hit the ball past him/her.

The distance of the ready position from the foul line is situation specific. In general, however, the third baseperson should be able to touch the glove to the foul line with one crossover step. The third baseperson could be positioned further away from the foul line for a left-handed batter known to pull the ball and closer to the foul line for a right-handed batter known to pull the ball.

#### Slow Pitch

Because bunting is not allowed in slow pitch softball, the third baseperson positions him/herself even with or several steps behind third base (see Figure 11-41).

### Fielding Responsibilities

The third baseperson's basic fielding responsibilities include (1) fielding all fly balls, ground balls, and bunts hit to the third-base area, (2) covering third base on balls hit to other fielders, (3) force plays at third base, and (4) tag plays at third base. A description of these responsibilities and techniques for execution are provided below.

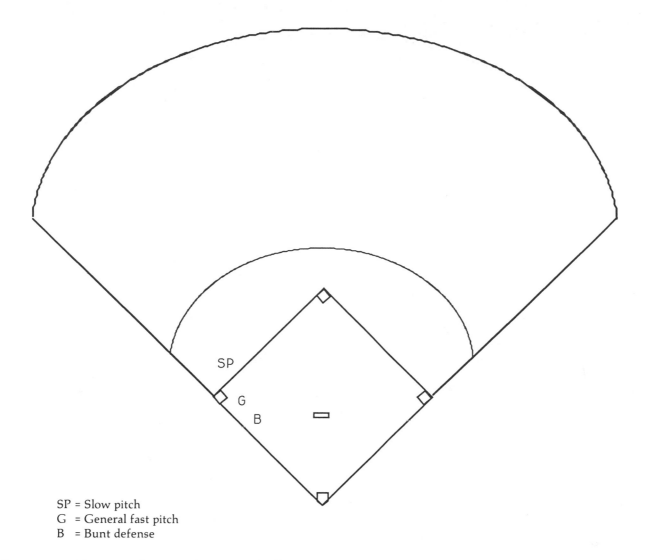

SP = Slow pitch
G  = General fast pitch
B  = Bunt defense

**Figure 11-41.** Various ready position locations—third base.

### Fielding Batted Balls

The third baseperson is responsible for fielding all fly balls, ground balls, and bunts hit to the third base area (see Figure 11-42). Because the third base area does not have exact boundaries, communication with other fielders is essential. The third baseperson has priority on fly balls hit between the pitching circle and the front part of third base. The shortstop has priority on fly balls behind third base. The third baseperson must also back up any ground balls hit to the third-base side of the pitcher, and field any slow-hit ground balls to the shortstop area.

### Base Coverage

The third baseperson must cover third base unless he/she is attempting to field the ball.

Even if there are no runners on base, it is wise to cover third base so that coverage becomes automatic. If the ball is hit to the pitcher, the third baseperson first backs up the play, and then immediately covers third base. If a fly ball is hit to right field, the third baseperson immediately covers third base. Defensive success is greater when the other fielders know the bases are covered! Once positioned at third base, the third baseperson prepares for either a force play or a tag play.

### Force Plays at Third Base

The technique of receiving the throw at third base is similar to that used at first base, with the exception of feet placement. The throws must be taken at the corners of the base as opposed to the infield edge of the base.

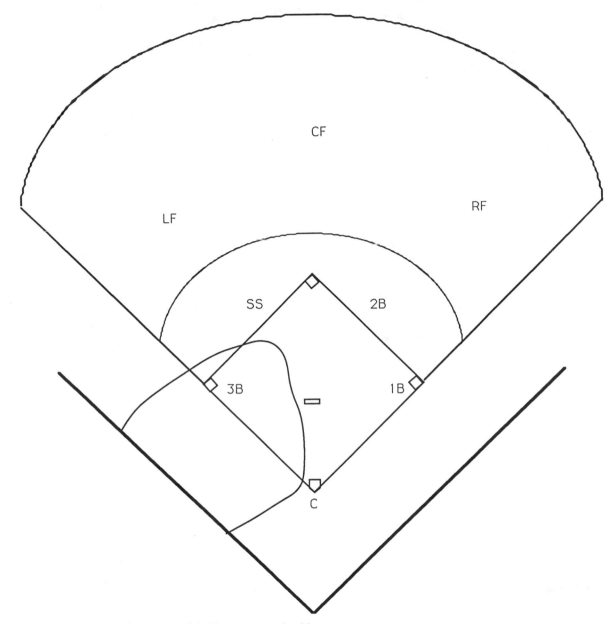

**Figure 11-42.** Position Play: General fielding areas—third base.

The third baseperson should straddle the corner of the base closest to the throw (see Figure 11-43). The shoulders are square to the fielder making the throw. The feet adjust to the flight of the ball (see Figure 11-44). Immediately following the catch, the third baseperson must check other runners and prepare to throw.

## Tag Plays at Third Base

### From the field

On tag plays at third base, the third baseperson straddles the base with the shoulders square to the throw (see Figure 11-45). The feet must be kept clear of the runner's side of the base in order to avoid injury. Upon catching the ball, the glove is placed on the ground in front of the base so that the runner slides into the tag. As the runner contacts the glove, the arm and hands should give with the force of the slide. Immediately following the tag, the third baseperson must check the other runners and be prepared to throw.

### From the catcher

The third baseperson may receive a throw from the catcher in order to tag a runner if: (1)

**Figure 11-43.** Straddle the corners of the base.

**Figure 11-44.** Foot adjustment to the ball.

**Figure 11-45.** Tag play at third base with an outfield throw.

the runner on second base is attempting to steal third base, or (2) the runner on third base is taking a big lead off the base. If a runner is attempting to steal third base, the third baseperson turns toward the infield, focuses on the action of the runner, and sprints to the base. He/she straddles the base and looks for the throw from the catcher. The third baseperson may want to plant the glove-side foot on the home plate side of the base (vs. straddling the base) to save a step. However, the runner must not be allowed to slide safely to the outfield side of the base.

If a runner on third base is taking a big lead and is slow in getting back to the base, the third baseperson turns to the foul line and takes 2-3 strides toward the base while watching for the throw. As the ball approaches, the third baseperson squares the shoulders to the throw, catches the ball, and tags the runner in one continuous motion (see Figure 11-46).

## SHORTSTOP

### Ready Position Location

The ready position for the shortstop is generally located halfway between second and third base, 5-10 ft. behind the basepath (see Figure

**Figure 11-46.** Preparing to receive a throw from the catcher to tag the runner returning to third base.

11-47). This general location varies, however, in relation to the hitting tendencies of the batter, the game situation, and the ability of the shortstop. For example, if a batter tends to hit up the middle, the shortstop would move a few steps toward second base. If a right-handed batter tends to pull the ball, the shortstop would move a few steps toward third base. In a situation where a runner must be prevented from scoring, the shortstop would move a few steps toward home plate in order to ensure time for the throw home. In general, the deeper the position, the greater the fielding range, and the more shallow the position, the more certain the throw.

## Fielding Responsibilities

The shortstop's basic fielding responsibilities include: (1) fielding all ground balls and fly balls hit to the shortstop area, (2) covering sec-

ond and third base, (3) force plays at second base, (4) tag plays at second base, (5) tag plays at third base, and (6) acting as a relay on throws from left and center field. A description of these responsibilities and techniques for execution is provided below.

### Fielding Batted Balls

The shortstop is responsible for fielding all ground balls and fly balls hit to the shortstop area (see Figure 11-47). The shortstop is the leader of the infield and, consequently, has priority on all ground balls and fly balls hit in his/her general area. For example, if a ball is hit on the ground up the middle of the infield, and the shortstop and the second baseperson have an equal chance of fielding the ball, the shortstop has priority and fields the ball while the second baseperson backs up the play. If a fly ball is simultaneously called for by the shortstop, third baseperson, and pitcher, the shortstop should make the catch. Outfielders, however, have priority over the shortstop. If a fly ball is called for by the left fielder and the shortstop, the shortstop must allow the left fielder to make the catch. Also, the shortstop must back up ground balls hit to the third baseperson or to the pitcher.

### Base Coverage

Generally, any time the ball is hit to the right side of the field, the shortstop covers second base. If a batter bunts the ball, with no runners on base, or with a runner on first base, the shortstop covers second base.

Any time a play is to be made at third base and the third baseperson is involved in fielding the ball, the shortstop covers third base. For example, with runners on first and second base, the shortstop would cover third base if the third baseperson is fielding a bunted ball. Similarly, if a ball is hit to the third baseperson and there is a runner on third base, the shortstop must cover third base in order to help hold the runner while the throw is made to first base. If the shortstop does not cover third base in this situation, the runner may get a big lead and either run home on the throw to first base or distract the third baseperson and allow the batter to safely reach first base.

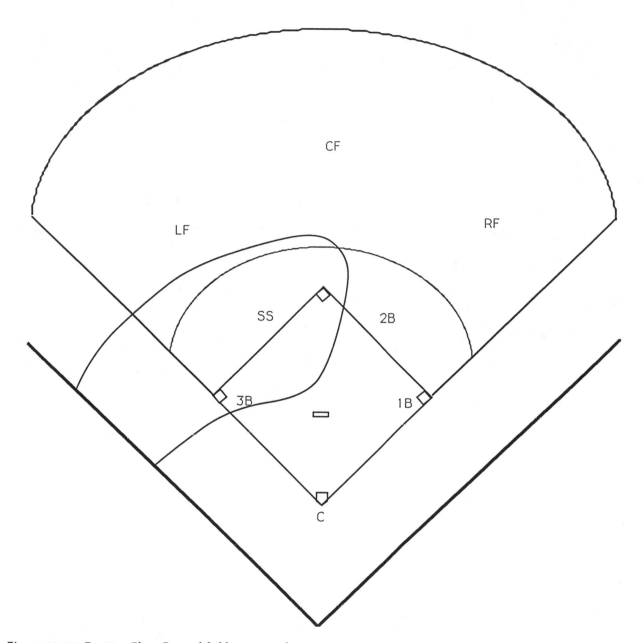

**Figure 11-47.** Position Play: General fielding areas-shortstop.

## Force Plays at Second Base
### *Turning the double play*

The simplest method for teaching youth softball players to turn a double play is to speed throw across the base (see Chapter 9). However, the shortstop must approach the base differently when a ball is fielded behind the basepath than when a ball is fielded in front of the basepath.

If a ball is initially fielded behind the basepath, the shortstop moves to the base in line with the fielder and: (1) steps on the base with the glove-side foot as the ball is caught, (2) steps across the base and plants the throwing-side foot perpendicular to the first baseperson, and (3) steps toward first base with the glove-side foot in order to complete the throw (see Figure 11-48). For safety reasons, the step across the base with the throwing-side foot (Step 2) should take the shortstop out of the basepath. An alternative to stepping on the base with the glove-side foot is to step across the base with the glove-side foot and drag the throwing-side foot over the base before plant-

(a)

(b)

(c)

(d)

**Figure 11-48.** Speed throwing across the base to receive a throw from behind the baseline.

(a)                          (b)                        (c)

**Figure 11-49.** Speed throwing across the base to receive a throw from in front of the baseline.

ing for the throw to first base (see "Second Base—Turning the Double Play").

If a ball is initially fielded in front of the basepath, the shortstop moves to the inside corner of the base and (1) touches the inside edge of the base with the glove-side foot, (2) steps away from the base with the throwing-side foot planting it perpendicular to the first baseperson, and (3) steps toward first base with the glove-side foot and completes the throw (see Figure 11-49). A shortstop who understands the speed throw will quickly learn how to turn the double play with a throw from either side of the basepath. If the force out at second base is the only play to be made, the shortstop receives the throw using the same technique as that described for the first baseperson.

## Tag Plays at Second Base

### From the Outfield

When receiving a throw from the outfield, the shortstop straddles the base, squares the shoulders to the throw, and catches the ball along the midline of the body. To prevent injury, the first-base side of second base must be left open for the runner. The shortstop keeps the glove low and allows the ball to come to the glove. In one continuous motion, the ball is caught, the glove is moved to the runner's side of the base, and the tag is made.

### From the Catcher

If a runner on first base is attempting to steal second base, the shortstop moves toward second base as soon as the ball crosses the strike zone. Upon approaching the base, the shortstop: (1) straddles the base, or (2) plants the glove-side foot next to the inside corner of the base in preparation for the throw (see Figures 11-50 and 11-51). It should be noted that setting up on the inside corner of the base is quickest but it often leaves the back edge of the base open for the runner. If the catcher's throw is on target, the shortstop keeps the glove low and allows the ball to come to the glove. As the ball is caught, the glove continues toward the ground on the runner's side of the base. Adjustments are made in relation to the path of the runner. If the catcher's throw is off target, the shortstop must move to catch the ball and attempt to tag the runner as quickly as possible.

## Tag Plays at Third Base

If the third baseperson is playing in front of third base, and there is a runner on second base, the shortstop must cover third base on a bunt, on a batted ball to the third baseperson, or on a steal attempt. In any of these situations, the shortstop must arrive at third base ahead of the runner and quickly straddle the base, facing the infield (see Figure 11-52). If the throw

**Figure 11-50.** Straddle the base.

**Figure 11-51.** Plant the glove-side foot next to the inside corner of the base.

**Figure 11-52.** Tag play at third base with a runner coming from second base.

**Figure 11-53.** Tag play at third base with a runner returning to the base.

is on target, the glove is kept low and the shortstop allows the ball to come to the glove. As the catch is made, the glove is placed on the ground on the runner's side of the base. If the throw is off target, the shortstop must move to catch the ball and tag the runner as quickly as possible.

If a runner is on third base, and the third baseperson is playing shallow, the runner often takes a large lead off of the base. If the catcher sees this and observes the runner slowly getting back to the base, a pickoff play may be called which requires the shortstop to take the throw. On this play, the third baseperson moves in another step to assure the large lead, and the pitcher pitches out. The shortstop moves toward third base on the release of the pitch, plants both feet on the inside of the third base line—hips toward the line, shoulders squares to the catcher—and, in a continuous motion, catches the ball and tags the runner (see Figure 11-53).

### Relays

When the ball is hit deep to left or center field, the shortstop positions him/herself in the outfield in order to receive the throw and relay the ball to the infield. The location of the relay depends upon the outfielder's throwing ability, the location of the ball, and the intended target. The shortstop relay is identical to the second baseperson relay. For an explanation of the technique, refer to "Second base—Relays."

## LEFT FIELD

### Ready Position Location

#### Fast Pitch

The general location of the ready position for the left fielder is in the center of the left-field area (see Figure 11-54). The left fielder's ready position may be adjusted in relation to

the hitting tendencies of the batter, the game situation, the field conditions, and ability. Obviously, a left fielder would play further back and closer to the foul line for a batter that consistently hits deep and down the line. However, if that same batter was at the plate with the game-winning run on third base, and there were less than two outs, the left fielder would continue to play close to the line but would play shallow enough to catch the ball in the air and throw the runner out at home plate. As far as field conditions, long thick grass has a slowing effect on ground balls. Thus, the left fielder may play more shallow than if the ground was hard and dry.

#### Slow Pitch

Generally, in slow pitch softball the left fielder positions him/herself deeper in the outfield than in fast pitch softball. The exact loca-

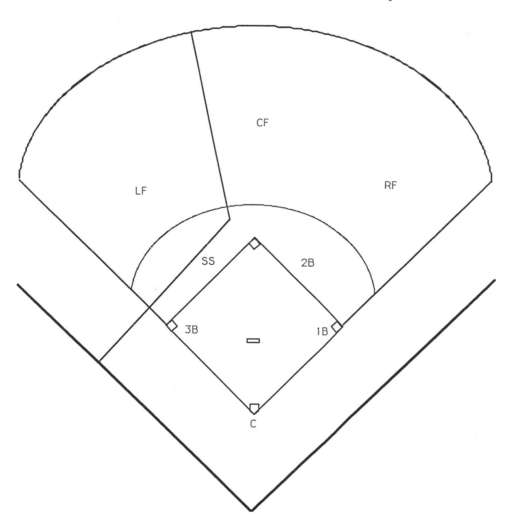

**Figure 11-54.** Position Play: General fielding areas—left field.

tion is dependent upon the same factors as in fast pitch. However, due to the nature of the game, the ball is consistently hit further in slow pitch softball.

## Fielding Responsibilities

The left fielder's basic fielding responsibilities include: (1) fielding all ground balls and fly balls hit to the left-field area, (2) backing up all infield throws to third base, (3) backing up all right field throws to second base, and (4) making accurate throws to the relay person. A description of these responsibilities and techniques for execution is provided below.

## Fielding Batted Balls

The left fielder is responsible for fielding all ground balls and fly balls hit to the left field area (see Figure 11-54). As with the infield, there are no exact boundaries in the outfield. Therefore, communication is essential. On fly balls, the left fielder has priority over all infielders. However, the center fielder has priority over the left fielder. If the left fielder and shortstop simultaneously call for a fly ball, the shortstop must allow the left fielder to make the catch. If the left fielder and the center fielder simultaneously call for a fly ball, the left fielder must allow the center fielder to make the catch. If a fly ball is hit foul, and the left fielder catches the ball, the batter is out. If, however, there is a runner on base, the runner has the option to tag the base, then advance immediately following the catch. The left fielder must be aware of this possibility and be prepared to throw the ball to the appropriate base.

In addition to fielding, the left fielder must back up all ground balls and fly balls hit to the center fielder. The left fielder should be positioned far enough behind the center fielder to be able to react to a missed ball. The left fielder must also back up any ground balls or fly balls hit to the shortstop or third baseperson. A successful catch by other fielders should never be assumed!

## Backing Up Infield Throws to Third Base

The left fielder is responsible for backing up third base on all throws from right field and on throws from the infield. When backing up throws, the left fielder should be positioned directly in line with the throw and third base. The left fielder should be far enough behind third base to allow him/her time to react to an overthrow or a deflected ball. The left fielder must also be sure to back up third base within the boundaries of the playing field. If an overthrow crosses the out of play line, the runners automatically advance. Also, if for any reason third base is not covered by an infielder, the left fielder should cover the base.

## Backing Up Second Base on Throws from Right Field

The left fielder should back up second base on all throws from the right-field area. If the throw is missed or deflected, the left fielder should be in a position to prevent the base runner(s) from advancing further.

## Throwing to the Relay Person

When retrieving a ball that has been hit beyond the outfielder, the first priority of the fielder is to gain possession of the ball. Therefore, as the outfielder moves toward the ball, it is essential that his/her eyes remain focused on the ball. As the outfielder retrieves the ball, he/she should listen for the location of the relay person. If the ball has stopped rolling, it may be fielded by planting the throwing-side foot just beyond the ball. After fielding the ball, the weight is immediately transferred to the glove-side foot and the eyes focus on the relay person (see Figures 11-55 and 11-56). The outfielder executes a crow hop and throws the ball to the relay person as quickly and as accurately as possible. If the ball is still rolling when the outfielder fields it, he/she must stop the body's momentum, execute a crow hop, and throw as soon as possible.

# CENTER FIELD

## Ready Position Location

The center fielder generally plays directly behind second base, in the middle of the outfield (see Figure 11-57). As with left field, the exact ready position location is dependent upon hitting tendencies of the batter, the game sit-

**Figure 11-55.** Planting the throwing-side foot beyond the ball.

**Figure 11-56.** Transferring the weight to the glove-side foot.

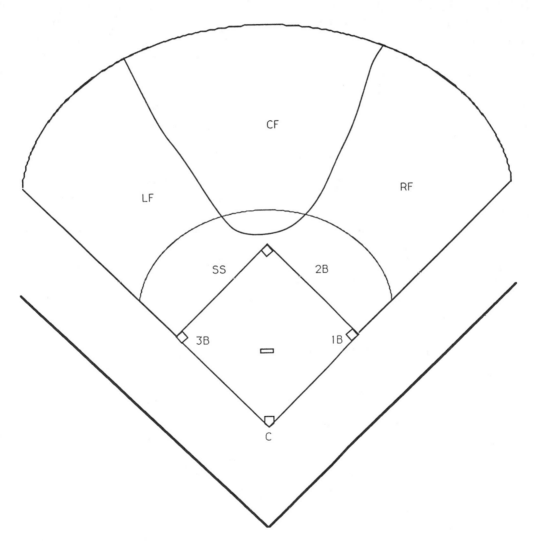

**Figure 11-57.** Position Play: General fielding areas—center field.

uation, the field conditions, and the center fielder's ability.

## Fielding Responsibilities

The center fielder's basic fielding responsibilities include: (1) fielding all ground balls and fly balls hit to the center-field area, (2) backing up all infield throws to second base, and (3) making accurate throws to the relay person (see "Left Field—Throwing to the Relay Person"). A description of these responsibilities is provided below.

## Fielding Batted Balls

The center fielder is responsible for fielding all ground balls and fly balls hit to the center-field area (see Figure 11-57). Because the center fielder is the leader of the outfield, he/she has priority on all ground balls and fly balls hit to the center-field area. If a ground ball is hit between left field and center field, the center fielder generally moves directly to the ball and the left fielder backs up the play. If the center fielder, left fielder, and shortstop simultaneously call for a fly ball, the shortstop and left fielder must allow the center fielder to catch the ball.

The center fielder is also responsible for backing up all ground balls and fly balls hit to the left fielder, right fielder, second baseperson, and shortstop. If the ball is hit to left field and the left fielder misses the ball, the center fielder must be in a position to field the ball. The left fielder must then look for the action of the baserunners and let the center fielder know what to do with the ball once it is fielded.

## Backing Up Infield Throws to Second Base

The center fielder is responsible for backing up all infield throws to second base. If the ball is being thrown to second base from the first base position, the center fielder moves to the left field side of second base. If the throw is made from the third base position, the center fielder moves to the right field side of second base. The center fielder must be positioned far enough behind second base to allow time to react to a missed or deflected ball. In addition, the center fielder must cover second base if no infielders are able to do so.

## RIGHT FIELD

### Ready Position Location

Because the majority of hitters are right-handed, the ready position for the right fielder is generally located in shallow right field. However, for left-handed batters, the right fielder usually plays deeper. The right fielder may adjust the ready position to specific game situations.

### Fielding Responsibilities

The right fielder's fielding responsibilities include: (1) fielding all ground balls and fly balls hit to the right field area, (2) backing up all infield throws to first base, (3) backing up outfield throws to second base, and (4) making accurate throws to the relay person (see "Left Field—Throwing to the Relay Person"). A description of these responsibilities is provided below.

### Fielding Batted Balls

The right fielder is responsible for fielding all ground balls and fly balls hit to the right field area (see Figure 11-58). Because the right fielder is generally positioned in shallow right field, communication with the second baseperson is critical. The right fielder has priority over the second baseperson on fly balls. The right fielder must also be prepared for the right-handed batter with a slow bat. If this batter hits the ball to right field, the ball will generally tail toward the foul line. If the ball hits the ground in front of the right fielder, it will generally bounce toward the foul line. An awareness of this possibility will help the right fielder move in to the correct position to field the ball. The same is true for the left-handed batter hitting to left field.

The right fielder is also responsible for backing up all ground balls and fly balls hit to the first baseperson, second baseperson, and center fielder. The center fielder generally fields balls hit between center and right field, while the right fielder backs up the play. Again, the right fielder must be positioned far enough behind the play to allow him/her time to react to a missed or deflected ball.

## Backing Up Infield Throws to First Base

The right fielder must back up first base on every infield throw to first base. Also, a catcher can relax and more easily throw to first base on pickoffs knowing that the right fielder will be there to back up the throw. As with all other back-ups, the right fielder must be lined up with the origin of the throw and first base and be far enough behind the base to be able to react to a missed or deflected ball. If for some reason first base is not covered by an infielder, the right fielder should move in to cover the base.

## Backing Up Outfield Throws to Second Base

Any time the left fielder throws the ball to second base, the right fielder must backup the throw even if the left fielder is only returning the ball to the infield. It must become a habit. Backing up is a critical role of all outfielders!

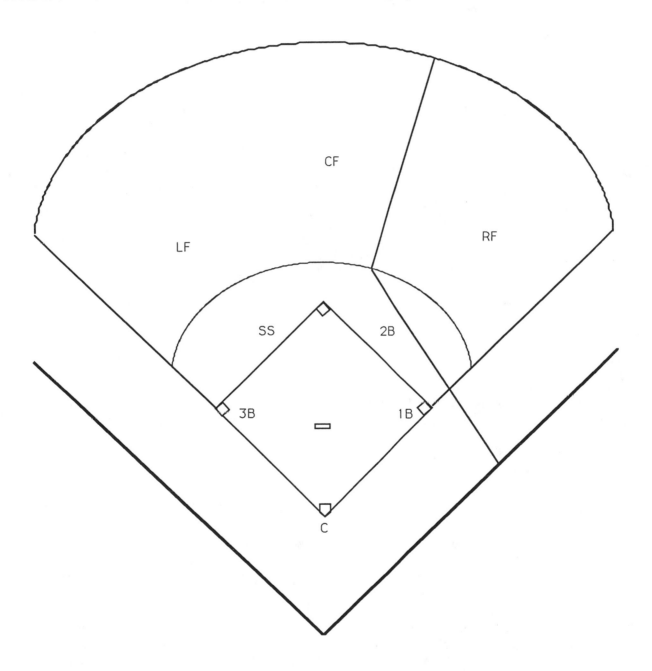

**Figure 11-58.** Position Play: General fielding areas—right field.

# 12
# Fundamentals of Pitching

*Jill Elliott, M.S.*

---

### QUESTIONS TO CONSIDER

- What is the position of the palm of the pitching hand as it enters the propulsive phase?
- What is the significance of opening and closing to the target?
- What two factors determine pitching accuracy?
- How can the development of pitching skills be problematic?
- How does a pitcher effectively mask a change-up?

---

## INTRODUCTION

The role of the pitcher is to consistently pitch the ball over home plate and through a designated area known as the strike zone. To be effective, the pitcher must do this in such a way that the batter cannot successfully hit the ball. Effective pitching is essential to defensive success.

This chapter contains a description of the basic mechanics involved in fast pitch pitching. Two pitches essential to pitching effectively will be discussed: (1) the fastball and (2) the change-up. The fastball, as its name implies, is a ball that is pitched as fast as possible. The basic mechanics involved in pitching the fastball serve as a basis for all other types of pitches and will be focused upon initially. The change-up is an off speed pitch to keep hitters from easily timing the fastball.

## PITCHING THE FASTBALL

Although it often takes many years, the ultimate goal of the pitcher is to deliver the ball forcefully and accurately. As in the overhand throw, the underhand throw or pitch can be broken down into four basic components or phases. These phases include: (1) the preparatory phase, (2) the propulsive phase, (3) the release phase, and (4) the follow-through. Slight variations occur depending on the type of delivery being used.

### Preparatory Phase

#### The Grip

A skilled pitcher has a different grip for every different kind of pitch. Only the basic grip for the fastball, however, will be presented in this chapter. The grip involves spreading two, three, or four fingers across the seams with the thumb in opposition around the ball (see Figure 12-1). Two or three fingers is most effective however, beginning pitchers with smaller hands may find it necessary to use four fingers for increased control. The ball is gripped with the fingers and thumb only. The ball does not contact the palm of the hand (see Figure 12-2).

## The Stance

As dictated by the rules (see Chapter 5, "Rule 6"), the pitcher must face the batter with one or both feet on the pitcher's plate and both feet within the 24-in. length of the plate. The feet are staggered with the glove-side foot comfortably behind (see Figure 12-3). The hands are apart with the ball in either hand as the pitcher initially assumes the stance on the pitcher's plate. The hands must then come together for a minimum of one second prior to the initiation of the pitching motion (see Figure 12-4).

## The Throwing Arm

The motion of the throwing arm depends on the type of delivery being used. There are two basic types of deliveries: (1) the windmill delivery, and (2) the slingshot delivery.

### Windmill Delivery

In the windmill delivery, the arms initially move downward to a position below the waist. The arms then begin to move forward and upward until they are extended horizontally to

**Figure 12-1.** 4-, 3-, or 2-finger grips.

**Figure 12-3.** Foot placement on the pitcher's plate.

**Figure 12-2.** Gripping the ball with the thumb and fingers only.

**Figure 12-4.** Bringing the hands together.

the ground (see Figure 12-5). The initial movement of the arms prior to the horizontal extension often varies from pitcher to pitcher. However, the greater the initial movement, the greater chance the pitching arm has to deviate from the plane to the plate and, thus, impair accuracy.

The glove arm remains horizontal, and the throwing arm continues upward until it is vertical. In its vertical position, the wrist is extended, the palm of the hand is out, and the thumb is under the ball (see Figure 12-6). Now the throwing arm is in a position to enter the propulsive phase.

### Slingshot Delivery

In the slingshot delivery, the throwing hand immediately comes out of the glove. The glove arm moves to extend horizontally to the target. The throwing arm initially moves in a downward and backward direction, then in an upward direction until the throwing hand is above and behind the head (see Figures 12-7 and 12-

**Figure 12-6.** Windmill: The vertical position of the throwing arm.

**Figure 12-5.** Windmill: The arms extended horizontally.

**Figure 12-7.** Slingshot: The throwing arm moving in a downward and backward direction.

8). At the height of the backswing, the wrist is extended, the palm of the hand is out, and the thumb, under the ball as the body prepares for the propulsive phase.

For either motion, the speed with which the preparatory arm action occurs is irrelevant to the force imparted on the ball. A rushed preparatory motion may cause excessive tension which will inhibit the total pitching motion.

### The Stride

As the pitching motion begins, the weight of the body is transferred to the throwing-side foot. With the weight on the throwing-side foot, the glove-side foot strides comfortably to the target. The stride occurs in such a way that the glove-side foot contacts the ground slightly to the glove side of the midline of the initial body position (see Figure 12-9). This will allow the hips to be fully rotated in the propulsive phase. The timing of the stride, however, is different depending on the style of delivery. These dif-ferences are small but significant to the style. WINDMILL: The weight is transferred onto the throwing-side foot as the arms move to extend horizontally. The throwing-side foot begins to forcefully push off the pitcher's plate and the glove-side foot begins to stride forward as the hands separate prior to the pivot on the throwing-side foot (see Figure 12-10). SLING-SHOT: The stride begins as the hands separate and occurs simultaneously with the backswing of the throwing arm and the pivot on the throwing foot.

### The Pivot

Following the initiation of the stride, the body pivots on the ball of the throwing-side foot until the foot is perpendicular to the intended path of the ball. The pivot opens the hips with the body sideways to the target, glove side in front (see Figures 12-11 and 12-12). The purpose of the pivot is to: (1) place the body in a position to use the muscles involved in hip

**Figure 12-8.** Slingshot: The throwing arm at the height of the backswing.

**Figure 12-9.** Position of the striding foot.

**Figure 12-10.** Windmill: Initiation of the stride.

**Figure 12-12.** Side view.

**Figure 12-11.** Pivot on the throwing-side foot to open the hips.

and trunk rotation effectively, and (2) create more distance through which the arm can move to generate greater force on the ball. As with the stride of the glove-side foot, the timing of the pivot on the throwing-side foot differs with the style of delivery. WINDMILL: The pivot begins as the throwing arm approaches vertical, after the stride has been initiated. SLING-SHOT: The pivot occurs simultaneously with the backswing of the throwing arm and the initiation of the forward stride of the glove-side foot. The pivot is completed, the striding foot contacts the ground, and the propulsive phase begins.

## Propulsive Phase

The propulsive phase begins as the glove-side foot fully contacts the ground and ends just prior to the release of the ball. The foot contact initiates a series of force-producing joint actions which begins with the larger joints and moves sequentially to smaller joints. The force producing joint sequence occurs as follows: hip rotation, trunk rotation, shoulder rotation, shoulder flexion, elbow extension, and wrist flexion. Although the joint sequence is a little more detailed than what is presented here, it is important to understand the general concept as it relates to throwing forcefully. The joint action is basically the same for the slingshot and the windmill deliveries and unless otherwise stated, the following applies to both.

### Rotation

The first action to occur in the propulsive phase is hip rotation. The hips rotate to bring the throwing-side hip to the target. As hip rotation reaches its greatest velocity, the trunk begins to rotate at an even faster rate. The shoulders then begin to rotate forward to contribute to the force production. When the hips, trunk, and shoulders are parallel (a result of the varied speeds of rotation), they continue to rotate to square or close to the target (see Figure 12-13). To assure complete closure, the throwing-side leg comes forward with the hip. The throwing-side foot, however, may not lose contact with the ground (see Chapter 5, "Rule 6"). The slingshot delivery requires a slight trunk lean to throwing side throughout the pitching motion to allow the ball to pass without hip interference (see Figure 12-14).

### Shoulder Action

The throwing shoulder begins to forcefully flex as the forces of body rotation bring it forward. The throwing arm, which begins its downward motion as the propulsive phase begins, remains relaxed with the elbow slightly flexed and the wrist extended. With the palm of the hand facing out, the elbow-wrist combination allows the ball and lower arm to trail the elbow in a whip-like motion (see Figure 12-15).

### Glove Side

A forceful pull of the previously extended glove arm sends the glove shoulder backward to increase the forward rotation of the throwing shoulder. The glove-side knee, previously flexed to absorb the impact of the stride, begins to forcefully extend just prior to the release of the ball. Both actions create an equal and opposite effect on the forward movement of the throwing side (see Figure 12-15).

### Arm Action

As the throwing arm nears the bottom of the arc, the elbow begins to extend and the wrist begins to flex completing the joint sequence. Immediately prior to the point of release, complete elbow extension and wrist flexion combine to snap the ball forward (see Figure 12-16). The ball is then released at an initial velocity equal to the velocity of the hand. Therefore, the greater the velocity of the hand, created by the joint sequence, the greater the velocity of the ball.

**Figure 12-13.** Complete rotation closes the hips to the target.

**Figure 12-14.** The slingshot delivery requires a slight trunk lean.

**Figure 12-15.** Forceful flexion of the throwing shoulder; the lower arm and ball trail in a whip-like motion.

**Figure 12-16.** Complete elbow extension and wrist flexion as the ball is released.

In summary, the force producing joint sequence occurs as follows: hip rotation, trunk rotation, shoulder flexion, elbow extension, and wrist flexion. Facilitating opposite actions are glove pull and glove knee extension.

### Release Phase

With the force production phase consistent, the path of the ball, or pitching accuracy, is determined by: (1) the path of the pitching arm prior to release, and (2) the exact point of release. If the path of the pitching arm goes from right to left prior to release, the ball will continue in this direction after release and end up to the left of the target. Likewise, if the path of the pitching arm goes from left to right prior to release, the ball will end up to the right of the target (see Figure 12-17). A pitcher who is consistently missing to the right or left of the target would be wise to check the path of the pitching arm.

If the path of the pitching arm prior to re-lease is directly in line with the target, and the force production phase is consistent, the height of the pitch is determined by the point of release. If the throwing side comes through properly, the midline of the thigh (stripe of pants) serves as an effective down-the-middle release point. Releasing the ball slightly behind the midline will direct the pitch lower. Releasing the ball slightly in front of the midline will direct the ball higher (see Figure 12-18). Because it is desirable to pitch to various locations in and around the strike zone, it is essential for the pitcher to understand the effects of various release points.

### Follow-Through Phase

The movement of the body which occurs immediately after the release of the ball is the follow-through. The purpose of the follow-through is to: (1) prevent any interruption of the joint sequence prior to release, and (2) avoid injury by safely reducing the force produced in

X – Target

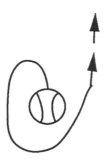

L – R = Right of the target

**Figure 12-17.** Path of the pitching arm prior to release.

X – Target

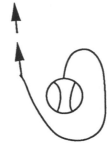

R – L = Left of the target

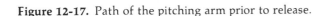

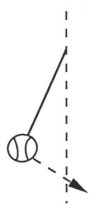

Early release—low pitch

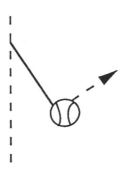

Late release—high pitch

**Figure 12-18.** Pitching release point—low, high..

the propulsive phase, following the release of the ball. The follow-through is a direct result of the actions of the propulsive phase. In general, the wrist continues to flex, the lower arm pronates or turns the palm of the hand to the ground, the upper arm continues upward, and the throwing-side leg continues forward (see Figure 12-19). From here, the pitcher can quickly enter a fielding position. Although the follow-through does not have any direct effect on the ball, a lack of follow-through is an indication of ineffective force production.

*Key Elements:*

• Preparatory actions via the windmill or sling-shot motion.

**Figure 12-19.** The follow-through.

- The pivot of the throwing-side foot to open the hips. The body is sideways to the target, glove side in front.
- A comfortable stride slightly to the glove-side of the midline of the initial body position.
- The sequential rotation of the hips, trunk, and shoulder.
- The whip-like motion of the throwing arm in the plane to the target.
- The equal and opposite action of the glove side.
- The throwing-side hip closing to the target to complete hip rotation and to provide a tangible release point.
- Release and follow-through.

*Common Errors:*

- No pivot on the throwing-side foot the hips fail to open to the target which results in an arm-only pitch with less than maximum velocity.
- The stride with the glove-side foot is too short which: (1) reduces the contribution of hip rotation and glove-knee extension, and (2) may be conducive to pitches above the strike zone.
- The stride is too long which: (1) interferes with the contribution of hip rotation, and (2) may be conducive to pitches in the dirt.
- The pitcher leans forward in an attempt to steer the ball to the target. The forward lean inhibits the sequential movement of joints and subsequently changes the point of release resulting in slower and less accurate pitches.
- The throwing arm deviates from the plane to the target to impair accuracy.
- The arm remains completely extended throughout the motion—this reduces the number of joints involved in force production and eliminates the whip effect of the pitching arm.
- The throwing-side hip fails to close to the plate as the ball is released which reduces the full effect of hip rotation.
- The throwing-side leg kicks behind the glove leg preventing hip closure.
- The trunk fails to lean to the throwing side throughout the slingshot motion resulting in: (1) the wrist getting out farther from the body than the elbow—illegal pitch; or (2) hip

interference as the ball comes through to the target.
- Little or no follow-through which: (1) minimizes the force applied to the ball prior to the release of the pitch, or (2) increases the chance for injury.
- A conscious effort to snap the wrist may be detrimental to the joint sequence. This sometimes causes the elbow to: (1) extend prematurely, then flex prior to release, or (2) fail to extend at all. The resulting shorter lever at release reduces the potential for greatest ball velocity.

## PITCHING ANALYSIS

Figures 12-20 to 12-22 show a pitching sequence from three pitchers. An analysis of these figures reveals several differences unique to each pitcher.

### Photos d

Pitcher 3 appears to be initiating the stride with a more forceful push off the pitcher's plate than either Pitcher 1 or 2.

### Photos e

As the arms extend horizontally, Pitchers 2 and 3 begin the turn on the pivot foot—Pitcher 1 has yet to begin the pivot.

### Photos f

With the arm of each pitcher near vertical, Pitchers 2 and 3 show a complete pivot and are fully open to the target. Pitcher 1 shows an incomplete pivot and is not fully open to the target. The incomplete pivot of Pitcher 1 is common among pitchers who tend to rely on strength and arm speed. Velocity would be further increased with a complete pivot and subsequent rotation.

### Sequence Photos—Pitcher 1, f & h; Pitcher 2, f & g; Pitcher 3, f & h

These photos clearly illustrate differences in arm speed. Although the vertical position is not identical for each pitcher, 1/9 of a second later Pitcher 1 and Pitcher 2 are approximately midway through the propulsive phase while Pitcher 3 is preparing to release the ball. All three pitchers pitch the ball with good velocity. However, as indicated by this sequence of

(a)                          (b)                          (c)

(d)                          (e)

**Figure 12-20.** Pitcher 1.

(f)

(g)

(h)

(i)

**Figure 12-20.** (continued)

(j)

(k)

**Figure 12-20.** (continued)

(a)

(b)

**Figure 12-21.** Pitcher 2.

(c)

(d)

(e)

(f)

**Figure 12-21.** (continued)

(g)                                                    (h)

(i)

**Figure 12-21.** (continued)

(a)

(b)

(c)

(d)

(e)

**Figure 12-22.** Pitcher 3.

**(f)**

**(g)**

**(h)**

**(i)**

**(j)**

**Figure 12-22.** (continued)

photos, Pitcher 3 consistently pitches with the greatest velocity. The key to arm speed is an effective sequence of joint actions and a relaxed throwing arm.

NOTE: There is only a slight difference between pitchers in the photos showing the velocity of the arm in the preparatory phase (photos d, e, f). The significant difference is in the velocity of the arm in the propulsive phase.

### Photos g

Although the photos do not show the exact moment the glove-side foot contacts the ground, Pitchers 1 and 3 show glove-side knee flexion which indicates an initial absorption of the impact of the stride. Pitcher 2 does not show glove-side knee flexion. Pitcher 2 is not only putting a lot of strain on the knee with the impact of the stride but is reducing the potential equal and opposite effect of glove-side knee extension.

### Photos h and i

Although Pitcher 2 (photo h) is slightly beyond the release of the ball, this photo shows a lack of complete rotation with the throwing-side hip well back of the release point. Pitcher 1 (photo i) has brought the hip through more than Pitcher 2, but note also that Pitcher 1 did not completely open the hips to the target. Pitchers 1 and 2 did not obtain the full effects of rotation. Pitcher 3 (photo h) has brought the throwing-side hip through with the release of the ball. Photos i and j illustrate the force with which the hip has come through as it has continued forward with the follow-through. Pitcher 3 completely opened to the target, then closed to the target, and thus, obtained an excellent effect of rotation.

## SUGGESTIONS FOR TEACHING PITCHING TO BEGINNERS

Developing a softball pitcher can be problematic. The rules of the game of softball require the pitcher to pitch three strikes for every four balls. This kind of pitching consistency, however, is usually not attainable early in a pitching career. If the beginning pitcher is required to perform in a game circumstance, one of two situations may result. The first situation involves a sacrifice of force production for accuracy. The pitcher stands square to the batter and aims the ball at the strike zone to achieve a higher percentage of strikes. Hitters improve and fielders improve but the pitching stays the same. A pitcher in this situation rarely sees an increase in velocity and often has to find a different position as the level of play increases.

The second situation involves a lack of pitching accuracy while attempting to apply maximum force to the ball. Because correct release points and maximum force production are still being learned, a tremendous number of walks, with few chances to hit and field the ball, result. A pitcher in this situation may be put under a lot of stress by teammates, coaches, and spectators—stress that may destroy the pitcher's confidence and motivation. Only the most determined pitchers survive this situation and continue with a pitching career. Also, this situation reduces the opportunity for learning offensive and defensive aspects of softball.

If these situations are to be avoided, it is essential to have a systematic approach to developing pitchers; an approach that begins years before the pitcher has to perform in a competitive game situation. The following are suggested progressions for such an approach.

### Preparatory Phase

As with any skill, the potential pitcher must first understand the basic mechanics of pitching. A clear understanding of the key elements of pitching will help the pitcher set goals and evaluate goals in a systematic manner. Also, a tremendous amount of learning takes place through imitation which makes it desirable to have a skilled[1] role model present during the various stages of learning.

Initially, pitching requires a slingshot or windmill motion to position the ball for the propulsive phase. The pitcher may choose either one of these deliveries depending on which motion is most natural. For example, those who cannot perform a smooth windmill motion may be better suited to the slingshot motion. The

[1]Velocity is not always an indication of mechanical efficiency. Many elite pitchers rely on strength and would further benefit from incorporating proper mechanics.

windmill motion, however, is a more efficient motion.

## Propulsive Phase

### Arm Motion

Once the pitching motion to be learned is determined, the pitcher must begin to work on motion efficiency. Initially, only the pitching arm motion is focused upon.

The pitcher must first learn the correct position of the elbow, wrist, and hand throughout the pitching motion. If the palm of the hand is on top of the ball or facing inward as the arm is going through the propulsive phase, the elbow and wrist will not be in a position to effectively contribute to the force production. The pitcher can easily learn the correct position of the pitching arm—without a complicated explanation—through the following drill:

The pitcher pairs up with another player who is about the same height. The players grasp hands in front of the pitcher's body with the palm out, thumb down (see Figure 12-23). The pitcher then executes the windmill motion. The players maintain the grasp until the pitcher reaches the release point. The hands separate and the pitcher follows through (see Figures 12-24 and 12-25). Because the propulsive phase of the slingshot delivery is virtually identical to the windmill delivery, the correct arm position

**Figure 12-24.** The pitcher executes the windmill motion.

**Figure 12-23.** The pitcher grasps the hands another player, palm out and thumb down.

**Figure 12-25.** The hands separate and the pitcher follows through.

learned in this drill will easily transfer to the slingshot preparatory phase.

As the correct position of the pitching arm becomes automatic, the pitcher is ready to focus on the arm motion. The pitcher stands sideways to the target, glove side in front, and executes the arm motion. The glove-side foot is angled slightly for a comfortable stance (see Figures 12-26 and 12-27). Although the pitcher is concentrating exclusively on the whip-like feeling of the pitching arm, the throwing hip should come through as the arm approaches the release point. Bringing the hip through will help develop correct hip closure right from the beginning. This exclusive focus on arm motion is first repeated many times without releasing the ball.

When it appears as though the pitcher is beginning to understand the arm motion, the same action is repeated with the release of the ball. A blindfold may be used to increase the focus on feeling the correct arm motion—slight flexion to extension to extension with the release. The blindfold is especially effective with pitchers who are determined to use accuracy as an evaluation of arm action.

### Glove Pull

Building on the pitching arm motion, the pitcher, still sideways to the target, extends the glove arm to the target, then pulls the glove to the glove shoulder as the arm motion is executed. The pitcher will need to repeat this many times before the glove pull is correctly timed and used effectively with the pitching arm motion. To help the pitcher understand the potential influence pulling the glove has on the throwing side, the coach or another player can hold the extended glove and instruct the pitcher to pull (see Figures 12-28 and 12-29). The importance of pulling the glove to the glove shoulder will become clear.

### Square, Pivot, Close

Next, the pitcher must learn to: (1) start square to the target; (2) pivot to the sideways

**Figure 12-26.** The pitcher stands sideways to the target and executes the arm motion.

**Figure 12-27.** This pitcher has brought the throwing-side hip forward. The next progression is to bring the whole leg THROUGH the release point and completely "close" to the target.

**Figure 12-28.** Another player holds the extended glove.

**Figure 12-29.** The pitcher "pulls" the glove to the glove shoulder.

**Figure 12-30.** Square.

**Figure 12-31.** Pivot.

**Figure 12-32.** Close.

position while striding to the target then, (3) close the throwing-side hip to finish square to the target (see Figures 12-30 to 12-32). Although the focus is on the square-pivot-close, the pitcher also executes the whip-like action of the throwing arm and glove pull. It is important for the pitcher to feel the throwing-side hip come through with the throwing arm. Bringing the hip through with the arm not only completes hip rotation, it also provides a consistent release point for the pitcher.

Again, the pitcher initially executes many repetitions of square-pivot-close without releasing the ball. Having the pitcher correctly execute this sequence the length of the baseline or any other specified distance provides an efficient method of repetition. As the pitcher begins to perform the correct basic movements automatically, the finer points of sequential rotation can become a part of the focus. Here, the pitcher throws as hard as possible and concentrates on remaining relaxed and correct throughout the motion. Remaining relaxed is essential to a smooth and efficient motion. Unnecessary tension interferes with the pitching motion, reduces velocity, increases effort, and impairs accuracy.

### Release Phase

The correct release points for specific pitch locations are developed through a kinesthetic or internal feeling of when to let go of the ball. The greater the velocity of the hand, however, the smaller the difference in release points has to be to make a difference in the height of the pitch. Therefore, if the pitcher slows down to become more accurate, the accuracy will only be learned at that slowed down velocity. For a potential pitcher to become truly effective, velocity and accuracy must be focused upon simultaneously.

Getting the feel of various release points can be accomplished by attempting to hit various targets (i.e., high, low). The targets provide the pitcher with immediate feedback. The pitcher should focus on the feel of each release point in relation to the direction of the pitch. If the pitching arm remains in the plane directly to the target and the throwing hip comes through correctly, the pitch released at the midline of the thigh will be directed down the middle of the strike zone. All things being equal, slightly in front of this point results in a higher pitch while slightly behind this point results in a lower pitch.

When accuracy adjustments can be consistently made without sacrificing force production, the pitcher is ready to enter game situations. At this stage, good days and bad days are usually the norm. Positive reinforcement, correct feedback, encouragement, and patience are crucial to the coaching role.

### PITCHING THE CHANGE-UP

To prevent being hit like a pitching machine in a game situation, the pitcher must develop a slower pitch or *change-up*. The purpose of a periodic change-up, or change-of-pace pitch, is to get the hitters to: (1) swing early, and/or (2) begin to think about the timing of their swing. A pitcher who can get the hitter to think in the batter's box has a tremendous advantage!

The key to pitching an effective change-up is to mask the pitch so it looks like every other pitch. Detectable changes in the pitching motion may give the hitter time to react and adjust to the slower speed. The following are suggestions for minor, undetectable changes in the: (1) grip, (2) stride, and (3) release that are conducive to throwing an effective change-up.

### Grip

There are several ways to grip the ball for a change-up. The most common grip is to place the ball deep in the palm of the hand and wrap the fingers around the ball, preferably off the seams (see Figure 12-33). Another grip is with the fingertips or first knuckles of the fingers buried into the ball. To use the knuckle grip, however, the pitcher's hand must be large enough to still control the release of the ball. Whatever the grip, it must allow the ball to inefficiently pop out of the hand at release.

### Stride

The pitcher also shortens the stride when throwing a change-up. A shorter stride reduces the distance the hips can rotate to generate force and subsequently reduces the amount of force to be applied to the ball. The shorter stride also requires less glove-side knee flexion to absorb the impact of the stride. Reduced glove-side knee flexion proportionally reduces the contribution of glove-side knee extension to again reduce the amount of force applied to the ball (see "Common Errors").

**Figure 12-33.** The change-up grip.

## Release

The arm motion must be identical to the fastball. As the pitching arm moves toward the release point, however, the wrist stiffens. Once at the desired release point, the fingers quickly extend so the ball can efficiently pop out of the hand and float to the plate. Once the pitch is released, the arm follows through as if throwing a fastball.

To further reduce the force applied to the ball, the pitcher may choose to tuck the throwing elbow into the side of the body as the release point is approached. The wrist remains stiff while the elbow continues to slightly flex until the hand is at the desired release point. At the instant the pitch is released, the elbow untucks and the arm follows through as if throwing a fastball.

### Key Elements:

- The grip on the softball changes to: (1) deep in the palm of the hand, or (2) with larger hands, with the fingertips or first knuckles securing the ball. The grip is preferably off the seams.
- The pitcher shortens the stride slightly.
- The pitcher throws hard, keeping the arm speed consistent.
- The wrist is stiff through the release of the ball. The pitcher may choose to tuck the elbow into the side as the release point nears.
- The hand continues to move forward to the desired point of release and the fingers quickly extend to allow the ball to pop out of the hand.
- The pitching arm follows through as if throwing a fastball.

### Common Errors:

- The pitcher slows the arm motion. The batter sees the pitch coming, waits patiently and hits the ball hard.
- The speed of the ball is TOO slow and the hitter has time to adjust.
- Incorrect adjustment of the release point. The pitcher should practice changing from the fastball to the change-up and back again.

Although the change-up can be thrown for a strike, it is most effective when thrown to drop out of the strike zone as it crosses the plate. If the batter begins to swing at a pitch that looks like a fastball strike, adjustment to the slower, low pitch is very difficult. To effectively mask the change-up, the pitcher must THROW HARD and know the subtle changes will reduce the speed of the pitch!

## PITCH VARIATIONS

Pitchers should not be concerned with throwing different types of pitches until they have developed correct pitching mechanics, good control, and good speed. Pitchers can be very effective with a good fastball/change-up combination and good location!

Once the pitcher has met the above criteria, he/she may begin to think about different types of pitches. The various pitches are dependent upon the rotation or *spin* of the ball. Although there are many different methods for imparting spin, the spin itself (in combination with optimal velocity) is responsible for the movement of the ball. Therefore, as an introduction to throwing various pitches, the pitcher can play with the spin of the ball—during practice. Spin from bottom to top is conducive to a *drop ball*, spin from top to bottom is conducive to a *rise ball*, spin from left to right is conducive to a *curve ball*, and no spin at all is conducive to a *knuckle ball* (see Figure 12-34). The spin of the drop ball is the easiest spin to learn!

Drop rotation

Rise rotation

Curve

**Figure 12-34.** The rotation of the ball necessary to produce various pitches.

## SLOW PITCH

The rules of slow pitch require the pitcher to begin with one or both feet in contact with the pitcher's plate. The throwing-side foot, however, must maintain contact with the plate throughout the delivery. Prior to the delivery of the pitch, the pitcher must come to a complete stop with the ball in front of the body, the body facing the batter. From this initial position, the pitcher pitches the ball with an underhand motion. The ball must be released at a moderate speed with a perceptible arc that is a minimum height of 6 ft. and a maximum height of 12 ft. Following the release of the pitch, the arc and speed of the ball allow the pitcher time to move a few steps back. The added distance from the batter will give the pitcher more time to react to a hit and, as a result, more time to move to the ball.

# 13
# Fundamentals of Hitting

*Jill Elliott, M.S.*

---

## QUESTIONS TO CONSIDER

- Where is the bat gripped by the hands for maximum flexibility and control?
- What is the significance of initially placing the hands at the top of the strike zone?
- What roles does the wrist action play in relation to the speed of the swing?
- What is the most significant error when hitting?
- What are three elements which affect the path of the ball following contact?
- How can hitting be evaluated to increase the opportunity for success for each player?

---

## INTRODUCTION

Hitting is the primary method of obtaining and advancing baserunners in order to score runs. A single hit, a home run, or several hits within the same inning may result in a run or runs being scored. In general, the more effective the team hitting, the more runs scored.

Swinging a bat effectively may be broken down into four components or phases. These components include: (1) the preparatory phase, (2) the propulsive phase, (3) the contact phase, and (4) the follow-through phase. Although slight variations exist depending on the goal of the hitter, a description of the basic principles underlying the four components of hitting is provided below.

## BASIC PHASES OF HITTING

### Preparatory Phase

#### The Grip

The bat is held with a firm but relaxed grip. The hands are held together with the back hand on top. Comfort, flexibility, and control are qualities of a good grip. In general, gripping the bat in the area where the fingers meet the palms allows maximum flexibility and control (see Figure 13-1). A grip held too deep in the palms reduces flexibility, whereas a grip held too far in the fingers reduces control. Also, lining up the second knuckles of both hands places the top hand in a good position to transfer maximum power to the ball at the point of contact (see Figure 13-2).

The location of the grip on the bat handle is also a factor. Gripping the bat just above the knob will allow maximum power. Gripping the bat handle 3-4 in. above the knob, or choking up on the bat, will increase the speed of the swing and control of the bat but will reduce power (see Figure 13-3 ). The location of the grip depends on the situation. Choking up is desirable in the following situations:

- the batter wants to hit the ball to a particular spot, known as place hitting
- the batter is having trouble getting around

179

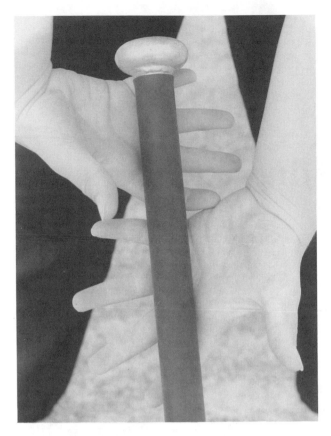

**Figure 13-1.** Bat placement in the hands.

**Figure 13-3.** Choke grip.

**Figure 13-2.** Power grip.

on the pitch because the pitcher is throwing faster than usual

- the batter has two strikes and has to be prepared to hit anything close to the strike zone
- the batter needs a lighter and shorter bat but none are available

The longer grip or power grip can be used in most other situations.

**The Ready Position**

The basic ready position for hitting in softball positions the feet approximately shoulder width apart and parallel. Both feet are an equal distance from the plate with the weight evenly distributed over the balls of the feet. The knees and trunk are slightly flexed. A conscious two-step process of flexing the trunk first and flexing the knees second ensures a weight distribution over the balls of the feet.

The arms are up and away from the body with the elbows bent. The hands are back and positioned at the top of the strike zone (approximately chest high). Positioning the hands at the top of the strike zone: (1) provides the batter with the knowledge that any pitch above the hands will be out of the strike zone, and (2) allows the most effective swing for hitting pitches within the strike zone. The bat is held still and angled at or between 0 and 45 degrees from horizontal. Above all, the stance is balanced, comfortable, and relaxed (see Figure 13-4).

**Eye Focus and Head Position**

The head is level and facing the pitcher, with the eyes initially focused on the pitcher's release point. The eyes pick up the center of the ball as it travels through the release point, and the eyes continue to follow the ball until it: (1) contacts the bat, or (2) enters the catcher's glove. Attempting to follow the ball prior to its release may disrupt the timing of the swing because each pitcher's motion is slightly different. Also, any unorthodox motion or added movement by the pitcher may serve as a distraction to the batter.

As the ball travels toward the batter, the head position remains relatively stationary while the face moves in a downward direction so that the eyes can focus straight ahead at contact. If the face does not move down to follow the ball, the batter has to rely on peripheral vision or no vision at all—neither is reliable! Following the ball into the catcher's glove when the batter does not swing: (1) reinforces the correct head movement and eye focus, and (2) aids in maintaining concentration and focus throughout an at bat (see Figure 13-5).

**Swing Initiation**

The initiation of the swing depends on the average speed of the pitcher and the speed of the batter's swing. In general, if the pitcher is slow, the swing begins after the pitcher releases the ball. If the pitcher is extremely fast, the swing may begin as the pitcher releases the ball. The faster the total swing speed, however, the longer the batter can wait to initiate the swing. A faster swing speed also allows the batter more time to evaluate the pitch (see Figure 13-6). Adjustments in the initiation of the swing

**Figure 13-4.** Hitting ready position.

**Figure 13-5.** Following the ball into the catcher's glove.

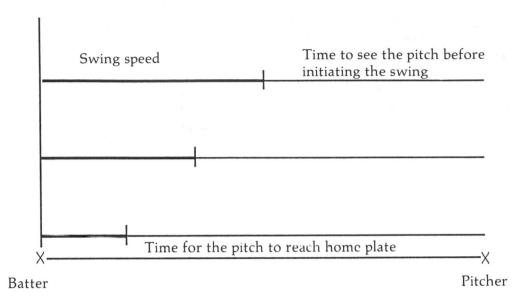

Swing speed

Time to see the pitch before initiating the swing

Time for the pitch to reach home plate

Batter

Pitcher

**Figure 13-6.** Swing initiation in relation to swing speed.

can be made as the batter's swing speed increases and as the batter becomes accustomed to the pitcher. From situation to situation, the total swing speed must be consistent; adjustments are made by varying the initiation of the swing.

## Weight Shift

The swing is initiated by shifting the weight to the back foot and taking a short stride toward the pitcher with the front foot. As the weight shifts inward toward the catcher. This inward shoulder rotation will put the hitting muscles "on stretch" which will result in a forceful contraction into the ball. The amount of inward rotation may vary depending on the goal of the batter and the speed of the pitcher. If the hitter's goal is to hit the long ball, the amount of inward rotation will be greater. However, if the pitcher is very fast in relation to the speed of the swing, the amount of inward rotation will be reduced.

## The Stride

With the weight shifted to the back leg, the front leg is free to stride forward (see Figure 13-7). The stride is fairly short, about 4-6 in., allowing the midline of the body and the position of the head to remain constant. The striding foot is planted at an angle approximately 45 degrees from its original position. Foot placement directly toward the pitcher, or 90 degrees, opens the hips too early and results in: (1) an early commitment to the pitch, which

reduces the time to make a decision and adjust to the pitch, or (2) an interruption of the joint sequence in an attempt to keep the hands back, which reduces the total force production. Foot placement parallel to its original position (0 de-

**Figure 13-7.** Weight shift and stride.

grees) inhibits the contribution of the hips to the joint sequence by reducing the distance the hips can be rotated, which again reduces the total force production.

If the batter perceives the pitch to be a non-desirable pitch, the swing may be terminated during any of the preparatory actions. The batter, however, should expect each pitch to be the perfect pitch. In a perfectly timed swing, the next phase, the propulsive phase, begins as the striding foot fully contacts the ground.

## Propulsive Phase

The propulsive phase begins as the front foot contacts the ground and ends as the bat contacts the ball. The stride initiates a series of force-producing joint actions which begins with the larger joints and ends with the smaller joints. Although this joint sequence is a little more detailed than presented here, it is important to understand the general concept as it relates to hitting.

## Rotation

As the weight is transferred to the front foot, the hips begin to rotate forcefully, with the back hip rotating forward (see Figure 13-8). When the hip rotation reaches its greatest velocity, the trunk begins to rotate at an even faster rate, adding to the force production. Shoulder rotation follows trunk rotation. The shoulders rotate forward at the fastest rate until they are parallel with the hips. When the shoulders and hips are approximately parallel, the arms, held back until now, begin to bring the hands and the bat forward (see Figure 13-9).

## Arm and Wrist Action

The front elbow leads the swing as the elbows begin to extend to the ball, bringing the bat forward, knob first. As the elbows near complete extension, the wrists, which until now have been cocked as a result of rotation, snap the bat into the ball. This wrist action occurs just prior to contacting the ball. *Cocked* and *snap* are the common terms used for the wrist action. In the context of hitting, these terms describe the action of the wrists from radial flexion (wrist flexion to the thumb side of the forearm) to ul-

**Figure 13-8.** Hip rotation: The shoulders and hands are still back.

**Figure 13-9.** The hips and shoulders are parallel; the hands begin to bring the bat forward.

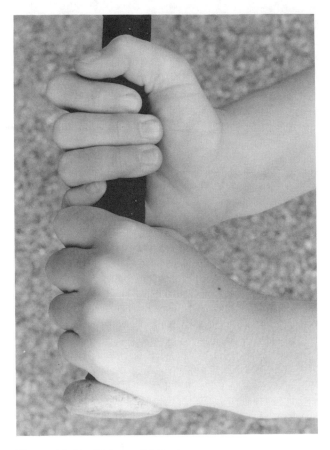

**Figure 13-10.** Wrist radial flexion.

**Figure 13-11.** Wrist ulnar flexion.

**Figure 13-12.** The shorter radius: The front shoulder to the hands.

nar flexion (wrist flexion to the little finger side of the forearm) (see Figures 13-10 and 13-11).

The action of the wrists in the swing is important for several reasons. First, the wrists are a final contributor to the joint sequence. Second, the wrist radial flexion that occurs as the shoulders rotate forward and the elbows begin to extend shortens the radius of the swing for maximum swing speed (see Figure 13-12). Finally, the wrist ulnar flexion that occurs as the bat comes through the strike zone increases the radius of the swing at contact for maximum power (see Figure 13-13). Also, keeping the hands back as long as possible provides a maximum amount of time to adjust the swing to the pitch.

Due to the force generated from the preceding joint sequence, the final wrist snap into the ball occurs at a very high speed. Because of the speed of the bat against the speed of the ball, the grip on the bat must tighten to increase the control of the bat at contact.

### Front Knee Extension

Just as the arms near complete extension, immediately prior to the bat contacting the ball, the front knee forcefully extends. This forceful extension acts to send the front side back. The

**Figure 13-13.** The radius is lengthening: The front shoulder to the end of the bat.

**Figure 13-14.** Front knee extension.

result is an equal and opposite action that increases the force with which the backside comes forward. Forceful knee extension, also known as hitting against the front leg, further contributes to the total force production (see Figure 13-14).

In summary, the force producing joint sequence in hitting occurs as follows: hip rotation, trunk rotation, shoulder rotation, elbow extension, and wrist ulnar flexion. Contributing to the total force production is the front knee extension just prior to contact. The weight

transfer up to the point of contact goes from a stance where the weight is evenly distributed over the toes of both feet, back to the back foot, then forward against the front foot. Although the weight is transferred from the back to the front foot, the midline of the body and the head position must remain relatively constant.

### Contact Phase

For the ideal swing, at the moment of contact:

1. the head is down and the eyes are focused on the point of contact
2. the arms and bat are extended completely to the ball as the bat contacts the ball (in front of the plate)
3. the hips, trunk, and shoulders are rotated forward (approximately 45 degrees—square to the point of contact)
4. the weight of the body is transferred against the front foot—midline of body constant
5. the front knee is completely extended
6. the toes of the back foot are pointing down with the laces of the shoe facing the pitcher, and the back knee is bent as a result of weight transfer and rotation
7. the center of the bat is contacting the center of the ball to send the ball right back through the middle of the field

However, pitchers try to limit the number of ideal pitches allowing an ideal swing. Therefore, it is important to understand the elements influencing the path of the ball after contact so that adjustments might be made according to the location of the pitch. With the force production phase consistent, the path of the ball after contact is basically dependent on three elements: (1) the path of the bat before contact, (2) the area of contact in relation to the plate ("going with the pitch"), and (3) the point of contact between the ball and bat.

#### Bat Path

Consider the first element, the path of the bat before contact. If the bat travels in an upward direction and contacts the center of the ball in the center of the bat, the ball will deflect off the bat in an upward direction. Conversely, if the bat travels in a downward direction and contacts the center of the ball in the center of the bat, the ball will deflect off the bat in a downward direction. Finally, if the bat travels in a direction parallel to the pitch and contacts the center of the ball in the center of the bat, the ball will deflect in the same parallel direction.

Generally, in softball, a slightly downward swing is desirable. With the hands starting at the top of the strike zone a slightly downward swing directly to the ball is the most efficient path for the bat. Also, a slightly downward swing increases the chances of hitting a line drive or a ground ball. Line drives and ground balls consistently result in a higher on-base percentage than fly balls. If an individual is consistently popping up or flying out, it would be wise to check the path of the bat prior to contact.

### Area of Contact

The second element of ball direction involves the area in which the bat contacts the ball. As mentioned previously, the ideal swing involves the center of the bat contacting the center of the ball. The area of the bat in which this ideal contact occurs is known as the *sweet spot*. In order to contact the ball on the bat's sweet spot and still keep the force production phase intact, the area of contact in relation to the plate must change according to the location of the pitch.

If the ball is pitched to the inside of the plate, the bat must contact the ball well in front of the plate. Although the force production phase remains the same, the hips must rotate further on an inside pitch for ideal contact to occur. If the ball is pitched down the center of the plate, the bat must contact the ball just in front of the plate. If the ball is pitched to the outside of the plate, the bat must contact the ball over the outside corner of the plate (see Figure 13-15).

Though the force production phase remains the same, the ball contacts the bat at different points of the swing which results in different bat angles at the point of contact. As a result, the inside pitch is generally the best pitch to pull, the center pitch is the best pitch to drive up the middle, and the outside pitch is the best pitch to hit to the opposite field.

### Point of Contact

The third element affecting the path of the ball after contact involves the point of contact between the bat and the ball. If the force production phase is correct, the path of the bat prior to contact is correct, and the ball has been contacted in the appropriate area in relation to the plate but the top of the bat contacts the bottom of the ball, the result will be a pop-up.

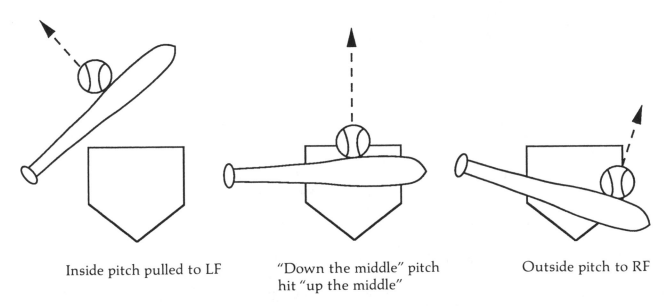

Inside pitch pulled to LF      "Down the middle" pitch hit "up the middle"      Outside pitch to RF

**Figure 13-15.** Location of the pitch in relation to the plate (for a right-handed batter).

If, in the same situation, the bottom of the bat contacts the top of the ball, the result will be a weak ground ball (see Figure 13-16). Many times coaches attempt to correct a swing when it is actually a matter of the correct perception of the path of the pitch. Coaches must be aware of this reality and understand that repetition is the only way to improve pitch perception. With the ball now having been contacted, the follow-through completes the swing.

## Follow-Through Phase

The movement which occurs immediately after the bat has made contact with the ball is the follow-through. The purpose of the follow-through is to: (1) prevent any interruption of the joint sequence prior to contact, and (2) avoid injury by safely reducing the force produced in the force production phase. The follow-through is a direct result of the actions of the propulsive phase. In general, the wrist of the top hand rolls over the top of the bat, the arms and shoul-

ders continue around, and the trunk and hips square to the pitcher (see Figure 13-17).

Although the follow-through does not have any direct effect on the ball, it is important to note because it may provide insight into possible errors occurring in the swing. For example, consistently following through with the hands finishing above the front shoulder may indicate an upward swing into the ball. If the hands begin to move up to the shoulder before contact, the batter will consistently hit the ball up in the air. Also, an incomplete follow-through indicates a breakdown in the force production phase of the swing. In this case, a less than forceful hit will result.

### Key Elements:

- A firm but relaxed grip which tightens at contact.
- A balanced and relaxed ready position.
- Hands holding the bat at the top of the strike zone, with the bat angle at or between 0 and 45 degrees from horizontal.

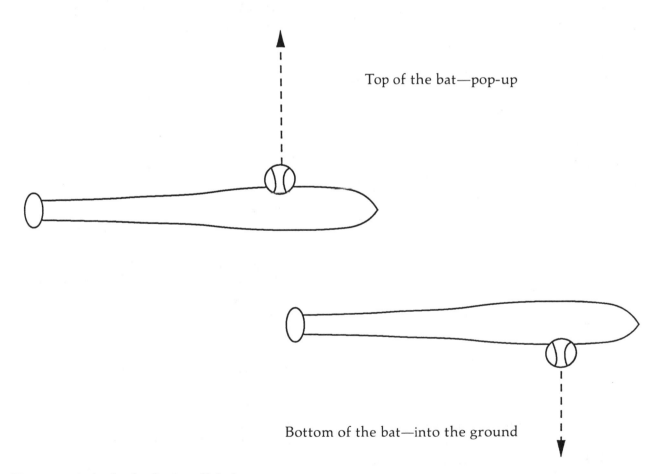

Top of the bat—pop-up

Bottom of the bat—into the ground

**Figure 13-16.** Angle of reflection off the bat.

**Figure 13-17.** Follow-through.

- A constant head position with the eyes focused on the ball from the pitcher's release point to either: (1) contact with the bat, or (2) to the catcher's glove—commonly referred to as keeping the head down.
- Initial weight transfer to the back foot and slight inward shoulder rotation toward the catcher.
- Stride, 4-6 in.; front foot, 45-degree angle from its original position.
- Weight transfer forward against the front leg initiating the following sequential movement of joints:
  1. hip rotation
  2. trunk rotation
  3. shoulder rotation
  4. elbow extension
  5. wrist ulnar flexion
- Contact.
- Follow-through.

*Common Errors:*

- Most common—the head position, turning the head with the shoulders as they rotate forward or pulling the head out (See Figure 13-18). Results:

**Figure 13-18.** ERROR: Pulling the head out.

  1. ends eye contact with the ball
  2. alters the path of the bat, usually causing the batter to miss above the ball
- The midline of the body and the head move toward the pitch as the stride is taken. Results:
  1. an impaired perception of the pitch, with the eyes and the ball moving in opposite directions
  2. an early complete weight transfer onto the front foot which reduces the contribution of the hips to the total production of force
- Striding too long. Results:
  1. an inability to rotate the hips effectively
  2. lowering the path of the bat, usually causing the batter to miss below the ball
  3. lengthening the time and distance required to swing the bat, resulting in a late swing or reduced decision time
  4. lowering the eyes, which causes a perception of ball movement
- Early arm extension and/or wrist flexion which lengthens the radius of the bat arc and results in a slower swing speed.
- Dropping the hands from their ready position as the swing is initiated (see Figure 13-19). Results:
  1. increased swing time

**Figure 13-19.** ERROR: Dropping the hands.

2. back shoulder also dropping to cause an upward bat path
3. an upward swing for pitches above the hands
- Ineffective force production through improper joint sequence for example:
  1. striding without rotating or an arms-only swing
  2. rotating the shoulders and hips simultaneously vs. sequentially. This error also brings the hands forward early which commits the bat to a path early and thus reduces the time to adjust to the pitch
  3. failing to extend the front knee also results in a lowering of the hands which leads to a swing below the ball or an upward swing to contact the ball
  4. incomplete arm extension at contact
- Incomplete follow-through which indicates a breakdown in the force production phase.

## SUGGESTIONS FOR TEACHING HITTING

### Redefining Success

The first step in teaching hitting is to understand how to define "successful hitting." If successful hitting is defined as reaching a base safely, then a good success rate for the best hitters is about three or four times out of every ten. This good success rate, however, means failing six or seven times out of ten. Also, some of the best swings may result in failure while some of the worst swings may result in success. The low success to number of attempts ratio along with the inconsistent outcome makes hitting one of the most difficult skills for a player to learn and understand. If successful hitting experiences are major factors influencing self-confidence and enhancing motivation, then hitting must be redefined in terms of success and failure.

Successful hitting can be defined individually, based on the skill level and ability of each player. Actual performance, not outcome, should be emphasized. For example, Player A may be able to swing hard but does not contact the ball because her head pulls out. For Player A, any swing with the correct head position and eye focus must, therefore, be evaluated as a successful swing. However, any ball that is hit hard when the player pulls her head must be evaluated as an unsuccessful swing. Player B may be able to keep his head down and contact the ball consistently but does not contact the ball forcefully. For Player B, success could be defined as hitting the ball with a progressively more forceful swing regardless of the outcome of that swing. Player C may have a mechanical flaw which alters the path of the bat. Any swing with this flaw corrected would be considered a successful swing regardless of the outcome of that swing.

By redefining success, each player has an increased opportunity to experience success. Defining successful hitting on an individual basis, however, makes it essential for the coach to understand the basic principles of hitting.

## COACHING GOALS

When teaching hitting, the goals of the coach are: (1) to help the individual clearly understand the requirements of hitting, (2) to properly evaluate the individual and determine priorities for learning, (3) to help set goals specific to the individual, and (4) to help evaluate success for that individual. Suggestions for reaching these coaching goals follows.

## BAT SELECTION

Hitting begins with bat selection. In general, the player should be able to hold the bat at the bottom of the handle with the bottom hand and extend the arm with the bat parallel to the ground. If this cannot be done comfortably, it is best to select a lighter bat (see Figure 13-20). Lighter bats lead to increased swing speed.

## THE EYE CONTACT

The phrase "keep your eyes on the ball" is probably the most common phrase in the game of softball. The importance of eye contact, however, cannot be underestimated! If every component of hitting is done incorrectly but the eyes follow the ball to the bat, the batter may still contact the ball. If every component of hitting is done correctly but the eyes do not follow the ball to the bat, the batter will not contact the ball consistently. Hitting success is hard to justify without contact. Therefore, eye focus and ball contact must be the first priorities in teaching hitting.

### Hitting a Stationary Ball

The hitting tee is an effective tool for helping the batter initially understand the head position and eye contact in relation to the swing. To use a tee correctly, the batter assumes the ready position behind and away from the tee so the arms can extend to the ball and contact can occur in front of the body (see Figure 13-21). From the ready position, the batter strides and swings to hit the ball off of the tee. The head

remains still as the bat is swung. The focus should be on head position and eye contact only. As the swing is repeated several times, the batter should become aware of how the head position feels in relation to the swing.

From the hitting ready position, it seems only natural to stride contralaterally or with the front foot. Many less experienced batters, however, will try to stride ipsilaterally or with the back foot. Correct head position and subsequent eye contact are very hard to maintain with an ipsilateral stride. If a batter attempts to hit a moving ball before the contralateral stride naturally occurs, she/he will experience limited success. Batters should not progress to hitting a moving ball until the contralateral stride occurs naturally.

### Tracking the Ball to the Bat

When hitting the ball off of the tee, the batter's head remains stationary throughout the swing. When hitting a pitched ball, however, the head must move down to follow the ball to the bat. Players should understand that the head and the hands move in opposite directions. If the head goes around with the hands, the eyes will not be in a position to see the ball. Put

**Figure 13-20.** Bat selection; this player should select a lighter bat.

**Figure 13-21.** Positioned too close to the tee, the batter cannot fully extend the arms at contact.

another way, the chin goes from the front shoulder to the back shoulder.

The following are ideas to reinforce the understanding of head movement in relation to the swing:

1. The players initially swing to hit an imaginary ball. If bats are limited, players can also use imaginary bats. The goal is to feel the head (face) movement in relation to the swing.
2. The batter stands at a plate while the coach carries the pitch to the plate. The batter watches the ball to the bat. For safety purposes, the coach should make sure the batter understands to swing easy to meet the ball rather than swing hard to hit the ball out of the coach's hand!
3. The ball is pitched to the batter from a distance shorter than the regulation pitching distance, at a relatively slow speed with little or preferably no arc. Again the focus is on the feel of the head position and eye action in relation to the swing. As the consistency of contact increases, the pitching distance gradually increases.

Along with the correct head movement and eye focus, the batter must develop a correct perception of the pitch and coordinate that perception with the swing. The following are ideas for developing pitch perception and hand-eye coordination:

1. Lower skilled players can begin by swinging at a larger and lighter ball with a large plastic bat.
   a. The ball is initially pitched from a short distance—then progressively pitched from longer distances. As skill increases, the ball size becomes progressively smaller and the plastic bat is eventually replaced by a regulation-size bat.
   b. The ball can be suspended on a rope from above home plate. The player puts the ball in motion on the initial hit. The batter then hits the ball forward either:
      (i) as it is on its way back to its original position
      (ii) after it has gone past its original position and is on its way forward again
   The ball should be soft enough to not cause injury to the batter.

2. "Soft Toss" is an excellent drill for facilitating hand-eye coordination. It requires a batter, a swinging implement, a tosser, and several balls. The batter either: (1) stands in the hitting ready position, or (2) kneels on the back knee with the front leg bent, the front foot angled 45 degrees. The tosser is on the home plate side of the batter and tosses the ball to the batter (see Figure 13-22). The ball is tossed so the batter can swing and hit the ball in front of the body. The ball can be hit to an open field or into an area of the fence that will give with the force of the hit.
   a. The batter uses a regulation bat; the tosser tosses a softball.
   b. The batter uses a bat; the tosser tosses a tennis ball.
   c. The batter uses a cut broomstick or dowel rod; the tosser tosses tennis balls.
   d. The batter uses a broomstick or dowel rod; the tosser tosses plastic golf balls.
3. The pitching machine can provide a fairly consistent pitch location and give the batter a high percentage of strikes to hit. The speed and distance can be set specific to the skill level of the batter.
4. Visual training can occur with balls that are half one color, half another color. The balls can be painted or colored with a permanent marker. Any one of the preceding suggestions can be done with half-colored balls. The batter swings to hit the ball as well as observes the color of the half that contacted the bat. If the batter does not follow the ball

**Figure 13-22.** Soft toss drill.

to the bat, he/she will not be able to determine the color that was hit.

Correct eye focus and head movement, along with repetition and variety, result in better bat contact with the ball. Skilled demonstrations at this early stage help the hitter understand eye contact throughout the swing. At the same time, these demonstrations are valuable in helping the hitter pick up other aspects of hitting without consciously focusing on them. Another valuable technique, generally used too little in teaching physical skills, is imagery. Asking the hitters to imagine themselves performing identically to the demonstration may facilitate learning. Many young players have great imaginations and can use imagery effectively.

## DIVIDING HITTING INTO ITS COMPONENTS

Anytime a batter has problems generating force because of a mechanical error, the batter should return to the hitting tee. The stationary ball allows the batter to focus exclusively on a specific component of the swing because adjustments to the pitch are non-existent. Once a batter correctly performs the component with a stationary ball on the tee, he/she can progress to focusing on the component with a moving ball. Again, the goal of the batter should be clearly identified and correctly evaluated.

### The Stride

The stride is very important as it initiates the sequence of actions to follow. To practice striding correctly, the batter assumes the ready position behind and away from the tee. While in the ready position, the batter marks the midline of the body. The midline can be marked by drawing a line in the dirt, placing a bat on the ground, or putting tape on a floor (see Figure 13-23). The batter strides and swings, and then checks the midline mark. If the stride has been executed correctly, the midline of the body will still be in line with the midline mark (see Figure 13-24). If the stride is too long or the weight has transferred over the striding foot, the midline of the body will be ahead of the midline mark. If the batter leans back on the swing or

**Figure 13-23.** The batter marks the midline with a line on the gym floor.

**Figure 13-24.** The batter swings, then checks the midline.

keeps the weight on the back foot, the midline of the body will be behind the midline mark.

As the stride is initiated, the batter may have a tendency to drop the hands below the top of the strike zone. If this is the case, the batter must focus on the hands and concentrate on keeping them at the top of the strike zone! Dropping the hands can cause problems with total swing time and correct swing adjustment (see Common Errors).

## Rotation

The batter assumes the ready position at the tee and strides to the ball, focusing on hitting the ball as hard as possible. If the batter's head pulls out as a result of swinging hard, a simple "head down" usually serves as a sufficient reminder. The focus, however, is on swinging hard. As the batter becomes more aware of the action of his/her body parts, it might help to think of pulling the shoulders around with the hips. The batter should note the feel of the rotation and continually try to increase its effectiveness.

## Arm and Wrist Action

The batting tee is placed in a position which requires the arms to be extended at contact. The batter needs only to be aware of the bent-to-straight action of the arms and wrists and the path of the bat. Again, without eliminating the previously practiced components, the batter focuses primarily on the arm action. Telling the batter to "lead with the knob of the bat," then "throw the barrel of the bat at the ball" is often effective in creating proper arm action. Remember, from the initial hand position to contact, the bat takes a slight downward arc. Becoming aware of how the proper action feels is very beneficial for increasing self-evaluation and practice efficiency.

## Knee Extension

If the striding knee extension does not occur naturally it can be practiced on the batting tee. The batter swings to hit the ball off the tee and concentrates on forcefully extending the front knee immediately prior to contact. Al-though the batter is executing the whole swing, the focus is on the front knee extension only!

## The Complete Swing

Timing of components, smoothness of execution, and swing speed will be improved over time through many repetitions, correct constructive feedback, and patience. If the batter is required to perform in a game situation before the entire swing is learned (which is usually the case), the batter and coach must remember the goal of execution and evaluate success accordingly.

## PERFORMANCE EVALUATION

Once the correct swing is internalized, usually after many years, the batter must learn to evaluate performance by differentiating between: (1) the degree of readiness for a pitch, (2) proper or improper execution of the swing, and (3) the effectiveness of the pitch. Many times failure to reach base safely is a result of an excellent pitch or a great defensive play. These factors are entirely out of the batter's control and should not lead to an evaluation of failure. Many times, however, failure to reach base safely is a result of improper swing execution or just not being ready. These factors are entirely in a batter's control and can be corrected! Also important is the evaluation of each individual's best hit. An effort to duplicate readiness and swing execution may result in greater consistency.

## ERROR CORRECTION

Due to the complexity of hitting, errors in swing execution may appear throughout a career. For this reason, it is important for coaches to remember that when two or more errors occur simultaneously, they must be prioritized and corrected one at a time. If two or more coaches are working with a team, each coach must be aware of these priorities and provide the same reinforcements. Many times one coach will point out one error while another coach—or helpful parent—will point out another error. Although both teachers may be correct in their analysis, they are providing the batter with two items to think about at the same time. The batter may attempt to correct both items simultaneously in an effort to please everyone and swing successfully. This will probably result in an unsuccessful attempt and may lead to increased anxiety and frustration, further inhibiting performance.

Coaches must also remember to save error corrections for practice. Verbal and visual cues or reminders (i.e., "head down," "extend your arms," "hands up") are helpful during games, but corrections are usually not possible and generally serve as a distraction to the batter during a game.

# 14
# Bunting—Fast Pitch

*Jill Elliott, M.S.*

---

QUESTIONS TO CONSIDER

- What are the four components of bunting?
- What are two reasons for positioning the bat at the top of the strike zone?
- Why is it important to "catch" the ball with the bat when executing a sacrifice bunt?
- What skill must the batter possess before attempting to learn the bunt for a hit?
- What are the goals of the batter when executing a slap hit?

---

## INTRODUCTION

Bunting in fast pitch softball is an alternative to hitting. Bunting can be used to obtain baserunners or advance baserunners. Although bunting is not an essential skill, its mastery greatly contributes to the offensive strategic possibilities. Also, as the pitching improves to the point of dominating a game, it becomes less likely that consecutive hits will occur to advance runners and produce runs. Therefore, as the level of play advances, the role of bunting becomes increasingly crucial to offensive production.

There are two basic types of bunts: the *sacrifice bunt* and the *bunt-for-a-hit*. Although the goals of these two bunts are different, there are basic components common to both types of bunts. The basic components are: (1) the hitting ready position, (2) the approach to the ball, (3) bat position, (4) adjustment to the pitch, and (5) contact. This chapter contains a description of the basic components of bunting and the various approaches to specific types of bunts.

Specific bunts include sacrifice bunts, bunts for a hit, and the fake bunt and hit or slap hit.

## BASIC COMPONENTS OF BUNTING

### Hitting Ready Position

Each bunt starts from the hitting ready position. In review, the feet are approximately shoulder width apart, the weight is evenly distributed over the balls of the feet, the knees and trunk are slightly flexed, the arms are up and out from the body, and the hands are back and positioned at the top of the strike zone. In general, the batter should assume the ready position in the front of the batter's box so each bunt has the optimal chance of being placed inside the foul lines. From this position, the batter is able to approach the pitch.

### Approach to the Ball

The footwork for the approach varies with each type of bunt. Therefore, footwork will be discussed in terms of each bunt variation. The hand positioning, however, is similar for each type of bunt. As the bunt is initiated with the various foot movements, the top hand slides up the bat handle on the thumb and forefinger to the middle of the bat. The fingers of the top hand form a shelf for the bat, and the thumb is placed safely behind the bat (see Figure 14-1). The fingers and thumb of the bottom hand remain wrapped around the base of the handle. The bottom hand serves as the control hand. Choking up on the bat handle can facilitate control.

## Bat Position

As the top hand slides up the bat handle, the shoulders square to the pitch. The elbows are slightly flexed as the arms extend the bat at the top of the strike zone. The bat is held horizontally with the barrel of the bat covering the width of the plate. The bat is positioned at the top of the strike zone for two important reasons: (1) only the pitches even with or below the bat are strikes or pitches to be bunted, and (2) the eyes are positioned "behind" the bat for an accurate view of the pitch (see Figure 14-2).

## Adjustment to the Pitch

As the pitch approaches the plate, the BODY adjusts the bat to the pitch location, while the arm, bat, and eye positions remain constant. The arms, bat, and head should form a triangle and remain in this position for every pitch location. If the pitch is lower than the top of the strike zone bat level, the triangle is lowered by further bending the knees. If the pitch is inside or outside, the triangle is adjusted by a shift of body weight (see Figure 14-3).

**Figure 14-2.** Position of the bat.

**Figure 14-3.** Adjustment to an outside pitch.

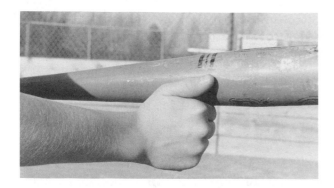

**Figure 14-1.** Position of the top hand.

The direction of the bunt is dictated by the angle of the bat in relation to the pitch. The bottom hand (control hand) is responsible for establishing the desired angle of the bat. If the hands are an equal distance from the body or perpendicular to the path of the pitch, the ball is deflected in the direction of the pitcher. For a right-handed batter, placing the control hand slightly further away from the body than the top hand will direct the ball toward the first-base side of the field. Placing the control hand closer to the body than the top hand will direct the ball toward the third-base side of the field (see Figure 14-4). The opposite will be true for a left-handed batter.

## Contact

The bunt must result in the ball being hit on the ground. To do this successfully, the batter attempts to contact the center of the ball with the center of the bat. The bat must be still as it contacts the ball. The instant the ball is contacted, the arms give to absorb the force of the ball. Both arms give equally as the batter thinks of "catching" the ball with the bat.

The amount of absorption depends on the speed of the pitch and the goal of the bunt. The bunt should require the fielders and the catcher to move a maximum distance. Too much absorption causes the ball to stop directly in front of the catcher, while too little absorption hits the ball directly to the fielders. Proper absorption, however, requires the fielders and the catcher to move to the ball and to decide who has the best chance of fielding and throwing the ball. As pitchers become more skilled and the speed of the pitches increases, the amount of absorption must also increase (see Figure 14-5).

Following contact, the batter must get to first base as efficiently as possible. When executing the *square around bunt*, the weight immediately transfers to the right foot and the left foot crosses over to take the initial step to first base. For all other bunts, the weight transfers to the front foot as the ball is contacted and the back foot takes the initial step to first base. As

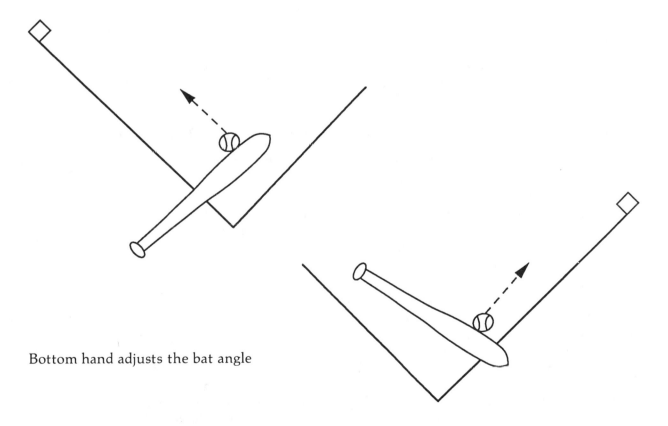

Bottom hand adjusts the bat angle

**Figure 14-4.** Bat angles for bunt placement.

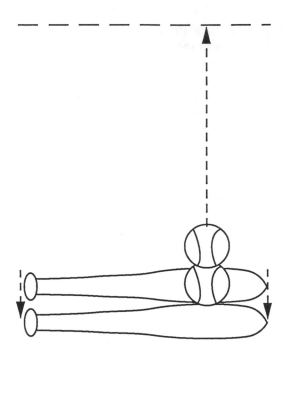
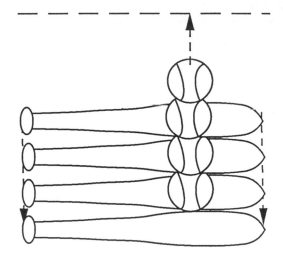

**Figure 14-5.** Distance of bunt in relation to give.

the initial step is taken, the bat is dropped, not thrown, to the third base side of the batter. Dropping the bat on the third base side will assure that the bat is not tripped over while running to first base.

## SACRIFICE BUNTS

The purpose of the sacrifice bunt is to advance a baserunner by sacrificing the batter. Because the baserunner can leave the base as the ball leaves the pitcher's hand, the baserunner can get to the next base before the bunter can get to first base. On a well executed bunt, the force out at first base is the only play the defense can execute. Thus, the batter is out but the baserunner is one base closer to home. It is important to note that the sacrifice bunt is only used with less than two outs in the inning.

There are two variations of the sacrifice bunt: (1) the square around bunt, and (2) the pivot bunt. The square around bunt is the most basic bunt. A batter should be able to correctly perform the square around bunt before attempt-

ing a pivot bunt or a bunt-for-a-hit. The major difference in the square around bunt and all other bunts occurs in the approach. This section will focus mainly on the differences in the approach.

## Square Around Bunt

The square around bunt begins from the hitting ready position at the front of the batter's box. The batter remains in this position until the pitcher's hands separate to begin the pitching delivery. As the pitcher's hands separate, the back foot moves forward to bring the back side of the body even with the front side of the body. A front foot pivot accompanies this back foot movement so that the toes of both feet point toward the pitcher. The feet are parallel and approximately shoulder width apart. The knees and hips are slightly flexed and the hips, trunk, and shoulders are square to the pitcher (see Figure 14-6). The bat positioning, adjustment to pitches, and contact ball are the same as previously described.

**Figure 14-6.** The square around bunt position in the front of the batter's box.

### Key Elements:

- Hitting ready position.
- Back foot moves forward and the front foot pivots to square the hips, trunk, and shoulders to the pitch.
- Simultaneously, the top hand slides up to the middle of the bat.
- The arms extend the bat out from the body at the top of the strike zone with the barrel of the bat covering the width of the plate.
- The eyes are behind the bat following the center of the ball.
- Adjustments to pitch location are made through body adjustments. The triangle formed by the bat, arms, and head are kept intact.
- The bunt direction is determined by the position of the control hand.
- Contact the center of the ball with the center of the bat. The arms give with contact.
- The weight is transferred to the right foot and the left foot crosses over to make the ini-

tial step toward first base (for both right-handed and left-handed bunters).
- The bat is dropped to the third base side of the batter to avoid interfering with the movement toward first base.

### Common Errors:

- The initial step with the back foot occurs after the ball has been released, giving the batter too little time to set up and adjust to the pitch.
- The back foot steps out of the batter's box when squaring the body to pitch—an out will result if the ball is contacted.
- The bat is held lower than the top of the strike zone. This results in: (1) the eyes farther from bat level which makes the proper point of contact harder to determine, and (2) having to move the bat up to contact a high strike. The upward movement of the bat may result in pushing the ball up in the air.
- The top hand wraps around the bat, increasing the chance of injury.
- The bottom of the ball contacts the top of the bat, resulting in a pop-up and possible double play.
- The arms push the ball rather than give with the ball. The ball gets to the defensive player quicker, increasing the chance of forcing out the lead runner.
- The arms (rather than the body) adjust the bat to the ball resulting in: (1) a moving bat at contact, making the point of contact less certain, (2) arms that are not in a position to give with the pitch because they are moving toward the ball, and (3) eyes that are no longer in a position to properly perceive the pitch.

## Pivot Bunt

The pivot bunt is a variation of the square around bunt. The batter assumes a similar hitting ready position in front of the plate, but closer to the plate than with the square around bunt. As the pitcher's hands separate to begin the delivery, the batter pivots forward on the balls of both feet (see Figure 14-7). To ensure a balanced bunting position, the batter may take a small step with the front foot away from the plate as the pivot occurs. The feet are staggered, the weight is more on the front foot, and the

**Figure 14-7.** Pivot bunt position.

hips, trunk, and shoulders are square to the pitcher.

Once the pivot has occurred, executing the bunt is identical to the square around bunt (see "Basic Components of Bunting").

*Key Elements:*

- Hitting ready position—closer to the plate than with the square around bunt.
- The body pivots forward on the balls of both feet to square the hips, trunk, and shoulders to the pitcher.
- The front foot takes a small step away from the plate during the pivot to ensure a balanced position.
- The body weight is distributed more on the front foot.
- Bunt execution is identical to the square around bunt key elements.

*Common Errors:*

- The feet are set too close together. This results in poor balance which inhibits the ability to adjust to the pitch.

- Stance too far from the plate results in an inability to reach the outside strike.
- Pivot occurs too late, resulting in insufficient time to extend, adjust, and give with the pitch.
- Others common to square around bunt.

## Suggestions for Teaching the Sacrifice Bunt

### Hand Position and Contact

The sacrifice bunt can be learned by placing a batter in a position square to the pitcher. In this squared position, the batter is shown the proper hand and bat positions. Once these positions are understood and can be consistently duplicated, the ball is pitched slowly to the top of the batter's strike zone from only 5 to 6 ft. away. The batter focuses only on "catching" the ball with the bat. The center of the bat contacts the center of the ball and the arms recoil upon contact. Because of the slow speed of the pitch, the ball will drop straight down when the bunt is executed correctly (see Figure 14-8).

If the batter is having trouble giving with the pitch, and instead pushes the bat at the pitch, the batter can practice the arm action without a bat. The arms are extended in front of the body at the top of the strike zone and the batter catches the ball with the top hand. Also,

**Figure 14-8.** The ball drops straight down with the slow speed of the pitch.

a glove may be placed on the end of the bat. The bunter must "give" to catch the pitch with the glove.

### Pitch Adjustment

The next step is to understand how to adjust to the pitch. Using the triangle concept—the bats, arms, and head as one unit—the batter attempts to "catch" pitches in various locations around the strike zone. The pitches are "caught" first with the top hand, then with the bat. Remember, at no time does the triangle break to allow the bat to fall below eye level!

### Square/Pivot to the Pitch

#### Without a ball

From the hitting ready position, the batter squares (via square around or pivot approach) to the pitcher, the hand slides up to the middle of the bat on the thumb and forefinger, and the arms extend the bat at the top of the strike zone. This process is repeated several times without a ball.

#### With a ball

The batter must understand that in executing a sacrifice bunt, an early indication of the bunt is intentional. The purpose of the bunt is not to fool the defense but to advance the baserunner by sacrificing the batter. When this concept is understood, the batter is ready to practice the square/pivot with a pitcher. From the regulation pitching distance, a player or coach imitates the pitching motion and pitches the ball for the batter to bunt. The batter practices squaring/pivoting as the pitcher's hands separate just prior to the delivery. The top hand slides up the bat handle simultaneously with the square/pivot and the batter executes the bunt as previously practiced.

### Bunt Placement

Once a batter correctly adjusts to various pitches, he/she can practice placing the ball in various locations. Early attempts at placing the ball often result in the batter changing the bat angle as the ball contacts the bat. This last second change results in pushing the ball. The push results in either the ball being hit too hard or in hitting the ball foul. The batter must under-

stand that the adjustment occurs before contact so that the bat can be stationary at contact.

To practice bunt placement, the ball is pitched to the batter and the batter practices the slight adjustment of the bottom hand necessary to direct the ball to the desired location. Everything that has been previously practiced remains the same. Only the relationship between the position of the bottom hand and the top hand changes, and that change occurs BEFORE the bat contacts the ball. As skill increases, the speed of the pitch is increased to simulate game situations.

## BUNTING FOR A HIT

The purpose of bunting for a hit is to reach base by surprising the defense. The element of surprise occurs by waiting until the last possible moment to place the bat in a bunting position and either give with the pitch when the defense is back, or push the pitch between fielders when the defense is drawn in. The bunt for a hit can be done from either the right or left side of the plate. A *drag* bunt from the left side of the plate, however, is more efficient because the batter starts closer to first base. Generally, the faster the running speed of the batter, the more effective the bunt for a hit.

### Right-Handed Push Bunt

The batter assumes the ready position slightly behind and away from the plate. The batter times the pitch and takes a short stride toward the pitcher with the front foot, similar to the regular hitting stride. At the last possible moment, the bat is lowered to the bunting position as the weight is transferred to the front foot, and the back foot strides toward first base. (see Figure 14-9). As the bat contacts the ball, the weight is moving onto the foot striding to first base. The ball can be pushed to either side of the infield, depending upon the situation.

Similar to the sacrifice bunt, the batter squares the shoulders to the ball and "catches" the ball with the bat. The bat must be stationary just prior to contact to allow controlled placement of the ball. Choking up with both hands during the initial grip can help increase control.

(a)

(b)

(c)

(d)

**Figure 14-9.** Right-handed push bunt.

## Left-Handed Drag Bunt

The left-handed batter assumes the ready position fairly close to the plate. The batter times the pitch, strides toward the pitcher, and lowers the bat to the bunting position at the last possible moment. Contact is made with the shoulders square to the pitch, the bat in front of the body and stationary, and the weight on the front foot (see Figures 14-10). Generally, the batter drags the ball down the first-base line. Immediately following contact, the back foot strides to continue the run to first base. The bat is dropped to the third-base side of the batter, and the run is continued to first base. Again, the bat must be stationary at contact, and the eyes must see the ball contact the bat.

### Key Elements:

- Hitting ready position: (1) behind and away from the plate on the right side, or (2) near the plate on the left side.
- Short stride toward the pitcher.
- Shoulders square to the pitch and bat lowered to bunting position at last possible moment.
- Eyes follow the ball to the bat.
- Bat is stationary at contact and "catches" the ball.
- The weight is moving onto the front foot as contact is made, and the back foot strides toward first base immediately following contact.

### Common Errors:

- The initial ready position is in the wrong area of the batter's box and may result in contact outside of the box.
- The initial step is toward first base rather than toward the pitcher, resulting in a right-handed batter being jammed with the inside strike and a left-handed batter unable to reach the outside strike.
- The eyes focus on first base before contact is made. The batter increases the chance of mis-hitting the ball (i.e., pop-up).
- Lowering the bat to the bunting position and squaring the shoulders to the pitch too late, resulting in a moving bat at contact; the ball goes foul or directly to the fielders.
- The bat is moving at contact, resulting in uncontrolled ball placement.

## Suggestions for Teaching the Bunt for a Hit

### Approach

The batter must be proficient at performing the sacrifice bunt before attempting to learn the bunt for a hit. Once the batter understands all of the components of bunting, the challenge then becomes incorporating the components while the body is in motion. The first priority is the approach or the footwork. From the hitting ready position, the batter practices the proper footwork using an imaginary pitcher and an imaginary ball. The batter imagines the pitcher beginning the pitching motion, focuses on the pitcher's release point, and concentrates on correct footwork to the pitch. At the last possible moment, the batter lowers the bat to the bunting position. The weight is on the front foot, the ball contacts the bat, and the back foot continues movement toward first base.

### Timing With a Pitched Ball

After several repetitions, the batter progresses to an actual pitcher and ball. The focus is now on timing the step into the pitch and properly executing the bunt. The body is in motion, yet the bat is stationary in order to absorb the impact of the ball. To aid in understanding the concept of the stationary bat, the bunt may also be practiced without a bat. The pitcher pitches the ball at a moderate speed and the batter: (1) strides, (2) places the arms in the bunting position, (3) catches the ball, giving with the hands, and (4) continues to run toward first base. The same process is then repeated with the bat. Again, the eyes must follow the ball to the bat!

As timing and skill improve, the batter can practice bunting with the team pitcher throwing pitches that approach game speed and accuracy. Many repetitions and correct constructive feedback are necessary for consistent success.

## THE SLAP HIT

The slap hit or "fake bunt and hit" is used in an attempt to reach base as a result of a base hit. The initial "fake bunt" is used to make the defense react to a bunt. If the defense moves early to cover the bunt, there is more room for the batter to hit away. On the other hand, if

(a)

(b)

(c)

(d)

**Figure 14-10.** Left-handed drag bunt.

the defense does not react to the initial bunt action, the batter can elect to execute the bunt.

The slap hit is an extension of the pivot bunt. Initially, the batter assumes the ready position with a choke grip on the bat. As the pitcher initiates the pitching motion, the batter pivots as if to bunt (see Figure 14-11). As the pitch approaches, the hands slide together at the top of the bat grip and the bat moves to the slap position. The slap position consists of the top hand being positioned just in front of the back shoulder (without rotating back) and the bat in a position to quickly hit the ball (see Figure 14-12). Simultaneous with the movement of the bat, the weight moves toward the front leg with the knee slightly flexed. The eyes follow the center of the ball and the batter quickly brings the bat forward to slap the ball. Just prior to contact, the front knee forcefully extends to increase the amount of force applied to the ball. The batter follows through with the swing and initiates the run to first base with the back foot.

Because the batter has choked up on the bat and is taking only a half swing, the batter has maximum control over the bat. The ideal ball placement is to the left side of the field between shortstop and third base.

## Slap Hitting Effectively

The initial goal of the batter is to make the defense believe the batter is bunting. To do this, the batter must first sell the bunt. Beyond selling the bunt, the batter must wait until the last possible moment to execute the slap hit. Waiting until the last moment leaves only enough time to take the bat back to the shoulder. Taking the bat BEYOND the shoulder means that the batter will not have enough time to get the bat around to hit the ball, or will reveal the slap earlier than necessary and give the defense more time to react. A short compact half swing, NOT a home run swing, is key to the success of the slap hit!

**Figure 14-11.** Pivot position.

**Figure 14-12.** Slap position.

*Key Elements:*

- The hitting ready position with a choke grip on the bat.
- Selling the pivot bunt.
- Waiting until the last moment to move the bat back to a slap position. The hands move to the back shoulder, but not beyond.
- Moving the weight toward the front foot as the bat is drawn back.
- Watching the ball to the bat!
- Taking a quick, compact half swing to slap the ball to the left side of the infield.
- Following through and initiating the run to first base with the back leg.

*Common Errors:*

- The batter attempts to return to the original hitting position and take a full swing.
- The batter shifts the weight over the back foot as the bat is drawn back. This creates greater body rotation back and subsequently a longer, more time-consuming swing.
- The batter waits too long before drawing the bat back and has to rush the swing.
- The batter's half swing is too slow.
- The batter gives the slap away by: (1) not completely squaring the shoulders to the pitcher on the pivot, or (2) taking the bat back to hit too soon.
- The batter does not watch the center of the ball to the bat.

## Suggestions for Teaching the Slap Hit

To slap hit effectively, the batter must first understand the half swing. Understanding the half swing starts with the batter learning the position of the hands at the beginning of the swing. Therefore, the first step is to place the feet in the pivot bunt position and the bat in the slap position with the top hand just in front of the back shoulder. The ball is tossed to the batter and the batter slaps the ball. This is repeated many times to reinforce exact slap position of the hands, eye contact with the ball, and a quick swing of the bat. At this stage, the batter also practices hitting the ball to specific locations.

The next step is to start in the pivot bunt position and practice taking the bat back to the previously practiced slap position. Once the correct slap position is consistently attained, the batter progresses to executing the entire slap. The batter assumes the hitting ready position, pivots to bunt the ball, and draws the bat back to slap. As the correct movement is understood, the batter progresses to slapping a pitch that simulates game speed. The focus should be on selling the bunt and correctly timing the slap. A batter highly skilled at slapping can also fake the slap and quickly move the bat back to the original bunting position and execute the bunt.

# 15
# Baserunning

*Jill Elliott, M.S.*

---

## QUESTIONS TO CONSIDER

- When running to first base, what is the significance of running outside the foul line?
- What is the purpose of the arc on an extra base hit?
- Why can a runner on second base take a longer lead than the runner on first base?
- What should the runner expect to do at the end of *every* steal?
- How would a runner slide into second base if the shortstop is receiving a throw from right-center field?

---

## INTRODUCTION

Baserunning is a prerequisite to scoring runs and, therefore, an essential aspect of the game of softball. Proper technique and good judgment employed while running the bases can greatly increase the chances of scoring and/ or keeping an inning alive.

A description of the techniques involved in various baserunning situations that may occur in each game are provided below. Situations include: (1) running through first base, (2) rounding the bases on base hits and extra base hits, (3) leading off the bases, (4) stealing, and (5) sliding.

## RUNNING THROUGH FIRST BASE

The run to first base begins immediately after the follow-through of the swing. With the weight on the front foot as a result of the swing, the initial step toward first base is taken

with the back foot. As the back foot strides to first base, the bat is dropped behind the runner, and the eyes are focused on the base (see Figure 15-1). The runner runs to first base on the outside of the foul line and, on about the third step, glances to see if the ball has been fielded by the infielder or if it has gone through to the outfield (see Figure 15-2).

If the ball has been fielded by the infielder, the runner continues to run straight and hard through first base. First base is contacted on the front, outside edge preferably with the front part of the left foot (see Figure 15-3). Although the runner does not jump or leap onto the base, a forward lean with the upper body just before contacting the base is desirable. To ensure full running speed through the base, the runner should not begin to slow down until two or three steps beyond the base. One or two steps beyond the base, the runner should look over the right shoulder for a possible overthrow (see

**Figure 15-1.** The bat is dropped behind the batter/runner.

**Figure 15-2.** The runner runs on the outside of the foul line.

(a)

(b)

**Figure 15-3.** Contacting first base with the left foot is preferable. Contact with the right foot increases the possibility of contact with the first baseperson.

Figure 15-4). Once past the base, the runner attends to the field action and coaching directions.

*Key Elements:*
- Initial step to first base with the back foot immediately after the follow-through of the swing.
- Run hard, on or just outside the foul line.

**Figure 15-4.** The runner checks for a possible overthrow.

- Third step, momentarily check to see if the ball has been fielded.
- Lean into base at contact.
- After contacting the base, look over right shoulder for possible overthrow.
- Run 8-10 ft. beyond the base before slowing down.
- Attend to field play and coaching directions.

*Common Errors:*

- Too many small steps to get started.
- Running inside the foul line—if the runner is hit with a thrown ball inside the foul line, the runner is out.
- Slowing down before reaching the base or stopping on the base.
- Leaping to the base—once in the air, only gravity can bring the runner down to the base—leaping is significantly slower than running through the base.
- Being unaware of field action after safely reaching the base.

## ROUNDING BASES

### One-Base Hits

If on the third step out of the batter's box the runner sees the ball has gone into the outfield, the runner begins an arc 10-20 ft. prior to first base (see Figure 15-5). The arc is approximately 4-7 ft. wide and allows the runner to run in a straight line to second base. Through the arc, the runner continues to run as fast as possible and without breaking stride. First base is contacted on the inside front corner preferably with the left foot (see Figure 15-6). On the next stride, the right leg crosses over and the right foot plants directly in line with second base. A slight lean and dip of the left shoulder throughout the arc will help the runner make the turn toward second base at full speed.

Once the base has been rounded, the runner attends to the field action, listens for coaching directions, and decides to: (1) continue to run straight to second base, or (2) stop, pivot, and return to first base (see Figure 15-7). If the decision is made to continue on to second base, the runner must run hard and prepare to: (1) slide, (2) stop on the base with no immediate play, or (3) begin another arc to round second base.

### Extra Base Hits

When the ball has clearly been hit for extra bases, the runner begins an arc before all but the last base. The runner contacts the inside corner of each base with the left foot (if possi-

**Figure 15-5.** The runner arcs to round the base.

**Figure 15-6.** Base contact with the left foot.

**Figure 15-7.** Attending to the action on the field.

ble) and crosses the right foot over to stride directly to the next base.

As first base is rounded, the runner listens for coaching directions and momentarily looks for the ball. As second base is rounded, the runner looks to the third-base coach to help evaluate the play—especially if the ball is not in the runner's field of vision. The coach will signal: (1) "Stay there," (2) "Come hard to third," or (3) "Look for home." As third base is approached, the runner pays close attention to the third-base coach and reacts accordingly. The coach will signal: (1) slide, (2) round the base and react, or (3) continue home. In general, the last base to be reached is run at hard and straight and unless otherwise informed (i.e., "round the base"), the runner should expect to slide.

*Key Elements:*
- 4-7 ft. arc initiated 10-20 ft. prior to each base to be rounded.

- Contact the inside corner of the base preferably with the left foot without breaking stride.
- Lean the body into the turn toward the next base—aided with a left shoulder dip.
- Right leg crosses over so that the right foot is in line with the next base.
- Attend to field action and coaching directions.
- Decide immediately whether to stop and return to the base or run hard in a straight line toward the next base.
- When running more than one base, make an arc before each base and run hard and straight toward the last base.

*Common Errors:*
- No arc prior to the base; results in slowing down to make the turn, or an uncontrolled arc after the base and a less than direct run to the next base.
- Contacting the base in the middle or outside corner; requires more time to get to the next

base, and results in possible foot slippage with the lean into the turn.

- Stutter step(s) to contact the base with the left foot; results in slowing the runner down—proper foot contact comes with focused repetition.
- Lack of attention to the field play and/or coaching directions. Example: the runner rounds first base then turns her/his back to the ball while returning to the base. Possible results include: (1) the shortstop misses the relay from the outfielder and an opportunity for advancement is lost, or (2) the shortstop catches the relay from the outfielder and throws the ball to first base before the runner returns and the runner is tagged out.

## LEADING OFF—FAST PITCH ONLY

Once a base has been safely reached and the ball has been returned to the pitcher, the runner cannot leave that base until the pitcher releases the ball on the next pitch. The moment the ball leaves the pitcher's hand, the runner is free to take a lead off the base. The lead is taken in such a way that the runner may advance to the next base as quickly as possible if the opportunity arises (e.g., wild pitch, hit). At the same time the runner must be able to return to the base as quickly as possible if the situation requires (e.g., pickoff attempt, infield line drive).

To best prepare for both possibilities, the runner should assume a balanced lead. The balanced lead can be broken down into three components: (1) the ready position, (2) movement off of the base, and (3) the set position/reaction.

### Ready Position

There are two basic options for the initial leadoff ready position.

*Option 1:*

The runner begins with the left foot in contact with the inside edge of the base. The feet are parallel and approximately shoulder width apart with the toe of the right foot slightly open toward the next base. The shoulders and hips are square to the infield (see Figure 15-8).

**Figure 15-8.** Option 1: Ready position.

**Figure 15-9.** Option 2: Ready position.

*Option 2:*

The runner begins with either foot in contact with the inside edge of the base and the other foot a comfortable step behind the base. The shoulders and hips are square to the next base (see Figure 15-9).

With either option, the knees and trunk are slightly flexed, the weight is evenly distrib-

**Figure 15-10.** Option 1: Weight transfer to the left foot.

**Figure 15-11.** Takeoff to the next base.

uted over the toes of both feet and the arms are ready to help propel the body off the base. From the leadoff ready position, the runner anticipates the pitcher's motion and the release of the ball.

## Movement Off of the Base

### Option 1:

As the pitcher begins the downward arc of the delivery, the runner transfers the weight onto the left foot contacting the base (see Figure 15-10). At the anticipated moment of release, the weight is transferred to the right foot and the left foot forcefully pushes off the base. The left foot then crosses over the right foot as the right foot pivots to the next base (see Figure 15-11).

### Option 2:

As the pitcher approaches the point of release, the runner transfers the weight onto the contact foot to allow the foot behind to begin to stride forward (see Figure 15-12). The initial stride is timed so that the weight is transferring onto the striding foot and the contact foot is pushing off the base exactly as the pitch is released.

With both options the arms are used to help propel the runner's body off the base and aid in maintaining balance throughout the lead.

**Figure 15-12.** Option 2: Weight transfer to the contact foot and takeoff initiation.

The steps are alternated until the desired distance is reached. When the weight transfers onto the left foot at the desired distance from the base, the right foot comes around to the set position.

## Set Position/Reaction

The runner resumes a position similar to the Option 1 ready position with the weight

**Figure 15-13.** Leadoff set position.

**Figure 15-15.** Pivot, return.

**Figure 15-14.** Pivot, advance.

**Figure 15-16.** Dive back to the base with the head turned away from the throw.

evenly distributed on both feet. In the set position, however, the feet are slightly greater than shoulder width apart, the toes of both feet are slightly open, the center of gravity is lower to the ground, and the arms are in front ready to help propel the body in either direction (see Figure 15-13). From the set position the runner is ready to continue on to the next base or move back quickly to the initial base.

If the opportunity for advancement arises, the runner pivots on the right foot and strides with the left foot directly toward the next base (see Figure 15-14). If the situation requires a return to the base, the runner pivots on the left foot and strides with the right foot directly toward the base (see Figure 15-15). If the runner chooses to dive back to the base, the left foot pushes off the ground and the arms extend toward the base. As the runner returns, whether standing or diving, the head and shoulders should turn away from the throw to shield the face from possible contact with the ball (see Figure 15-16).

*Key Elements:*

- Leadoff ready position; the player may choose either option, but the player's choice should be consistent.
- Weight transfers to foot in contact with the base as the pitcher begins the downward motion to the release.
- Anticipate the pitcher's release.
- The foot contacting the base forcefully pushes off on the pitcher's release.
- The arms are used to help propel the body off of the base and aid in maintaining balance.
- At the desired leadoff distance, the right foot continues around to the set position.
- Left foot crossover to advance to the next base.
- Right foot crossover to return to initial base; head and shoulders turn slightly to the left upon the return for safety.

*Common Errors:*

- Waiting to see the release instead of anticipating it—results in lost time to prepare for advancement or return.
- Leaving before the pitch is released—results in the runner being called out.
- The weight is back on the heels as the pitcher approaches release—results in loss of momentum into the lead and less distance during the lead.
- The first step is taken with the right foot when executing Option 1—results in a very short initial step and wasted time.
- The set position is not balanced—may result in momentum going opposite of desired direction (i.e., leaning toward second base and getting picked off of first base).
- The runner looks for the ball when returning to the base—may result in injury.
- The runner decides to advance, then hesitates—the runner has a disadvantage going to either base.

## BASE SPECIFIC LEADS AND REACTIONS

### First Base

With a right-handed batter at the plate, a catcher's easiest pickoff attempt is to first base. For this reason, the runner on first base must be aware of the catcher's ability to throw, the movement of the first baseperson, and the movement of the second baseperson. If the first baseperson is playing close to the base, the lead is shorter. If the first baseperson is playing well in front of the base, the lead can be longer. However, the runner should be aware of the movement of the second baseperson. If the second baseperson moves toward first base, the runner must prepare to return. Table 15-1 shows the reactions of the runner on first base to various game situations.

### Second Base

The throw to second base is a longer and less reliable throw for the catcher. Therefore, the runner on second base can afford to take a longer lead. The runner on second base, however, must be aware of the movement of the second baseperson and the shortstop. If either defensive player moves toward the base after the pitch, the runner must quickly return. If neither player moves to cover the base after the pitch, the lead may be increased. The runner must also be aware of the center fielder. Although having the center fielder cover the base is somewhat of a gamble, some teams are able to execute this play effectively. Table 15-2 shows the reactions of a runner on second base to various game situations.

### Third Base

When taking a lead at third base, the ready position consists of the left foot touching the front, outside corner of the base and the right foot outside the foul line (either option). The lead is then taken outside the foul line. If the runner leads inside the foul line and a batted ball hits the runner, the runner is out. A lead inside the foul line also increases the possibility of contact with the third baseperson attempting to field a ball hit down the line. When determining the size of the lead, the runner must be aware of the catcher's ability to throw to third, the initial position of the third baseperson, and the movement of the shortstop. In general, the runner at third base takes a lead even with the third baseperson while the coach keeps an eye on the shortstop. If the third baseperson is playing even with or behind the base, the lead must be relatively small. Table 15-3

**Table 15-1.** Reactions of the runner on first base to various game situations.

| Situation | Possibility With Each Pitch | Runner's Reaction |
|---|---|---|
| Less than two outs, runner on 1 only | Passed ball/wild pitch | Evaluate, advance, or return |
| | Ground ball to infield | Must go to second |
| | Single to outfield | Run to second, look to third |
| | Line drive to infield—fielded | Immediately return to first |
| | Pop-up to infield | If fielded, return to first; if missed, must advance to second |
| | Fly ball to outfield | Position self halfway between the bases, if caught—return to first, if missed—advance to second |
| | Foul fly ball | Immediately tag up, look to advance if caught |
| R1, R3 | Fly ball to outfield | Halfway, or look to tag and advance to second on throw home depending on: (1) probability of a catch, and (2) probability of a play at the plate |
| Less than two outs, runners on: 1-2, or 1-2-3 (unless situation listed again, same reaction as above) | Passed ball/wild pitch | Watch other runners, react to their movement |
| | Pop-up to infield | Infield-fly rule, tag up, look to advance |
| | Fly ball to outfield | Halfway—if caught, tag up and look to advance with throw to third or home |
| Two outs | | Run to second with any contact, evaluate to advance further |
| Two outs, full count (3 balls, 2 strikes) | | Run to second with the release of the pitch |

R = Runner; 1 = First base; 2 = Second base; 3 = Third base

shows the reactions of the runner on third base to various game situations.

## SUGGESTIONS FOR TEACHING BASERUNNING

### Game Situations

The techniques of baserunning discussed so far do not involve complex skills. Simply telling the runner of these techniques, however, is not enough. The runner must experience each situation many times in order to gain a complete cognitive understanding of these techniques. For example, telling the runner to "run through first base" may seem sufficient—even to the runner. When the situation arises in a game, however, the runner attempts to stop on the base and neither the coach nor the runner can figure out why. Often, the coach repeats his/her instructions to run through the base,

and the runner acknowledges these instructions, only to stop on the base again. The frustration of this scenario can be avoided by setting up each baserunning situation during practice. Each runner must repeatedly experience all baserunning situations in order to make correct decisions in more stressful game situations.

### Learning Progressions

When learning to run "through" first base, the runner first experiences running just outside the foul line PAST first base. When the runner has learned to run past first base every time, more technical elements can become the focus—one element at a time. The runner enters the hitting ready position at home plate; the coach goes through the pitching motion and delivers an imaginary pitch; and the runner swings the bat, then slowly executes the proper footwork to initiate the run to first base. Once

**Table 15-2.** Reactions of the runner on second base to various game situations.

| Situation | Possibility With Each Pitch | Runner's Reaction |
|---|---|---|
| Less than two outs, runner on: 2 only | Passed ball/wild pitch | Evaluate, advance, or return |
| | Ground ball to infield | Do not have to advance, evaluate and react (i.e., ground ball to shortstop; return, look to advance on throw to first base; ground ball to first base or second base, look to advance immediately) |
| | Single to outfield | Advance to third, look to coach, be prepared to continue toward home |
| | Line drive to infield—fielded | Immediately return to second |
| | Pop-up to infield | If caught, return to second; if missed, look to advance to third (optional) |
| | Fly ball to outfield | Option 1: tag, look to advance— especially if hit to right field; Option 2: halfway, return if caught; look to score if it drops in |
| | Foul fly ball | Tag up, look to advance if caught |
| Less than two outs, runners on: 2-3 | Passed ball/wild pitch | Watch runner on third, react to his/her movement |
| | Fly ball to outfield | Tag up, look to advance on throw home |
| Less than two outs, runners on: 1-2, 1-2-3 | Ground ball to infield | Must advance to third |
| | Pop-up to infield | Infield-fly rule, tag up, look to advance |
| Two outs | | Run to third with any contact, evaluate to advance |
| Two outs, full count | | Run to third with the release of the pitch |

**Table 15-3.** Reactions of the runner on third base to various game situations.

| Situation | Possibility With Each Pitch | Runner's Reaction |
|---|---|---|
| Less than two outs, runner on: 3, 2-3, 1-3 | Passed ball/wild pitch | Evaluate, advance, or return |
| | Ground ball to infield | Do not have to advance, evaluate and react (e.g., ground ball to second base, second base playing deep; go on the hit) |
| | Single to the outfield | Score |
| | Line drive to infield—fielded | Immediately return to third |
| | Pop-up to infield | If caught, return to third; if missed, look to score (optional) |
| | Fly ball to outfield | Tag up, listen for "GO" from coach to score |
| | Foul fly ball | Immediately tag up, look to score |
| Less than two outs, runner on: 1-2-3 | Ground ball to infield | Must advance to home; attempt to break up potential double play |
| | Pop-up to infield | Infield-fly rule, tag up, look to score |
| Two outs | | Run to score with any contact |
| Two outs, full count | | Run to score with the release of the pitch |

the proper footwork is learned, the runner practices glancing at the ball on about the third step out of the batter's box. Progressing further, the runner practices looking over the right shoulder after reaching first base and reacts to any overthrows. Infielders actually overthrowing the ball help to create a more realistic situation.

A similar progression can be set up for each baserunning situation. The less experienced runners can work to gain an understanding of baserunning techniques while the more experienced runners can work to improve baserunning techniques. Specific baserunning practice not only provides an opportunity to understand and improve technique, it also enhances conditioning specific to softball.

## STEALING

In softball, stealing is an attempt to advance on the bases without the benefit of a hit, sacrifice, or passed ball/wild pitch. The steal is a strategic move that is signaled prior to the pitch. If successful, the steal advances the runner one base closer to scoring and eliminates the possibility of an easy double play. There are two basic types of steals in softball: the straight steal and the delayed steal. A description of these two types follows.

### Straight Steal

For the straight steal, the runner advances to the next base on the release of the pitch. The runner prepares for the straight steal in the leadoff ready position. At the anticipated release of the pitch, the contact foot forcefully pushes off of the base to initiate the movement toward the next base. The runner runs as hard as possible and prepares to slide 10-15 ft. from the base. To prevent sliding injuries due to a runner's indecisiveness, every steal ends with a slide!

*Key Elements:*
- Leadoff ready position.
- Contact foot pushes off of the base on the anticipated release of the pitch.
- Run hard!
- 10-15 ft. prior to the next base, prepare to slide.

*Common Errors:*
- The runner waits to see the ball released rather than anticipating the release; results in less time to get to the next base.
- The first step is too short or is taken with the right foot (Option 1); results in less distance covered with the initial step and less momentum in initiating the run.
- The runner hesitates after the initial step, resulting in lost time.
- Indecision about the slide at the next base— expect to slide every time!

### Delayed Steal

The delayed steal is dependent upon a lack of readiness on the part of the defense (vs. lack of skill) and should only be used in advanced levels of play. For the delayed steal, the runner leads off the base on the release of the pitch and advances to the next base on the return throw from the catcher to the pitcher. The delayed steal can be accomplished with the runner assuming a normal lead. The runner leads off the base on the release of the pitch, the catcher receives the pitch, and just as the catcher releases the ball on the return throw to the pitcher, the runner sprints to the next base. The sprint is initiated with the left foot crossing over the right foot and the right foot pivoting to square the body to the upcoming base. With proper timing, the runner can beat the ball to the base even with a quick response from the pitcher and infielder. Again, the runner slides to complete the steal.

*Key Elements:*
- Leadoff ready position.
- Normal leadoff on the release of the pitch.
- Crossover step to initiate sprint to the next base as the catcher releases the ball to the pitcher.
- Body squares to the next base.
- 10-15 ft. from the next base, prepare to slide.

*Common Errors:*
- Lead is too large, requiring a catcher's response.
- Lead is not large enough, leaving too much distance to be covered after the catcher's release.

- Leaving for the next base too soon, giving the catcher time to react before releasing the ball.
- Leaving for the next base too late, giving the pitcher and the infield time to react.
- Hesitating after the initial step.
- Attempting the delayed steal too often—the defense is prepared and reacts appropriately.

## SLIDING

Quite often, the baserunner must run as hard as possible to a base and stop on that base. Slowing down to stay on the base may result in an out. Yet, maintaining full speed will result in overrunning the base and may also result in an out. Sliding allows maximum speed into the base while minimizing the chances of continuing beyond the base. If executed properly, sliding reduces the possibility of injury by eliminating collisions between the fielder and the baserunner.

A runner must evaluate the situation and decide whether or not to slide when she/he is about half the distance to the base. At the same time, the runner must also determine which type of slide will be executed. There are three basic types of slides recommended for youth softball. These types of slides include: (1) the bent-leg slide, (2) the pop-up slide, and (3) the head-first slide. A description of the techniques involved in executing these slides is presented below.

### Bent-leg Slide

The bent-leg slide is the most basic and most common type of slide. Also, proper execution of the bent-leg slide is a prerequisite to the pop-up slide. The takeoff for the bent-leg slide begins 8-12 ft. prior to the base. The exact distance of the takeoff from the base is specific to each individual runner's skill level, size, and speed. In general, as skill, size, and speed increase, the distance from the base increases. Although the runner may be successful taking off from either leg, a left leg takeoff is preferble. The left leg takeoff will put the runner in a better position to advance to the next base if the opportunity arises.

Immediately after takeoff, the takeoff leg bends under the lead leg. The lead leg simultaneously extends (but does not lock at the knee) to the base with the foot slightly elevated (6-10 in.) above the ground. As this leg action occurs, the arms move upward to help the runner quickly reach a horizontal position. The chin is tucked to the chest to prevent the head from hitting the ground and to keep the action at the base in sight (see Figure 15-17). The bent leg contacts the ground with the outside of the lower leg, thigh, and hip (see Figure 15-18). The foot of the extended leg makes the initial contact with the base. The extended leg gives as the base is contacted to absorb the momentum of the body (see Figure 15-19).

Generally, the lower the runner is during the slide, the more evenly distributed the weight is over the contact area. A more even weight distribution results in fewer strawberries and other sliding injuries. Also, the lower the runner remains until the base is contacted, the harder the fielder must work to make a successful tag.

In the event that the runner needs to avoid a tag from a particular side of the base, the runner executes a bent-leg slide to the opposite side of the base and grabs the base with the hand. If the fielder is positioned on the inside of the base to make the tag, the runner slides to the outside of the base and grabs the base with the left hand. If the fielder is positioned on the outside of the base to make the tag, the runner

**Figure 15-17.** Bent-leg slide position.

**Figure 15-18.** Bent-leg slide contact area.

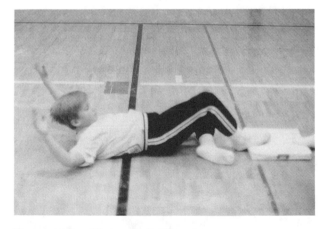

**Figure 15-19.** The extended leg gives.

slides to the inside of the base and grabs the base with the right hand (see Figure 15-20).

### Key Elements:

- Slide is initiated 8-12 ft. prior to the base.
- Takeoff leg bends under as the lead leg extends to the base.

**Figure 15-20.** The runner slides to the side of the base and reaches with the hand.

- The extended leg is 6-10 in. above the ground to prevent catching the cleats or the bottom of the shoe on the ground.
- The arms are thrown upward to help gain horizontal position.
- The arms, hands, and head are off the ground with the arms relaxed and overhead and the chin tucked to the chest.
- The body is laid back and low to the ground through the slide.
- The base is contacted with the foot of the extended leg—the extended leg then gives (the knee bends) to absorb the momentum of the slide.
- To avoid a tag, slide to the opposite side of the base and grab the base with the hand.

### Common Errors:

- Indecision! A runner's last-second decision to slide results in improper technique and many times leads to injuries.
- Slide initiation too far from the base—the runner stops before reaching the base.
- Slide initiation too close to the base—the leg jams into the base leading to possible injury.
- Sliding position too upright—weight fails to distribute evenly, potential for injury—also allows for an easier tag.
- The extended foot is not elevated—shoes or cleats catch on the ground.
- Hands and arms drag along the ground—tends to slow the slide and results in injuries.
- The chin does not tuck onto the chest—the head falls back and hits the ground as a result.

- The extended knee is locked and does not give upon contact with the base, resulting in injury.

## Pop-up Slide

The pop-up slide is initially the same as the bent-leg slide. For the pop-up slide, however, the runner is positioned more vertically as the base is approached. As the foot of the extended leg contacts the base, the bent leg extends by pushing the lower part of the leg against the ground. As the bent leg extends, the upper body continues to move forward and the arms are thrown downward (see Figure 15-21). The momentum of the slide along with the action of the legs, arms, and torso cause the runner to complete the slide in a standing position. If the opportunity for advancement occurs, the runner with the right foot extended to the base simply pushes off the base with the right foot and strides to the next base with the left foot. The runner with the left foot extended pivots on the right foot to square the body to the next base, then strides to that base with the left foot (see Figure 15-22). The second runner will require more time to advance.

### Key Elements:
- Initially the same as the bent-leg slide.
- As the base is approached, the runner begins to sit up.
- As the base is contacted, the bent leg extends, the upper body continues forward, and the arms are thrown downward (equal and opposite reaction helps the runner stand).
- The runner with the right foot extended pushes off the base with the right foot then strides to the next base with the left foot.
- The runner with the left foot extended pivots on the right foot to square the body to the next base, then strides to that base with the left foot.

### Common Errors:
- The runner comes to a complete stop at the base and then tries to get up—results in lost time to the next base.
- The runner puts the hands on the ground to push the body upward—slows the runner and tends to place the runner slightly off balance.
- The runner slows down before executing the

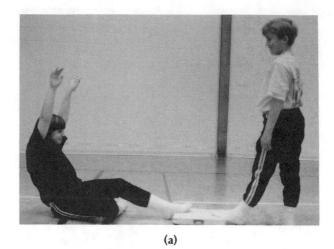

**(a)**

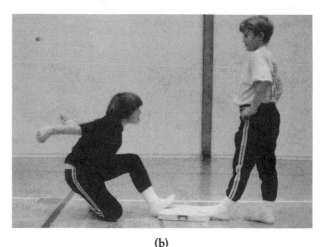

**(b)**

**(c)**

**Figure 15-21.** The pop-up slide.

slide—not enough momentum is generated to bring the body to a standing position.
- The runner initiates the slide too soon—results in reduced momentum as the base is contacted.

**Figure 15-22.** The runner with the left foot extended initiates the run to the next base.

**Figure 15-23.** Head-first slide takeoff.

## Head-First Slide

The head-first slide involves positioning the upper body forward rather than backward as in the bent-leg and pop-up slides. As a result, the legs are in a position to drive the body forward. The added drive from the legs results in little loss of forward speed, and consequently, less time in getting to the base. The head-first slide tends to be a natural movement and fairly easy to learn. This slide, however, puts the runner in a rather vulnerable position and, therefore, must be executed correctly to avoid injury.

Because of the added leg drive, the head-first slide begins 10-14 ft. from the base. The takeoff foot, which can be either foot, pushes forcefully against the ground in order to thrust the body forward. At takeoff, the head and shoulders lower and the arms forcefully extend

**Figure 15-24.** Head-first slide contact area.

to the base (see Figure 15-23). The ground is simultaneously contacted with the arms, abdomen, and upper thighs (see Figure 15-24). The head, upper chest, and knees are elevated off the ground with the knees slightly flexed to prevent the feet from dragging. The arms and wrists are extended toward the base (but not locked at the elbows) and the fingers are relaxed and curled down. The top of the base is contacted with the hands, which continue across the base with the momentum of the slide. As the base is approached, the head turns in the opposite direction of the tag. For example, if the tag is coming from the left, the head turns to the right. The runner, however, should do so in such a way that the base is still in sight (see Figure 15- 25).

*Key Elements:*
- Takeoff foot forcefully pushes against the ground to thrust the body forward.
- Head and shoulders lower on the takeoff.

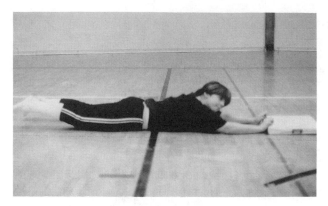

**Figure 15-25.** Initial contact with the base.

- Arms forcefully extend toward the base on the takeoff.
- Ground contact with the upper arms, abdomen, and upper thighs.
- Head, chest, and knees elevated with the knees slightly flexed to prevent foot drag.
- The fingers are curled and relaxed and the wrists are extended.
- The head turns opposite the direction of the tag.
- The base is contacted with the hands which continue across the base with the momentum of the slide.

*Common Errors:*

- The slide is initiated too close to the base, the runner goes into the base with the chest or stomach, or lands on the base—potential for injury.
- The head drops as the body slides across the ground—results in a scraped chin or injury to the face.
- The fingers extend to the base—potential for jammed or broken fingers.
- The hands contact the front edge of the base rather than the top of the base—the body continues to slide over the stationary hands and wrists resulting in possible injury.
- The head does not turn opposite the tag—the runner is tagged in the face.

## Progressions for Teaching Sliding

### Sliding Position

Whether teaching the bent-leg slide or the head-first slide, the runner must first understand body position during the slide. Without any movement toward a base, the runner en-

ters the sliding position on the ground. When teaching the bent-leg slide to a beginner, a bent left leg is recommended. A runner already accustomed to a bent right leg and resistant to change can continue to bend the right leg. The runner, however, should be aware of the disadvantage when progressing to the pop-up slide. The runner should become aware of what body part goes where and what area of the body contacts the ground. Learning the sliding position and what it feels like will aid the runner in evaluating moving slides. The runner should stand up and drop down to the sliding position several times until the correct position can be duplicated with minimal instruction. Once correct positioning is established, entry into the slide should become the focus. (Also see Appendix A, "Finding Your Sliding Leg Drill.")

### Entry into the Slide

Learning to enter into the slide requires a soft and smooth or slippery surface. Placing a base in the outfield grass or on a gym floor are two options. A long piece of cardboard in front of the base in the grass will help reduce friction. Cardboard that is the desired length of the slide will help the runner learn when the slide should begin. Also, for injury prevention in the learning process, sliding should be practiced with long pants and without shoes.

The runner starts several steps prior to the cardboard, alternates steps to the spot where the slide is to begin, and enters the slide. For example, the runner thinks "right, left, right, left—takeoff, slide." This process may not allow the runner to reach the base, but it will allow the runner to work on timing and technique. The number of steps prior to the slide may be gradually increased, and the speed with which they are taken is gradually increased. Eventually, the runner will run the entire distance between bases at full speed. Some runners will require more time to learn proper technique than other runners and should not progress until they are ready. Again, the progression discussed here may be used for both the bent-leg slide and the head-first slide.

### Pop-up Slide

The runner should be proficient at the bent-leg slide before attempting to learn the pop-up slide. The pop-up slide requires full momentum to finish in a standing position. Using the same smooth, soft surface, the runner enters the slide and on contact with the base thinks "push the lower leg (bent leg) against the ground; throw the arms down." If the base is not stationary, another player may stand on the opposite side of the base to prevent it from moving on contact. Once success at popping up has been achieved, the runner practices reacting to a defensive mistake by continuing on to the next base.

# Section IV
# Basic Strategies of Softball

# 16
# Offensive Strategies

*Jill Elliott, M.S.*

QUESTIONS TO CONSIDER

- Under what circumstances is a sacrifice bunt effective?
- What is the purpose of "taking" a pitch?
- How can you create a situation for batters to practice concentration?
- What pitch should the batter look for if the count is 0 balls, 2 strikes?
- What are the characteristics of a no. 1 (in the batting order) hitter?

## INTRODUCTION

As skill increases and players become familiar with the general play of softball, various strategies may be employed to create greater offensive opportunity. Many factors must be taken into account when determining the "best" offensive strategy for a particular situation.

Various offensive strategies and factors that may influence choice of strategy are presented below. Offensive strategies to be discussed are: (1) the bunt—sacrifice bunt, bunt and run, bunt-for-a-hit, and slap, (2) the steal—straight steal and delayed steal, (3) the hit and run, and (4) the take. Following the discussion of these situational strategies, ideas on the strategic aspect of hitting and suggestions for determining batting order are presented.

For specific offensive drills, see Appendix A.

## THE BUNT

Generally, bunting becomes more important as the level of play increases. The bunt pro-

vides several options in terms of strategy. A description of the various options is presented below.

### Sacrifice Bunt

The purpose of the sacrifice bunt is to sacrifice the batter in order to advance a baserunner. The batter squares around or pivots early to assure that the bat is stationary as it contacts the ball. The runner assumes a normal leadoff of the base with the pitch, and moves toward second base with the bunt. The bunt must be placed so that the fielder's only option is to throw to first base.

Several factors must be considered when using the sacrifice bunt. There should be: (1) less than two outs, (2) a close score such that one run is meaningful, (3) a runner with good speed on base in order to eliminate the possibility of a play on the lead runner, (4) a batter possessing the ability to bunt, and (5) a batter(s) following the bunter possessing good hitting ability. The bunter must be able to bunt the ball directly to the ground. A bunt caught in the air may give the defense a chance to throw out the runner leading off the base. Also, the batter(s) following the bunter must have the potential to advance the runner. A strong hitter should probably not be sacrificed if the next batter tends to be a weak hitter.

## Bunt and Run

Also known as the bunt and steal, the bunt and run requires the baserunner to run toward the next base on the release of the pitch. Because the runner is moving with the pitch, the batter must bunt that pitch. The advantage of the bunt and run is that the baserunner has an early start toward the next base, decreasing the likelihood of being thrown out. Occasionally, a defense caught off guard will leave a base uncovered, allowing a fast runner to advance an extra base. The disadvantage of the bunt and run is the almost certain double play resulting from a ball bunted into the air. Also, a good pitch to bunt cannot be guaranteed. The bunt and run is most effective when: (1) the pitcher is consistently throwing strikes, (2) the batter is highly skilled at bunting a variety of pitches, and (3) the baserunner has good speed.

## Bunt-for-a-Hit

The purpose of the bunt-for-a-hit is to enable the batter to reach base. There are several factors to consider when calling the bunt-for-a-hit: (1) the speed of the batter, (2) the hitting ability of the batter, and (3) the position of the defense. Obviously, the faster the runner, the greater the chance for success. If a batter is not likely to get a hit off of a pitcher, the bunt-for-a-hit provides another option.

In relation to the position of the defense, when the first and third basepersons are playing near their bases and do not appear to be expecting a bunt, an opportunity for the bunt-for-a-hit exists. This situation requires that a bunt be placed down either line in which the catcher, pitcher, or infielder must move a maximum distance to field the bunt. A bunt too soft will allow the catcher to easily field the ball, whereas a bunt too hard will allow an infielder to easily field the ball.

If the first and third basepersons are expecting the bunt and position themselves close to home plate, another bunting opportunity arises. This situation requires a firm bunt that is "pushed" past the charging defense. Generally, because the batter begins to move toward first base as the ball is contacted, a bunt between the pitcher and first baseperson is the easiest to execute. When properly done, the ball either goes untouched or is fielded by the second baseperson. If the second baseperson fields the ball, first base must be covered by the right fielder or be left uncovered. Either gives the advantage to the bunter!

Because the goal of bunting-for-a-hit is to allow the batter to reach base, the number of outs is not a factor. The number of strikes on the batter, however, is a factor. If the batter attempts to bunt with two strikes, anything except a "fair" bunt results in an out. Generally, having the batter swing away with two strikes is more effective.

## Slap Hit

The purpose of the slap hit is to advance the baserunner(s) and/or allow the batter to safely reach first base. The slap hit is typically executed as an alternative in any bunt situation. The slap hit can also be used if a batter is having trouble getting the bat around to hit the pitch with a full swing. Because the slap is a half swing, it is a quicker swing. Also, a good fake slap will freeze the defense and leave bases uncovered, allowing runners to steal.

A successful slap hit early in a game tends to keep the defense guessing in future bunt situations. A guessing defense is at a disadvantage over the offensive team—especially if each defensive person guesses differently! The key to the slap hit or any other offensive strategy is its unpredictability.

## THE STEAL

The purpose of the steal is to advance the baserunner without involving a batter. There are two types of steals: the straight steal and the delayed steal. A description of each follows.

## Straight Steal

On the straight steal, the runner attempts to advance to the next base with the release of the pitch. There are several factors to consider when calling the straight steal. First, the game situation must be assessed. Because stealing is a gamble, it is preferable to be even or ahead in the score. It is also more affordable to risk an out through stealing early in the game. Also, the speed of the runner, the condition of the field, the number of outs in the inning, and the skill of the batters are factors to consider. A wet and slippery field, for example, will reduce the chance for success for even the fastest runners. Also, if the next few batters are skilled (i.e., 2, 3, 4 in the batting order) and there are two outs in the inning, being caught stealing for the third out would result in the team's best hitters leading off the next inning. A successful steal, however, would place the runner in scoring position with a skilled batter at the plate.

When expecting a straight steal with less than two outs, the batter does not swing to hit the pitch. The batter may: (1) stand and watch the pitch go by, (2) swing and intentionally miss the pitch, (3) square around and fake a bunt, or (4) fake a slap hit. Regardless of the option chosen, the batter cannot contact the ball. If the batter contacts the ball and the ball is caught in the air, the runner is not in a position to react and return to the base. A double play will likely be the result.

## Delayed Steal

For the delayed steal, the runner assumes a normal lead, and advances to the next base as the catcher throws the ball back to the pitcher. The success of the delayed steal is largely dependent on the opposing team. Factors to consider are: (1) the catcher is throwing the ball back to the pitcher slowly, (2) the pitcher receives the ball and looks toward the ground, and/or (3) the infielders are not prepared to cover the desired base. Any one factor or combination of factors will present an opportunity for the delayed steal. Many times, if the runner steals just as the catcher commits to the throw back to the pitcher, the base may be stolen before the pitcher has time to receive the ball and relay it to the base—even if the pitcher reads the steal.

As with the straight steal, the delayed steal is best employed when the score is close and the runner on base is intelligent and fast. Also, the success of the delayed steal is dependent upon the lack of readiness of the opposing team rather than a lack of skill. This strategy is not advisable until players have attained a fairly advanced level of play!

## THE HIT AND RUN

The hit and run is another option for advancing a baserunner. The hit and run requires the runner(s) to leave the base as the pitch is released and the batter to hit the ball. Ideally, the fielders will move to cover the "steal," allowing more room for the batter to hit. If the ball is hit to the outfield (especially right field), a fast baserunner can often advance two bases. Even if the ball is hit to an infielder, forcing the lead runner(s) out is usually very difficult. The hit and run is typically employed when the score is close, a fast runner is on base, a skilled hitter is at the plate, and the pitcher is behind in the count (e.g., 2 balls, 1 strike).

When attempting the hit and run, there is always the risk of a double play. If the batter pops the ball up or lines the ball to an infielder, the runner has little time to react and return to the base. Also, if the pitcher is having control problems, it is hard to predict when a good pitch to hit will be thrown. Finally, if the batter does not hit the ball, the runner takes the risk of being caught stealing. Each player should be aware of these risks and evaluate her/his performance in relation to their role. For example, a runner that leaves for the next base with the pitch but is doubled off on a line drive has performed the strategy correctly.

## THE TAKE

If the batter is given a take sign, the batter is not to swing at the pitch. The purpose of a take is to create a variety of offensive opportunities. For instance, taking the first pitch while remaining in the hitting ready position may move the infield back and provide the batter with more room to bunt on the next pitch. Taking a pitch by squaring and faking a bunt may draw the infield in and create more room with which to hit on the next pitch. As mentioned earlier, the batter must take a pitch when the baserunner is stealing. Taking a pitch by starting but not finishing a swing may freeze the infielders and allow the runner on first base more time to steal second base. Taking a pitch by squaring around may draw the third baseperson in and leave the runner on second base with only the shortstop to beat in order to steal third base.

Many times the purpose of a take sign is misunderstood by youth coaches. Some feel if the pitcher is having a hard time throwing strikes, taking pitches will draw walks and increase the number of baserunners. Although walks do increase the number of baserunners, several negative things happen with this type of strategy. First, a potentially good pitcher may get discouraged and lose the desire to continue to work on pitching. Second, the batters do not increase their hitting skills because they do not swing the bat. And third, the fielders do not increase their fielding skills because the batters do not learn to hit.

From an offensive perspective, a walk will only move the baserunners one base at a time, but a well hit ball can move the baserunners several bases at a time. A team that swings the bat regardless of a pitcher's control will learn to: (1) understand the strike zone and discriminate more easily between balls and strikes, (2) make swing adjustments necessary to hit pitches in various locations in or around the strike zone, (3) be ready to hit every pitch and not let that perfect pitch get by, and (4) swing the bat with confidence and authority in those must-hit situations.

## THE STRATEGIC ASPECT OF HITTING

### Strategy in Relation to the Count

As pitch discrimination is learned, strategies in relation to the count (balls/strikes) on the batter can be employed to help increase hitting success. After several seasons of batting practice, the batter should begin to be aware of the location of the pitches that he/she hits best.

These high-percentage pitches will not be the same for each batter. Also, the batter should become aware of the perfect pitch, or that pitch the batter hits better than any other pitch. Hitting success may be enhanced by knowing the high-percentage pitches and the perfect pitch, and being able to first visualize these pitches out of the batter's box and then react to the desired pitch once in the batter's box.

Table 16-1 is a guide for hitting strategies in relation to the count on the batter. Again, the high-percentage pitches must be learned through several seasons of hitting before these strategies can be employed.

The batter must also remember to "go with the pitch." The outside pitch is best hit to the opposite field and the inside pitch is best hit when "pulled." Understanding this will increase the batter's number of high-percentage pitches and decrease the pitcher's advantage with a two-strike count.

### Strategy in Relation to the Pitcher

In addition to count strategies, the batter must also make adjustments in relation to the pitcher. The batter must:

1. Adjust the ready position in the batter's box in relation to the pitcher.
   a. If the pitcher throws straight and fast, the batter will benefit from moving back in the box.
   b. If the pitcher throws a variety of pitches (e.g., drop, curve, rise, etc.), the batter will benefit from moving up in the box giving the ball less distance to move.

**Table 16-1.** Hitting strategies in relation to the count on the batter.

| Count (balls/strikes) | Strategy |
|---|---|
| 0-0 | Look for a high-percentage pitch |
| 1-0, 0-1, 1-1, 2-1 | Same high-percentage pitch |
| 2-0 | Even more selective (perfect pitch) |
| 3-0, 3-1 | Look for one pitch—the "perfect" pitch |
| 0-2, 1-2, 2-2 | Have a clear mental picture of the "umpire's" strike zone and prepare to react to any pitch within that zone |
| 3-2 | Prepare to swing; KNOW the strike zone |

2. Be aware of the pitcher's ability to throw a *change-up*. The batter's chances of experiencing a change-up increase:
   a. after two quick strikes
   b. after swinging hard and missing
   c. after pulling a long foul ball
   d. if the pitcher has good control and is consistently ahead in the count
   e. if there are no runners on base

If the batter recognizes the change-up after the swing has been initiated, the batter can:

   a. immediately terminate the swing
   b. interrupt the joint sequence and delay the forward movement of the hands to hit the pitch.

If the batter can successfully hit the change-up, its effectiveness is greatly reduced!

3. Know the pitcher's strengths (e.g., "good drop ball pitcher"), and look for patterns in the pitcher's pitch selection. Again, the faster the batter's swing speed and the longer the batter keeps the hands back, the more time the batter has to adjust the swing to the pitch.

### Strategy in Relation to Concentration

When hitting, the batter's complete focus must be on the ball at the pitcher's release point. Many times the batter will watch the perfect pitch go by and then realize that was the perfect pitch. The batter then steps into the batter's box and prepares for the next pitch while still thinking about that last pitch. If the same pitch is thrown, the batter is not prepared to hit. Thinking about the last pitch, an umpire's call, or a mechanical change will significantly reduce the batter's likelihood of a successful hit.

The concentration necessary for successful hitting must be practiced just as frequently and intensely as the physical aspects of hitting. Creating distractions in practice similar to those that arise in a game will aid in developing concentration. For example, calling controversial balls and strikes during batting practice can help the batter learn, with a concentrated effort, to focus on the next pitch rather than on the last pitch. Having some players create verbal and/or

physical distractions can help the batter learn to focus on the pitch rather than the distractions. For consistent success, the batter must expect every pitch to be hittable. The batter must know the situation and step into the batter's box only when completely focused and ready to react and hit—EVERY TIME!

## SUGGESTIONS FOR DETERMINING A BATTING ORDER

During the early years of softball participation, the first priority should be to increase skill. During this time the batting order is less important. If every player is allowed the opportunity to swing the bat and run the bases, the offensive goals will be met. As skill increases, however, and the game becomes more competitive, a strategically determined batting order can have a significant effect on offensive production.

Generally, the first hitters in the batting order have more plate appearances during the course of a game than those hitters in the lower part of the batting order. Therefore, the most consistent hitters should be placed at the beginning of the order. The batters in the middle of the order often hit with runners on base. For this reason, the batters most likely to get extra base hits are placed in the middle of the order. The remaining batters are placed at the end of the batting order. Although different opponents may require different batting orders, a general guide for determining a batting order is presented in Table 16-2.

Because of player inconsistencies, the best order is not totally predictable. Sometimes instinct produces the most productive batting orders! However, theoretically, if the no. 1 batter reaches first base, the no. 2 batter can advance the no. 1 batter with a hit or sacrifice. With the no. 1 batter on second base, the no. 3 batter has a chance to advance the no. 1 batter to third base or home. If the no. 3 batter is unsuccessful at advancing the no. 1 batter, the no. 4 batter has a second chance. Because the no. 4 batter is a power hitter, it is likely that any runner on third base, second base, and possibly first base can score on a hit. If the no. 1 batter does reach first base, the no. 2 batter should have the ability to reach base safely. Depending upon the

**Table 16-2.** A guide for determining batting order.

| Batting Position | Desirable Characteristics |
|---|---|
| 1 | Most consistent singles hitter, highest on-base percentage, fast, good baserunner |
| 2 | Consistent hitter, good bunter, high-contact percentage |
| 3 | Best overall hitter, highest average,* good power |
| 4 | "Clean up" hitter, most power—long ball hitter* |
| 5 | Next most powerful hitter, good contact |
| 6 | Third most powerful hitter if available, or similar to the no. 2 hitter |
| 7-9 | More inconsistent hitters in order from 7-9, good bunters, good speed, ability to make things happen; no. 9 hitter—good bunter, good speed |

*If there is only one player for both the no. 3 and no. 4 role, the player will average more at bats in the 3 position.

strength of the no. 3 and the no. 4 batters, the no. 3 batter can hit or sacrifice the no. 2 batter to second base. The no. 4 hitter is still in a position to score the runner(s). If the first three batters are out in the first inning, the no.'s 4, 5, and 6 hitters are in a position to start the cycle over.

The possibilities are endless. The culmination of all the possibilities and all of the situations leaves room for a variety of philosophies, actions, and results. Because of the room for variety, there are no right or wrong strategies, and the game is forever unpredictable and interesting.

# 17
# Defensive Strategies

*Jill Elliott, M.S.*

## QUESTIONS TO CONSIDER

- What is the most important rule for defensive success?
- What general strategy should a pitcher use until the batter's strengths and weaknesses are better known?
- Under what circumstances does the shortstop assume the relay position?
- In a rundown, why does the chaser run full speed toward the runner?
- Which position player is responsible for calling the throw when the pitcher fields a bunt?

## INTRODUCTION

Although the defensive strategies may become more complicated as the skills increase, there are basic situations and strategies that occur at every level. This chapter contains a description of basic defensive situations and strategies, beginning with general defensive rules. The general rules are followed by specific defensive situations and strategies. Sample game situations can be found in Supplement 17-1 at the end of this chapter. Specific defensive drills can be found in Appendix A.

## GENERAL DEFENSIVE RULES

The most important rule for defensive success in softball is: EVERY PLAYER MUST BE INVOLVED IN EVERY PLAY! Each player must: (1) field the ball, (2) cover a base, or (3) back up the play or a base. If every base is covered and backed up, and every play is backed up, baserunners will be less likely to advance more than a minimum number of bases. For example, the third baseperson should make it a habit to cover third base even if the only play is at first base. If, for some reason, the play is not made at first base and the runner advances to second base, the runner will be less likely to attempt to advance to third base if third base is covered. If the runner does try to advance, the third baseperson is in a position to make a play on the runner.

Several general rules of defensive softball strategy apply to all defensive players.

1. Each player must always know the number of outs in the inning, the count on the batter, and the potential defensive plays—BEFORE THE PITCH is thrown.
2. The defense generally attempts to make the play on the lead runner if at all possible.
3. If the defensive team is sufficiently ahead in the later innings of the game, the defense

plays for the easiest out, regardless of the lead runner.

4. For lower skilled players, the defense should play for the easiest out. Remember, however, that learning occurs by doing. When possible, the defense should attempt to make a play on the lead runner.

5. If there are two outs in the inning, the defense plays for the easiest out. Unless an infielder can make an unassisted play at another base, the play should be made at first base!

6. If the winning run is on third base and there are less than two outs, the outfield moves closer to the infield. This will place the outfielder in a position to make a throw home following a catch, causing the runner to remain at third base or enabling a play at the plate to be made on a tagging runner.

Specific to Position:

7. The shortstop covers second base on a ball hit to the right side of the field. The second baseperson covers second base on a ball hit to the left side of the field. A ball hit up the middle of the field requires communication between the shortstop and second baseperson. However, the shortstop usually attempts to field the ball and the second baseperson covers the base.

8. If the ball is hit to the outfield and there is no immediate play at a base, the outfielder may run the ball to the infield—always prepared to throw!

Above all else, defensive strategy should not be complicated!

## SPECIFIC DEFENSIVE SITUATIONS AND STRATEGIES

In addition to the general defensive rules, there are specific defensive strategies associated with specific situations. A description of various defensive strategies and possible adjustments according to team personnel is provided below. Defensive strategies presented include: (1) basic pitching strategy, (2) cutoffs, (3) relays, (4) rundowns, (5) first and third situations, (6) pick offs, and (7) bunt defense/base coverage.

## Basic Pitching Strategies

In addition to the mechanics of pitching, the pitcher should learn and employ several basic pitching strategies. The following are basic strategies to help increase a pitcher's effectiveness in a game situation:

1. The pitcher's best pitch should be thrown for a strike on the first pitch of the game. The pitcher focuses on the catcher's glove, relaxes, visualizes the pitch for a strike, then throws the strike.

2. Most hitters will not swing at the first pitch they face. The pitcher should, therefore, attempt to throw a strike on the first pitch to each batter.

3. The pitcher should focus on the corners of the strike zone and avoid pitching the ball in the middle of the strike zone (especially when ahead in the count). Also, corner pitches versus down-the-middle pitches should be emphasized during practice.

4. A pitcher's effectiveness will increase with the ability to vary the speed of the pitch. At the very least, a pitcher should develop a fastball and a change-up. A change-up is more effective when:
   a. the pitcher is consistently ahead in the count throughout the game
   b. the hitter is swinging hard—pulls several pitches foul
   c. the hitter is in the top of the batting order—weaker hitters tend to be good change-up hitters
   d. the bases are empty—the slower pitch makes it tough for the catcher to throw out a stealing runner
   e. the hitter appears to be frustrated and thinking in the batter's box.

5. The pitcher should avoid patterns in pitch selection. For example, an occasional change-up on the first pitch may keep the batters guessing.

6. If the pitcher has an 0-2 count (no balls, 2 strikes) on the batter, the next pitch should be a *waste pitch*. A waste pitch is a pitch thrown just outside the strike zone. It is thrown to tempt the batter into swinging at a bad pitch. As a pitcher's control increases, two or three waste pitches may be thrown.

7. A pitch is only a strike if the umpire calls it a strike. For this reason, the pitcher must adjust and pitch to the UMPIRE'S strike zone. The pitcher cannot be distracted by what he/she perceives to be an incorrect call! A pitcher's complete focus must always be on the upcoming pitch.

As a pitcher gains experience throwing to specific hitters, he/she should become aware of the hitter's strengths and weaknesses. Obviously, the pitcher throws to the hitter's weaknesses and avoids his/her strengths. However, until the hitter's strengths and weaknesses are known, the pitcher should PITCH TO THE CORNERS AND VARY THE SPEED. The pitcher must remember that the strike zone is a zone of hittable pitches. A pitcher should not expect to strike out every batter!

## The Cutoff

Any time the ball has been hit to the outfield and there is a potential play on the lead runner at the plate, the first baseperson becomes the cutoff person. The instant it is known that there will be no play at first base, the first baseperson moves to an area even with the front of the pitching circle and lines up directly between the fielder making the throw and home plate (see Figure 17-1).

Outfielders should attempt to throw the ball to home plate by throwing the ball DIRECTLY AT THE CUTOFF PERSON. The throw must be low and hard so that the cutoff person can receive the throw about chest high or the catcher can catch the ball in the air or on one bounce. If it is determined that the throw is off target or will not permit a play on the runner at the plate, the catcher directs the first baseperson to cut the throw. If there is an opportunity to make a play on a runner at another base, the catcher then directs the first baseperson to throw to that base.

EXAMPLE: A ball is hit to center field, and a runner on second base rounds third base and attempts to score. The first baseperson, knowing there will be no play at first base, moves to the cutoff position directly between the center fielder and home plate. The center fielder fields the ball and throws low and hard toward home

plate. The batter decides to run to second base on the the center fielder's throw home. The catcher determines that the throw from the center fielder will arrive too late to tag the runner at home, but sees a chance for a play at second base. The catcher yells "Cut-2!" and the cutoff person intercepts the center fielder's throw and throws to second base. If there is no cutoff person and the throw travels all the way to home, the defense has no play on the batter advancing to second base.

*Key Elements:*
- The first baseperson moves immediately to the cutoff position—directly between the fielder making the throw and home plate. (The pitcher usually backs up the catcher but may assume the cutoff position as an alternative.)
- The fielder throws low and hard to home so that the ball may be cut off if necessary.
- If the throw is weak or off target, the cutoff person intercepts the throw and listens for a possible relay home or to another base.
- The catcher communicates the directive early enough for the cutoff person to react.
- All bases must be covered.

*Common Errors:*
- The first baseperson is not lined up with the catcher, which either causes the throw to be off line or takes the cutoff person out of the play.
- The cutoff person is too close to the catcher and blocks the catcher's view of the ball and the playing field.
- The throw home is thrown over the head of the cutoff person.
- The catcher waits too long to direct the cutoff person, and he/she does not have time to react.

## Relays

When a ball has been hit beyond the outfielders, the defense must work together to get the ball to the infield as quickly and efficiently as possible. The outfielder closest to the ball moves to the ball, while the back-up outfielder follows in order to help if necessary and communicates the direction of the relay throw. Sim-

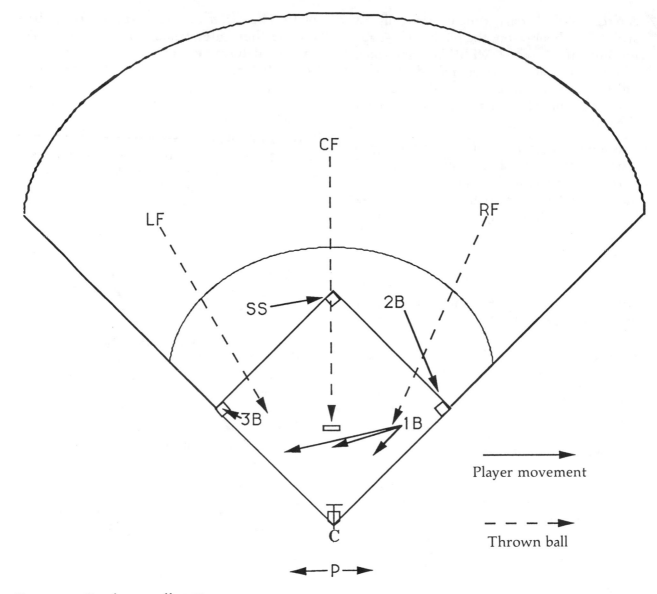

**Figure 17-1.** First-base cutoff position.

ultaneously, the second baseperson or shortstop moves toward the outfielder in a position to relay the ball to the eventual target. The exact relay position is dictated by the origin of the throw, the strength of the outfielder's throwing arm, and the target of the relay.

From the relay position, the relay person yells "Relay, relay!" with the arms extended overhead, in order to help the outfielder locate the relay position. The relay person then listens for the direction of the upcoming throw, receives the ball, and throws to the appropriate location. If the throw is to go to home plate, the first

baseperson moves to the cutoff position and prepares to react as directed by the catcher.

Generally, if the ball has been hit to the center or left side of the field, the shortstop becomes the relay person. If the ball has been hit to the right side of the field, the second baseperson acts as the relay person. Because the shortstop usually has the stronger throwing arm, it is possible for the shortstop to serve as the relay person in all situations.

If the shortstop is the relay person, the second baseperson may move to back up the shortstop in a tandem relay position or move to cover second base. If the second baseperson is the relay person, the shortstop backs up the second baseperson or covers second base. Generally, the stronger the outfielder's throwing arm, the more important it is to set up in a tandem relay. A hard throw beyond the relay person is harder to recover quickly and is therefore more costly than a weaker throw beyond the relay person.

*Key Elements:*

- The outfielder must listen for the location of the relay person while fielding the ball.
- The relay person must know each outfielder's throwing ability and adjust accordingly.
- The throw from the outfielder to the relay person must be catchable—the outfielder should not bypass the relay person and attempt to throw directly to a base.
- The relay person listens for the location of the upcoming throw—if nothing is said or if there is conflicting communication, the relay person should look for the best play.

*Common Errors:*

- The outfielder looks for the relay person before fielding the ball, which results in misplaying the ball.
- The relay person is out too far or not out far enough as dictated by the situation—results in a less efficient relay.
- The relay person attempts to relay the ball before catching it—the eyes focus on the upcoming target too early or the glove moves away from the ball too early.
- Ineffective communication—effective communication comes with correct practice!

## Rundowns

An effective rundown involves a minimum of four, or preferably five, fielders in the play. These four or five fielders include: (1) a fielder with the ball, or the *chaser*, (2) a fielder to receive the ball, or the *receiver*, (3) a fielder to back up the receiver, and (4) one or two fielders backing up and/or at the base behind the chaser. Ideally, the runner should always be chased back toward a base rather than toward the next base closer to home.

For example, a rundown between home plate and third base would include:

1. the catcher with the ball, chasing the runner back toward third base
2. the third baseperson to receive the ball
3. the shortstop to back-up the third baseperson
4. the first baseperson at home plate ready to receive the ball and chase the runner back toward third base

The left fielder should back up third base and the pitcher should back up home plate. The back-up fielders must be in a position to react to an errant throw (see Figure 17-2).

Upon receiving the ball from a fielder, the chaser immediately moves to one side of the baseline. The chaser carries the ball near the ear in plain sight of the receiver and runs as hard as possible toward the runner. If an immediate tag is not possible, the receiver moves in front of the base on the same side of the baseline as the chaser. Throws from a chaser to a receiver should not cross the baseline! As the runner nears the receiver, the receiver yells "Now!" and moves toward the baserunner. At that time, the chaser executes a quick snap throw to the receiver. Because the runner is moving at full speed, it is not likely that he/she will be able to change directions quickly enough to avoid the tag by the receiver.

If the tag is not immediately made, however, the receiver becomes the chaser and the first back-up fielder at the opposite end of the rundown becomes the second receiver. The original chaser continues in the same direction to become the second back-up, or changes directions and returns to the original base. If the second chaser cannot quickly tag the runner, the throw should go to the second receiver, who becomes the third chaser, to chase the runner back to the original base. This cycle is continued until the runner is tagged out. If properly executed, however, one throw is all that is necessary. The more throws required, the greater the possibility of error!

*Key Elements:*

- Each rundown requires a chaser, a receiver, and at least one back-up for each base.
- The chaser immediately chooses a side of the baseline and the receiver moves to the same side of the baseline and in front of the base.

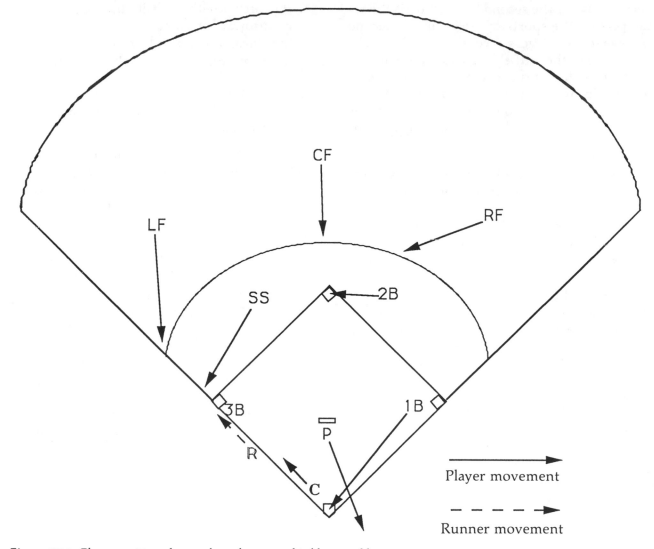

**Figure 17-2.** Player positions for rundown between third base and home.

- The chaser runs at full speed toward the runner with the ball near the ear, in clear view of the receiver.
- From the ear, a snap throw is executed to the receiver upon the receiver's request.
- If the tag is not made, the first chaser continues in the same direction, or returns to the original base. The chaser becomes the back-up player at that base.
- The back-up fielders must be prepared for an errant throw and play far enough away from the base to react.

*Common Errors:*

- The chaser does not run at full speed, giving the runner time to react and change direction on the throw to the receiver.

- The chaser and the receiver are on opposite sides of the baseline, placing the runner in a position to interfere with and/or deflect the throw.
- The chaser holds the ball in the glove, which takes more time to complete the throw and hides the ball from the receiver.
- The receiver catches the ball on the base or behind the base, giving the runner an opportunity to reach the base safely.
- The chaser throws the ball and does not move to assume a back-up role.
- The runner is chased to an advanced base rather than to the original base (i.e., home plate versus third base).
- The back-up is positioned too close to the base and an overthrow results in extra bases.

## First and Third Situations

Runners on first and third base with less than two outs can be one of the most frustrating situations in softball. If the runner on first base attempts to steal second base and the catcher throws to second base, the runner on third base scores. If the catcher does not throw to second base, the runner on third base does not score but the runner on first base advances easily to second base. There are, however, several options available to prevent either of these results.

A catcher must be aware of the runner's actions at all times. When a catcher knows the runner on first base is stealing, he/she receives the pitch and immediately glances toward third base to check the runner. If the runner on third base has a significant lead off of the base, the catcher immediately throws to the third baseperson in order to tag the runner. If the third-base runner is on or close to the base, the catcher must choose another option. He/she may:

1. Fake a throw to second base, then attempt to pick off the runner moving off of third base.
2. Throw quickly to the pitcher, hoping to get the runner on third base to break for home.
3. Throw directly to the second baseperson, positioned behind the pitching circle, in an attempt to get the runner on third base to move significantly off of the base.
4. Throw to the shortstop at second base in an effort to tag the stealing runner. If the runner on third base attempts to run home on the throw, the second baseperson (positioned behind the pitching circle) may intercept the throw and react to the runner (see Figure 17-3). If the runner anticipates the cut and returns to third base, the throw is made to third base. If the runner continues home, the throw is made to home. Finally, if the runner stops significantly off of the base, the second baseperson runs directly at the runner to: (1) tag the runner out, or (2) get the runner to commit to either base and execute a rundown.

Often the second baseperson and the shortstop are better suited for the opposite roles. In this situation, the shortstop may move to the cutoff position and the second baseperson may receive the throw at the base. However, it is a more difficult play for the shortstop because his/her back is to the runner on third base. The shortstop must react to verbal cues rather than visual cues.

If there are two outs, the runner on first base may attempt to force a prolonged rundown to allow the runner on third base time to score. In this situation, the first baseperson trails the runner toward second base and the right fielder covers first base. The catcher checks the runner on third base, then throws to the first baseperson for a quick tag of the runner. An effective rundown will produce an out before the third-base runner scores. However, if the runner on first base has created a rundown situation and the runner on third base breaks to home, the player with the ball immediately throws the ball to the catcher in an effort to tag the runner out.

### Key Elements:

- The catcher must be aware of the action of the runners.
- The catcher must first check the runner on third base before choosing another option.
- The second baseperson must read the runner on third base in order to correctly cut the throw and return the ball to home or third base. If unsure, the second baseperson should: (1) cut the ball and make a play on the runner at third base if the score is close, or (2) allow the ball through to second base when the score is not close.
- The first baseperson trails the stealing runner from first base in case the runner attempts to create a rundown situation.
- To aid in decision-making, the third baseperson must yell "Going!" if the runner on third base runs home.

### Common Errors:

- The catcher does not check the runner on third base before throwing to second base. If the runner on third base has taken a big lead, a return throw home will not be successful.
- Improper timing—improved through repetition.

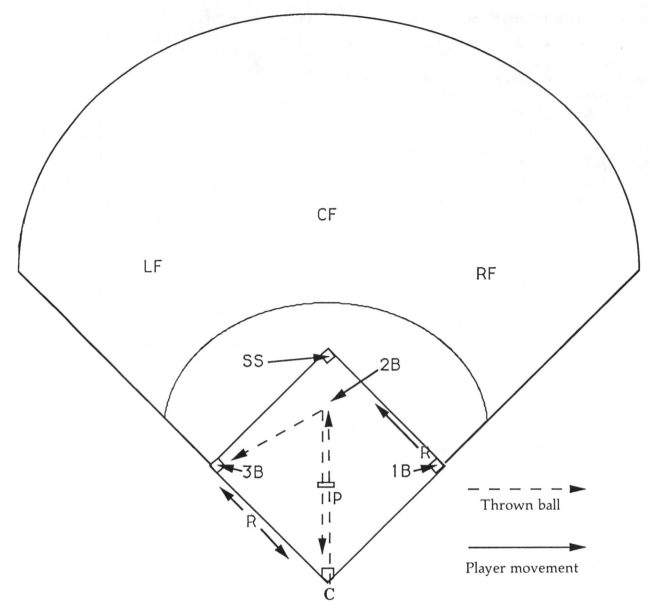

**Figure 17-3.** Second-base cutoff with runners on first and third.

- Not knowing the situation (i.e., the importance of the out versus the run).

## Pickoffs

If the runner on first base is taking a large lead off of the base and is slow in returning to the base, there are two basic options designed to pick the runner off base. The first option requires the first baseperson to take the throw at first base. The second option requires the second baseperson to take the throw at first base. Both options are advanced strategies.

*Option 1:*

The catcher gives a sign to communicate the Option 1 play to the first baseperson. The first baseperson positions him/herself close to first base and moves to the base as the ball passes the batter (see Chapter 11—"First Base"). The catcher throws the ball to first base and the first baseperson tags the runner. Even if the runner is safe, the runner will be less likely to take a lead on future pitches. With the first baseperson back, however, the pitcher must be prepared to cover bunts to the first-base side.

*Option 2:*

The catcher gives a different sign to communicate the Option 2 play to the pitcher and infielders. For the play to work, the following events must occur:

1. the pitcher pitches the ball high and outside the strike zone, or pitches out
2. the second baseperson moves to first base on the release of the pitch
3. the first baseperson moves a few steps toward the batter to help decoy the runner and prepares to avoid the throw
4. the right fielder moves to a position to back-up the throw to first base
5. the catcher throws to first base, knowing the second baseperson will be there on time

Because the second option requires a pitchout, the play is best called when the pitcher is ahead in the count (e.g., 1 ball, 2 strikes). Also, the second baseperson must move quickly and quietly (see Chapter 11—"Second Base"). Again, even if the runner is safe, the lead on the next pitch may not be as large.

*Key Elements:*

- The runner must be taking a large enough lead to allow the catcher's throw to be effective.
- Each option must be communicated effectively! The sign must be clear and visible.
- The second baseperson moves to first base on the release of the pitch (Option 2).
- The right fielder must be prepared to recover any overthrow!
- The catcher must throw to first base without hesitation!

*Common Errors:*

- The player receiving the ball at the base is not prepared to throw to the next base in the event that the runner tries to advance after recognizing the pickoff.
- The catcher does not react to the runner attempting to steal and throws behind the runner.
- The catcher throws to the player moving to cover the base rather than to the base. The throw is behind the player.
- Lack of effective communication.

## Pickoffs at Second and Third

A runner on second base may be picked off or held close to the base by the second baseperson, the shortstop, or the center fielder. The option for the center fielder requires a pitchout and is quite risky because there is no immediate back-up. A runner on third base may be picked off or held close with the third baseperson or shortstop covering the base. The option with the shortstop requires a pitchout.

## Bunt Defense

The bunt plays an important role in offensive softball strategy, and, therefore, an effective bunt defense is essential. Although a bunt is not totally predictable, the following guidelines may aid in predicting and defending the bunt more effectively.

1. The first and third basepersons must always think bunt and be in a position to field the bunt. A bunt may occur on any pitch.
2. If the catcher arrives at a bunted ball simultaneously with other fielders, the catcher makes the play. The catcher moving into the throw has the easiest play.
3. Because the catcher is the only player facing the runners, he/she makes the decision on where the ball should be thrown.
4. The defense should move to cover the bunt as the ball is contacted rather than before the ball is contacted to be sure the batter's "square" is not a decoy for something else (i.e., steal, slap—especially if the slap is within the opponent's ability).

The defense should also be aware of what to anticipate and how to react depending on the situation (see Tables 17-1 and 17-2).

Very few bunts will be attempted in a high-scoring game. Bunts usually occur in games with a low score or a close score where one run is meaningful. If the run is not meaningful and the other team bunts, play the easiest out.

## Bunt Defense Responsibilities

Table 17-2 presents a variety of bunt situations and the responsibility of each position in those situations.

**Table 17-1.** When to anticipate a bunt and how to react.

| Situation | Anticipation/Reaction |
|---|---|
| *Runner on 1:* | |
| 0 outs | Anticipate bunt; 1 and 3 move in halfway |
| 1 out | Know the batter's hitting ability and/or the place in the batting order for potential strategy |
| Less than 2 outs, 2 strikes | Bunt not as probable; 1 and 3 in general ready position |
| *Runner on 2:* | |
| 0 outs | Bunt probable with tag necessary for out at third |
| 1 out | Bunt still probable; know the batter's ability and place in the batting order |
| *Runners on 1, 2:* | |
| 0 or 1 out | 1 and 3 may move in close depending on the batter's ability; look for the force out at third on a bunt |
| *Runner on 3:* | |
| 0 or 1 out | Know the runner's speed and the batter's bunting ability—to anticipate squeeze bunt |
| *Any Situation:* | |
| 2 outs | Bunt not likely, 1 and 3 move to general ready position—remain ready to react to a bunt attempt |

**Table 17-2.** Responsibility of each position when a bunt is expected in a variety of situations.

**Situation: No runners on base or a runner on first base**

| Position | Reaction |
|---|---|
| Pitcher (P) | Charge the bunt and communicate with C, 1, and 3. Look to cover third base if 3 fields the bunt. |
| Catcher (C) | Move to field the bunt; communicate with P, 1, and 3. Know the runners position and call the throw. |

**Table 17-2. (continued)**

**Situation: No runners on base or a runner on first base**

| Position | Reaction |
|---|---|
| First base (1) | Charge the bunt and communicate with P, C, and 3. |
| Second base (2) | Move to receive the throw at first base. |
| Shortstop (SS) | Move to receive the throw at second base. |
| Third base (3) | Charge the bunt and communicate with P, C, and 1. Return to cover third base if P, C, or 1 fields the bunt. |
| Left field (LF) | Back up third base; prepare to cover the base if left unattended. |
| Center field (CF) | Back up second base. |
| Right field (RF) | Back up first base. |

**Situation: Runner on first and second base, or second base only**

| Position | Reaction |
|---|---|
| Pitcher | Charge the bunt and communicate. |
| Catcher | Move to the bunt, communicate, call the throw to third base or first base. |
| First base | Charge the bunt and communicate. |
| Second base | Move to receive the throw at FIRST BASE. |
| Shortstop | Move to receive the throw at THIRD BASE and tag the base (force out) or the runner. |
| Third base | Charge the bunt and communicate. |
| Left field | Back up third base. |
| Center field | COVER second base. |
| Right field | Back up first base. |

**Situation: Runner on third base**

**Reaction:** All reactions are the same as the previous situation (runner on 1, 2 or 2 only) except for the catcher's reaction. With a runner on third base, the catcher must remain at the plate in order to receive the throw home. The catcher watches the runner moving from third base and calls the throw either to home or to first base. A fast runner and a well placed bunt may force the play to be made at first base, and the catcher must communicate this. The catcher must also be aware of whether a tag play or a force play at the plate is required (see Chapter 11—"Catcher").

**Supplement 17-1.**
# Defensive Coverage—Sample Situations

Defensive coverage should be simple and logical. If the position responsibilities make sense
to the fielder, the fielder is more likely to respond correctly. The following are sample situations and the basic position responsibilities
of each player. If adjustments to these responsibilities are necessary due to team personnel,
the adjustments should remain logical and
simple.

## Situation 1: No runners on base, ground ball to infield

| Position | Responsibilities |
|---|---|
| Pitcher | (1) Field the ball if hit directly to the mound, or (2) relax, stay clear of the throw, and (3) prepare for any overthrows or errors |
| Catcher | (1) Field the ball if hit to the home-plate area, or (2) backup the infield side of first base, and (3) call the throw (i.e. "1") |
| First base | (1) Field the ball if hit to first-base area, or (2) quickly cover first base |
| Second base | (1) Field the ball if hit to second-base area, or (2) cover first base if hit in the first-base area—communicate with first baseperson for the putout, or (3) move to cover second base if hit to the left side of second base |
| Third base | (1) Field the ball if hit to the third-base area, or (2) cover third base |
| Shortstop | (1) Field the ball if hit to the short-stop area, or (2) backup the third base-person if hit to the third-base area, or (3) cover second base if hit to the right side of the infield |
| Left field | (1) Backup if hit to the left side of the infield, or (2) backup left-field side of second base |
| Center field | (1) Backup any ground ball hit to the center of the infield, or (2) backup any throw to the right side of second base |
| Right field | (1) Backup any hit to the right side of the infield, or (2) backup infield throws to first base |

Even if there is no immediate play at
second base or third base, the bases
should be covered and backed up!
Automatic coverage will be beneficial
over time.

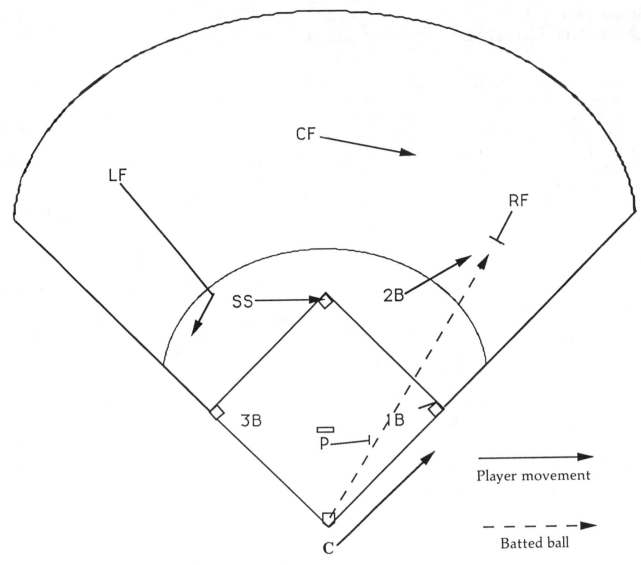

**Figure 17-1s.** Hit to right field with no runners on base.

## Situation 2: No runners on base, single to right field (see Figure 17-1s)

| Position | Responsibilities |
|---|---|
| P | Backup errant throw on infield side of first base |
| C | Backup throw to foul side of first base |
| 1B | Receive the throw at first base |
| 2B | React to hit, communicate with right fielder |
| 3B | Cover third base |
| SS | Cover second base |
| LF | Prepare to backup possible throw to second base and/or third base |
| CF | Backup ground ball to right fielder |
| RF | Field the ball; look for play at first—if no play at first, throw the ball to shortstop at second base or run the ball to the infield |

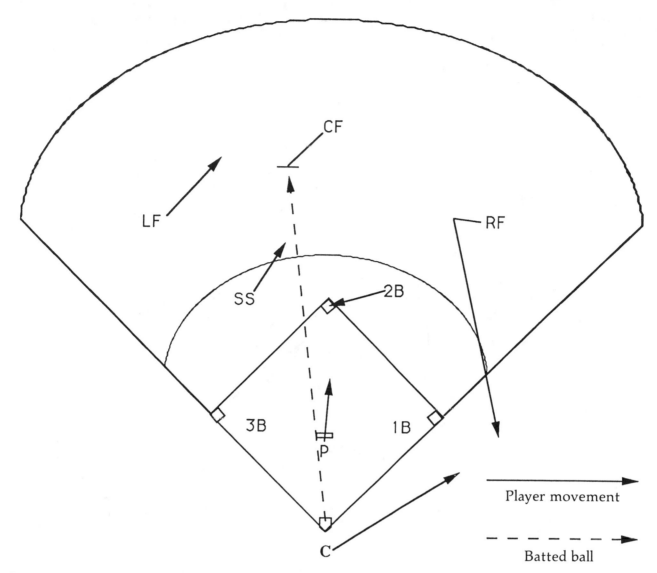

**Figure 17-2s.** Hit to left-center field with no runners on base.

## Situation 3: No runners on base, single to left or center field (see Figure 17-2s)

| Position | Responsibilities |
|---|---|
| P | Backup throw to second base |
| C | Backup infield side of first base for possible relay to first |
| 1B | Cover first base for possible play on runner rounding first base |
| 2B | Cover second base; look to relay the ball to first base |
| 3B | Cover third base |
| SS | React to the hit; communicate with the left or center fielder; assume cut-off position |
| LF | Field the ball and throw to second base or run the ball into the infield; or backup the center fielder |
| CF | Field the ball and throw to second base or run the ball into the infield; or backup the left fielder |
| RF | Backup first base for possible relay from second base |

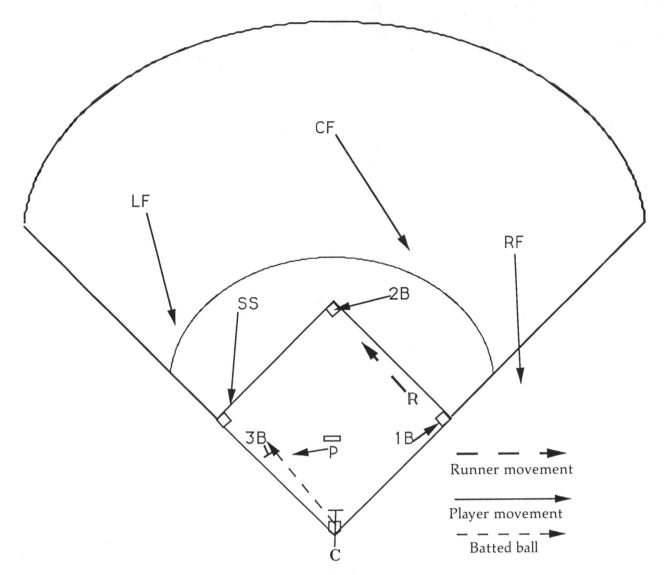

**Figure 17-3s.** Ground ball to third base with a runner on first base.

## Situation 4: Runner on first, less than 2 outs—ground ball to third base (see Figure 17-3s)

| Position | Responsibilities |
|---|---|
| P | React to bobbled ball in the pitching area |
| C | Call the throw—second base or first base |
| 1B | Cover first base |
| 2B | Cover second base |
| 3B | Field the ball; anticipate the force play at second base; if not possible, throw to first base |
| SS | Backup third baseperson, then cover third base |
| LF | Backup third baseperson and any throws to third base |
| CF | Backup the RF side of 2B, in line with possible throw from third base |
| RF | Backup any throw to first base |

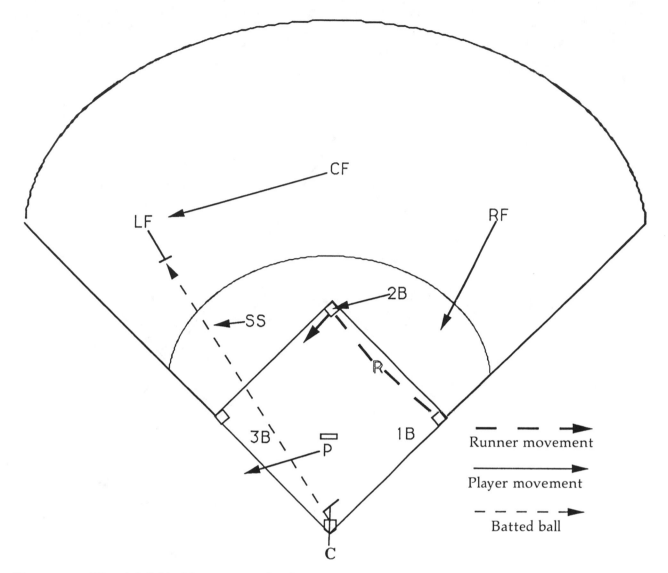

**Figure 17-4s.** Hit to left field with a runner on first base.

## Situation 5: Runner on 1, single to left field (see Figure 17-4s)

| Position | Responsibilities |
|----------|------------------|
| P | Backup any throw to third base |
| C | Call the throw, remain at home plate |
| 1B | Cover first base, ready to backup throw to second base |
| 2B | Cover second base |
| 3B | Cover third base |
| SS | React to hit, communicate with left fielder |
| LF | Field ball, listen and react to runner—look for throw to second base to tag runner rounding or throw to third base if the runner continues to third |
| CF | Backup LF |
| RF | Backup throw to second base |

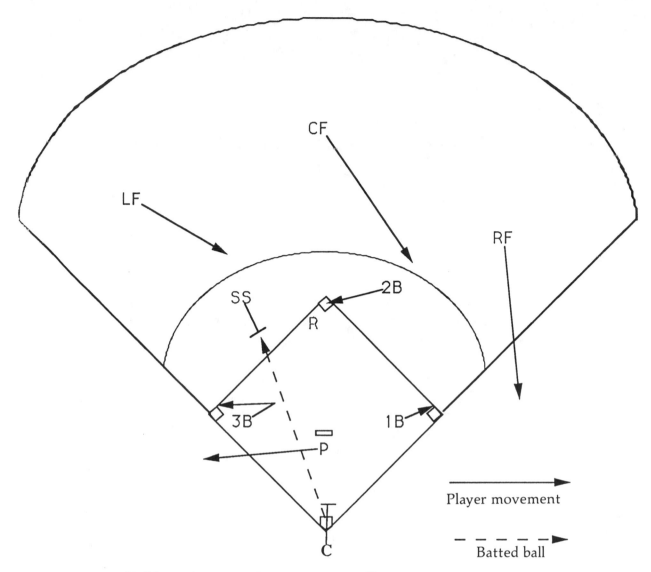

**Figure 17-5s.** Ground ball hit to shortstop with a runner on second base.

## Situation 6: Runner on 2, less than two outs, ground ball to shortstop (see Figure 17-5s)

| Position | Responsibilities |
|---|---|
| P | React to bobbled ball in the pitching area; backup potential throw to third base |
| C | Cover home plate |
| 1B | Cover first base |
| 2B | Cover second base |
| 3B | React to ball; cover third base |
| SS | Field ball; look runner back to second base, and throw to second base or tag the runner if the runner is off of the base, or quickly throw to first. Throw to third if runner runs on the hit |
| LF | Backup ground ball to SS |
| CF | Backup possible throw to second base |
| RF | Backup throw to first base |

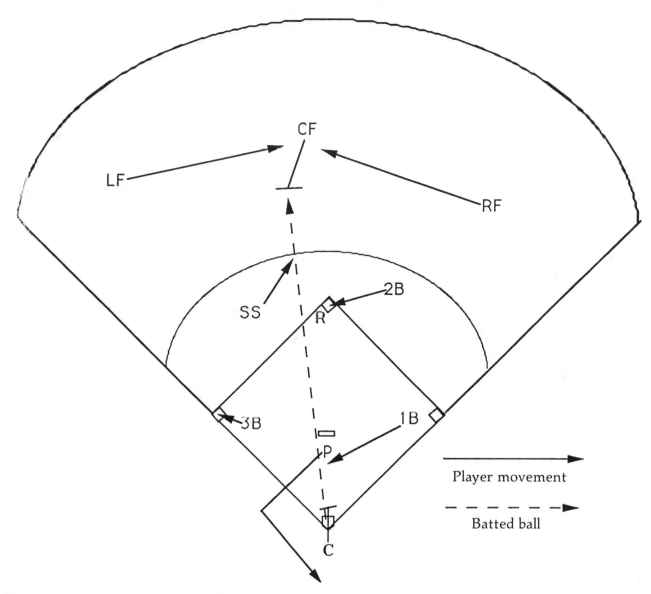

**Figure 17-6s.** Ground ball to center field with a runner on second base.

## Situation 7: Runner on 2, single to center field (see Figure 17-6s)

| Position | Responsibilities |
|----------|------------------|
| P | Backup throw to home; react to back-up possible throw to third |
| C | Cover home plate; watch the runner; call the throw |
| 1B | Assume cutoff position; listen for cut |
| 2B | Cover second base |
| 3B | Cover third base |
| SS | React to hit; relay the ball if it gets by the CF |
| LF | Backup the CF |
| RF | Backup the CF |

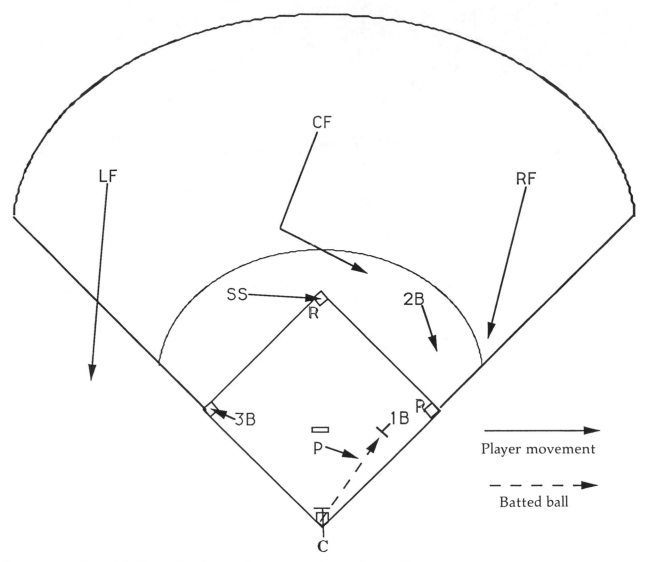

**Figure 17-7s.** Ground ball hit to first base with runners on first and second base.

## Situation 8: Runner on 1–2, less than two outs, ground ball to first base (see Figure 17-7s)

| Position | Responsibilities |
|---|---|
| P | React to bobbles in the pitching area; stay clear of throw to third |
| C | Stay near home, call the throw |
| 1B | Field the ball; throw to third for force out; or look for a play on the runner running to first base |
| 2B | Backup first baseperson; cover first base |
| 3B | Cover third base—look for possible second out at first or second base |
| SS | Cover second base for possible throw |
| LF | Backup throw to third base |
| CF | Backup possible throw to second base; if throw goes to third base, move to RF side of second base |
| RF | Backup first baseperson and possible return throw to first base |

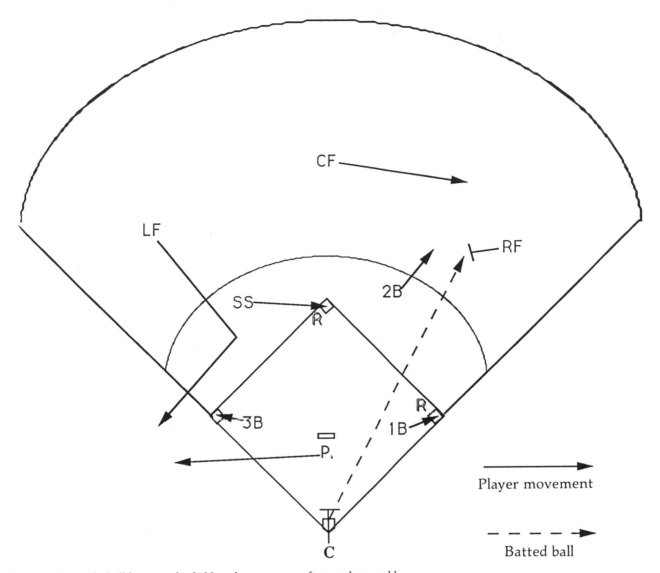

**Figure 17-8s.** Fly ball hit to right field with runners on first and second base.

## Situation 9: Runner on 1-2, less than two outs, fly ball to right fielder (see Figure 17-8s)

| Position | Responsibilities |
|----------|------------------|
| P | Backup third base |
| C | Cover home plate; watch runners; call throw |
| 1B | Cover first base |
| 2B | React to fly ball; communicate with RF |
| 3B | Cover third base |
| SS | Cover second base |
| LF | Backup second base if runner has to return on the catch; backup third base if runner advances to third base on the catch |
| CF | Backup RF |
| RF | Catch the ball; look and listen for potential plays |

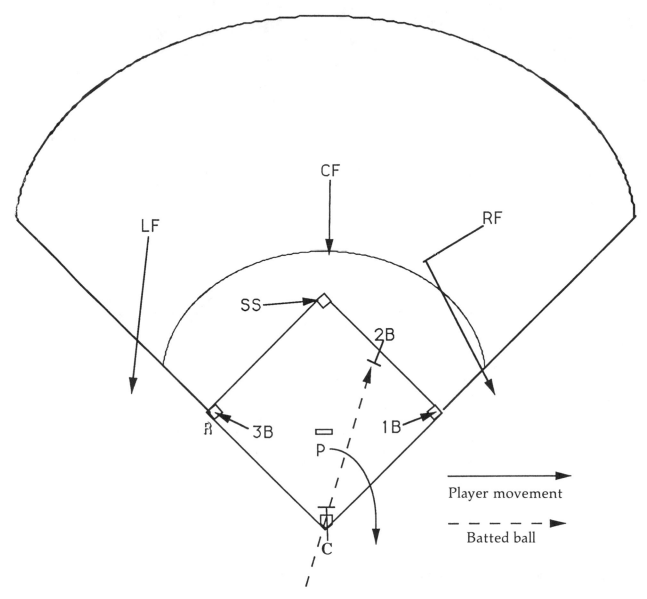

**Figure 17-9s.** Ground ball hit to second base with a runner on third base.

## Situation 10: Runner on 3, less than two outs, ground ball to second baseperson (see Figure 17-9s)

Note: If the run is insignificant, play to get the out at first

| Position | Responsibilities |
|----------|------------------|
| P | React to ball; stay clear of possible throw to third base or home plate—once the ball is by, move to backup home plate |
| C | Watch runner; call throw—cover home plate |
| 1B | Cover first base, catch the throw and prepare to throw home |
| 2B | Field the ball; (1) Look the runner back to third base, throw to first base, (2) throw to third base if the runner has a significant lead, (3) look to throw home if the runner advances on the hit—if throw will be late, throw to first base, or (4) run directly at the runner if the third baserunner is stopped between bases |
| 3B | Cover third base |
| SS | Cover second base |
| LF | Backup third base |
| CF | Backup any throws to second base |
| RF | Backup second baseperson and backup throw to first base |

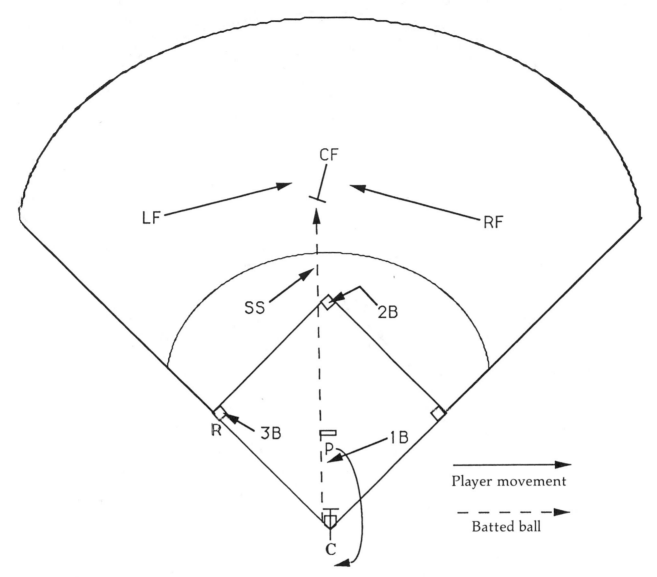

**Figure 17-10s.** Fly ball hit to center field with a runner on third base.

## Situation 11: Runner on 3, less than two outs, fly ball to center field (see Figure 17-10s)

| Position | Responsibilities |
|----------|------------------|
| P | Backup home plate |
| C | Watch runner; call the throw; cover home plate |
| 1B | Assume cutoff position |
| 2B | React to hit; cover second base |
| 3B | Cover third base |
| SS | React to hit; communicate with outfield |
| LF | Backup CF |
| CF | Move into the catch; immediately throw home! |
| RF | Backup CF |

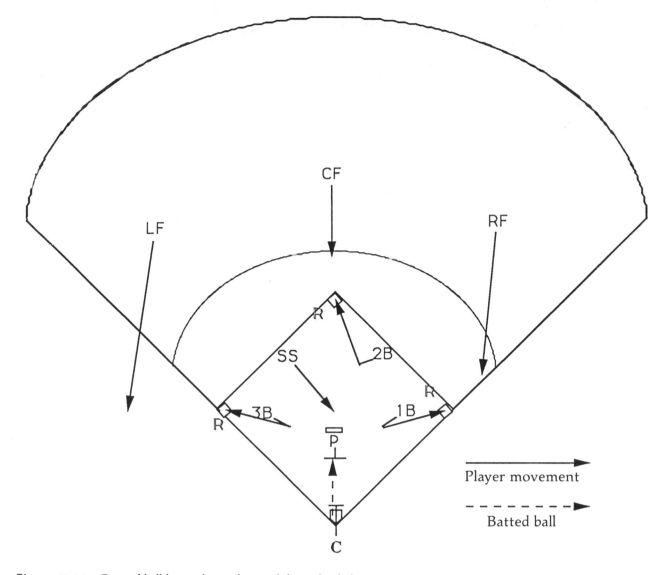

**Figure 17-11s.** Ground ball hit to the pitcher with bases loaded.

## Situation 12: Runner on 1-2-3, less than two outs, ground ball to pitcher (see Figure 17-11s)

| Position | Responsibilities |
|---|---|
| P | Field the ball; immediately throw home |
| C | Receive the throw home; anticipate potential to double play throw at first base |
| *1B | React to ground ball; cover first base |
| *2B | Backup pitcher; move to cover second base |
| *3B | React to ground ball; cover third base |
| *SS | Backup pitcher |
| LF | Backup possible throw to third base |
| CF | Back up second base; cover if left open |
| RF | Backup first base throw from C |

*All infielders move initial ready position in to assure force out at the plate. If the run is insignificant, remain in general ready position.

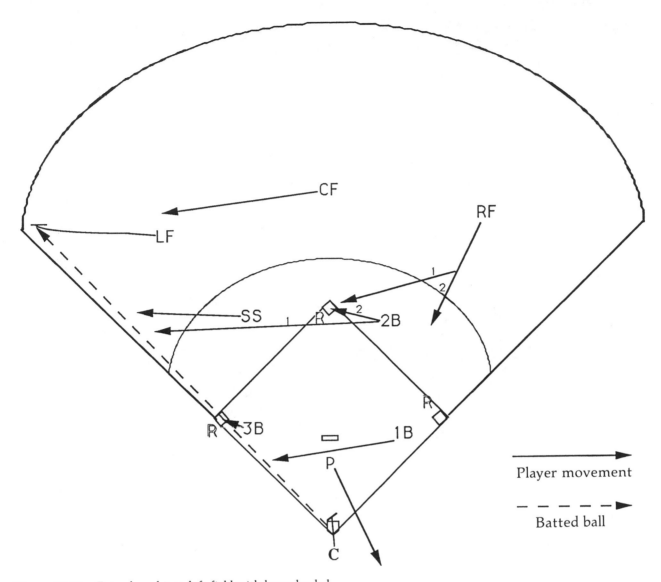

**Figure 17-12s.** Extra-base hit to left field with bases loaded.

## Situation 13: Runner on 1-2-3, extra-base hit down left-field line (see Figure 17-12s)

| Position | Responsibilities |
|---|---|
| P | Backup home plate |
| C | Cover home plate; watch runners—call throw from relay person; call possible cut and return throw |
| 1B | Assume cutoff position; listen for cut and throw |
| 2B | Backup relay person, or cover second base |
| 3B | Cover third base |
| SS | Assume relay position; call for the ball; listen for upcoming throw |
| LF | Move to ball; listen for location of relay person |
| CF | Help LF |
| RF | Cover second base if the second baseperson is backing up the relay person, or backup second baseperson covering second base |

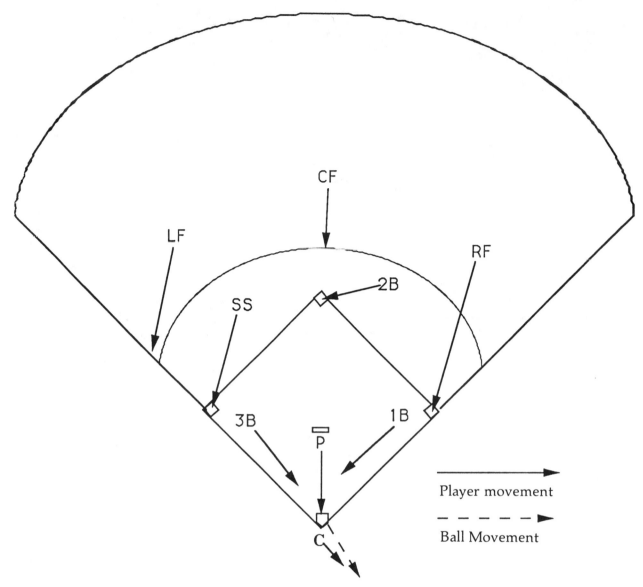

**Figure 17-13s.** Player positioning on a passed ball or wild pitch.

## Situation 14: Runner on 3, 1–3, 2–3, or 1–2–3, wild pitch/passed ball (see Figure 17-13s)

| Position | Responsibilities |
|----------|------------------|
| P | Cover home plate |
| C | Immediately recover pitch |
| 1B | Backup deflected or errant throw to first-base side of infield |
| 2B | Cover 2B |
| 3B | Backup catcher's throw to the pitcher on the third-base side of infield |
| SS | Cover third base |
| LF | Backup possible throw to third base |
| CF | Backup possible throw to second base |
| RF | Cover first base |

# Section V
# Methods of Effective Coaching

# 18
# Working Effectively with Parents

*Martha Ewing, Ph.D.*
*Deborah Feltz, Ph.D.*
*Eugene W. Brown, Ph.D.*

---

## QUESTIONS TO CONSIDER

- How can I obtain the information and help needed from parents to do a good job?
- What is my responsibility to the parents of the players on my team?
- How can I avoid the negative influence some parents have on a team or program?
- What are the responsibilities of the players and their parents to this program?

---

## INTRODUCTION

Support and assistance from parents can be very helpful. Some parents, however, through lack of awareness, can weaken the effects of your coaching, and thus reduce the benefits softball can provide to their children.

These negative influences can be minimized if you tell parents:

- how you perceive your role as the coach
- the purpose and objectives of the softball program
- the responsibilities they and their children have in helping the team run smoothly

*Some parents, through lack of awareness, can weaken the effects of your coaching.*

The most effective way of communicating the purposes and needs of your program is through a parents' orientation meeting. A parents' orientation meeting can be used to:

- teach parents the rules and regulations of softball so they understand the game
- provide details about the season
- provide a setting for collecting and distributing important information

At the parents' orientation meeting, you have the opportunity to ask for their assistance and discuss other items that are specific to the team. A meeting for parents is also an excellent way for them to get to know you and each other. A face-to-face meeting and a few short remarks go a long way toward uniting coaches and parents in a cooperative endeavor that benefits the players. Many potential problems can be eliminated by good communication that begins before the first practice.

## CONTENT OF A PARENTS' ORIENTATION MEETING

Parents usually have a number of questions concerning their child's softball program. With proper preparation and an outlined agenda, you should be able to answer most questions. A sample agenda is provided. This agenda can be supplemented with items you and/or the parents believe to be important.

## Sample Agenda
## Parents' Orientation Meeting

1. Introductions
2. Goals of the team and program
3. Understanding the sport of softball
4. Dangers and risk of injury
5. Emergency procedures
6. Equipment needs
7. Athletes' responsibilities
8. Parents' responsibilities
9. Season schedule
10. Other

Each agenda item and its relationship to the softball program is explained in the following paragraphs.

### Introductions

Parents should be informed about who administers the softball program. They should become acquainted with the coaches and the parents of the other players. As the coach, you should introduce yourself, briefly describing your background, coaching experience, and reasons for coaching.

The parents should also introduce themselves, identify where they live, and perhaps indicate how long their children have been involved in the program and the objectives that they have for their child's involvement in softball. Learning who the other parents are makes it easier to establish working relationships for specific tasks and to initiate sharing of responsibilities (e.g., carpooling and bringing refreshments to games).

Finally, the purpose of the meeting should be explained to communicate important information about each agenda item. If handouts are available, they should be distributed at this time. We suggest that at least one handout, an agenda, be distributed to provide order to the meeting, a sense of organization on your part, and a place for parents to write notes.

Information about the players and their families should be collected (see Supplement 18-1). A team roster and telephone tree (see Supplement 18-2) could be compiled from the information collected, then typed and distributed to each of the families at another time.

### Goals of the Team and Programs

The goals of the sponsoring organization, as well as your personal goals, should be presented. Parents then will be able to judge whether those goals are compatible with their beliefs regarding what is appropriate for their child. Goals that have been identified by young softball players as most important are:

• to have fun
• to improve skills and learn new skills
• to be on a team and to make new friends
• to succeed or win

Most educators, pediatricians, sport psychologists, and parents consider these to be healthy goals that coaches should help young athletes achieve. Parents should be informed of the primary goals of the team and the amount of emphasis that will be placed on achieving these goals.

*Parents should be informed of the primary goals of the team.*

Other areas that should be addressed are your policies on eliminating players, the consequences of missing practices, and recognizing players through awards. You may be asked to answer many questions about how you will function as a coach. Some examples are:

• Will players be allowed to compete if they missed the last practice before a game?
• Will players be excluded from contests or taken off the team if they go on a two-week vacation?
• Will players receive trophies or other material rewards?
• How much emphasis will be placed on rewards?
• Are the rewards given only to good performers or are they given to all participants?

Chapter 19 discusses the issue of appropriate use of rewards. You may wish to comment on several points explained in Chapter 19 as you address this issue.

## Understanding the Sport of Softball

Many times spectators boo umpires, shout instructions to players, or contradict the coach because they do not know the rules or strategies of softball. This is particularly true if the rules of play have been modified for younger age groups. Informing parents about basic rules, skills, and strategies may help those who are unfamiliar with softball and will prevent some of this negative behavior.

The information may be presented in the form of a film, brief explanation, demonstration of techniques, and/or interpretations. In addition, parents could obtain copies of Section II, "Youth Softball Rules of Play" to learn more about the rules of the game. If you'd rather not use the meeting to cover this information, you could invite parents to attend selected practice sessions where a demonstration and/or explanation of positions, rules, and strategies will be presented to the team.

## Dangers and Risk of Injury

Parents should be told what they can expect in terms of possible injuries their child may incur in softball. As noted in Chapter 2, failure to inform parents of potential injuries is the most frequent basis for lawsuits involving coaches and players.

Tell them, for example, that generally the injuries are confined to sprains, bruises, and contusions, but that there is a possibility for broken bones, concussions, and catastrophic injuries. Supplement 18-3 provides information on sites of injuries in youth softball. This information should be reviewed with parents. Let them know if a medical examination is required before their child's participation. If so, tell them what forms or evidence of compliance is acceptable, to whom it must be provided, and when it is due.

*Parents should be told what they can expect in terms of possible injuries in youth softball.*

Tell the parents what will be done to prevent injuries and assure them that the playing/practice area and equipment will be checked to help keep players safe and free from exposure to hazards.

Lastly, the program's policy of accident insurance should be described. Inform parents if the program maintains athletic accident coverage or whether parents are required to provide insurance coverage for injuries that happen during their child's athletic participation.

## Emergency Procedures

Have the parents provide you with information and permission necessary for you to function during an emergency. The Athlete's Medical Information Form (Supplement 18-4) and Medical Release Form (Supplement 18-5) were designed for these purposes. You should have the parents complete these forms and keep them with you at all team functions. These forms will provide you with information to guide your actions in an emergency.

## Equipment Needs

Explain what equipment the players need and where it can be purchased. Advice on the quality of particular brands and models and an indication of how much parents can expect to pay for specific items is also welcomed by the parents.

If an equipment swap is organized, tell them where and when it will be held. A handout describing proper equipment should be provided. Supplement 18-6 provides a list and guidelines for the selection of softball equipment. This supplement could be reproduced and used as a handout to the parents for properly outfitting their child.

## Athletes' Responsibilities

The "Bill of Rights for Young Athletes," (Martens and Seefeldt 1979) reminds adults that the child's welfare must be placed above all other considerations. Children and their parents must realize, however, that along with rights, they must meet certain responsibilities. Young athletes must be responsible for:

- being on time at practices and games with all of their equipment
- cooperating with coaches and teammates
- putting forth the effort to condition their bodies and to learn the basic skills
- conducting themselves properly and living with the consequences of inappropriate behavior

These responsibilities should be discussed so parents may help reinforce them at home.

### Parents' Responsibilities

Parents of young athletes must assume some responsibilities associated with their child's participation on the softball team. This should be discussed at the parents' orientation meeting. Martens (Martens 1978) has identified a number of parental responsibilities. You may wish to cover all or a portion of the following responsibilities in the parents' orientation meeting.

- Parents should learn what their child expects from softball.
- Parents should decide if their child is ready to compete and at what level.
- Parents should help their child understand the meaning of winning and losing.
- Parents are responsible for disciplining their child and ensuring that their child meets specific responsibilities for participating on the softball team.
- Parents should not interfere with their child's coach and should conduct themselves in a proper manner at games.

Parents should also be sensitive to fulfill the commitment they and their child have made to the team. This often requires that parents displace other important tasks in order to get their child to practice on time, publicly support the coach, encourage players to give their best effort, reward players for desirable efforts, and participate in the social events of the team.

*Children and their parents must assume certain responsibilities.*

If called upon, parents should be willing to assist the coach to carry out some of the many tasks required to meet the needs of the team. If you, as the coach, can anticipate and identify tasks with which you will need assistance, these should be presented to the parents at the orientation meeting.

It is surprising how many parents will volunteer to help you if the tasks are well-defined. See Supplement 18-7 for a description of some qualifications required of assistants and some possible responsibilities. You may not be able to

anticipate all the tasks. However, by developing an expectation of shared cooperation at the orientation meeting, parents who are not initially called upon for assistance are more likely to provide help as the need arises.

One conflict that sometimes arises results from parents falsely assuming your responsibility as coach. They may attempt to direct the play of their child and/or others during practices and games. This type of action by a parent undermines your plans for the team. It may also create a conflict in the mind of the athlete as to which set of instructions to follow.

You must inform parents that their public comments should be limited to praise and applause and that you will be prepared to coach the team. There are many ways to coach young athletes and different strategies that can result in success. You should inform parents that, if they disagree with your coaching, you will be open to their suggestions when they are presented in private.

### Season Schedule

Fewer telephone calls and memos will be needed later in the season if you prepare and distribute a schedule of events for the season at the orientation meeting. The most efficient way to provide parents with the entire season schedule is with a handout.

The schedule should inform the parents about the length of the season; the dates, sites, and times when practices and games will be held; lengths of practices and games; number of games; number of practices; and other events for the season. Maps and/or instructions about where team events will occur are often helpful.

## GETTING PARENTS TO ATTEND AN ORIENTATION MEETING

After you have received your team roster and, if possible, before the first practice, you should make arrangements to schedule a parents' orientation meeting. If you do not personally have sufficient space to accommodate the parents, a room in a neighborhood school usually can be scheduled free of charge for an orientation meeting.

Before scheduling the time and date for the meeting, the parents should be asked about the times that they could attend. This information, as well as items of parental concern for an agenda, can be obtained through a telephone conversation with the parents. Once the time and date have been determined, the parents should be notified about this information by telephone or brief letter.

If a letter is sent, the agenda for the meeting should be included. If possible, this notification should occur about two weeks before the meeting and should be followed by a courteous telephone reminder on the night before the meeting.

In your communication with the parents, you should stress the importance of the meeting and the need for each family to be represented at the meeting.

## ORGANIZING THE PARENTS' ORIENTATION MEETING

If you are well-prepared and organized, conducting a parents' orientation meeting will be an enjoyable and useful event. Before this meeting, you should complete the agenda and write down key points you plan to communicate under each item. Next, assemble the handouts that will be distributed at the meeting. At the very least, the handouts should include an agenda for the parents to follow.

Other suggested handouts and forms for distributing and collecting information include: information on common softball injuries, medical examination form (if provided by your program), accident insurance form and information (if provided through your program), athletic medical information form, medical release form, description of proper equipment, list of team assistants and responsibilities, season schedule, telephone tree, and player and parent roster. The items in Supplements 18-1 through 18-7 are suitable for duplication (permission is granted) and could be distributed at the orientation meeting.

## FOLLOW-UP ON THE PARENTS' ORIENTATION MEETING

After having conducted the parents' orientation meeting, you should contact the families who were unable to attend and briefly inform them about what was discussed. They should be given the handouts that were distributed at

the meeting, and you should collect whatever information is needed from them. Once your records are completed, you may compile additional handouts (e.g., telephone tree).

*Keep the lines of communication open between you and the parents.*

No matter how many questions you answer at the parents' orientation meeting, it will not solve all of the problems. Thus, it is important to keep the lines of communication open. You should indicate your willingness to discuss any problems that were not discussed at the first meeting. This might be done with a telephone call or at a conference involving the coach and parent, or the coach, parent, and athlete. Immediately before or after a practice is often an appropriate time to discuss major issues with parents. You could even have another meeting for parents midway through the season to provide an update on the team's progress, to discuss any problems, or to listen to parent's comments. By inviting parents to talk with you, they will become a positive rather than negative influence on the players and the team.

## SUMMARY

Parents can be an asset to your program, but some parents can have a negative influence on your program. Communicating to parents about how you perceive your role as the coach, the purpose of the softball program, and the responsibilities that they and their children have to the softball program can minimize these negative influences. The most effective way to communicate this information is through a parents' orientation meeting. The time and effort you put into developing a well-organized meeting will save you considerably more time and effort throughout the season.

In a parents' orientation meeting, you have the opportunity to explain to parents that they have responsibilities to you and the team, such as deciding if their child is ready to compete, having realistic expectations, disciplining, and not interfering with coaching or playing. Children's responsibilities of promptness, cooperation, commitment, and proper conduct can also be outlined for parents.

In addition, other agenda items can be discussed and information can be gathered at a parents' orientation meeting that may make your job run more smoothly throughout the season. Be sure to discuss such items as danger and risk of injury, equipment needs, emergency procedures, and the season schedule.

The agenda items outlined in this chapter may not cover all the issues you need to address with the parents of your players. Therefore, you must organize a specific meeting that meets the needs of your team.

## REFERENCES

Martens, R. (1978). *Joys and sadness in children's sports*. Champaign, IL: Human Kinetics Publishers

Martens, R. & Seefeldt, V. (Eds.). (1979). *Guidelines for children's sports*. Reston, VA: AAHPERD.

## SUGGESTED READINGS

American College of Sports Medicine, American Orthopaedic Society for Sports Medicine & Sports Medicine Committee of the United States Tennis Association. (1982). *Sports injuries—An aid to prevention and treatment*. Coventry, CT: Bristol Myers Co.

Foley, J. (1980). *Questions parents should ask about youth sports programs*. East Lansing, MI: Institute for the Study of Youth Sports.

Jackson, D. & Pescar, S. (1981). *The young athletes' health handbook*. New York: Everest House.

Micheli, L.J. (1985). Preventing youth sports injuries. *Journal of Health, Physical Education, Recreation and Dance, 76*(6), 52-54.

Mirkin, G. & Marshall, H. (1978). *The sportsmedicine book*. Waltham, MA: Little Brown, & Co.

Rotella, R.S., & Bunker, L.K. (1987). *Parenting your superstar: How to help your child get the most out of sports*. Champaign, IL: Leisure Press.

Smith, R.E., Smoll, F.L., & Smith, N.J. (1989). *Parents' complete guide to youth sports*. Reston, VA: AAHPERD.

# Team Roster Information

| | Player's Name | Birth Date | Parents' Names | Address | Phone #'s Home/Work |
|---|---|---|---|---|---|
| 1. | | / / | ——— | ——— | ——— |
| 2. | | / / | ——— | ——— | ——— |
| 3. | | / / | ——— | ——— | ——— |
| 4. | | / / | ——— | ——— | ——— |
| 5. | | / / | ——— | ——— | ——— |
| 6. | | / / | ——— | ——— | ——— |
| 7. | | / / | ——— | ——— | ——— |
| 8. | | / / | ——— | ——— | ——— |
| 9. | | / / | ——— | ——— | ——— |
| 10. | | / / | ——— | ——— | ——— |
| 11. | | / / | ——— | ——— | ——— |
| 12. | | / / | ——— | ——— | ——— |
| 13. | | / / | ——— | ——— | ——— |
| 14. | | / / | ——— | ——— | ——— |
| 15. | | / / | ——— | ——— | ——— |
| 16. | | / / | ——— | ——— | ——— |
| 17. | | / / | ——— | ——— | ——— |
| 18. | | / / | ——— | ——— | ——— |

# Telephone Tree

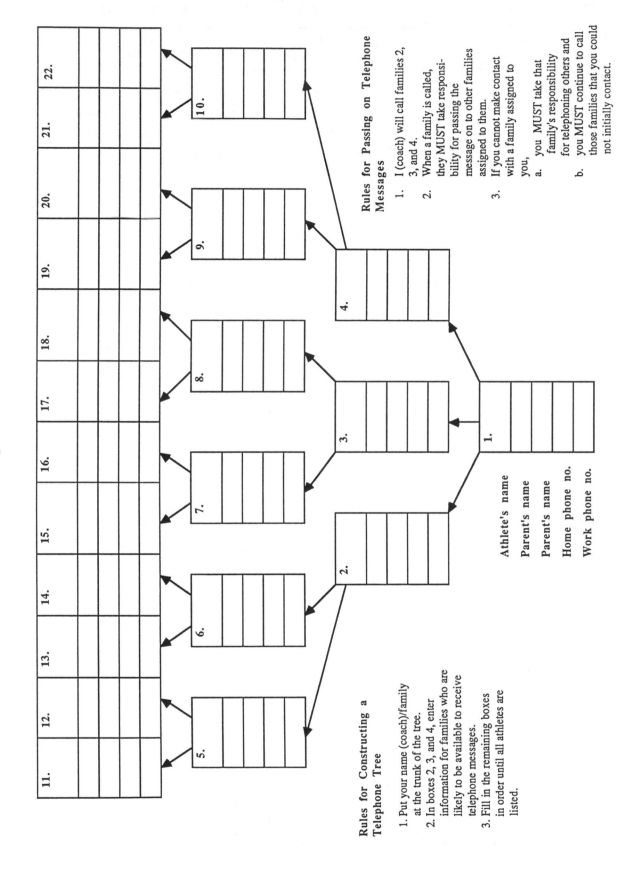

**Rules for Constructing a Telephone Tree**

1. Put your name (coach)/family at the trunk of the tree.
2. In boxes 2, 3, and 4, enter information for families who are likely to be available to receive telephone messages.
3. Fill in the remaining boxes in order until all athletes are listed.

Athlete's name

Parent's name

Parent's name

Home phone no.

Work phone no.

**Rules for Passing on Telephone Messages**

1. I (coach) will call families 2, 3, and 4.
2. When a family is called, they MUST take responsibility for passing the message on to other families assigned to them.
3. If you cannot make contact with a family assigned to you,
   a. you MUST take that family's responsibility for telephoning others and
   b. you MUST continue to call those families that you could not initially contact.

**Supplement 18-3.**

# Sites of Injuries in Youth Softball and Baseball

### Age Group[a]

| | Total | 0-4 Years | | 5-14 Years | | 15+ Years | |
|---|---|---|---|---|---|---|---|
| | | Number | Percent | Number | Percent | Number | Percent |
| Head and Face | 112,362 | 5,299 | (87%) | 48,306 | (40%) | 58,757 | (19%) |
| Shoulder and Trunk | 40,340 | 129 | (2%) | 7,509 | (6%) | 32,702 | (10%) |
| Arms and Hands | 137,799 | 317 | (5%) | 44,601 | (37%) | 92,881 | (30%) |
| Legs and Feet | 150,469 | 383 | (6%) | 21,034 | (17%) | 129,052 | (41%) |
| Other | 1,603 | ---- | ------- | 200 | ------- | 1,403 | ------- |
| Totals | 442,573 (100%) | 6,128 ---- | (100%) | 121,650 (28%) | (100%) | 314,795 (71%) | (100%) |

| | Total All Ages | Age Group 5-14 Years |
|---|---|---|
| A. Medically attended injuries, 1980 | 1,236,800 | 359,400 |
| B. Hospital emergency room-treated injuries, 1980 | 442,900 | 121,700 |

a  Distribution of Estimated Baseball/Softball-Related Injuries Treated in U.S. Hospital Emergency Rooms, by Body Part Injured and Age Group of Victim, 1980.

Source:  National Electronic Injury Surveillance System, U.S. Consumer Product Safety Commission/EPHA

# Athlete's Medical Information
(to be completed by parents/guardians and athlete)

Athlete's Name: _____ Athlete's Birthdate: _____

Parents' Names: _____ Date: _____

Address: _____

Phone No's.: (____)_____ (____)_____ (____)_____
           (Home)                (Work)                (Other)

**Who to contact in case of emergency (if parents cannot be immediately contacted):**

Name: _____ Relationship: _____

Home Phone No.: (____)_____ Work Phone No.: (____)_____

Name: _____ Relationship: _____

Home Phone No.: (____)_____ Work Phone No.: (____)_____

Hospital preference: _____ Emergency Phone No.: (____)_____

Doctor preference: _____ Office Phone No.: (____)_____

## MEDICAL HISTORY

**Part I. Complete the following:**

| | Date | Doctor | Doctor's Phone No. |
|---|---|---|---|
| 1. Last tetanus shot? | _____ | | |
| 2. Last dental examination? | _____ | _____ | _____ |
| 3. Last eye examination? | _____ | _____ | _____ |

**Part II. Has your child or did your child have any of the following?**

| General Conditions: | Circle one | | Circle one or both | | Injuries: | Circle one | | Circle one or both | |
|---|---|---|---|---|---|---|---|---|---|
| 1. Fainting spells/dizziness | Yes | No | Past | Present | 1. Toes | Yes | No | Past | Present |
| 2. Headaches | Yes | No | Past | Present | 2. Feet | Yes | No | Past | Present |
| 3. Convulsions/epilepsy | Yes | No | Past | Present | 3. Ankles | Yes | No | Past | Present |
| 4. Asthma | Yes | No | Past | Present | 4. Lower legs | Yes | No | Past | Present |
| 5. High blood pressure | Yes | No | Past | Present | 5. Knees | Yes | No | Past | Present |
| 6. Kidney problems | Yes | No | Past | Present | 6. Thighs | Yes | No | Past | Present |
| 7. Intestinal disorder | Yes | No | Past | Present | 7. Hips | Yes | No | Past | Present |
| 8. Hernia | Yes | No | Past | Present | 8. Lower back | Yes | No | Past | Present |
| 9. Diabetes | Yes | No | Past | Present | 9. Upper back | Yes | No | Past | Present |
| 10. Heart disease/disorder | Yes | No | Past | Present | 10. Ribs | Yes | No | Past | Present |
| 11. Dental plate | Yes | No | Past | Present | 11. Abdomen | Yes | No | Past | Present |
| 12. Poor vision | Yes | No | Past | Present | 12. Chest | Yes | No | Past | Present |
| 13. Poor hearing | Yes | No | Past | Present | 13. Neck | Yes | No | Past | Present |
| 14. Skin disorder | Yes | No | Past | Present | 14. Fingers | Yes | No | Past | Present |
| 15. Allergies | Yes | No | | | 15. Hands | Yes | No | Past | Present |
| Specify:_____ | | | Past | Present | 16. Wrists | Yes | No | Past | Present |
| _____ | | | Past | Present | 17. Forearms | Yes | No | Past | Present |
| 16. Joint dislocation or | | | | | 18. Elbows | Yes | No | Past | Present |
| separations | Yes | No | | | 19. Upper arms | Yes | No | Past | Present |
| Specify:_____ | | | Past | Present | 20. Shoulders | Yes | No | Past | Present |
| _____ | | | Past | Present | 21. Head | Yes | No | Past | Present |
| 17. Serious or significant ill- | | | | | 22. Serious or significant in- | | | | |
| nesses not included above | Yes | No | | | juries not included above | Yes | No | | |
| Specify:_____ | | | Past | Present | Specify: _____ | | | Past | Present |
| _____ | | | Past | Present | _____ | | | Past | Present |
| 18. Others:_____ | | | Past | Present | 23. Others: _____ | | | Past | Present |
| _____ | | | Past | Present | _____ | | | Past | Present |

**Part III.** Circle appropriate response to each question. For each "Yes" response, provide additional information.

|  | Circle one | Additional information |
|---|---|---|

1. Is your child currently taking any medication? If yes, describe medication, amount, and reason for taking.  Yes  No  _____
_____

2. Does your child have any allergic reactions to medication, bee stings, food, etc.? If yes, describe agents that cause adverse reactions and describe these reactions.  Yes  No  _____
_____
_____

3. Does your child wear any appliances (e.g., glasses, contact lenses, hearing aid, false teeth, braces, etc.)? If yes, describe appliances.  Yes  No  _____
_____
_____

4. Has your child had any surgical operations? If yes, indicate site, explain the reason for the surgery, and describe the level of success.  Yes  No  _____
_____
_____

5. Has a physician placed any restrictions on your child's present activities? If yes, describe restrictions.  Yes  No  _____
_____

6. Does your child have any existing and/or past medical or emotional conditions that require special concern and attention by a sports coach? If yes, explain.  Yes  No  _____
_____
_____

7. Does your child have any deformities (e.g., abnormal curvature of the spine, heart problems, one kidney, blindness in one eye, one testicle, etc.)? If yes, describe.  Yes  No  _____
_____
_____

8. Is there a history of serious family illnesses (e.g., diabetes, bleeding disorders, heart attack before age 50, etc.)? If yes, describe illnesses.  Yes  No  _____
_____
_____

9. Has your child lost consciousness or sustained a concussion?  Yes  No  _____
_____

10. Has your child experienced fainting spells or dizziness while exercising?  Yes  No  _____
_____

**Part IV.** Has your child or did your child have any of the following personal habits?

| Personal Habit | Circle one | | Circle one or both | | Indicate extent or amount |
|---|---|---|---|---|---|
| 1. Smoking | Yes | No | Past | Present | _____ |
| 2. Smokeless tobacco | Yes | No | Past | Present | _____ |
| 3. Alcohol | Yes | No | Past | Present | _____ |
| 4. Recreational drugs (e.g., marijuana, cocaine, etc.) | Yes | No | Past | Present | _____ |
| 5. Steroids | Yes | No | Past | Present | _____ |
| 6. Others | | | | | |
| Specify: _____ | Yes | No | Past | Present | _____ |
| _____ | Yes | No | Past | Present | _____ |
| _____ | Yes | No | Past | Present | _____ |

**Part V.** Please explain below any "Yes" responses in Parts II, III, and IV or any other concerns that have present implications for my coaching your child. Also, describe special first aid requirements, if appropriate. An additional sheet may be attached if necessary.

_____
_____
_____
_____
_____
_____

# Medical Release Form

I hereby give permission for any and all medical attention necessary to be administered to my child in the event of an accident, injury, sickness, etc., under the direction of the people listed below until such time as I may be contacted.  My child's name is _____.
This release is effective for the time during which my child is participating in the _____
_____ softball program and any tournaments for the 19___/19___
season, including traveling to or from such tournaments.  I also hereby assume the responsibility for payment of any such treatment.

PARENTS' OR GUARDIANS' NAMES: _____

HOME ADDRESS: _____

                          Street              City          State       Zip

                                         (_____)_____(W)

HOME PHONE: (_____)_____  (_____)_____(W)

INSURANCE COMPANY: _____

POLICY NUMBER: _____

FAMILY PHYSICIAN: _____

PHYSICIAN'S ADDRESS: _____ PHONE NO. (_____)_____

In case I cannot be reached, either of the following people is designated:

COACH'S NAME: _____ PHONE NO. (_____)_____

ASS'T. COACH OR OTHER: _____ PHONE NO. (_____)_____

SIGNATURE OF PARENT OR GUARDIAN _____

SUBSCRIBED AND SWORN BEFORE ME THIS _____ OF _____, 19 ____

SIGNATURE OF NOTARY PUBLIC _____

Supplement 18-6.

# Working Effectively with Parents

## Guidelines for Selecting Softball Equipment

### • Ball

There are a variety of softballs available for purchase in sporting goods stores. The softballs vary in size, weight, and material. Softballs should be selected for their compatibility with the physical characteristics and needs of the youth player. Softball-size "Incrediballs" or RIF (Reduced Injury Factor) Level I balls are made of a softer material and are recommended for six- to eight-year-old softball players. The RIF ball or Incrediball will allow the beginning player to grip the ball more easily and play the game without fear of injury. The RIF and Incrediball are also recommended for any type of indoor use. The 11-in. Level 10 RIF softball is recommended for 9- to 11-year-old players. The smaller, lighter ball is easier for the youth player to grip and throw. The 12-in. regulation softball is recommended for 11- to 18-year-old players.

### • Bat

Bats are available in many different materials (e.g., wood, aluminum, graphite, and ceramic). The length and weight of the bat should be appropriate for the size and strength of the player. In general, a lighter bat is conducive to a faster swing speed. For safety, a sponge-covered bat should be considered for six- and seven-year-old players.

### • Glove

The glove is the most important piece of equipment for the youth softball player. The glove should be large enough to enclose the ball yet not so large that the fielder cannot easily control it. The glove should be broken in in such a way that the thumb-side edge of the glove naturally closes to the small-finger edge of the glove. If the thumb-side edge of the glove naturally closes to any other finger, the pocket will not effectively hold a softball. Also, the glove should be flexible enough to allow the player to easily open the glove to the ball! Between games or practices, a ball should be placed in the pocket of the glove to help maintain the glove's correct form.

### • Shoes

Softball cleats are not a required piece of equipment and are not necessary for the young ages. Generally, a supportive basketball or tennis type of shoe will due. A basketball or tennis shoe will provide support for the starting, stopping, and change of direction moves required in softball. However, as skill increases, cleats will add to the player's ability to maneuver on the field. Plastic or multi-purpose cleats are recommended. Metal spikes are not.

### • Batting Helmet

All hitters, baserunners, and on-deck batters must wear a batting helmet. Helmets are often provided by the league or team. However, coaches, league officials, and parents should be sure all helmets are NOCSAE (National Operating Committee on Standards for Athletic Equipment) approved. Helmets should be checked periodically for wear of the inside padding or cracks in the helmet itself.

### • Catcher's Equipment

The catcher should wear a catching helmet with a face mask and throat protector, a body protector, and shin guards. The equipment must be adjusted to fit each player. When changing catchers, time must be taken to adjust the equipment to the new catcher. Also, extra face masks with throat protectors should be available for any player catching for a pitcher in the catching position—even if it is only practice!

## • Clothing

Unless uniforms are provided, typical attire (T-shirts, shorts/sweats, and athletic socks) will function well for youth softball. Clothing should not inhibit movement or get in the way of the player. If the player is highly likely to slide during the course of a practice or game, long pants and/or knee pads will reduce the chance for injury.

NOTE: All equipment should be regulation softball equipment (see Chapter 5).

Supplement 18-7.

# Descriptions of Team Assistants and Their Responsibilities*

*Assistant coach*—aids the coach in all aspects of coaching the team during practices and games.

*Team manager*—keeps game statistics, completes line-up cards, and makes arrangements for practice sites and times; works approximately one hour per week.

*Team treasurer*—collects fees from players, identifies sponsors, maintains financial records; works approximately five hours at the beginning of the season and a few hours throughout the remainder of the season.

*Team doctor/nurse/paramedic*—establishes a plan to respond to possible emergencies for each practice and game site, prepares and updates a medical kit, assists the coach in responding to injured players by providing first aid, collects and organizes completed medical history forms and reviews these with the coach, maintains records of completed on-site injury reports and completes a summary of season injuries, delegates other parents to bring ice to games for initial care of certain injuries; works approximately five hours at the beginning of the season and approximately ½ hour per week throughout the remainder of the season. Note that only a certified medical doctor, trainer, nurse, or paramedic should assume some of these defined responsibilities. See Chapters 26 and 27 for more details.

*Team social coordinator*—plans team party and team social functions; works approximately five hours per season.

*Team refreshments coordinator*—contacts parents to assign them the shared expense and responsibilities of providing refreshments at all games (see Chapter 25); works approximately two hours per week.

*Team secretary*—prepares and duplicates handouts, types, sends out mailings; works approximately 10 hours per season.

*Note that these are only suggestions for assistants and their responsibilities. The way you organize your team may result in the need for different and/or additional assistants.

# 19
# Motivating Your Players

*Martha Ewing, Ph.D.*
*Deborah Feltz, Ph.D.*

---

### QUESTIONS TO CONSIDER

- Why do children play softball?
- What techniques can you use to minimize the number of "dropouts" from your team?
- What are the four elements of "positive" coaching?
- What can you do to help your players set realistic goals for themselves?

---

## INTRODUCTION

The key to understanding your athletes' motivation is to understand each of their needs. As a coach, you play an important role in determining whether an athlete's needs are fulfilled. Previous research indicates that motivation will be high and young athletes will persist in a sport if their needs are met by that sport. But what are those needs and why do children desire to participate in sports?

## WHY YOUNG ATHLETES PARTICIPATE IN SOFTBALL

In order to help your players maintain or improve their motivation in softball, you must understand why they participate and why some of them stop participating. Based on interviews with young athletes who participated in a variety of sports, the following reasons for playing were identified and are listed in the order of their importance.

1. To have fun
2. To improve skills and learn new ones
3. For thrills and excitement
4. To be with friends or make new friends
5. To succeed or win

While these research findings provide some insight as to why most children play softball, they are only general guidelines. The best information available to you is to learn from the athletes on your team why they are participating in the softball program.

*To improve your players' motivation, you must know why they participate in softball.*

## WHY YOUNG ATHLETES DROP OUT OF SOFTBALL

Knowing why some youngsters stop playing softball can help you find ways to encourage them to continue playing. From a survey of 1,773 young athletes (Youth Sports Institute 1977) who dropped out of softball and other sports, we learned that the reason for dropping out was that they did not achieve the goals they set when they initially enrolled to play.

This is not surprising if you consider that their reasons for getting involved in sports represent goals that can only be achieved through participation. When these goals are not being met, withdrawal occurs. Some of the reasons most often cited for dropping out of sports are discussed in the following paragraphs.

## Other Interests

Children are often very good at assessing their relative ability in various activities. They may "shop around" and participate in several sports and other activities before deciding which ones provide them the greatest chance of being successful.

Dropping softball to achieve in other activities such as music, soccer, swimming, dance, and scouting is acceptable. When children tell you or their parents that they want to pursue other activities, they should be encouraged to do so but welcomed to return to softball later if they desire.

## Work

Many children who would like to participate in softball discontinue because their help is needed at home or they desire to obtain a job. If it is possible, practices and games should be arranged at times that allow all individuals to stay involved. Attempt to find a creative alternative so that having a job does not preclude participation in softball. Although much can be learned from work, the lessons that can be learned in sport are also valuable.

Another compelling reason for sports participation during childhood is that this experience may be a prerequisite for successful performance in later years. However, children who find that they must discontinue their participation should be assured that they may return to softball at a later time.

## No Longer Interested

For many children, playing softball is a prestigious achievement. However, once they get involved, some may determine that softball is not as glamorous as it first appeared. Although these children may have enjoyed their sport experience, they may decide that other interests are more important and/or enjoyable.

Children with interests in other activities should not be forced by parents or pressured by coaches and peers to continue participation in a softball program. Doing so often transforms a normally well-behaved child into one who becomes a discipline problem. Parents and coaches should give children a chance to explore other activities and return to softball if they so decide.

## Not Enough Playing Time

Children sign up for softball because they anticipate the enjoyment and skill development that will result from their involvement. Many young athletes who cited "not playing enough" as a reason for dropping out were telling coaches that they needed more playing time to achieve their goal. These children are not usually asking to be starters or even to play the majority of the time. However, to be told indirectly that they aren't good enough to play during a game can be devastating to a child's feelings of self-worth. Coaches of young athletes need to ensure that a fair and equitable pattern of play occurs both during practices and games.

## Skills Were Not Improving

Young athletes want to learn skills and see themselves improving in those skills. Coaches need to recognize that each athlete is different in his/her skill level. Instruction should be designed to help each athlete on the team improve in performance abilities.

It is important to show athletes how they have improved. Too often, young athletes compare their skills to the skills of other athletes rather than their own past performances. This type of comparison is destructive to the self-esteem of unskilled players. Players of all ability levels should be taught to evaluate their performance based on the progress they are making.

*Young athletes expect to see improvement in their skills if they are to remain in softball.*

## Did Not Like the Coach

This reason for dropping out may be another way for athletes to tell coaches that they were not playing enough and their skills were not improving. In a study of youth sport participants, the athletes who did not like the coach said they did not like being yelled at, thought the coaches played only their favorite players, and did not think the coaches were fair.

To be effective, coaches must treat young athletes with the same respect that coaches expect from the athletes. It is not necessary or effective to yell at athletes to communicate with them. Avoid all sarcastic and degrading comments. Use a positive approach to create an enjoyable and motivating environment for players to learn and have fun playing the game.

## HOW TO HELP MOTIVATE YOUR PLAYERS

Athletes are most highly motivated when they obtain what they seek from their participation in sport. Therefore, motivational techniques that you select should be based on the reasons athletes have for joining the team. The following strategies may help you improve your players' motivation.

### Know Why Your Athletes Are Participating

Young athletes differ in their personalities, needs, interests, and objectives for playing softball. You must, therefore, get to know your athletes as individuals to determine why they participate. One way to accomplish this is through a team meeting at the start of the season.

Ask your players why they are participating and what their personal objectives are for the season. They may be asked this question before, during, and after practices and special events or whenever you have a chance to talk one-on-one with your players.

### Help Your Athletes Improve Skills and Learn New Skills

Skill improvement is a very important reason for joining a softball team. Therefore, practice sessions should focus on skill development, with regular opportunities for players to measure their progress. In addition, you can help athletes set performance goals that are appropriate for them. For example, as young players first learn to field a ground ball, they should practice fielding balls rolled to them at a slow pace. More advanced players should be encouraged to field balls rolled at a faster pace or to field balls that are hit to them by a coach who can control the pace and location of the hit. Finally, players should practice fielding balls hit or rolled to both their glove-side and non-glove-side and to field balls with runners on base to provide athletes a chance to practice making appropriate decisions. As players improve, they can understand and measure their progress both in practice and in game situations.

### Make Practices and Games Enjoyable

As indicated by various studies, young athletes want to have fun. This means they want to play; they do not want to sit on the bench or stand in long lines waiting their turn at a drill. One of the best ways to ensure that practices are enjoyable is to use short, snappy drills that result in all players being involved most of the time. You can also keep your players' interest by incorporating new and challenging drills. Your players may even be able to invent useful drills of their own.

*Having a chance to display their skills during a game is an excellent motivator of young athletes.*

In games, too, all players can be involved, even if they are sitting on the bench. Team members can be watching the individuals who are playing similar positions to learn from their good techniques or their mistakes. They can also watch for strategies used by the other team. Most importantly, however, they should all have a chance to play in every game. The knowledge that they will have a chance to display their skills during the course of the contest is a primary source of motivation before and after the experience. Players who sit on the bench, unable to test their skills in a game, are not likely to have fun.

## Allow Players to be with Their Friends and Make New Friends

Many athletes view their softball participation as a chance to be with their friends while doing something they enjoy. Allowing your players to have fun with their friends does not mean your practices have to be disruptive. You can encourage an esprit de corps within the team. Social activities, such as a mid-season pizza party, require more time on your part but may foster rewarding friendships among players and coaches.

Remember, many of your players' friends may be on opposing teams. Encourage athletes to continue their friendships with players on opposing teams and even develop new friendships with opponents.

## Help Players Understand the Meaning of Success

Children learn at an early age to equate winning with success and losing with failure. If athletes win a game, they feel good or worthy. If they lose, they feel incompetent or unworthy. This attitude toward winning can be discouraging to players, unless they are always winning. One of your most important roles, therefore, is to help your players keep winning in perspective. One way to accomplish this is to help your players understand that winning a game is not always under their control. For example, after losing a game, you may explain the loss to your team this way: "We hit the ball well today, but their team played very good defense, so we didn't get as many runs as we expected."

Your players also need to know that, although striving to win is an important objective in softball, being successful in softball also means making personal improvements and striving to do one's best. This attitude can be developed by:

- encouraging maximum effort during practices and games
- rewarding effort
- helping players set important but realistic goals that they can attain and thus feel successful when they are achieved

In helping your players understand the meaning of success, it is also important not to punish them when they fail, particularly if they gave a maximum effort.

*Your coaching approach is the factor with the greatest influence on player motivation.*

## Use the Positive Approach to Coaching

Probably the most important factor that influences your players' motivation is the approach you take in coaching. There are many different styles or approaches used by coaches, but most fall into either of two categories: the negative approach and the positive approach.

- ### Negative Approach

The negative approach is the most visible model of coaching. The negative approach, demonstrated by some professional, college, and even high school coaches, is often highlighted in the media. This approach is one in which the coach focuses on performance errors and uses fear, hate, and/or anger to motivate players.

The negative approach doesn't work very well with young athletes. Constant criticism, sarcasm, and yelling often frustrate young athletes, deteriorate their self-confidence, and decrease their motivation. Remember that young athletes are just beginning to develop their skills, and they have fragile self-concepts.

*Focus on correct aspects of performance and use liberal amounts of praise and encouragement.*

- ### Positive Approach

The positive approach, in contrast, is one where the coach focuses on the correct aspects of performance and uses plenty of encouragement and praise for the tasks that players perform correctly. When errors occur, a coach who uses the positive approach corrects mistakes with constructive criticism.

A positive, supportive approach is essential when coaching young athletes if high levels of motivation are to be maintained. Key principles for implementing a positive approach to coaching are listed and explained in the following paragraphs.

## Key Principles for Implementing a Positive Approach to Coaching (Smoll & Smith 1979)

- ### Be liberal with rewards and encouragement.

The most effective way to influence positive behavior and increase motivation is through the frequent use of encouraging statements and rewards. The single most important difference between coaches whom young athletes respect most and those they respect least is the frequency with which coaches reward them for desirable behaviors.

The most important rewards you can give are free. They include a pat on the back, a smile, applause, verbal praise, or a friendly nod. The greater your use of encouraging statements and rewards, the more your players will be motivated.

- ### Give rewards and encouragement sincerely.

For rewards to be beneficial, they must be given sincerely. It will mean little to your players to tell them they played well if, in fact, they played poorly. This does not mean that you should not give them positive feedback about their performance when they make mistakes. You can point out their errors and at the same time praise them for the plays they performed well. It is important to be positive but also honest.

- ### Reward effort and correct technique, not just results.

It is easy to praise a player who just hit a home run, but it is less natural to praise a player who swung hard but missed the ball. Sometimes, too, we forget to reward correct technique when it does not result in scoring runs. It is important, however, to reward players' efforts and the use of correct technique if you want this behavior to continue. A solid hit that is stopped by a defensive player who makes a spectacular play should be recognized as if the hit was successful. Occasionally, spend a few extra minutes with the lesser skilled players, before or after practice, to help them learn the correct techniques. This extra attention and caring will greatly increase their motivation to keep trying.

- ### Have realistic expectations.

Base your rewards and encouragement on realistic expectations. Encouraging your softball players to strive for college standards, without the feelings of success associated with achieving the many levels of performance leading to such standards, will probably make them feel as though they have failed. It is much easier for you to give honest rewards when you have realistic expectations about your players' abilities.

## Help Players Set Goals

Young athletes learn from parents and coaches that success is equated with winning and failure is equated with losing. Adopting this view of success and failure confuses the players. Let's take, for example, the play of Mary and Kara, members of the winning and losing teams, respectively.

Both girls played about half of the game. Mary's unsporting conduct was noticed quickly by the umpire. The umpire cautioned her about running into fielders unnecessarily. Early in the third inning, she pushed the first baseman who was attempting to catch a throw from the shortstop and was disqualified from further play due to the continued rough play. Kara, on the other hand, masterfully used her practiced skills to assist her teammates in defense and hit her first triple of the season. However, since Mary was a member of the winning team, she was able to "laugh-off" her behavior and revel in the success of her team. On the other hand, Kara felt that her efforts were insignificant and worthless and joined her teammates in the disappointment of a 6-3 loss.

As adults, we recognize the inaccuracy of these perceptions. But, our actions at the end of a contest may tell our players that a winning score is what really matters.

*Equating success with winning and failure with losing results in mixed messages to the athlete.*

Athletes need a way to compare their current performances with their past performances to determine whether they are successful. This can be accomplished through goal setting. You as a coach can help each of your athletes establish individual goals. By doing this, each athlete can regain control over personal success or failure. In addition to removing the mixed messages, remind your players that there are some factors that are out of their control that may determine the outcome of a game. For example, the pitcher may be throwing the best game of her career. Although your athlete is hitting very well, there is just no hitting the opposing pitcher today. Or, due to injury or illness, a player is forced to play an unfamiliar position. These examples highlight the need to establish goals for personal improvement that are consistent with the objective of winning, but not entirely dependent on their achievement, to maintain player motivation. There are several guidelines for goal setting that can markedly help performance.

## Guidelines for Goal Setting

### • Success should be possible for everyone on the team.

When implementing a goal setting program, each athlete must experience some success. In other words, each athlete should perform at a level that demands a best effort for the existing conditions. Help each athlete realize that effort equals success by focusing rewards on such efforts.

### • Goals under practice conditions should be increasingly more challenging and goals during competition should be more realistic.

When you set up drills to work on fielding or hitting, help your players set goals for practice that will challenge each of them to exceed a previous effort. For example, when practicing batting, you may ask your "star" to make solid contact with the ball 7 out of 10 times in practice, while another player may be challenged with making solid contact 4 out of 10 times! You should not expect the same level of performance in a game because neither you nor the players control all the factors. With this approach, motivation at practice is increased and players have a realistic chance of experiencing self-worth in a game.

### • Goals should be flexible.

If goal setting is to be effective, goals must be evaluated frequently and adjusted depending on the athlete's success ratio. If an athlete is achieving the set goal, raise the goal to provide a greater challenge and motivation. If the goal is too difficult and the athlete is feeling frustration or failure, the goal should be lowered rather than have the athlete continue to experience failure. Having to lower the level of a goal may also be frustrating. Therefore, it is important to be as accurate as possible when initially setting goals for individual players.

### • Set individual goals rather than team goals.

In general, team goals should not be made. This is because team goals are not under anyone's control, and they are often unrealistic. It is too difficult to assess accurately how a team will progress through a season. Will your team improve faster than other teams, at the same pace, or be a latecomer? If you set winning a certain number of games (e.g., 8 of 10 games) as a goal and the team loses their first three games, you cannot achieve the goal even by winning the remaining seven games. This will only cause greater discouragement among team members. Work on individual improvement through goal setting, and let the team's improvement reflect the individual's improvement.

Goal setting can be very effective in improving a player's performance, confidence, and self-worth. To be effective, however, you must know your players well enough to know when they are setting goals that are challenging, controllable, and realistic. In addition, goals must be adjusted to ensure feelings of self-worth.

## DEALING WITH COMPETITIVE STRESS

Some coaches believe the best way to motivate a team for competition is to get them "psyched-up" before the game. With young athletes, however, getting psyched-up is not usually the problem; rather, the problem for them is getting "psyched out."

Competitive stress in young athletes can originate from many sources—the athlete, the teammates, the coach, and the parents. When young athletes were asked what caused them to worry, among the most frequently given answers were:

1. improving their performance

2. participating in championship games
3. performing up to their level of ability
4. what their coach and parents would think or say

Thus, young softball players are most likely to be worried about performance failure. This worry about failure may increase players' anxieties, which, in turn, may cause poor performance, and eventually may decrease motivation. Figure 19-1 illustrates this cycle.

A good way to help your players avoid the effects of competitive stress is to reduce their fear of failure. This can be achieved by encouraging them to enjoy the game and to do their best. When your players lose or make a mistake, do not express displeasure; rather, correct their mistakes in a positive way by using the following sequence:

1. Start with a compliment. Find some aspect of the performance that was correct.
2. Tell the player what was wrong and how to correct it.
3. Give another positive statement such as, "Everyone makes mistakes. Keep working at it and you will get it."

This approach allows players to keep practicing their skills without the fear of making a mistake. The following guidelines may be helpful in preventing competitive stress.

## Guidelines for Preventing Competitive Stress

- Set realistic goals.
- Use the positive approach when correcting mistakes.

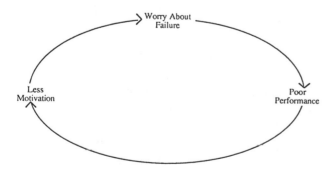

**Figure 19-1.** A cyclic representation of performance failure.

- Eliminate the type of "pep talks" that communicate overemphasis on the game and the outcome.

## APPROPRIATE USE OF TEAM TROPHIES, MEDALS, AND OTHER AWARDS*

Anyone who has ever attended a post-season softball team party is aware that presenting trophies and awards is a common practice. Young athletes may receive any number of external awards, ranging from small ribbons to large trophies. However, whether it is appropriate to give children these awards is a controversial issue.

The advocates of awards such as medals, trophies, ribbons, certificates, and jackets indicate that they increase the children's desire and motivation to participate. Critics, in contrast, suggest that giving rewards to young athletes for activities in which they are already interested turns play into work and decreases their desire to participate. What is the answer: Awards or no awards?

While the advocates and critics of this issue would have us view it as a simple one, researchers have found that no simple answer exists. The purpose of this section is to provide you with information on how and in what situations external rewards influence young athletes' self-motivation to participate in sports.

## Understanding Rewards

An activity is defined as intrinsically motivating if an individual engages in that activity for personal interest and enjoyment, rather than for external reasons such as receiving a trophy, money, or publicity. In essence, young athletes are intrinsically motivated when they play for the sake of playing. Until recently, coaches assumed that if external rewards are given for activities that are already intrinsically motivating, the result will be a further increase in intrinsic motivation.

However, research has shown that this is not always the case. The presentation of extrinsic rewards for an already self-motivated activity may result in reduced intrinsic motiva-

*Much of the material presented in this section has been adapted from the work of Gould (1980).

tion. The following adapted story (Casady 1974) illustrates how rewards can undermine intrinsic motivation.

*An old man lived next to an open field that was a perfect location for the neighborhood children's "pick-up" baseball games. Every afternoon the children would come to the field, choose sides, and engage in a noisy game. Finally, the noise became too much for the old man, so he decided to put an end to the games. However, being a wise old man who did not want to stir up trouble in the neighborhood, he changed the children's behavior in a subtle way.*

*The old man told the children that he liked to hear them play, but because of his failing hearing, he had trouble doing so. He then told the children that if they would play and create enough noise so he could hear them, he would give each of them a quarter.*

*The children gladly obliged. After the game, the old man paid the children and asked if they could return the next day. They agreed, and once again they created a great deal of noise during the game. However, this time the old man said he was running short of money and could only pay them 20 cents each. This still satisfied the children. However, when he told them that he would be able to pay only 5 cents on the third day, the children became angry and indicated that they would not come back. They felt that it was not worth the effort to make so much noise for only 5 cents apiece.*

In this example, giving an external reward (money) for an already intrinsically motivating activity (playing baseball and making noise) resulted in decreased intrinsic motivation in the children. Hence, when the rewards were removed, the amount of participation decreased.

An increasing number of individuals have suggested that this phenomenon also occurs in organized youth sports such as softball. In many programs, young athletes are presented with a substantial number of external awards (trophies, jackets, ribbons, etc.) for participating in an already desirable activity. Critics of external awards feel that giving these rewards decreases the youngsters' intrinsic motivation and when the rewards are no longer available, they no longer participate. Thus, external rewards may be one cause of discontinued participation in softball.

## Effects of Intrinsic Awards

There are two aspects of every reward that can influence a young athlete's intrinsic motivation (Deci 1975). These are:

1. the controlling aspect of the reward
2. the informational aspect of the reward

### • Controlling Aspects of Rewards

Extrinsic rewards can decrease intrinsic motivation when they cause players to perceive that their reasons for participation have shifted from their own internal control to factors outside (or external to) themselves. This was illustrated clearly in the story of the old man and the children. The children's reasons for playing shifted from internal factors (fun and self-interest) to external factors (money). Then, when the rewards were diminished, they no longer wanted to play. In essence, the children were no longer participating for the fun of it but were participating solely for the reward. If young softball players are made to feel that their primary reason for participating is to receive a trophy or a medal to please their parents, their intrinsic motivation will probably decrease.

### • Informational Aspects of Rewards

External rewards can also communicate information to individuals about their competence and self-worth. If the reward provides information that causes an increase in a child's feelings of personal worth and competence, it will increase intrinsic motivation. If it provides no information about self-worth or competence or reduces these feelings about oneself, it will decrease intrinsic motivation.

*Seek to elevate feelings of self-worth in the awards you give.*

A "Most Improved Player" award is a good example of how material rewards can enhance motivation. This award usually tells the player that he/she has worked hard and learned a lot. This award would probably increase intrinsic motivation. Constant failure and negative feedback, however, would decrease a young player's feelings of competence and self-worth and, in turn, would decrease intrinsic motivation. Consequently, you must help children establish realistic goals. When rewards are given, they should be based upon some known criteria (performance, effort, etc.). This helps to ensure that rewards provide the recipients with information to increase feelings of self-worth and competence.

## • Informational Versus Controlling Aspects of Rewards

Because most rewards in children's athletics are based upon performance, thus conveying information about the recipient's self-worth, giving external rewards should never undermine intrinsic motivation. However, this may not always be true. Even though external rewards may convey information about a child's sense of personal competence, the child may perceive the controlling aspect as being more important than the information conveyed (Halliwell 1978). Thus, instead of increasing the young athletes' intrinsic motivation, the extrinsic rewards undermine children's interest in sports by causing them to perceive their involvement as a means to an end. They are pawns being "controlled" by the pursuit of winning the reward.

## Practical Implications

Extrinsic rewards have the potential to either increase or decrease intrinsic motivation. Two key factors determine which will occur:

1. If children perceive their softball involvement as being controlled primarily by the reward (e.g., they are participating only to win the trophy or to please Mom or Dad), intrinsic motivation will decrease. In contrast, if children feel they are controlling their involvement (playing because they want to), then intrinsic motivation will increase.
2. If the reward provides information that increases the young players' feelings of self-worth and competence, intrinsic motivation will increase. If, however, the reward provides no information at all or decreases a person's feelings of competence or self-worth, then intrinsic motivation will decrease.

These findings have important implications for you as the coach. Be very careful about using extrinsic rewards! These rewards should be relatively inexpensive and not used to "control" or "coerce" children into participation in already desirable activities. Moreover, because you play such a vital role in determining how children perceive rewards, you must keep winning in perspective and stress the non-tangible values of participation in softball (fun and personal improvement) as opposed to participating solely for the victory or the reward.

*The frequent use of inexpensive or "free" rewards will increase player motivation.*

One way to increase intrinsic motivation is to give your players more responsibility (more internal control) for decision-making and for rule-making (Halliwell 1978). This could be done by getting input from your athletes about making team rules or letting them help organize practices. Younger players could be selected to lead a drill or favorite warm-up exercise and given some playing time at positions they desire. Older, more experienced players could help conduct practices and make actual game decisions (allowing players to call some plays without interference, for example).

Intrinsic motivation can also be increased by ensuring that when external rewards are given, they provide information that increases your players' feelings of self-worth and competence. The easiest way to accomplish this is to have realistic expectations of the players. Not all children will have a winning season or place first in the tournament. However, some realistic goals can be set with each athlete in terms of improved personal skills, playing time, etc., and the players can be rewarded for achieving their goals. This could be accomplished through the use of "Unsung Hero" and/or "Most Improved Player" awards.

These "official" rewards are not nearly as important, however, as the simple ones that you can give regularly. Remember, some of the most powerful rewards are free (pat on the back, friendly nod, or verbal praise). These rewards should be frequently used to acknowledge each athlete's contribution to the team, personal improvement, or achievement of a personal goal.

Finally, remember that the rewards must be given for a reason that has meaning to your players. Rewards not given sincerely (not based upon some criteria of success) may actually decrease intrinsic motivation. Therefore, coaches must set realistic, attainable goals and reward children when they attain those goals.

## SUMMARY

Children play softball because they want to improve their skills, have fun, be with friends, and be successful. Children who drop out of softball typically do so because one or more of their goals was not met. You can maximize your players' desire to participate, and help prevent them from dropping out, by getting to know them as individuals.

Learn why they are participating. Focus on skill development in practice sessions and make sure the practices are enjoyable. Allow time for friendships to develop by creating a cordial environment both on and off the field. Help players understand the meaning of success and have them set realistic goals.

Using a positive approach to coaching is the most effective way to improve players' performance. Positive coaching also makes playing and coaching more enjoyable. Be sure to reward effort and correct techniques in addition to the results that meet your expectations.

Having realistic expectations of players' performances will provide more opportunities to give rewards. However, when players make mistakes, use the positive approach to correcting errors. The positive approach involves issuing a compliment, correcting the error, and then finishing with another positive statement. Using a positive approach and helping players reach their goals are effective ways to motivate your players toward maximum performance.

Extrinsic rewards have the potential to either increase or decrease intrinsic motivation. Extrinsic rewards are most effective when they are kept in perspective, are inexpensive, and are used to reflect improvements in personal competence. The non-tangible values of participation in softball should be stressed, as opposed to participating only for winning or for the reward.

---

### REFERENCES

Casady, M. (1974). The tricky business of giving rewards. *Psychology Today*, 8(4): 52.

Deci, E.L. (1975). *Intrinsic motivation*. New York: Plenum.

Gould, D. (1980). *Motivating young athletes*. East Lansing, MI: Institute for the Study of Youth Sports.

Halliwell, W. (1978). Intrinsic motivation in sport. In W.F. Straub (Ed.), *Sport psychology: An analysis of athlete behavior*. Ithaca, NY: Movement Publications.

Smoll, F.L. & Smith, R.E. (1979). *Improving relationship skills in youth sport coaches*. East Lansing, MI: Institute for the Study of Youth Sports.

Youth Sports Institute. (1977). *Joint legislative study on youth sports program, phase II*. East Lansing, MI: Institute for the Study of Youth Sports.

---

### SUGGESTED READINGS

Orlick, T. (1980). *In pursuit of excellence*. Ottawa, Ontario: Coaching Association of Canada.

Singer, R.N. (1984). *Sustaining motivation in sport*. Tallahassee, FL: Sport Consultants International, Inc.

Smoll, F.L., & Smith, R.E. (1979). *Improving relationship skills in youth sports coaches*. East Lansing, MI: Institute for the Study of Youth Sports.

# 20
# Communicating With Your Players

*Martha Ewing, Ph.D.*
*Deborah Feltz, Ph.D.*

---

## QUESTIONS TO CONSIDER

- How can you send clear messages to your players?
- What is the positive approach to communication?
- What are the characteristics of a good listener?
- How can good communication skills improve your ability to coach?

---

## INTRODUCTION

The most important skill in coaching is the ability to communicate with your players. It is critical to effectively carry out your roles of leader, teacher, motivator, and organizer. Effective communication not only involves skill in sending messages but skill in interpreting the messages that come from your players and their parents.

## SENDING CLEAR MESSAGES

Any means you use to convey your ideas, feelings, instructions, and/or attitudes to others involves communication. Thus, when communicating with your players, your messages may contain verbal as well as nonverbal information. Nonverbal messages can be transmitted through facial expressions such as smiling, or through gestures and body movements.

When you send messages to your players, you may, without thinking, send unintentional nonverbal information as well as your inten-

tional verbal message. If your nonverbal message conflicts with what you say, your message will probably be confusing. For example, when you tell your players that they have done a good job and let your shoulders slump and heave a heavy sigh, don't be surprised if your players are less receptive to your next attempt at praise.

Another example of mixed messages occurs when you tell your players they should never question umpires' calls and then you denounce an umpire's decision. If the need should arise to question an umpire's call, you should ask the umpire for clarification in a professional manner.

### Using a Positive Approach to Communicate

Communication is more effective when you use the positive approach. The positive approach to communication between you and your athletes involves establishing:

- mutual trust
- respect

283

- confidence
- cooperation

## Essential Factors in Sending Clear Messages

### • Getting and Keeping Attention

Getting and keeping your athletes' attention can be accomplished by: (1) making eye contact with them, (2) avoid potential distractions, (3) being enthusiastic, and (4) emphasizing the importance of what you have to say. For example, when you want to instruct your players on a new skill, organize them so everything you do is visible to them. Be sure that they are not facing any distractions, such as children playing at the other end of the field. It is also helpful to use a story, illustration, or event that will highlight the importance or focus attention on the instruction that is to follow.

### • Using Simple and Direct Language

Reduce your comments to contain only the specific information the player needs to know. For example, when a player makes a mistake in a defensive strategy drill, make sure your feedback is simple, focuses on one error at a time, and contains only information that the player can use to correct the mistake. Keep information simple and specific.

*The positive approach to communication is an essential element of good coaching.*

### • Checking With Your Athletes

Make certain that your players understand what you are saying. Question them so you will know if they understood the key points of your message. For example, let's say you are trying to explain how to run the basic slide drill. After showing them the drill, you can save time and frustration by asking your players before they practice the drill what are the key points of proper technique, where is the appropriate area to initiate the slide, and how should the baserunner respond to the throw to the base. If your athletes cannot answer these questions, they will not be able to participate effectively in the drill.

### • Being Consistent

Make sure your actions match your words. When a discrepancy occurs between what you say and what you do, players are affected most by what you do. "Actions speak louder than words." You need to practice what you preach if you wish to effectively communicate with your players and avoid the loss of credibility that comes with inconsistent behaviors.

### • Using Verbal and Nonverbal Communication

Your athletes are more likely to understand and remember what you have said when they can see it and hear it at the same time. Using the previous example, simultaneously demonstrating the basic slide drill while explaining the key points will result in clearer instructions.

## BEING A GOOD LISTENER

Remember, too, that you must be a good listener to be an effective communicator. Communication is a two-way street. Being receptive to your players' ideas and concerns is important to them and informational to you.

*Part of good coaching involves listening to your players.*

By listening to what your athletes say and asking them how they feel about a point, you can determine how well they are learning. Their input provides you the opportunity to teach what they do not understand.

## Essential Factors in Good Listening Skills

### • Listening Positively

Players want the chance to be heard and to express themselves. You can encourage this by using affirmative head nods and occasional one- to three-word comments (e.g., "I understand") while you're listening. The quickest way to cut off communication channels is by giving "no" responses or negative head nods.

### • Listening Objectively

Avoid prematurely judging the content of a message. Sincerely consider what your players have to say. They may have good ideas! A good listener creates a warm, non-judgmental atmosphere so players will be encouraged to talk and ask questions.

## • Listening With Interest

Being a good listener means being attentive and truly interested in what your players have to say. Look and listen with concern. Listen to what is being said and how it is being said. Establish good eye contact and make sure your body also reflects your interest in your player's message. Be receptive to comments that are critical of you or your coaching. Criticism is the most difficult communication to accept, but it is often the most helpful in improving our behavior.

## • Checking for Clarity

If you are uncertain of what your athletes are communicating to you, ask them what they mean. This will help to avoid misinterpretation.

*Being receptive to your players' thoughts and comments is important to them, and it also provides you with essential information.*

## SUMMARY

The ability to communicate with your players is critical in your role as a coach. It is a skill that involves two major aspects: speaking and listening. Coaches who are effective communicators get and keep the attention of their players, send clear and simple messages, and check to make sure their message is consistent with their actions. They also have good listening skills, which involve listening positively, helpfully, objectively, and with concern.

---

### SUGGESTED READINGS

Martens, R. (1987). *Coaches guide to sport psychology*. Champaign, IL: Human Kinetics.

# 21
# Maintaining Discipline

*Martha Ewing, Ph.D.*
*Deborah Feltz, Ph.D.*

---

### QUESTIONS TO CONSIDER

- What is the best way to prevent misbehavior?
- Should players be involved in establishing team rules?
- How should team rules be enforced?
- What are the key points of an effective plan for handling misconduct?

---

## INTRODUCTION

Coaches often react to their athletes' misbehaviors by yelling, lecturing, or using threats. These verbal techniques are used because we often do not know what else to do to regain control. Many discipline problems could be avoided, however, if coaches anticipated misbehavior and developed policies to deal with them.

*Harsh comments may prevent misbehavior, but they often create a hostile, negative environment that reduces learning and motivation.*

## PLAN FOR SOUND DISCIPLINE

Although threats and lectures may prevent misbehavior in the short term, they create a hostile, negative atmosphere. Typically, their effectiveness is short-lived. Hostility between a coach and team members neither promotes a positive environment in which it is fun to learn the game of softball nor motivates the players to accept the coach's instructions.

Sound discipline involves a two-step plan that must be in place before the misbehaviors occur. These steps are: (1) define team rules, and (2) enforce team rules.

Athletes want clearly defined limits and structure for how they should behave. You can accomplish this without showing anger, lecturing, or threatening. As the coach, it is your responsibility to have a systematic plan for maintaining discipline before your season gets under way. If you have taken the time to establish rules of conduct, you will be in a position to react in a reasonable manner when children misbehave.

*Athletes want clearly defined limits and structure for how they should behave.*

### Define Team Rules

The first step in developing a plan to maintain discipline is to identify what you consider to be desirable and undesirable conduct. This list can then be used to establish relevant team rules. A list of potential behaviors to consider when identifying team rules is included in Table 21-1.

Your players (especially if you are coaching individuals who are 10 years of age or older) should be involved in establishing the rules for the team. Research has shown that players are more willing to live by rules when they have had a voice in formulating them (Seefeldt et al. 1981). This can be done at a team meeting, early in the season. The following introduction has been suggested (Smoll & Smith 1979) to establish rules with players:

> *"I think rules and regulations are an important part of the game because the game happens to be governed by rules and regulations. Our team rules ought to be something we can agree upon. I have a set of rules that I feel are important. But we all have to follow them, so you ought to think about what you want. They should be your rules, too."*

Rules of conduct must be defined in clear and specific terms. For instance, a team rule that players must "show good sportsmanship" in their games is not a very clear and specific rule. What, exactly, is showing good sportsmanship? Does it mean obeying all the rules, calling one's own errors, or respecting umpires' decisions? The Youth Sports Institute has adopted a code of sportsmanship which defines sportsmanship in more specific terms (Seefeldt et al. 1981). This code has been reprinted in Table 21-2. You may wish to use some of the items listed as you formulate your team rules.

*Players are more willing to live by rules when they have had a voice in formulating them.*

Remember, you are a part of the team and you should live by the same rules. You should demonstrate the proper behaviors so the children will have a standard to copy. As a coach, you must also emphasize that behaviors of coaches as seen on television (such as screaming, throwing bats out of the dugout, and belittling and embarrassing players) are also examples of undesirable conduct!

## Enforce Team Rules

Not only are rules needed to maintain discipline, but these rules must be enforced so reoccurrences are less likely. Rules are enforced through rewards and penalties. Players should be rewarded when they abide by the rules and penalized when they break the rules. The next step, therefore, in developing a plan to maintain discipline, is to determine the rewards and penalties for each rule. Your players should be asked for suggestions at this point because they will receive the benefits or consequences of the decisions. When determining rewards and penalties for the behaviors, the most effective approach is to use rewards that are meaningful to your players and appropriate to the situation. Withdrawal of rewards should be used for misconduct. A list of potential rewards and penalties that can be used in softball is given in Table 21-3.

**Table 21-1.** Examples of desirable and undesirable behavior to consider when making team rules.

| Desirable Behavior | Undesirable Behavior |
|---|---|
| Making every effort to attend all practices and games except when excused for justifiable reasons | Missing practices and games without legitimate reasons |
| Being on time for practices and games | Being late or absent from practices and games |
| Attending to instructions | Talking while the coach is giving instructions |
| Concentrating on drills | Not attending to demonstrations during drills |
| Treating opponents and teammates with respect | Pushing, fighting, and/or using abusive language with opponents and teammates |
| Giving positive encouragement to teammates | Making negative comments about teammates |
| Bringing required equipment or uniform to practices and games | Forgetting to bring required equipment or uniform to games and practices |
| Reporting injuries promptly | Waiting till after the team roster is set to report an injury |
| Helping to pick up equipment after practices | Leaving equipment out for others to pick up |

**Table 21-2.** Youth sportsmanship code

| Area of Concern | Sportsmanlike Behavior | Unsportsmanlike Behavior |
|---|---|---|
| Behavior toward umpires | No disqualifying arguments | Arguing with umpires |
| | When questioning umpires, do so in the appropriate manner (e.g., lodge an official protest, have only designated individuals such as a captain address umpires) | Swearing at umpires |
| | Treat officials with respect and dignity at all times | Being ejected from game |
| | Thank umpires after game | |
| Behavior toward opponents | Treat all opponents with respect and dignity at all times | Arguing with opponents |
| | Talk to opponents after the game | Making sarcastic remarks about opponents |
| | | Making aggressive actions toward opponents |
| Behavior toward teammates | Give only constructive criticism and positive encouragement | Making negative comments or sarcastic remarks |
| | | Swearing at or arguing with teammates |
| Behavior toward spectators | No talking | Arguing with spectators |
| | | Making negative remarks/swearing at spectators |
| Behavior toward coach | Share likes and dislikes with the coach as soon as possible | |
| Rule acceptance and infraction | Obey all league rules | Intentionally violating league rules |
| | | Taking advantage of loopholes in rules (e.g., everyone must play, so coach tells unskilled players to be ill on important game days) |

The best way to motivate players to behave in an acceptable manner is to reward them for good behavior. When appropriate behavior is demonstrated, comment accordingly or be ready to use nonverbal interactions such as smiling or applauding. Some examples are:

- "We only hit into three double plays in that game; that's the fewest we ever had. Way to be!"
- "I know you are all very disappointed in losing this game. I was real proud of the way you congratulated and praised the other team after the game."
- "Do you realize that for our first five practices everyone was dressed and ready to play at 3 o'clock, our starting time? That helped make the practice go better. Keep it up! Let's see if we can make it a tradition!"

Penalties are only effective when they are

**Table 21-3.** Examples of rewards and penalties that can be used in softball.

| Rewards | Penalties |
|---|---|
| Being a starter | Being taken out of a game |
| Playing a desired position | Not being allowed to start |
| Leading an exercise or part of it | Sitting out during practice: <br> • until ready to respond properly <br> • a specific number of minutes <br> • rest of practice or sent home early |
| Praise from you <br> • in team meeting <br> • to media <br> • to parents <br> • to individual | Dismissed from drills: <br> • for half of practice <br> • next practice <br> • next week <br> • rest of season |
| Decals | Informing parents about misbehavior |
| Medals | |
| Certificates | |

meaningful to the players. Examples of ineffective penalties include showing anger, giving a player an embarrassing lecture, shouting at the player, or assigning a physical activity (e.g., running laps or doing push-ups). These penalties are ineffective because they leave no room for positive interactions between you and your players. Avoid using physical activity as a form of punishment; the benefits of softball, such as learning skills and improving cardiovascular fitness, are gained through activity. Players should not associate these types of beneficial activities with punishment.

*Rewards and penalties that are meaningful to your players and appropriate to the situation are most effective.*

Sometimes it is more effective to ignore inappropriate behavior if the infractions are relatively minor. Continually scolding players for minor pranks or "horseplay" can become counterproductive. If team deportment is a constant problem, the coach must ask, "Why?" Misbehavior may be the players' way of telling the coach that they need attention or that they do not have enough to do. Coaches should check to see if the players are spending a lot of time standing in lines while waiting for a turn to practice. Try to keep your players productively involved so they don't have time for inappropriate behavior. This is accomplished through well-designed practice plans. A lack of meaningful softball activity in your practices could lead to counterproductive or disruptive behavior.

*Misbehavior may be the players' way of telling the coach that they need attention or do not have enough to do.*

When the rules for proper conduct have been outlined and the rewards and penalties have been determined, they must then be stated clearly so the players will understand them. Your players must understand the consequences for breaking the rules and the rewards for abiding by the rules. Violators should explain their actions to the coach and apologize to their teammates. You must also follow through, consistently and impartially, with your application of

rewards for desirable conduct and penalties for misconduct.

Nothing destroys a plan for discipline more quickly than its inconsistent application. Rules must apply to all players equally and in all situations. Thus, if your team is in a championship game and your star player violates a rule that requires that he or she not be allowed to start, the rule must still be enforced. If not, you are communicating to your players that the rules are not to be taken seriously, especially when the game is at stake.

It is impossible to predetermine all rules that may ultimately be important during the season. However, by initiating several rules early in the season, a standard of expected behavior will be established. Positive and negative behaviors that are not covered by the rules can still be judged relative to these established standards and appropriate rewards or punishment can be given.

## Key Points to An Effective Discipline Plan

- Specify desirable and undesirable conduct clearly in terms of rules.
- Involve players in establishing the team rules.
- Determine rewards and penalties for rules that are meaningful to players and allow for positive interaction between you and your players.
- Apply rewards and penalties consistently and impartially.

## SUMMARY

Although threats, lectures, or yelling may deter misbehavior in the short term, the negative atmosphere that results reduces long-term coaching effectiveness. A more positive approach to handling misbehavior is to prevent it by establishing, with player input, clear team rules and enforcement policies. Use fair and consistent enforcement of the rules primarily through rewarding correct behaviors rather than penalizing wrong behaviors.

### REFERENCES

Seefeldt, V. Smoll, F., Smith, R.E., & Gould, D. (1981). *A winning philosophy for youth sports programs.* East Lansing, MI: Institute for the Study of Youth Sports.

Smoll, F., & Smith, R.E. (1979). *Improving relationship skills in youth sport coaches.* East Lansing, MI: Institute for the Study of Youth Sports.

# 22
# Developing Good Personal and Social Skills

*Annelies Knoppers, Ph.D.*

---

### QUESTIONS TO CONSIDER

- Which personal and social skills should youth softball coaches attempt to foster?
- Why are personal and social skills important?
- How can a coach bolster the self-esteem of athletes?
- How important is fun in youth sports?
- What can a coach do to ensure that sport participation is an enjoyable experience for athletes?
- What strategies can be used to help young athletes develop positive interpersonal skills?
- What is sportsmanship and how can it be taught?

---

## INTRODUCTION

Youth sport experiences can play, and often do play, a crucial role in the development of personal and social skills of children. The learning of these skills is different from that of physical skills in the following ways:

- Athletes will learn something about these skills whether or not we plan for such learning. If we do not plan for this learning, however, it is possible that the sport experience will be a negative one for some of the athletes. If we do plan, then it is more likely that the sports experience will be positive. Obviously then, this is different than the learning of physical skills. If you don't teach your players to do a specific sport skill, they will not learn anything about these skills. In contrast, at every practice and game, players are learning something about the personal and social skills regardless of planning.

- You as the coach continually model these skills. You may never have to model certain physical skills, but personal and social skills always show.

- The learning of these skills is also different from learning physical skills in that you cannot design many drills for the personal and social skills. These skills are a part of every drill and experience.

Coaches, therefore, can have an influence on children that goes well beyond the sport setting. The extent of this influence is increased when:

- the coach and athletes work together over a long period of time
- the athletes are participating in sport because they want to

290

• the coach is respected and liked by the athletes

Research has also shown that many parents want their children to participate in sports so their daughters and sons can develop personal and social skills through their sport experiences. Thus, coaches can and should work on the development of these skills in athletes.

The basic skills on which a beginning coach should focus are: self-esteem, fun in sport, interpersonal skills, and sportsmanship. Although self-esteem and interpersonal skills are not solely developed through sport, sport experiences can play a crucial role in the enhancement of these skills. In contrast, having fun in sport and showing sportsmanlike behavior are elements specific to the sport setting. Therefore, the coach is often held responsible for their development.

Regardless of the type of personal and social skills emphasized, the more coaches are liked and respected by the athletes and the more they work to create a positive atmosphere, the more likely it is they will influence the development of those skills in their players. The development of these skills is also likely to be enhanced when there is respect for teammates, opponents, officials, the spirit and letter of the rules, and the sport. Consequently, coaches who are very critical when athletes practice and compete, who are angry after a game or after errors, or who will do anything for a win, should change their ways or get out of coaching. Coaches who are unhappy or angry with athletes who make mistakes or lose contests retard the development of personal and social skills.

# PERSONAL AND SOCIAL SKILLS

## Self-Esteem

Self-esteem is the extent to which an individual is satisfied with oneself, both generally and in specific situations. The level of your athletes' self-esteem will affect their performance, relationships with others, behavior, enjoyment, and motivation. Thus, self-esteem plays a large part in the lives of your athletes as well as in your own life.

All of the players on your team will have feelings about themselves and their ability to do the things you ask of them. Those feelings were developed through experience. They will tend to behave in a way that reflects how they feel about themselves, making that behavior a self-fulfilling prophecy.

*The level of self-esteem in young athletes influences their performance level.*

### Examples

If Chris feels clumsy when playing first base, he is likely to mishandle the balls thrown to him frequently, which reinforces for him that he is clumsy.

If adults or kids always laugh at Susan's hitting technique, then she may be very self-conscious about hitting and always takes the pitch rather than swing at the ball.

A combination of a sense of failure and the derisive or negative comments from others can, therefore, lower self-esteem. Luckily, the level of self-esteem is not something that is fixed forever. It can be changed, not overnight nor with a few comments, but over a period of time with a great deal of encouragement. Consequently, enhancing levels of self-esteem requires consistent and daily planning by a coach. Positive changes in the self-esteem of players come about through the implementation of a coaching philosophy that places a priority on this change. Mere participation in sport will not automatically enhance Susan's self-esteem; her coach must plan for experiences and develop strategies that promote self-esteem.

• **Show Acceptance of Each Athlete**

Showing acceptance of each athlete means you must take a personal interest in each of your players regardless of their ability, size, shape, or personality. You need to be sensitive to individual differences and respect those differences. Coaches have to accept their athletes as they are. This does not mean that you have to accept or condone all their behaviors and actions. It means you should still show an interest in Tom even though he seems to whine a lot. You can talk to him about his whining, but you still should give him the same amount of attention as the other players, praise him for good behavior, encourage his effort, chat with him about his non-sport life, and compliment him when he does not whine.

You also can show your acceptance of each

player by demonstrating an interest in them as people, not just as athletes. Show an interest in their school life and their family as well as in the things they like and dislike. Take the time to make each athlete feel special as both a player and a person. All athletes should know that without them the team would not be such a great place to be.

- **React Positively to Mistakes**

In practice, be patient. Don't get upset with errors. Instead, focus on the part of the skill that was correctly performed and on the effort made by the player. Give positive suggestions for error correction. Helpful hints on how to do so are given in Chapter 4. Often in games, it is best to let mistakes go by without comment; simply praise the effort and the part of the skill that was performed correctly.

Kids usually know when they make mistakes and do not need an adult to point them out publicly. A coach who constantly corrects errors publicly not only embarrasses the players but may also be giving them too much information. Ask them privately if they know why the error occurred. If they know, then no correction needs to be given. Encourage them also to ask for help when they need it: "Coach, why did I miss that runner going home?" This type of questioning encourages self-responsibility and ensures that an athlete is ready to respond to your helpful suggestions.

- **Encourage Athletes**

Encouragement plays a vital role in building self-esteem. Coaches can never encourage their athletes enough. Athletes benefit most from coaches who are encouraging. Also, athletes who have supportive coaches tend to like sports more and are more likely to develop a positive self-image in sports. Encouragement is especially crucial for athletes who have low self-esteem, who have difficulty mastering a skill, who make crucial errors in a game, who are not highly skilled, and who are "loners." Encouragement conveys to athletes that the coach is on their side, especially if that encouragement is individualized.

*Appropriate Times for Encouragement*
- when a skill performance is partially correct
- when things aren't going well (the more dis-

couraging the situation, the more encouragement is needed)
- right after a mistake; focus on the effort, not the error
- when any effort is made to do a difficult task
- after each game and practice; do not let players leave feeling upset or worthless

*How to Give Encouragement*

In general, give encouragement by publicly naming the athlete so that recognition is directly received for the effort. If an athlete is struggling with something personal, then encourage the athlete privately.

- Publicly acknowledge each athlete's effort and skill as they occur
- Recognize each athlete as they come off the field in either a verbal way: "Good hustle in going for that ball, Joan!" or in a non-verbal way: a smile, pat on the back, or wink
- Praise players who encourage each other
- Monitor your behavior or have someone else observe a practice or game
- Be sincere; make the encouragement both meaningful and specific

*Examples*

After a player fails to catch a fly ball, instead of saying "Nice try, John!" say "Way to go back for the ball, John! Good hustle!"

After a player fell, instead of saying "I'm sorry you fell, Sue!" say "Way to get back up on your feet so quickly, Sue! I like your determination!"

Before a game, instead of saying "Play well in this game, OK?" say "I want all of you to try to do a little better than you did in the last game. I know you can do it!"

## Additional Tips for Enhancing Self-Esteem

- Credit every player with the win
- Applaud physical skills (or parts of them) that were performed correctly
- Praise the use of appropriate social skills and effort
- Be more concerned that each player gets a substantial amount of playing time than whether or not the team wins
- Give special and more attention in practices and games to non-starters
- Give athletes responsibilities; ask for help in

setting up team rules and in creating new drills

- Never call athletes by degrading names; poke fun at their physiques, abilities, or gender; or use ethnic, racial, or gender stereotypes or slurs

### Examples

Instead of saying (in a derogatory manner) "John runs like a girl!" say "John needs to improve his running."

Instead of saying (in a derogatory manner) "You played like a bunch of sissies!" say "We're going to have to work on being a bit smarter and more aggressive on the bases!"

Instead of saying "Paula really looks funny the way she runs the bases!" say "Of all the kids on this team, Paula seems to show the most determination in running to first. Good for her!"

## FUN IN SPORT

One of the main reasons why youngsters participate in sport is to have fun. Conversely, if they do not enjoy being on the team, players are more likely to drop out. Fun, therefore, is a crucial element in participation. Even though fun occurs spontaneously in sport, each coach should plan carefully to ensure that each athlete is enjoying the sport experience. The following ideas, when put into practice, increase the likelihood that the athletes and you will enjoy the team experience.

*A primary reason young athletes participate in sports is to have fun.*

- Conduct well-organized practices. Plan so all of the players have the maximum amount of physical activity that is feasible in conjunction with your objectives for a practice. Try to eliminate standing in line and waiting for turns as much as possible. If you have a large group, use the station method to keep all the players busy (see Chapter 4).
- Select drills that are suitable for the skill level of the players.
- Create enjoyable ways of learning skills; use innovative drills and games for practicing fundamental skills; and ask the players for suggestions and innovations.
- Watch the players' faces; if you see smiles

and hear laughter, your players are enjoying practice!

- Project fun yourself; tolerate some silliness; avoid sarcasm; and be enthusiastic!
- Use games or drills that end when each person has won or has performed a skill correctly a specific number of times.
- Give positive reinforcement.
- Encourage athletes to praise, compliment, and encourage each other; do not allow them to criticize each other nor use degrading nicknames.
- Make sure athletes regularly change partners in drills.
- Allow each child to learn and play at least two positions, if possible, and to play a lot in every game.
- Keep the atmosphere light; don't be afraid to laugh and to gently joke .
- Smile; show that you enjoy being at practice or at the games. Say "I really enjoyed this practice!" or "This is fun!"
- Take time to make each athlete feel very special. "The team could not function as well as it does without YOU!"

## INTERPERSONAL SKILLS

Since sport involves teammates, opponents, officials, and coaches, it can be a great place to develop good interpersonal, or people, skills. Sport, however, can also be a place where athletes learn poor interpersonal skills. The type of skills that the athletes learn depends on the coach. If you, for example, praise Deb because she encouraged Donna, then you are reinforcing a positive interpersonal skill and creating a cooperative environment. If you say nothing when you hear Mike call one of the Hispanics on the team Chico, then you are reinforcing a racial slur and an inequitable climate. Just as youngsters need to be taught the proper technique for fielding a ball, they also need to be taught how to relate to others in a way that bolsters self-esteem and sensitivity.

### • The Coach as Model

If you want your athletes to develop good people skills, you must consistently model the skills you wish them to develop. If you explain to them that they are not to yell and scream at each other and yet you yell and scream at them, you are giving a conflicting message: "Do as I say, not as I do." Similarly, if you state that your athletes may never criticize each other because it shows lack of respect and yet you criticize officials, you are sending a mixed message.

The greater the inconsistencies in your messages (that is, between what you say and what you do), the less likely that the players will develop good people skills. When you send mixed messages, players are likely to ignore what you say and imitate your behavior. Thus they will yell, scream, and criticize if you yell, scream, and criticize. As part of practice and game plans, therefore, you should give serious thought to the type of behaviors you wish your athletes to show to each other, opponents, officials, and coaches.

*The overriding principle that should guide your planning and behavior is to show respect and sensitivity to all others without exception.*

What does respectful behavior look like? According to Griffin and Placek, a player who shows respect for others:

- follows rules
- accepts officials' calls without arguing
- compliments good play of others including that of opponents
- congratulates the winner
- plays safely
- says "my fault" if it was
- accepts instruction
- will hold back rather than physically hurt someone
- questions coach and officials respectfully

Players show sensitivity to the feelings of others when they:

- pair up with different teammates each time
- cheer teammates on, especially those who are struggling
- help and encourage less skilled teammates
- stand up for those who are belittled or mocked by others
- are willing to sit out sometimes so others can play
- feel OK about changing some rules so others

can play or to make the competition more even
- refrain from using abusive names and stereotypic slurs, and from mocking others

The above behaviors are those you must model, teach, discuss, and encourage to enhance the people skills of your players. When you catch your players using these skills, praise them! Praise as frequently, if not more, the use of these skills as you would praise correct physical performance.

However, modeling, teaching, discussing, and encouraging these behaviors is not enough. You must also intervene when players use poor interpersonal skills. If you see such actions and ignore them, you are giving consent and approval.

When should you intervene? Griffin and Placek suggest that you should act when a player:

- criticizes teammates' play
- yells at officials
- pushes, shoves, or trips teammates or opponents
- ignores fellow teammates
- gloats and rubs it in when the team wins
- baits opponents, e.g., "you're no good"
- bosses other players
- will hurt someone just to win
- makes fun of teammates because of their shape, skill, gender, race, or ethnic origin
- calls others names, like "wimp," "stupid," "klutz," etc.
- blames mistakes on others
- complains to officials
- shares a position unwillingly
- ignores less skilled players
- complains about less skilled players
- gets into verbal or physical fights
- uses racial, ethnic, or gender slurs

Obviously, the lists of desirable and undesirable behaviors could be much longer. Their overall theme suggests that everyone should show respect and sensitivity to all people. This includes coaches, officials, teammates, and opponents. Coaches should be firmly committed to this "people principle" and should try to express it in their coaching.

### • Tips for Enhancing People Skills

- Explain the *people principle* and establish a few basic rules as examples of the principle (e.g., praise and encourage each other).
- Discuss how you feel when you are encouraged and when you are hassled. Ask them how they feel.
- Praise behavior that exemplifies the people principle.
- Work to eliminate stereotypic grouping of players for drills; don't let players group themselves by race, gender, or skill level. They should rotate so all will have a chance to work with everyone else.
- Call the entire team's attention to an undesirable behavior the first time it occurs and explain or ask why that behavior does not fit the people principle.
- Talk to the team about the use of racial jokes and slurs such as calling a Native American "Chief," an Asian American "Kung Foo," and an Hispanic "Taco," and the derogatory use of gender stereotypes such as "sissies," "playing/throwing like a girl," and "wimp." Explain how these behaviors convey disrespect and insensitivity and cannot be tolerated. Remember, too, that often these verbalizations by players echo those they have heard used by adults.
- Assign drill partners on irrelevant characteristics such as birthday month, color of shirt, number of siblings, etc.
- Stress the "one for all and all for one" concept.
- Monitor your own behavior.

## SPORTSMANSHIP

Sportsmanship is a familiar term that is difficult to define precisely. When we talk about sportsmanship, we usually are referring to the behavior of coaches, athletes, and spectators in the competitive game setting, especially in stressful situations. Thus, it is easier to give examples of sportsmanlike and unsportsmanlike behaviors than to define sportsmanship. For some examples, see Table 21-2 in Chapter 21.

### • Displaying Sportsmanship

#### Treatment of Opponents

*Sportsmanlike behaviors*

- At the end of the game, athletes shake hands sincerely with their opponents and talk with them for a while.
- An opponent falls, and Joan helps her back on her feet.
- John forgets his game shoes, and the opposing team lends him a pair.
- A team brings orange slices and shares them with their opponents.
- After the game, a coach praises the play of both teams.

*Unsportsmanlike behaviors*

- Joan stomps away in disgust after her team loses.
- An athlete verbally hassles an opponent, saying "You dummy! We're going to run right over you!"
- A player swears after the opponents score.
- After a player on the Stars is tripped by an opposing player, the Stars players decide they have to "get physical" too.

#### Treatment of Officials

*Sportsmanlike behaviors*

- The Stars coach saw a Blazers player touch the softball in fair territory before it went out of bounds. When the hit is ruled a foul ball, because the official thought the ball was touched by a player on the Stars, the Stars coach says nothing.
- The only Stars player who asks the official to explain a call is the captain. When other Stars players have a question, they ask the captain to speak for them.
- When the captain or coach speaks to an official, they do so in a respectful and courteous manner.

*Unsportsmanlike behaviors*

- The coach of the Stars throws the clipboard into the fence after an official calls a runner attempting to steal second safe on a close play.
- When an official makes two calls in a row against the Blazers, the coach yells "Homer!"

## Reaction to Rules

### *Sportsmanlike behaviors*

- Since league rules permit only one practice per week, the coach of the Tigers holds only one practice and schedules no "secret" practices.
- One league requires that all its players play an equal amount of time. Although some coaches ask lesser skilled players to "be sick" on important game days, the coach of the Panthers continually stresses that all players are expected and needed for every game.

### *Unsportsmanlike behaviors*

- The players on the Eagles are taught by their coach how they can break the rules without being detected.
- In order to get play stopped to allow the substitute pitcher more time to warm-up, the coach of the Falcons tells an athlete to fake an injury.
- Having the pitcher throw inside to the batter who follows the hitter who hit a home run.

## • Creating a Positive Climate

Because one of the goals of youth sports is to teach sportsmanship, a coach should know in which situations unsportsmanlike actions are most likely to occur. Often these situations are under the control of the coach and by changing them, the likelihood of unsportsmanlike behavior occurring decreases.

Situations when unsportsmanlike behavior is most likely to occur are those in which coaches, parents, and athletes view:

- competition as war rather than as a cooperative, competitive game;
- opponents as enemies rather than as children playing a game;
- abusive language towards opponents and officials as part of the game rather than as disrespectful and intolerant behavior;
- errors by officials as proof that they favor the other team rather than as evidence that officials make mistakes, too;
- winning as the only important part of the game rather than as being only a part of the game; and

- every game as serious business rather than as a playful, fun-filled, and skillful endeavor.

Obviously, then, a coach can decrease the likelihood of the occurrence of unsportsmanlike behavior by viewing youth sport as a playful, competitive, cooperative activity in which athletes strive to be skillful and to win and yet know that neither winning nor perfect performance are required. This type of attitude creates a positive climate and tends to enhance sportsmanship.

## • Teaching Sportsmanship

Stress-filled situations are the second type of condition under which unsportsmanlike behaviors tend to occur. These situations are created by the game rather than by the coach. As a coach, therefore, you must teach the athletes how they should behave in these situations. Sportsmanship can be taught.

### Role Modeling

Often the behavior of athletes in a stress-filled situation reflects that of their coach. If you stay calm, cool, and collected when the score is tied in the championship game, so will your players. To do so, however, you need to keep the game in perspective, which you can do by answering "no" to the following questions:

- Will the outcome of the game matter a month from now?
- Will it shake up the world if our team wins or loses today?
- Is winning more important than playing well and having fun?

Once you begin to answer "yes" to these questions, the game has become so important to you that you will be more likely to snap at the players and argue with the officials. Perhaps then you should ask yourself whether you should stay in youth sports.

On the other hand, if you can answer "no" to the above questions, you are probably approaching the game from a healthy perspective and are more likely to stay calm, cool, and collected and exhibit good sportsmanlike behavior.

### Using the People Principle

If children are to behave in a sportsmanlike

manner, they must be told specifically what is expected of them and must be praised for doing so. The people principle that was described in an earlier section requires all to show respect and sensitivity to others.

*The people principle is the basic guideline for sportsmanlike behavior.*

### Use Praise

When athletes follow the people principle, they should be praised.

### Examples

Sally helps her opponent back up to her feet. Coach immediately says "Way to be, Sally!"

You know Johnny thinks the official made a mistake, but Johnny says nothing. You immediately say "Way to stay cool, Johnny!"

### Eliminate Unsportsmanlike Behaviors

Ideally, when an athlete behaves in an unsportsmanlike way, you should say something immediately, and if possible, pull the child aside. Firmly indicate:

- that the behavior was inappropriate
- how it violates the people principle
- that you expect everyone to follow this principle
- that the athlete will be in trouble if the behavior is repeated
- that you know the athlete will try hard not to do it again

If the behavior is repeated, remind the athlete of the previous discussion and give an appropriate penalty. For examples of penalties see Chapter 21.

If athletes are to develop sportsmanship, you must not tolerate any unsportsmanlike actions. Sometimes it is easy to ignore a youngster's outburst because you feel the same frustration. By ignoring it, however, you are sending the message that at times such behavior is acceptable. Consequently, athletes will not acquire a clear sense of sportsmanship.

### Discuss Sportsmanship

Young athletes need to have time to discuss sportsmanship because it is so difficult to define precisely. Team meetings before or after a practice provide a good opportunity for discussion. The following tips should help you facilitate such a discussion:

- Ask opening questions such as "Who can give an example of sportsmanlike behavior? Unsportsmanlike behavior? Why is one wrong and not the other?"
- Read the examples from this section of both types of behaviors, and ask the athletes to label them as sportsmanlike and unsportsmanlike. Ask them to explain their reasoning.
- Encourage role playing. "What would it be like to be an official who is trying to do what's best and to have a coach or players yelling at you?"
- Discuss the relationship between the importance attached to winning and sportsmanship.
- Point out examples from college and professional sports. Ask the players to classify the behaviors and to give a rationale.

During these discussions, refrain from lecturing. Think of yourself as a facilitator who attempts to encourage discussion and an exploration of the people principle.

The extent to which your athletes display or react to sportsmanlike or unsportsmanlike behavior will determine the frequency with which you should hold such discussions at practice. To reinforce these discussions, you should point out examples of both types of behaviors at the brief team meeting after some game. Publicly praise each player who acted in a sportsmanlike manner and remind those who acted otherwise of your expectations. Remember also to continually examine your own behaviors to ensure that you are demonstrating the type of actions in which you want your players to engage.

## SUMMARY

The extent to which athletes develop personal and social skills through the sport experience depends a great deal on you. Just as physical skills cannot be mastered without planned and directed practice, neither can personal and social skills be developed without specific strategies and guidelines. If a coach does not plan such strategies nor set guidelines for the development of these skills, then the sports experience may be a negative one for the athletes. They may lose self-esteem, develop a dislike for sport participation, and drop out. Conversely, those athletes who feel good about themselves, their teammates, and the sports experience are more likely to stay in sport. Thus a coach has a responsibility to develop these skills.

## REFERENCES

Berlage, G. (1982). Are children's competitive team sports socializing agents for corporate America? In A. Dunleavy et al. (Eds.), *Studies in the sociology of sport*. Fort Worth, TX: Texas Christian University Press.

Coakley, J. (1986). *Sport in society* (3rd ed.). St. Louis, MO: Times/Mirror Mosby.

Griffin, P., & Placek, J. (1983). *Fair play in the gym: Race and sex equity in physical education*. Amherst, MA: University of Massachusetts.

## SUGGESTED READINGS

Martens, R. (Ed.). (1978). *Joy and sadness in children's sports*. Champaign, IL: Human Kinetics.

National Coaching Certification Program (NCCP I). (1979). *Coaching theory, level one*. Ottawa, Ontario: Coaching Association of Canada.

National Coaching Certification Program (NCCP II). (1979). *Coaching theory, level two*. Ottawa, Ontario: Coaching Association of Canada.

Orlick, T. & Botterill, C. (1975). *Every kid can win*. Chicago: Nelson Hall.

Tutko, T. & Burns, W. (1976). *Winning is everything and other American myths*. New York: Macmillan, Inc.

Yablonsky, L. & Brower, J.J. (1979). *The little league game*. New York: Times Books.

# 23
# Evaluating Coaching Effectiveness

*Paul Vogel, Ph.D.*

---

**QUESTIONS TO CONSIDER**

- Why evaluate coaching effectiveness?
- What should be evaluated?
- Who should evaluate coaching effectiveness?
- What steps can be used to conduct an evaluation?

---

## INTRODUCTION

Evaluation of coaching effectiveness should be based on more than being a good person, working the team hard, or having a winning season. The important question is: "Did the players make significant progress in individual technique, knowledge, tactics, fitness, and personal/social skills that were identified as objectives for the season?" The coaching evaluation described in this chapter provides a systematic but relatively simple procedure for estimating the effects of your coaching efforts and ways to improve your coaching effectiveness.

Coaches who have not benefited from coaching education programs, sport-specific clinics, high quality coaching as a participant, and/or have not had sufficient prior coaching experience are particularly susceptible to using the ineffective coaching methods. Although beginning coaches may benefit most from evaluating their coaching effectiveness, even experienced professionals can significantly improve their coaching abilities by completing an evaluation and then acting on the results.

*All coaches can significantly improve their coaching effectiveness by completing an evaluation and then acting on the results.*

Because the results of participation in athletics can produce positive and/or negative effects, it is important to determine the degree to which both are occurring.

1. Was the coaching effective in achieving its purpose(s)?
2. What changes can be made to improve the quality of coaching?

The evaluation described herein provides a relatively simple procedure for estimating the effects of your coaching efforts. It will also help you identify ways to improve your techniques.

## WHAT SHOULD BE EVALUATED?

The most important information concerning the effectiveness of your coaching activities can be obtained by determining the degree to which you meet the objectives identified for your players at the beginning of the season (see

Chapter 3), including technique, knowledge, tactics, fitness, and personal/social skills. The worksheet in Figure 23-1 (also included in reproducible form in Supplement 23-1) provides an example of how you can identify what should be evaluated.

*Coaching effectiveness should be judged by the degree to which players meet their objectives.*

For a discussion on how to use Supplement 23-1, see "Step 2: Collect the Evaluation Data."

## WHO SHOULD EVALUATE?

Initially, you should evaluate your own effectiveness. To ensure a broader and more objective evaluation, however, you should have others participate in the evaluation. For example, by using the worksheet illustrated in Figure 23-1, you might rate the majority of your players as achieving one or more objectives in the areas of sport skills, knowledge, tactics, fitness, and personal-social skills. Another person, however, may feel that what you thought was appropriate was in fact an inappropriate technique, an incorrect interpretation of a rule, an improper tactic, a contraindicated exercise, or an improper attitude. Obtaining such information requires courage on your part but it often yields important information to help you improve your coaching effectiveness.

*Self-evaluation is a valuable means for improving your coaching effectiveness.*

To obtain the most useful second party information, use individuals who meet the following three criteria:

1. They are familiar with your coaching actions.
2. They know the progress of your players.
3. They are individuals whose judgment you respect.

A person fulfilling these criteria could be an assistant coach, parent, official, league supervisor, other coach, local expert, or even one or more of your players.

The evaluation form illustrated in Supplement 23-2 provides another way to obtain information relative to coaching effectiveness as perceived by others. This form can be used for individual players (one form per player) or for the team as a whole (one form for the entire team). The purpose of the form is to obtain information that will reveal areas of low ratings. Follow-up can be completed in a debriefing session with the rater to determine the reasons for low ratings and to identify what can be done to strengthen the ratings. Debriefing sessions with this type of focus have proven to be highly effective in identifying ways to improve programs and procedures.

## WHAT STEPS CAN BE USED TO CONDUCT AN EVALUATION?

Four steps can be used to complete an evaluation of your coaching effectiveness. These are:

1. Identify the objectives
2. Collect evaluation data
3. Analyze the evaluation data to identify reasons why some coaching actions were ineffective
4. Implement the needed changes

### Step 1: Identify Objectives

The form illustrated in Supplement 23-1 can be used to identify the objectives you have for your players. Simply list the specific sport skills, knowledges, tactics, fitness abilities, and personal/social skills that you intend to develop in your players. Completion of this step clearly identifies what you believe is most important for your players to master and it provides a basis for later evaluation.

*A prerequisite to conducting an evaluation of coaching effectiveness is to clearly identify the objectives that you want your players to achieve.*

Once the objectives are identified, the remaining evaluation steps can be completed. This step also provides a good opportunity for you to obtain information from others regarding the appropriateness of your season's objectives for the age and experience level of your players.

Let your players know what the objectives are. Clearly specifying the objectives for your season has two other important benefits. First,

Coach *Sally Smith* Season *Summer* Date *August 15, 1992*

**EVALUATION QUESTION:** **Did significant, positive results occur on the objectives included in the performance areas listed below?**

| CATEGORIES — SEASON OBJECTIVES / ROSTER | Karen | Patty | Amanda | Corey | Dana | Sheronda | Marie | Keisha | Alana | Rika | Chris | Marty | Gail | Diane | | | | | Total (% yes) | Other notes |
|---|---|---|---|---|---|---|---|---|---|---|---|---|---|---|---|---|---|---|---|---|
| *Softball skills* | | | | | | | | | | | | | | | | | | | | |
| *Hitting* | Y | N | Y | Y | Y | N | Y | N | N | Y | Y | Y | N | Y | | | | | 64 | |
| *Bunting* | N | N | Y | Y | Y | Y | N | Y | N | Y | N | N | Y | Y | | | | | 82 | |
| *Fielding* | Y | Y | Y | Y | Y | Y | Y | Y | Y | N | N | Y | N | Y | | | | | 79 | |
| *Throwing* | Y | Y | N | N | Y | Y | Y | N | Y | Y | Y | Y | Y | N | | | | | 71 | |
| *Pitching* | N | Y | Y | Y | N | N | Y | Y | N | Y | Y | N | Y | Y | | | | | 64 | |
| *Catching* | Y | Y | Y | Y | N | Y | N | Y | Y | Y | N | Y | N | Y | | | | | 71 | |
| *Position play* | N | Y | Y | N | Y | Y | N | Y | Y | N | Y | Y | N | Y | | | | | 64 | |
| *Offensive strat.* | Y | Y | Y | N | Y | Y | Y | Y | N | Y | N | Y | Y | N | | | | | 71 | |
| *Defensive strat.* | | | | | | | | | | | | | | | | | | | | |
| *Lead runner* | Y | Y | Y | N | N | Y | Y | N | Y | Y | N | Y | Y | Y | | | | | 71 | |
| *Throw to cut* | N | Y | Y | Y | Y | N | Y | Y | Y | N | Y | N | Y | Y | | | | | 71 | |
| *Conditioning* | Y | Y | Y | Y | Y | Y | N | Y | Y | N | Y | Y | Y | Y | | | | | 86 | |
| *Personal skills* | | | | | | | | | | | | | | | | | | | | |
| *Cooperative* | Y | Y | N | Y | Y | Y | Y | Y | N | Y | Y | Y | Y | Y | | | | | 86 | |
| *Support team* | Y | Y | Y | Y | Y | Y | Y | Y | Y | Y | N | N | Y | Y | | | | | 86 | |
| *Resp. officials* | Y | Y | Y | Y | Y | Y | Y | Y | Y | Y | Y | Y | Y | Y | | | | | 100 | |
| *Good sports* | Y | Y | Y | Y | N | Y | Y | Y | Y | Y | Y | N | Y | Y | | | | | 86 | |
| Total (% yes) | 73 | 87 | 87 | 73 | 73 | 80 | 73 | 80 | 67 | 73 | 60 | 67 | 73 | 87 | | | | | | |

**EVALUATIVE RESPONSES:** Record your assessment of player outcomes for each objective by answering the evaluative questions with a "Y" ("YES") or "N" ("NO") response.

**Figure 23-1.** Coach's evaluation of player outcomes.

it clarifies in your mind what the player outcomes should be, and, therefore, provides a guide to organize your season and its practices. Second, effectively communicating to your players the objectives selected for the season will help them understand what you are trying to teach. Research on effective instruction reveals that clear specification of intended outcomes is strongly related to improved achievement.

## Step 2: Collect the Evaluation Data

The primary source of evaluative data should be your self-evaluation of the results of all or various parts of the season. However, assessments by others, combined with self-assessment, are more valuable than self-evaluation alone. Both approaches are recommended.

### • Completing the Coach's Assessment of Player Performance

After you have identified objectives and entered them in the first column of the "Coach's Evaluation of Players' Outcomes" form, enter the names of your players in the spaces on the top of the form. Next, respond either Y (Yes) or N (No) to the question, "Did significant improvements occur?" as it relates to each of the season objectives for each player.

Your decision to enter a Y or N in each space requires you to define one or more standards. For example, all of your players may have improved on a particular season objective but you may feel that several of those players did not achieve enough to receive a Y. However, an N may also seem inappropriate. To resolve this difficulty, clarify the amount of player achievement for each objective that you are willing to accept as evidence of a significant positive improvement. There is no exact method of determining how much gain is enough; therefore, you need to rely on your own estimates of these standards. The procedures suggested on the following pages of this chapter allow for correction of erroneous judgments. It is also possible to use a scale to further divide the response options: 0 = none, 1 = very little, 2 = little, 3 = some, 4 = large, and 5 = very large. Given ratings of this type, you may establish 4 and/or 5 ratings as large enough to be categorized as a Y and ratings of 3 or less as an N.

It is important to remember that players who begin the season at low levels of performance on various objectives have the potential for more improvement than players who are near mastery. Players who begin the season at high levels of performance often deserve Y rather than N for relatively small gains.

Injury, loss of fitness, or development of inappropriate sport skills, knowledge, tactics, or personal/social skills are detrimental effects that can occur and should be identified. In this situation the appropriate entry is an N circled to distinguish it from small or slight gains.

*You must decide if your players achieved significant gains on the outcomes you intended to teach.*

Completion of the coach's evaluation form will reveal your perception of the degree to which your players achieved important objectives. By looking at one objective across all players as well as one player across all objectives, patterns of your coaching effectiveness will emerge. (This is explained in more detail in Step 3.)

### • Obtaining Information from Selected Other Persons

To obtain information from others about your coaching effectiveness, use the form illustrated in Supplement 23-2. Remember, the form can be used for individual players or for an entire team. Note that the estimates of performance are relative to other players of similar age and gender participating in the same league. When using the form to rate individual players, ask the evaluator to simply place a check in the appropriate column (top 25 percent, mid 50 percent, or bottom 25 percent) for each performance area. When using the form to rate the entire team, estimate the number of players judged to be in each column.

Ratings of players' performance at the end of the season (or other evaluation period) are not very useful without knowing your players' performance levels at the beginning of the season. Changes in performance levels are the best indicators of your coaching effectiveness. To determine change in players' performance, it is necessary to estimate performance before and after coaching occurred. Pre and post ratings may be difficult to obtain, however, because of the time it requires of your raters.

A good alternative is to have the evaluators record pre and post ratings at the end of the evaluation period. For example, if three of your players were perceived to be in the top 25 percent of their peers at the beginning of the season and seven players were perceived to be in that performance category at the end of the season, the net gain in performance would be 4. Your desire may be to have all of your players move into the top 25 percent category during the course of the season. Such a desire is, however, probably unrealistic. Having 50 percent of your players move from one performance level to the next would be an excellent achievement.

It would be nice to look at your evaluations of player performance and the evaluations of their performance by others and see only Y responses or ratings in the top 25 percent. Such a set of responses, however, would not be helpful for improving your coaching effectiveness. An excessive number of high ratings probably signals the use of a relaxed set of standards.

All coaches vary in their ability to change behavior across stated outcome areas and across various individual players on a team. The incidences where individual players do not attain high ratings on various objectives are most useful to reveal principles of coaching effectiveness that are being violated. Accordingly, use standards for your self-ratings (or for the ratings by others) that result in no more than 80 percent of the responses being Y on the "Coach's Evaluation of Players' Outcomes" or moving from one category of performance to another when rated by others. As you will see in Step 3, ratings that are more evenly distributed among the response options are the most helpful for determining how your effectiveness may be improved.

Use of the form "Evaluation of Player/Team Performance Relative to Others" (Supplement 23-2) provides you with an estimate of changes in player performance as viewed by other persons whose judgment you respect. The relatively broad performance areas upon which the evaluation is based does not, however, provide enough detailed information to fully interpret the data obtained. Simply stated, more information is needed. Additional information can be obtained by using the technique of debriefing.

A debriefing session, based upon the information included in the completed evaluation form, provides a good agenda for discussing potential changes in your coaching procedures with the person who completed the evaluation. The debriefing should include these elements:

- Thank the individual for completing the evaluation form and agreeing to discuss its implications.
- Indicate that the purpose of the debriefing session is to identify both strengths and weaknesses, but that emphasis should be focused on weaknesses, and how they may be improved.
- Proceed through the outcome areas and their corresponding ratings, seeking to understand why each area resulted in large or small gains. For example, if a disproportionate number of the players were rated low relative to their peers on offensive skills, and there were very small gains from the beginning to the end of the evaluation period, you need more information. Attempt to determine what offensive skills were weak and what might be changed to strengthen them in the coming season.
- In your discussion, probe for the things you can do (or avoid doing) that may produce better results. Make a special attempt to identify the reasons why a suggested alternative may produce better results.
- Take careful notes during the discussion. Record the alternative ideas that have good supporting rationales and how they might be implemented.

The information collected in this way is invaluable for helping to identify good ideas for increasing your ability to help players achieve future season objectives.

*Coaching strengths are pleasing to hear, but identified weaknesses are more helpful for improving effectiveness.*

## Step 3: Analyze the Data

The first step necessary to analyze the information collected is to total the number of Y responses entered for each player across all season objectives. As a coach, you should seek to have all of your players make significant gains on all of the season's objectives.

However, from a coaching improvement viewpoint, it is necessary to have a mixture of Y and N responses across both the objectives and players. It is important that no more than 80 percent of your ratings be Y responses on the coaches' self-evaluation form. Tell other raters of your performance that no more than 80 percent of the players can be listed as showing improvement from one performance level to another in their pre/post estimates. It may be necessary to "force" the appropriate number of Y and N responses to meet this requirement.

When you have met the criteria of no more than 80 percent positive answers, divide the number of Y responses by the total number of objectives and enter the percent of Y responses in the row labeled "Total" for each player. Similarly sum the number of Y responses across players for each objective and enter the percent of Y responses in the column labeled "Total" for each season objective.

The pattern of Y and N responses that emerges from "forced ratings" can be very helpful in identifying the season's objectives and/or the kinds of players for which your coaching is most or least effective. By looking at the characteristics of the players who obtained the highest ratings versus those who achieved the lowest ratings, you may obtain good insight into things you can change to be more effective with certain kinds of players. This same type of comparison provides similar insight into how to be more effective in teaching certain objectives.

The real benefits of this kind of analysis come with evaluating the reasons why no or few players received Y responses. Answers to these "Why?" questions reveal changes you can make to improve your coaching effectiveness.

To help you determine why you were (or were not) successful with your coaching in certain player performance areas, a "Checklist of Effective Coaching Actions" was developed (Supplement 23-3). It provides a number of items you can rate that may help you identify ways to increase your coaching effectiveness. For example, if several of your players made insufficient progress in the offensive technique

of bunting, you could review the checklist to help determine coaching actions you used (or did not use) that may be related to helping players of similar skill level, fitness, or qualities of character. As you identify coaching actions that may have detracted from player improvement, note these and then alter your subsequent coaching actions accordingly.

- **Interpreting Unmet Expectations**

The above suggestions provide a systematic method for you to identify ways to improve your coaching ability. There are, however, other ways to interpret lack of achievement. The first and foremost (and nearly always incorrect) is to blame lack of performance on lack of talent or lack of player interest.

*Be sure to consider all possibilities for self improvement before accepting other reasons for unmet expectations.*

Effective coaches can improve the ability of their players, even those with only average abilities. The most helpful approach you can use to improve your coaching effectiveness is to assume that when the performances of your players do not meet your expectations, the solutions to the problems will be found in your coaching actions. This assumption may prove to be wrong, but you must be absolutely sure that you have considered all possibilities for self-improvement before accepting other reasons for unmet expectations.

If you determine that insufficient players' achievement is not likely to be due to ineffective coaching, it is possible that the expectations you hold for your players are unrealistic. Remember, motivation is enhanced when players perceive that they are improving. Expectations that are too high can have a negative effect on motivation and improvement. Reasonable expectations divided into achievable and sequential steps will result in appropriate standards of performance.

Allotment of insufficient time for teaching and learning the objectives selected for the season can also result in poor players' achievement, even when performance expectations and other coaching actions are appropriate. Players must have sufficient time to attempt a task, make errors, obtain feedback, refine their attempts, and habituate the intended actions before it is reasonable to expect them to demonstrate those actions in competition. Attempting to cover too many objectives within limited practice time is a major cause of insufficient achievement.

*If the changes identified to improve coaching effectiveness are not implemented, evaluation is a waste of time.*

### Step 4: Act on the Needed Changes

The primary reason for conducting an evaluation of your coaching effectiveness is to learn what can be done to improve the achievement levels of your players. Identifying the changes that will lead to improvements, however, is a waste of time if those changes are not implemented. Improvements can occur in planning, instruction, motivation, communication, knowledge of the game, and evaluation. Regardless of your level of expertise, by systematically evaluating your coaching actions, you can find ways to become more effective and more efficient.

### SUMMARY

By systematically evaluating players' performance on the intended outcomes of the season, you can estimate the effectiveness of your coaching actions. Limited achievement of players in some performance areas can signal a need to change some coaching actions. Use of the forms and procedures outlined in this chapter will reveal changes you can make to improve your coaching effectiveness. By taking action on the changes that are identified, you can make significant steps toward becoming a more effective and efficient coach.

**Supplement 23-1.**

# Coach's Evaluation of Players' Outcomes

Coach _____ Season _____ Date _____

| | EVALUATION QUESTION: | Did significant, positive results occur on the objectives included in the performance areas listed below? | | | | | | | | | | | | | | | | | |
|---|---|---|---|---|---|---|---|---|---|---|---|---|---|---|---|---|---|---|---|
| **CATEGORIES** | **SEASON OBJECTIVES** | R O S T E R | | | | | | | | | | | | | | | | Total (% yes) / Other notes |
| | | | | | | | | | | | | | | | | | | | |
| | | | | | | | | | | | | | | | | | | | |
| | | | | | | | | | | | | | | | | | | | |
| | | | | | | | | | | | | | | | | | | | |
| | | | | | | | | | | | | | | | | | | | |
| | | | | | | | | | | | | | | | | | | | |
| | | | | | | | | | | | | | | | | | | | |
| | | | | | | | | | | | | | | | | | | | |
| | | | | | | | | | | | | | | | | | | | |
| | | | | | | | | | | | | | | | | | | | |
| | | | | | | | | | | | | | | | | | | | |
| | Total (% yes) | | | | | | | | | | | | | | | | | | |

| EVALUATIVE RESPONSES: | Record your assessment of player outcomes for each objective by answering the evaluative questions with a "Y" ("YES") or "N" ("NO") response. |
|---|---|

Supplement 23-2.

# Evaluation of Player/Team Performance Relative to Others

Evaluator _____    Player/Team _____    Season _____

| EVALUATION QUESTION: | In comparison with other players in this league, how does the player (or team) listed above perform in the areas listed below? | | | | | | |
|---|---|---|---|---|---|---|---|
| **PERFORMANCE AREAS** | **PLAYER OR TEAM PERFORMANCE LEVELS** | | | | | | **COMMENTS** |
| | **SEASON START** | | | **SEASON END** | | | |
| | TOP 25% | MID 50% | BOTTOM 25% | TOP 25% | MID 50% | BOTTOM 25% | |
| | | | | | | | |
| | | | | | | | |
| | | | | | | | |
| | | | | | | | |
| | | | | | | | |
| | | | | | | | |
| | | | | | | | |
| | | | | | | | |
| | | | | | | | |
| | | | | | | | |
| | | | | | | | |
| | | | | | | | |
| | | | | | | | |
| | | | | | | | |
| | | | | | | | |
| | | | | | | | |

**INDIVIDUAL EVALUATION:**
For each performance area indicate, by placing a check in the top, mid, or bottom column, the start and end of the season performance level of the player.

**TEAM EVALUATION:**
For each performance area estimate the number of players (% or actual numbers) in the top, mid, or bottom performance levels at the start and end of the season.

## Supplement 23-3.
# Checklist of Effective Coaching Actions[1]

## Introduction

This checklist can be used to identify coaching actions that may be related to player achievement (or lack of achievement) of objectives. It, therefore, serves as an aid to identify the reason(s) why a player(s) did not achieve one or more of your expected outcomes. To use the checklist in this way, read the items in each content category (i.e., coaching role, organization, effective instruction) and ask yourself the question, "Could the coaching actions (or inactions) implied by this item have contributed to the unmet expectation?" Answer the question by responding with a "Yes" or "No." If you wish to rate the degree to which your actions (inactions) were consistent with the guidelines implied by the items, use the 5 point rating scale described below. Items which result in "No" or low ratings suggest that you are in discord with effective coaching practices. The process of seeking answers to specific concerns identified by your reaction to checklist items is an excellent way to obtain information most likely to help you become more effective as a coach.

## Directions

Rate the degree to which you incorporate each of the following items into your coaching activities. Check "Yes" or "No" or use the following 5 point scale where: 1 = Strongly Disagree, 2 = Disagree, 3 = Neutral, 4 = Agree, 5 = Strongly Agree.

| Item | Rating |
|---|---|
| | Disagree                    Agree |

**Coaching Role**

1. My primary purpose for coaching was to maximize the benefits of participation for <u>all</u> of the players.    (NO) 1 2 3 4 5 (YES)

2. The beneficial (individual techniques, knowledge, tactics, fitness, attitudes) and detrimental (time, money, injury, etc.) of participation were constantly in mind during planning and coaching times.    (NO) 1 2 3 4 5 (YES)

3. I communicated through actions and words that I expected each player to succeed in improving his/her level of play.    (NO) 1 2 3 4 5 (YES)

**Organization**

4. I completed a plan for the season to guide the conduct of my practices.    (NO) 1 2 3 4 5 (YES)

[1] Modified from: Vogel, P.G. (1987). Post season evaluation: What did we accomplish? In V.D. Seefeldt (ed.) *Handbook for youth sport coaches.* Reston, VA: American Alliance for Health, Physical Education, Recreation and Dance.

5. Performance expectations set for the players were realistic and attainable.　　(NO)　1　2　3　4　5　(YES)

6. I conscientiously decided which objectives must be emphasized in the pre, early, mid, and late season.　　(NO)　1　2　3　4　5　(YES)

7. Objectives for developing my practices were drawn from those identified and sequenced from pre to late season.　　(NO)　1　2　3　4　5　(YES)

8. The amount of total practice time allocated to each season objective was sufficient.　　(NO)　1　2　3　4　5　(YES)

9. My practices would be characterized by others as orderly, safe, businesslike, and enjoyable.　　(NO)　1　2　3　4　5　(YES)

10. Objectives were broken down as necessary to allow players to achieve them in several small steps.　　(NO)　1　2　3　4　5　(YES)

## Knowledge of the Sport

11. I am familiar with the rationale for each season objective selected and clearly communicated to my players its purpose and described how it is to be executed.　　(NO)　1　2　3　4　5　(YES)

12. I was able to identify the key elements of performance necessary for achievement of each season objective.　　(NO)　1　2　3　4　5　(YES)

## Effective Instruction

13. I clearly communicated (by word and/or example) the key elements to be learned for each objective included in a practice.　　(NO)　1　2　3　4　5　(YES)

14. Practice on an objective was initiated with a rationale for why the objective is important.　　(NO)　1　2　3　4　5　(YES)

15. Instruction did not continue without players' attention.　　(NO)　1　2　3　4　5　(YES)

16. Practice on an objective provided each player with many practice trials and with specific and positive feedback.　　(NO)　1　2　3　4　5　(YES)

17. During practice, I regularly grouped the players in accordance with their different practice needs on the season's objectives.　　(NO)　1　2　3　4　5　(YES)

18. I used questions to determine if the    (NO)  1  2  3  4  5  (YES)
    players understood the objectives
    and instruction.

19. The players sensed a feeling of control    (NO)  1  2  3  4  5  (YES)
    over their own learning which resulted
    from my emphasis of clearly identify-
    ing what they needed to learn and then
    encouraging maximum effort.

20. My practices were pre-planned and    (NO)  1  2  3  4  5  (YES)
    clearly associated the use of learning
    activities, drills, and games with the
    season objectives.

21. I evaluated my practices and incorpor-    (NO)  1  2  3  4  5  (YES)
    ated appropriate changes for subsequent
    practices.

## Motivation

22. My practices and games resulted in the    (NO)  1  2  3  4  5  (YES)
    players achieving many of their goals
    for participation.

23. I taught the players how to realistically    (NO)  1  2  3  4  5  (YES)
    define success in terms of effort and self-
    improvement.

24. An expert would agree, upon observing    (NO)  1  2  3  4  5  (YES)
    my practices, that I use a positive, rather
    than negative, coaching approach.

## Communication

25. There was no conflict between the verbal    (NO)  1  2  3  4  5  (YES)
    and non-verbal messages I communicated
    to my players.

26. I facilitated communication with the    (NO)  1  2  3  4  5  (YES)
    players by being a good listener.

27. Accepted behaviors (and consequences    (NO)  1  2  3  4  5  (YES)
    of misbehavior) were communicated to
    players at the beginning of the season.

28. Players were involved in developing    (NO)  1  2  3  4  5  (YES)
    or confirming team rules.

29. Enforcement of team rules was consistent    (NO)  1  2  3  4  5  (YES)
    for all players throughout the season.

### Involvement with Parents

30. Parents of the players were a positive, rather than negative, influence on player's achievement of the season objectives.  (NO)  1  2  3  4  5  (YES)

31. I communicated to the parents my responsibilities and the responsibilities of parents and players to the team.  (NO)  1  2  3  4  5  (YES)

### Conditioning

32. The intensity, duration, and frequency of the physical conditioning I used was appropriate for the age of the players.  (NO)  1  2  3  4  5  (YES)

33. I routinely used a systematic warm-up and cool-down prior to and after practices and games.  (NO)  1  2  3  4  5  (YES)

34. The physical conditioning aspects of my practices appropriately simulated the requirements of the sport.  (NO)  1  2  3  4  5  (YES)

### Injury Prevention

35. I followed all recommended safety procedures for the use of equipment and facilities.  (NO)  1  2  3  4  5  (YES)

36. I did not use any contraindicated exercises in my practices.  (NO)  1  2  3  4  5  (YES)

### Care of Common Injuries

37. I established and followed appropriate emergency procedures and simple first aid as needed.  (NO)  1  2  3  4  5  (YES)

38. I had a well stocked first aid kit at each practice and game, including players' medical history information and medical release forms.  (NO)  1  2  3  4  5  (YES)

### Rehabilitation of Injuries

39. None of the players experienced a recurrence of an injury that could be attributed to inappropriate rehabilitation.  (NO)  1  2  3  4  5  (YES)

**Evaluation**

40. I completed an evaluation of player improvement on the season objectives.

(NO)  1  2  3  4  5  (YES)

41. I identified the coaching actions (or inactions) that appeared most closely related to unmet player expectations.

(NO)  1  2  3  4  5  (YES)

42. I made the changes in coaching action needed to improve my coaching effectiveness.

(NO)  1  2  3  4  5  (YES)

# Section VI
# Sports Medicine and Training

# 24
# Conditioning Youth Softball Players

*Jean Foley, Ph.D.*
*Paul Vogel, Ph.D.*
*Eugene W. Brown, Ph.D.*
*Martha Ewing, Ph.D.*

QUESTIONS TO CONSIDER

- What are the energy production systems and how important are they to performance in softball?
- What are muscular strength, power, endurance, and flexibility and how important are they to performance in softball?
- What are the five principles of training that should be used when conditioning youth softball players?
- What are interval training, circuit training, and weight training and how can they be used to enhance the conditioning of your athletes?

## INTRODUCTION

Aerobics, anaerobics, strength, power, and endurance are some of the many terms that may lend confusion to your understanding of sport conditioning. The goals of this chapter are to provide you with an understanding of the basic principles of conditioning and how these principles apply to softball. The information will provide you with a more detailed understanding of the process involved in conditioning so that you can appropriately integrate these concepts into your coaching.

*Sport conditioning is the participation in physical activity, intended to enhance the energy production and muscular systems of the body, which may supplement and improve the performance of learned sport skills in future play.*

## ENERGY PRODUCTION SYSTEMS

Anyone who has played or watched softball knows that much energy is required to participate in the game. Sport scientists have discovered that the body can produce energy for physical activity by two different systems—the aerobic system and the anaerobic system. Muscle cells, which use the energy, can only store enough reserves for a few seconds of all-out exercise. When this immediate energy supply is used up, new energy is generated by one of these two energy "refill" systems.

## Aerobic System

The aerobic system is sometimes called the "endurance" system. In this system, food, the body's fuel, is converted into energy in the presence of oxygen. The aerobic system functions during long-duration, low-intensity exercise. This type of activity allows the body plenty of time to react effectively to the energy needs of the working muscle.

The aerobic system is very efficient because it converts fuel into energy with relatively little waste and produces little unnecessary heat. The aerobic system can function for extended periods of time because it can produce energy from fats, carbohydrates, and protein.

*Protein is not a major source of energy for exercise except in cases of extreme starvation.*

*Carbohydrates are stored in a limited supply in the muscles and liver, and can be used for both aerobic and anaerobic work.*

*Fats can be used only by the aerobic system. The virtually unlimited supply of this fuel, stored as adipose tissue or fat, is the basis for the long-term functioning of the aerobic system.*

Conditioning the aerobic system is a necessary base for energy system conditioning in softball. The reasons for this are twofold:

1. **Softball has an endurance component, particularly for pitchers and when playing doubleheaders.**

The softball player with a well-conditioned aerobic system is not as susceptible to fatigue toward the end of a contest. The delayed onset of fatigue in an aerobically fit athlete can also be a factor in determining how much high quality work can be accomplished during lengthy practice sessions and games.

2. **The body learns to "spare" carbohydrates.**

As the aerobic system is trained, the body learns to use more fat for fuel and to conserve carbohydrates for high-intensity (anaerobic) activities.

## Anaerobic System

High-speed or sprint-type activities require a refilling of the muscle cells' energy supplies at a faster rate than is possible by the aerobic system. In this situation, energy production switches over to a special, faster operating system that converts carbohydrates into energy without using oxygen. This system is called anaerobic, meaning "without oxygen." As with any emergency procedure, there are trade-offs that must be made. In order to gain the advantage of quicker replenishment of energy supplies, the anaerobic system suffers two limitations:

1. **Reduced energy yield.**

For each sugar (carbohydrate) unit consumed, the anaerobic system can produce only three basic energy units. On the other hand, the aerobic system can produce 39 energy units from each sugar unit. Therefore, the aerobic system yields 13 times more energy (per fuel unit utilized) than the anaerobic system.

2. **Lactic-acid build-up.**

The anaerobic system produces a byproduct called lactic acid that is not produced by the aerobic system. This chemical quickly builds up in fast-working muscles, causing temporary fatigue, discomfort, and impaired performance. The only way the body can get rid of lactic acid is to slow down and use the aerobic system to convert the lactic acid into usable fuel.

The anaerobic system can produce energy at high speed for about 30 to 90 seconds or at a moderate speed for about 90 seconds to three minutes before the oxygen debt forces the body to slow down so it can switch to the aerobic system. After a recovery period, the anaerobic system can be turned on again to give another short burst of high-speed work. This alternating of sprint work and recovery periods can be continued only until the body's stores of carbohydrates are used up or until the lactic acid removal system can no longer keep up with the rate of anaerobic work.

The energy production system responds to anaerobic training in three major ways:

*1. By learning to tolerate larger amounts of lactic acid*

The body physiologically adapts to tolerate larger amounts of lactic acid. Therefore, high-intensity work can be maintained for longer periods of time.

*2. By reducing the recovery period*

The body adapts by reducing the recovery time required before the anaerobic system can be used again.

*3. By increasing the rate at which the anaerobic system can operate*

Training adaptations increase the speed at which the system can produce energy.

A summary of the two energy production systems is presented in Figure 24-1.

## USE OF THE ENERGY SYSTEMS IN SOFTBALL

Now that the basic principles of the energy production systems have been presented, let's look at the sport of softball and determine where its requirements fit on the energy scale from aerobic to anaerobic. In analyzing the relative importance of the two energy systems in softball, the main concept to keep in mind is that performance time and effort determine the extent to which the aerobic, anaerobic, or both systems are called upon.

Softball generally can be considered a sport that places a moderate demand on the anaerobic system and a small demand on the aerobic system. The anaerobic system is used during high-intensity work such as sprinting around the

| Energy Production Systems | Characteristics |
|---|---|
| Aerobic | • produces energy from fuel with oxygen<br>• can use fats, carbohydrates, or protein for fuel<br>• high energy yield per fuel unit<br>• no lactic acid produced<br>• slow rate of energy production |
| Anaerobic | • produces energy from fuel without oxygen<br>• can only use carbohydrates for fuel<br>• low energy yield per fuel unit<br>• produces lactic acid as a byproduct<br>• fast rate of energy production |

**Figure 24-1.** Energy production summary.

bases. The aerobic system is used during recovery between the short bursts of activity and during longer periods of low-intensity work. Thus, it is important to condition both of these energy systems to be prepared best for the various demands of softball.

## MUSCULAR SYSTEM

In addition to requiring large amounts of energy, softball calls upon the muscles to produce forces for various activities. Throwing the ball requires upper body strength while hitting requires explosive power.

Muscles can produce force only by shortening or contracting. All muscle forces, therefore, are pulling forces and not pushing forces. For example, if you forcefully bend (flex) your knee, the muscles in the back of the thigh (hamstrings) are active. On the other hand, forcefully straightening (extension) the knee results in contraction of the muscles in the front of the thigh (quadriceps). Almost all muscles in the body operate in this paired fashion. As one muscle (or muscle group) shortens to pull a body part in a particular direction, the paired muscle (or muscle group) relaxes and allows the movement to take place. To cause movement in the opposite direction, the muscles simply reverse their roles. If it is desirable to hold a body part in a fixed position, both muscles in the pair exert force to stabilize the joint.

When planning to condition the muscular system for softball, several factors need to be addressed. In addition to the "muscle pair" concept, the components of muscular power, endurance, and flexibility; age and ability level of the players; and the specific muscular needs for participation in the sport must be carefully considered. These factors are covered in the sections that follow.

### Muscular Power

The force that a muscle can apply is called muscular strength. In softball, many of the movements not only require large muscular forces, but these forces must be exerted during short periods of time. This concept of rate of application of muscular force is called muscular power.

## Muscular Endurance

Power is the high-intensity component of muscular conditioning. There is also a low-intensity aspect, the muscular endurance component. Muscular endurance refers to the ability of a muscle to exert a sub-maximal force for a prolonged period of time.

Scientists have shown that there are actually different types of muscle fibers within a muscle. Some of these fibers, called fast-twitch or white fibers, are used primarily for brief, powerful muscular movements. Other fibers, called slow-twitch or red fibers, are mainly used for longer, low-intensity movements. As with the aerobic and anaerobic energy systems, the power and endurance components of the muscular system require different types of conditioning.

## Flexibility

Flexibility refers to the range of motion of a joint or the range through which the muscle groups can move the bones of a joint without causing injury.

Stretching exercises, used as part of a conditioning program to maintain or increase flexibility, are often ignored by coaches and athletes. However, flexibility exercises are an important component of a softball conditioning program. They may reduce the occurrence of certain injuries and enhance the performance of certain techniques.

### • Reducing injury potential

When muscles are worked hard, there is a temporary breakdown in their tissue. This breakdown is quickly repaired, but the muscle fibers become shortened unless they are stretched. A shortened, inflexible muscle on one side of the joint won't be able to readily stretch when its muscle pair on the opposite side of the joint fully contracts. The result may be a muscle tear (strain) or damage to the connective tissues of the joint (sprain). Flexibility exercises may reduce the occurrence of these types of injuries.

### • Enhancing performance

Lack of flexibility may inhibit or prevent the performance of certain techniques. For example, limited hip flexibility may retard a player's ability to field ground balls and move into throwing position. This is only one of the many examples of the influence of flexibility on performance.

## USE OF THE MUSCULAR SYSTEM IN SOFTBALL

Picture again a typical game of softball. How would you rate the three muscular factors of power, endurance, and flexibility in terms of their importance to successful performance? (See Figure 24-2.) Clearly, most of the actions in softball can be characterized as powerful movements. Along with powerful, high-force actions come a high risk of injury, so flexibility should also be a high priority in conditioning for softball. Finally, for the same reasons aerobic fitness is necessary in conditioning the energy systems for softball, a muscular endurance base is required by the repetitive nature of the movements.

## How to Condition for Softball

Now that we have examined conditioning, we can turn to the problem of how to develop programs to promote the kind of conditioning needed for softball.

You should now have a basic knowledge of the underlying concepts of conditioning. The contrasts between the aerobic and anaerobic ends of the energy production continuum have been described. Three critical aspects of the muscular system continuum (power, endurance, and flexibility) have been explained. Both the energy production systems and the muscular system have been analyzed in relation to their specific applications to softball. Now we come to the practical application of this information. How can you as a coach use the discoveries of the sport scientists to develop better softball players?

## Five Principles of Training

The following five principles of training should be used as guidelines for conditioning both the energy production and muscular systems.

**Where should the various positions in softball be placed?**

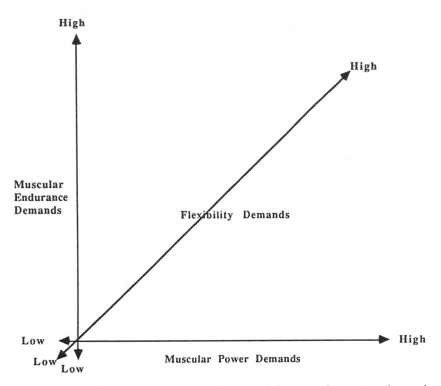

**Figure 24-2.** Graph showing the continuum of the muscular system demands.

## 1. Warm-Up/Cool-Down

Before beginning a training session or game, use jogging, calisthenics, softball-specific exercises, and stretching to prepare the body for more strenuous activity. A program for accomplishing this goal, as well as cooling down the body after strenuous exercise, is outlined in Supplement 24-1. Warm-up activities increase the breathing rate, heart rate, and muscle temperature to exercise levels. Warm-up also causes cartilage pads in the joints to absorb fluids, thereby increasing their shock-absorbing capabilities. It is a period in which the athlete becomes more aware of his/her surroundings (the field, fences, lights, etc.) and gradually reacquainted with the demands of more vigorous activity to follow. Providing the opportunity for your athletes to become aware of their surroundings and sensitive to the demands of the sport are important factors in reducing the potential for injury.

Proper warm-up can thus improve performance and reduce the likelihood of injury to the athlete. Note that the warm-up should not be used as a conditioning period. Having your players exercise too hard during warm-ups defeats the purpose of this period and may cause, rather than prevent, injuries. Stretching exercises are appropriate after a warm-up.

As the age of the athlete group increases, a greater amount of time is needed to warm up for exercises. Seven-year-olds may only need five minutes to warm up, whereas 18-year-olds may need as much as 10 to 15 minutes of warm-up exercises. It is, however, important to include a warm-up interval before practices and games even with the youngest athletes because this proper approach to training is more likely to persist as they grow older.

After a workout session or game, the body should be cooled down. This process should include light, aerobic activity (e.g., jogging) to help the body clear out any remaining lactic acid from the muscles and to reduce the pooling of blood in the extremities. This will reduce soreness and speed the recovery process in preparation for the next day's activities. The cool-down should also be followed by stretching exercises, as emphasized earlier, to help maintain flexibility.

## 2. Overload

In order to cause a change to take place in the energy production and muscular systems, a stress must be applied to these systems. Repeatedly demanding more than usual of a bodily system causes the system to respond by changing to a state in which it can more easily handle that stress. Overload does not mean placing an impossibly heavy work load on the system, but rather, asking the system to work harder than it is normally accustomed to doing, without reaching a work load at which injury may occur.

*Regulation of the overload is the basis of all conditioning programs.*

There are five factors that can be manipulated to produce an exercise overload within a workout:

### • Load

This is the resistance to muscular force. It can be the body, a body part, or any object, such as a weight, which is to be moved. Systematic variation of resistance (load) can be used to create an exercise overload to enhance the development of muscular strength.

### • Repetitions

This is the number of times muscular force is applied in moving a load. Conditioning of the aerobic energy-production system and enhanced muscular endurance result from progressively increasing the number of repetitions of muscular contraction.

### • Duration

This is the length of time muscular force is applied in performing a set (bout) of repetitions. Similar to a systematic increase in repetitions, increasing duration of exercise can be used to enhance the aerobic energy-production system and muscular endurance.

### • Frequency

The rate of exercise (number of repetitions for a given time unit) is the frequency. As frequency increases, exercises shift from having a conditioning effect on the aerobic energy-production system and muscular endurance to having a conditioning effect on the anaerobic energy-production system and muscular power.

### • Rest

The recovery interval between bouts of exercise, during which a muscle or muscle group is moderately inactive to inactive, is the rest period.* Note that rest for the anaerobic system also may occur when the frequency of exercise is reduced so the demands of the exercise are placed upon the aerobic system.

## 3. Progression

The overload principle must be applied in progressive stages. Conditioning must start with an exercise intensity the body can handle, allowing time for recovery from the physical stress before progressing to an increased work level. Overloading your athletes too rapidly or failing to allow sufficient time for them to recover between workouts can cause injury or illness rather than enhance their fitness.

A good example to keep in mind is the method by which muscles get stronger. A training overload actually causes a temporary breakdown of the muscle fibers, which are then repaired to an even stronger state. If the muscles are overloaded again before the repair period is over, the result may be further damage instead of adaptation. Coaches should be familiar with the signs of overtraining as outlined in Chapter 26 and should monitor their athletes closely to make sure they are progressing at a rate their bodies can handle.

## 4. Specificity

In order to activate the energy production systems, the muscular system must also be activated. Even though this relationship exists, it is important to carefully consider the desired nature of conditioning when selecting physical activity to achieve these goals.

Physical exercises have specific conditioning effects. Stretching the hip joints will have little, if any, influence on increasing the power of the muscles that move these joints. Exercises to strengthen the calf muscles will not increase the strength of the stomach muscles. Similarly, a well-conditioned gymnast is not likely to possess the type of fitness required for softball. Thus, when planning a conditioning program, it

*Longer rests are required for short, high-intensity exercise bouts. Shorter rests are required for long, low-intensity exercise bouts.

is important to first assess the demands of softball on your players in order to select exercises and manipulate the overload factors to help condition your players to meet these specific demands.

The specific components of the energy and muscular systems can be conditioned by application of the following general guidelines to overload these systems. However, these guidelines must be applied in conditioning the energy and muscular systems associated with the specific demands of softball.

### Training the Energy Production Systems

- Aerobic system—use endurance activities involving moderate exercise intensity of large body segments or the whole body. Some examples include running the perimeter of the field, swimming laps, running, and bicycling long distances.
- Anaerobic system—use "sprint" type activities involving very intense exercise of large body segments or the whole body. The same exercises, as listed for aerobic training, are appropriate activities for anaerobic training. However, distances must be reduced and the intensity increased. Sprinting the bases would have a more specific training effect for softball. By sprinting the bases, players would be concomitantly developing their techniques along with anaerobic conditioning.

### Training the Muscular System

- Power—use exercises, by specific muscle groups, involving the rapid application of relatively large forces and few repetitions.
- Endurance—use exercises, by specific muscle groups, involving the application of relatively small forces and many repetitions.
- Flexibility—use slow and sustained (6 to 30 seconds) stretching of specific muscle groups to the point of slight discomfort. Don't bounce!

### 5. Reversibility

It is not enough to plan and carry out a developmental conditioning program. Once an athlete's body attains a certain fitness level, a maintenance program is necessary to prevent the conditioning benefits from being lost.

Studies on athletes have shown that even starting players will experience a decrease in fitness level during the competitive season unless provisions are made to maintain conditioning throughout the season. The maintenance program does not have to be as frequent or as intense as the build-up program, but without a minimal program of this type, the hard-earned fitness will gradually be lost.

## METHODS FOR CONDITIONING

*Regulation of the exercise overload is the basis for all conditioning programs.* As previously stated, this can be accomplished by manipulating the factors of load, repetition, duration, frequency, and rest. There are three distinct training methods that can be used to effectively manipulate these factors to enhance conditioning. These methods are *interval training, circuit training,* and *weight training.*

### 1. Interval Training

This type of training was first used in training runners. Interval training, however, has been used in many sports, including softball. Interval training involves a period of vigorous exercise followed by a recovery period. It functions by using aerobic and anaerobic activities to condition the energy production systems. By gradually increasing the duration, intensity, and number of exercise bouts and by decreasing the rest interval between bouts, an overload can be achieved.

Interval training can be adapted to softball by alternating bouts of intense practice on basic skills, such as throwing, with recovery periods. In fact, a series of practice sessions can be structured with an interval training basis. The first session would consist of relatively low-intensity exercises of short duration with relatively long rest intervals; whereas, in subsequent practice sessions, the exercise intensity and duration would be increased and the number and duration of rest intervals would be decreased. It should be noted that in interval training, rest periods can be used for rest, water breaks, strategy sessions, team organization, and light aerobic activity.

The specific conditioning components enhanced by an interval training program depend upon the nature of the exercises included in the program. A systematic interval training program can improve the energy production systems (aerobic and anaerobic) as well as the strength and endurance of specific muscle groups that are exercised. A year-round interval training program for highly skilled and motivated players who are 14 years of age or older is included in Supplement 24-2.

## 2. Circuit Training

This type of training involves participation in a variety of activities in rapid succession. These activities are conducted at various locations (stations) around the softball field. The team is divided so that an equal number of players are at each station. When the circuit begins, all players attempt to perform their best at the tasks assigned to each station within a set time. Successive stations should differ in the demand they place on the body. For example, an intense arm exercise (e.g., swinging a heavy bat) should not be followed by a throwing drill. Recovery occurs as the groups rotate, within a specified time interval, to the next station and as subsequent stations differ in their demands upon the body.

In circuit training an exercise overload is produced by:

- increasing the number of stations in the circuit
- increasing the number of repetitions or work intensity at one or more stations
- increasing the time for exercise at each station
- increasing the number of times the circuit is completed
- decreasing the recovery period between stations

The variety of activities that can be included in a circuit provides the opportunity to be flexible in creating different and specific exercise overloads as well as simultaneously enhancing skill. Supplement 24-3 contains an example of a softball training circuit and recording form, which can be photocopied as is, as well as a blank form upon which you can implement your own training circuit to meet the specific needs of your players.

## 3. Weight Training

This type of training involves the lifting of weights to produce an exercise overload. In weight training, a variety of sub-maximal lifts are performed to produce increased strength, power, and endurance in the specific muscle groups that are exercised. In general, weight training involves applying the "Five Principles of Training" to produce increases in muscular strength.

Following the "Five Principles of Training," the first part of a weight training routine is the warm-up and stretching program. The weight resistance is the overload, which is increased in a progression as the athlete's workout record indicates gains in strength. Analysis of the strength requirements of softball (specificity) has resulted in the list of exercises outlined in Supplement 24-2. The cool-down and post-lifting stretching routine decreases muscle soreness and prevents loss of flexibility. Finally, once strength gains are achieved, the maintenance program must be used to avoid reversal of strength increases acquired during the developmental program.

In weight training, an exercise overload can be produced by varying the:

- exercise load
- number of repetitions per set
- frequency of exercise during each set
- number of sets
- length of rest interval between exercise sets

The exercise load determines the number of repetitions of an exercise an athlete can perform during each set. Generally, no fewer than eight repetitions per set of each exercise are recommended when attempting to increase muscular strength for softball. However, if increased muscular endurance is the goal of a particular weight training exercise, (a) the load should be decreased to permit a much greater number of repetitions, (b) the number of sets should be increased to three or more, and (c) the rest intervals between sets should be decreased. On the other hand, if increase in muscular power is the goal, this can be achieved by rapidly and repeatedly lifting a relatively heavy load 8 to 12 repetitions per set.

It should be noted that it is possible to train

some muscle groups to increase power and others to increase endurance. The degree to which either component increases depends upon the specific nature of the overload condition.

Several factors should be carefully considered before engaging your players in a weight training program. These factors include:

- **Age of the athletes**

A weight training program for softball is not recommended for players under 14 years of age.

- **Level of interest**

A weight training program is not an essential element for participants in a recreational league. However, a weight training program can be beneficial to highly skilled players who are interested in participating in a very competitive league.

- **Availability of facilities and equipment**

Sites and equipment for weight training may not be accessible. Before encouraging your athletes to participate in a weight training program, some investigation of availability is needed.

- **Availability of qualified adults**

Before encouraging your players to participate in a particular weight training program, a qualified adult must be available to supervise the weight room and to provide instruction in proper spotting and performance techniques for each of the suggested exercises.

Because of the great variety of weight training equipment and the availability of many books and guides to weight training, only general guidelines are presented here. A suggested program of weight training exercises appropriate for the highly skilled softball player who is 14 years of age or older is included in Supplement 24-2. These exercises can be done using either free weights or weight machines. The guidelines given cover training schedules and how to fit a weight training program into the overall plan of the season. Specific techniques and explanations of weight training exercises can be found in manuals available in most local bookstores. Some references are:

- *Strength Training by the Experts* by Daniel P. Riley

(2nd edition, Leisure Press, 1982). Covers a variety of equipment, including free weights, Nautilus, and Universal. Explains which muscle groups are used in each exercise.
- *Weightlifting for Beginners* by Bill Reynolds (Contemporary Books, 1982). Designed primarily for free weights and at-home weight training.

## ECONOMICAL TRAINING

The relative importance of conditioning for softball must be put into perspective with the importance of meeting the cognitive, psycho-social, strategy, and sport techniques needs of your players. As a softball coach, you must address all of these needs, to varying degrees, during practices and games. However, because of the limited amount of time available to meet the needs of your players, whenever possible, you should plan activities that simultaneously meet needs in more than one area. This approach is referred to as economical training. If practice sessions are carefully planned, it is possible to devise activities that simultaneously meet needs in more than one area. For example, the intensity, duration, and structure of a fielding drill could be organized to enhance components of conditioning and strategy, as well as techniques of fielding.

*It is easier to get 14-year-olds in condition to play than it is to make up for the years in which they were not taught the techniques of the game.*

The concept of economical training is presented here because many coaches erroneously set aside blocks of time within their practices for conditioning-only activities. Push-ups, sit-ups, sprints, and distance running are typical of what is included in these conditioning-only blocks of time. With youth players who have not achieved a high level of mastery of the techniques of the game, conditioning-only activities are not recommended. Practice time needs to be spent on learning the techniques and strategies of the game of softball, with conditioning an accompanying outcome as the result of planned economical training. As players develop a higher level of mastery of the techniques of softball, conditioning-only activities could be included in practices. However, they should be made as closely related to softball as possible.

## SUMMARY

In this chapter you have learned how the energy and muscular systems work, how they are used in softball, and how to condition these systems. Although separate conditioning-only workouts were not recommended for the under-14 age group, guidelines were given for incorporating the principles of training into the regular practices for the double purpose of skill improvement and enhanced conditioning (economical training). Athletes begin to require and benefit from supplementary programs for conditioning the energy and muscular systems around the age of 14. Examples of such programs have been provided, with guidelines for varying the training at different points in the year. Suggested schedules and workout routines to guide this training are provided in the supplements.

A basic knowledge of the scientific principles of physical conditioning will help you design effective practices and training sessions. It will also help you communicate to your athletes the importance of each type of conditioning activity you use. Conveying this understanding to your players will not only make them more knowledgeable, but will also help them develop good lifelong habits and attitudes towards exercise and fitness.

### SUGGESTED READINGS

Fox, E.L. (1979). *Sports physiology.* Philadelphia: W.B. Saunders.
Lamb, D.R. (1984). *Physiology of exercise* (2nd ed.). New York: Macmillan.
Sharkey, B. (1984). *Physiology of fitness* (2nd ed.). Champaign, IL: Human Kinetics Publishers.
Stone, W.V., & Knoll, W.K. (1978). *Sports conditioning and weight training.* Boston: Allyn and Bacon.

Supplement 24-1.

# Warm-Up, Cool-Down, and Stretching Activities for Softball

## Introduction

The players' preparation for each practice and game should begin with a warm-up session and should be followed by a cool-down period. Warm-up and cool-down activities should be conducted at light to moderate intensities and should be followed by stretching exercises.

## Warm-up

Warm-up activities should be performed to increase the breathing rate, heart rate, and muscle temperature to exercise levels. These are done to prepare the body for the demands of subsequent strenuous activities. Additionally, warm-ups enhance the players' awareness for their surroundings. Warm-ups can also be used as a valuable introduction in setting the tone of the players' attitude toward the activity to follow. Warm-ups for sport should involve the regions of the body upon which more intense exercise demands will be placed during training for and participation in the sport. Thus, with softball, virtually all regions of the body should be prepared. The following categories included some examples of warm-ups that can be used for softball.

### Light Aerobic/General Warm-ups

- Jogging
- Jogging in place
- Jumping jacks

### Light Aerobic/Softball-Specific Warm-ups

- Jogging the bases
- Playing catch with a partner

### Body Region-Specific Warm-ups

- Neck rolls—The head is rolled from shoulder, to chest, to opposite shoulder, and the procedure is reversed and repeated. (Note: Do not make complete head circle. There is potential for compression of the vertebrae when the neck is hyperextended.)

- Shoulder circles—With arms horizontal and to the side of the body, small circular rotations of the arms are made. These circles are gradually increased. This pattern is then repeated; however, the arms are rotated in the opposite direction.
- Trunk circles—While standing with the feet shoulder-width apart and the hands on the hips, the trunk is moved in a circular manner. (Note: Avoid an excessive arch of the low-back by keeping the head in an upright position.)

## Stretching

Stretching should be performed by slowly and gently extending each muscle group and joint to the point of slight discomfort. This position should be held for 6 to 30 seconds. The stretch should then be released and repeated in the same manner two or more times. Bouncing or fast, jerky movements are inappropriate in that they activate the muscles' stretch reflex mechanism and, therefore, limit rather than enhance flexibility.

Stretching exercises, used as part of a softball conditioning program to maintain or increase flexibility, may reduce the occurrence of certain injuries, such as muscle strains and joint sprains, and may enhance performance of certain techniques. Because softball involves virtually all major muscle groups and joints of the body, a variety of flexibility exercises, targeted at these regions, should be a part of each pre- and post-practice and game. The following flexibility exercises are some examples that are appropriate for softball.

- Calf stretch—With the legs straddled in a forward-backward alignment, the knee of the back leg is bent while the entire sole of the back foot maintains contact with the ground. By switching the position of the feet, the other calf is stretched.
- Kneeling quad stretch—From a kneeling position, the hip is pressed forward. By switching the positions of the legs, the other quadriceps muscle and hip joint are stretched.

Note that this exercise also stretches the trunk.

- Seated straddle (groin stretch)—From a seated position with the legs straddled, the trunk is moved forward. The head should be kept upright to reduce pressure on the lower back.
- Butterfly (groin stretch)—In a seated position, place the soles of the feet together with the knees bent no more than 90 degrees. Grasp the ankles with the hands and apply pressure with the elbows to the inside of the legs to rotate the legs outward. Keep the back straight with the head in an upright position.
- Trunk and hip stretch—From a supine position, both arms are placed 90 degrees from the trunk. The head is turned toward one of the outstretched arms while bringing the opposite leg (90 degrees from the trunk) over the midline of the body and toward the ground. This exercise should be performed on both sides.
- Shoulder stretch—Bend the elbow and position the arm behind the head. The hand of the opposite arm grasps the bent elbow and slowly pulls it toward the midline of the trunk. To stretch the other shoulder, the roles of the arms are switched.
- Shoulder stretch—Stand with your side to the fence and extend your arm and grasp the fence as far behind you as possible to feel stretch of the pectoral muscles (across the front of the chest). To stretch the other shoulder, the roles of the arms are switched.
- Shoulder stretch—Extend one arm straight ahead at shoulder height. Use opposite arm to hook extended arm between the elbow and shoulder and pull to stretch the muscles across upper back. Switch the role of the arms to stretch the other shoulder and arm.

## Cool-Down

The importance of cooling down has not received sufficient emphasis among coaches of young athletes. Cool-down sessions are infrequently used to end a practice session and are rarely used following a game. A cool-down period helps to:

- clear out lactic acid accumulated in the muscles

- reduce the pooling of blood in the extremities
- prevent the loss of flexibility that may accompany intense muscular exercise

Like the warm-up, cool-down activities should include movements similar to those included in the practice or game. Thus, the warm-up and stretching activities, previously listed, are appropriate for the cool-down. Have your athletes perform the cool-down exercises first, then the stretching activities.

## Supplement 24-2.

# Year-Round Conditioning Program

## Introduction

This supplement contains information on a year-round conditioning program. It is directed at conditioning the energy production system, through a program of interval training, and the muscular system, through a weight training program. This year-round program is appropriate for the highly motivated player who is 14 years of age or older. It is for players who have chosen to concentrate on softball and wish to maximize their performance through enhanced conditioning on a year-round basis. This program is NOT for beginning players and/or players below the age of 14 years who would derive greater benefit by devoting their time to learning and perfecting the techniques of softball.

## Interval Training Program

Interval training is a method for developing the anaerobic energy-production system while maintaining and/or enhancing a previously established base of aerobic fitness. This type of training uses alternating periods of short-duration, high-intensity anaerobic ("sprint" type) exercises with longer periods of moderate-to low-intensity aerobic exercises.

The training outlines provided in this supplement can be used with different modes of exercise, depending on individual preference and the availability of equipment and facilities. Swimming, jogging and running, and/or bicycling are modes of exercise suggested for interval training in softball. Specific distances are not indicated in this supplement because of the variety of exercises possible and because of variations in individual fitness. All players should, however, maintain a record of distances covered on individual forms provided in this supplement so their progress can be assessed. Distance records can be kept in yards, meters, miles, kilometers, blocks, or laps.

An important concept to keep in mind when planning an interval training program is that the program should progress to a point where it places a similar aerobic and anaerobic demand on the athlete as that of a hard-played game of softball. This type of work load in an interval training program conditions the athletes to the demands they will be confronted with during competition. Regulation of the duration and intensity of exercise, as well as the rest intervals, are the components of an interval training program that can be manipulated to achieve the desired exercise levels.

The interval training program included in this supplement is divided into five phases. These phases are briefly described and followed by forms that can be used by athletes to keep records of their progress.

- Pre-season Aerobic/Anaerobic Transition Program—This four-week program is used to prepare athletes for high intensity anaerobic conditioning after they have developed a good aerobic fitness base (see Table 24-1s).
- Pre-season Anaerobic Developmental Interval Training Program—This is an eight-week program to be started 10 weeks before the first game (see Table 24-2s). The program should be preceded by anaerobic training and the four-week "Aerobic/Anaerobic Transition Program."

- In-Season Anaerobic Maintenance Program—This program should be completed once, a week starting two weeks before the first game and continuing through the end of the season (see Table 24-3s).
- Post-Season Aerobic Program—This program involves rhythmical, low intensity aerobic activities such as swimming, jogging, running, and bicycling for three days per week to enhance aerobic fitness (see Table 24-4s).
- Post-Season Anaerobic Maintenance Program—This program should be done once a week to maintain anaerobic fitness levels during the aerobic phase of off-season conditioning (see Table 24-4s).

## Weight Training Program

Weight training for softball should focus on the development of muscular power, or the ability to quickly exert large muscular force. The load should be lifted explosively, then returned to the starting position slowly. Generally, the larger muscle groups should be exercised first. Also, the same muscle groups should not be exercised in succession. Table 24-5s contains weight-lifting exercises that can be used to meet the specific requirements of softball. They are arranged in an appropriate order.

Since the weight training exercises listed can be done using a variety of equipment, details of technique and an explanation of procedures for each exercise will not be given here. Many good guides for weight training are available in local bookstores. A few examples of such guides that contain explanations of correct technique and details for each specific exercise are:

- *Sports Conditioning and Weight Training* by William J. Stone and William A. Kroll (Allyn & Bacon, 1978). This book is designed to offer sound, systematic training programs for those who wish to apply strength and conditioning techniques to specific sports.
- *Strength Training by the Experts* by Daniel P. Riley (2nd edition, Leisure Press, 1982). This book covers a variety of lifting equipment, including free weights, Universal equipment, and Nautilus equipment, and explains which muscle groups are used in each exercise.
- *Weightlifting for Beginners* by Bill Reynolds (Contemporary Books, 1982). This book is designed primarily for free weights and at-home weight lifting.

Year-round conditioning for muscular power can be divided into three parts: pre-season (developmental), in-season (maintenance), and post-season (developmental). Pre-season and post-season workouts have improvement in muscular power as their goals. In-season workouts are done less frequently and should be used to maintain the muscular fitness developed during the off-season.

## Pre-season Weight Training

Athletes new to weight training should start a developmental program at least three months before the first competition. Overloaded muscles require about 48 hours to repair and recover sufficiently, so a lifting schedule of three days per week with a minimum of one day off between workouts will give best results.

For the first one to two weeks, the athlete should do one exercise 8 to 12 times (repetitions), then move on to the next exercise until each exercise in the weight training program has been covered. This series of repetitions of each exercise is called a set.

The appropriate weight load or resistance is a load the athlete can lift properly a minimum of 8 times, but is not so light that it can be lifted more than 12 times. Some experimenting with weight loads will be necessary to determine correct starting weights for each exercise. Once these weight loads are determined, they should be recorded on the "Weight Training Program Checklist" included in this supplement (see Table 24-6s).

During this first phase of the weight training program (two weeks), the athlete should master the proper lifting technique and work through the initial muscle soreness that accompanies learning the correct weight loads. After this initial phase, the work can be increased to two sets while maintaining the initial weight levels for 8 to 12 repetitions per exercise. Two sets of the same exercise are completed before the next exercise is done. This second phase also lasts two weeks.

In the third phase, three full sets are done during each workout. Three full sets of 8 to 12

**Table 24-1s.** Pre-Season Aerobic/Anaerobic Transition Program.

**(To be started 14 weeks before the first game)**

Name_____

The information at the top of each week's schedule specifies a suggested duration and intensity of the work-out for that week. Space is provided for a coach or player to write an alternate workout for each week. The frequency of workouts is three per week, on an every-other-day basis. Each workout should be preceded and followed by stretching exercises. Work intensity is specified in terms of percentage of effort as follows:

| LM | = Light to Moderate | 50% of maximum effort* |
|----|---------------------|------------------------|
| H  | = Hard              | 80% of maximum effort |
| S  | = Sprint            | 100% of maximum effort |

For example, **3x(2:H,2:LM)** means do three sets of (two minutes at 80% of effort followed by two minutes at 50% of effort). For each workout completed, record the **date** and the **total distance covered**.

| WEEK | | Day 1 | Day 2 | Day 3 |
|------|---|-------|-------|-------|
| **1** | **[9:LM,3x(2:H,2:LM),9:LM]** alternate workout: [ | | | ] |
| | Date: | | | |
| | Distance: | | | |
| **2** | **[7:LM,4x(2:H,2:LM),7:LM]** alternate workout: [ | | | ] |
| | Date: | | | |
| | Distance: | | | |
| **3** | **[5:LM,5x(2:H,2:LM),5:LM]** alternate workout: [ | | | ] |
| | Date: | | | |
| | Distance: | | | |
| **4** | **[3:LM,6x(2:H,2:LM),3:LM]** alternate workout: [ | | | ] |
| | Date: | | | |
| | Distance: | | | |
| | **TOTAL TIME FOR EACH WORKOUT = 30 MINUTES** | | | |

Pre-season Aerobic/Anaerobic Transition Program

*If the intensity of the hard and sprint portions of the exercise intervals cannot be maintained, the athlete should reduce the intensity of the light to moderate intervals.

**Table 24-2s.** Pre-Season Anaerobic Developmental Interval Training Program.

**(To be started 10 weeks before the first game)**

Name_____

The information at the top of each week's schedule specifies a suggested duration and intensity of the workout for that week. Space is provided for a coach or player to write an alternate workout for each week. The frequency of workouts is three per week, on an every-other-day basis. Each workout should be preceded and followed by stretching exercises. Work intensity is specified in terms of percentage of effort as follows:

| | | |
|---|---|---|
| **LM** | = Light to Moderate | **50% of maximum** effort* |
| **H** | = Hard | **80% of maximum** effort |
| **S** | = Sprint | **100% of maximum** effort |

For example, **4x(:20S,2:LM)** means do four sets of (20 seconds at maximum effort followed by two minutes at 50% of effort). For each workout completed, record the **date** and the **total distance covered**.

| WEEK | | Day 1 | Day 2 | Day 3 |
|---|---|---|---|---|
| **1** | [4:LM,2x(1:H,2:LM),4x(:20S,:40LM),4:LM] | | | |
| | alternate workout: [ | | ] | |
| | Date/Distance | | | |
| **2** | [4:LM,2x(1:H,2:LM),5x(:20S,:40LM),4:LM] | | | |
| | alternate workout: [ | | ] | |
| | Date/Distance | | | |
| **3** | [4:LM,2x(1:H,2:LM),6x(:20S,:40LM),4:LM] | | | |
| | alternate workout: [ | | ] | |
| | Date/Distance | | | |
| **4** | [4:LM,2x(1:H,2:LM),7x(:20S,:40LM),4:LM] | | | |
| | alternate workout: [ | | ] | |
| | Date/Distance | | | |
| **5** | [4:LM,3x(1:H,2:LM),8x(:20S,:40LM),4:LM] | | | |
| | alternate workout: [ | | ] | |
| | Date/Distance | | | |
| **6** | [4:LM,3x(1:H,2:LM),9x(:20S,:40LM),4:LM] | | | |
| | alternate workout: [ | | ] | |
| | Date/Distance | | | |
| **7** | [4:LM,3x(1:H,2:LM),6x(:10S,:20LM),2:LM,6x(:10S,:20LM),4:LM] | | | |
| | alternate workout: [ | | ] | |
| | Date/Distance | | | |
| **8** | [4:LM,3x(1:H,2:LM),8x(:10S,:20LM),2:LM,8x(:10S,:20LM),4:LM] | | | |
| | alternate workout: [ | | ] | |
| | Date/Distance | | | |

The table caption "Pre-season Anaerobic Developmental Interval Training Program" spans the top of the table.

*If the intensity of the hard and sprint portions of the exercise intervals cannot be maintained, the athlete should reduce the intensity of the light to moderate intervals.

**Table 24-3s.** In-Season Anaerobic Maintenance Program.

**(To be started two weeks before the first game)**

Name_____

A suggested workout is provided at the top of the In-Season Aerobic Maintenance Program form. Space is provided for the coach or player to write an alternate workout. The frequency of workouts is one per week. Workouts should be completed at the end of a practice but not on a day before a game. Each workout should be preceded and followed by stretching exercises. Intensity is specified in terms of percentage of effort as follows:

| | | | |
|---|---|---|---|
| **LM** | = Light to Moderate | **50% of maximum effort*** |
| **H** | = Hard | **80% of maximum effort** |
| **S** | = Sprint | **100% of maximum effort** |

For example, **3x(2:H,2:LM)** means do three sets of (two minutes at 80% of effort followed by two minutes at 50% of effort). For each workout completed, record the **date** and the **total distance covered.**

| In-Season Anaerobic Maintenance Program | | | | | |
|---|---|---|---|---|---|
| [2:LM,2x(1:H,2:LM),2x(:20S,:40LM),8x(:10S,:20LM),4:LM] | | | | | |
| alternate workout: [                                               ] | | | | | |
| MONTH | WEEK | | | | |
| | 1 | 2 | 3 | 4 | 5 |
| **1** Date: | | | | | |
| Distance: | | | | | |
| **2** Date: | | | | | |
| Distance: | | | | | |
| **3** Date: | | | | | |
| Distance: | | | | | |
| **4** Date: | | | | | |
| Distance: | | | | | |
| **5** Date: | | | | | |
| Distance: | | | | | |

*If the intensity of the hard and sprint portions of the exercise intervals cannot be maintained, the athlete should reduce the intensity of the light to moderate intervals.

**Table 24-4s.** Post-Season Aerobic and Anaerobic Maintenance Program.

**(To be started two to four weeks after the last game)**

---

### AEROBIC PROGRAM

Aerobic capabilities should be developed during the post-season to provide the base for building the more intense anaerobic work capacity required for top performance during the season. Aerobic work combined with muscular strength/power work on alternate days is a good variation from the typical season routine. In the post-season time period, the development of aerobic capacity and muscular strength/power become primary, rather than secondary, objectives.

Begin three days of aerobic activity (swimming, jogging and running, bicycling, or other rhythmical, low intensity, long duration activities) alternated with three days of weight training. Progress up to 40 minutes of continuous aerobic activity and then work on increasing the speed or intensity at which the 40 minutes of work is done. Each workout should be preceded and followed by stretching exercises. Record the date and workout time on the Year-Round Conditioning Checklist in the portion of the checklist devoted to Post-Season.

---

### ANAEROBIC MAINTENANCE PROGRAM

A suggested workout is provided at the top of the Post-Season Anaerobic Maintenance Program form. Space is also provided for the coach or player to write an alternate workout. The post-season anaerobic maintenance program should be done once a week. It should not be completed on the same day as an aerobic workout. Each workout should be preceded and followed by stretching exercises. Intensity is specified in terms of percentage of effort as follows:

| | | |
|---|---|---|
| **LM** | = Light to Moderate | **50% of maximum effort*** |
| **H** | = Hard | **80% of maximum effort** |
| **S** | = Sprint | **100% of maximum effort** |

For example, **4x(:20S,:40LM)** means do four sets of (20 seconds at maximum effort followed by 40 seconds at 50% of effort). For each workout completed, record the **date** and the **total distance covered**.

| Post-Season Anaerobic Maintenance Program | | | | | |
|---|---|---|---|---|---|
| [4:LM,2x(1:H,2:LM),4x(:20S,:40LM),4x(:20S,:40LM),4:LM] | | | | | |
| alternate workout: [                                                              ] | | | | | |
| **MONTH** | | **WEEK** | | | | |
| | | 1 | 2 | 3 | 4 | 5 |
| **1** | Date: | | | | | |
| | Distance: | | | | | |
| **2** | Date: | | | | | |
| | Distance: | | | | | |
| **3** | Date: | | | | | |
| | Distance: | | | | | |
| **4** | Date: | | | | | |
| | Distance: | | | | | |

*If the intensity of the hard and sprint portions of the exercise intervals cannot be maintained, the athlete should reduce the intensity of the light to moderate intervals.

**Table 24-5s.** Conditioning activities for softball players.

| Order | Exercise | Comment |
|---|---|---|
| 1 | Neck flexion | This exercise can be done on specially designed weight machines or can be accomplished by wrapping a towel around the forehead and having a partner provide resistance. |
| 2 | Squat lift | The angle at the back of the knee should not be allowed to become less than 90 degrees. An upright position of the head should be maintained, and the back should be kept as close to vertical as possible throughout the lift. Trained spotters must be used. If using free weights, wrap a towel or foam pad around the center of the bar to lessen the discomfort of the bar across the back of the neck. |
| 3 | Bench press | Trained spotters must be used. |
| 4 | Bent knee sit-ups | A weight can be held high on the chest and/or the sit-up can be done on an incline to increase resistance. The feet should be held down by a partner or restraining structure. |
| 5 | Finger flexion | Grip strength exercises can be done with a spring hand gripper. |
| 6 | Hip abduction | This exercise can be done on a specially designed weight machine or by having a partner provide resistance. Both legs should be exercised. |
| 7 | Bent over row | The head should be supported, and the back should be in a horizontal position. |
| 8 | Neck extension | This exercise can be done on specially designed weight machines or can be accomplished by wrapping a towel around the head and having a partner provide resistance. |
| 9 | Hip abduction | This exercise can be done on a specially designed weight machine or by having a partner provide resistance. Both legs should be exercised. |
| 10 | Toe rise | If using free weights, wrap a towel or foam pad around the bar to lessen the discomfort of the bar across the back of the neck. Trained spotters must be used. A block of wood can be used under the toes to increase the range through which the muscles must exert force in lifting the body. |
| 11 | Arm curl | A rocking motion of the body should not be used to aid the arms in lifting the resistance. |
| 12 | Knee flexion | |
| 13 | Lat pull-down | Keep the hips extended and do not use hip flexion to aid in the pull-down motion. |
| 14 | Back hyperextension | A partner or restraining structure is needed to hold the legs down. |
| 15 | Knee extension | |
| 16 | Reverse forearm curl | |

repetitions on an exercise are completed, then the next exercise is done. This phase should last for eight or more weeks and should end about two weeks before the first competition. It is during this third phase that weight levels are adjusted upward as strength increases. This information is summarized in Table 24-7s.

When 12 repetitions of a given exercise have been completed for each of the three sets for two successive workouts, the weight load for that exercise can be increased to the next level for the following workout. The athlete should be able to do a minimum of 8 repetitions for each of the three sets at the new weight level. If this is not possible, a smaller weight increase is indicated.

# Table 24-6s. Weight Training Program Checklist.

Name _____

**INSTRUCTIONS:**
- Record the weight load only when there is a change in load.
- Record the number of repetitions for each set (example: 12/10/10)
- Increase the weight load when you have done 12 repetitions for each of three sets for two consecutive workouts.
- Use a smaller load increase if you cannot do a minimum of eight repetitions per set at a new load.

| Date | | Neck flexion | Squat lift | Bench press | Bent knee sit-up | Finger flexion | Hip abduction | Bent over row | Neck extension | Hip adduction | Toe rise | Arm curl | Knee flexion | Lat pull-down | Back hyperextension | Knee extension | Reverse forearm curl |
|---|---|---|---|---|---|---|---|---|---|---|---|---|---|---|---|---|---|
| | WT. | | | | | | | | | | | | | | | | |
| | REPS. | / / | / / | / / | / / | / / | / / | / / | / / | / / | / / | / / | / / | / / | / / | / / | / / |
| | WT. | | | | | | | | | | | | | | | | |
| | REPS. | / / | / / | / / | / / | / / | / / | / / | / / | / / | / / | / / | / / | / / | / / | / / | / / |
| | WT. | | | | | | | | | | | | | | | | |
| | REPS. | / / | / / | / / | / / | / / | / / | / / | / / | / / | / / | / / | / / | / / | / / | / / | / / |
| | WT. | | | | | | | | | | | | | | | | |
| | REPS. | / / | / / | / / | / / | / / | / / | / / | / / | / / | / / | / / | / / | / / | / / | / / | / / |
| | WT. | | | | | | | | | | | | | | | | |
| | REPS. | / / | / / | / / | / / | / / | / / | / / | / / | / / | / / | / / | / / | / / | / / | / / | / / |
| | WT. | | | | | | | | | | | | | | | | |
| | REPS. | / / | / / | / / | / / | / / | / / | / / | / / | / / | / / | / / | / / | / / | / / | / / | / / |
| | WT. | | | | | | | | | | | | | | | | |
| | REPS. | / / | / / | / / | / / | / / | / / | / / | / / | / / | / / | / / | / / | / / | / / | / / | / / |
| | WT. | | | | | | | | | | | | | | | | |
| | REPS. | / / | / / | / / | / / | / / | / / | / / | / / | / / | / / | / / | / / | / / | / / | / / | / / |
| | WT. | | | | | | | | | | | | | | | | |
| | REPS. | / / | / / | / / | / / | / / | / / | / / | / / | / / | / / | / / | / / | / / | / / | / / | / / |
| | WT. | | | | | | | | | | | | | | | | |
| | REPS. | / / | / / | / / | / / | / / | / / | / / | / / | / / | / / | / / | / / | / / | / / | / / | / / |
| | WT. | | | | | | | | | | | | | | | | |
| | REPS. | / / | / / | / / | / / | / / | / / | / / | / / | / / | / / | / / | / / | / / | / / | / / | / / |
| | WT. | | | | | | | | | | | | | | | | |
| | REPS. | / / | / / | / / | / / | / / | / / | / / | / / | / / | / / | / / | / / | / / | / / | / / | / / |
| | WT. | | | | | | | | | | | | | | | | |
| | REPS. | / / | / / | / / | / / | / / | / / | / / | / / | / / | / / | / / | / / | / / | / / | / / | / / |
| | WT. | | | | | | | | | | | | | | | | |
| | REPS. | / / | / / | / / | / / | / / | / / | / / | / / | / / | / / | / / | / / | / / | / / | / / | / / |
| | WT. | | | | | | | | | | | | | | | | |
| | REPS. | / / | / / | / / | / / | / / | / / | / / | / / | / / | / / | / / | / / | / / | / / | / / | / / |
| | WT. | | | | | | | | | | | | | | | | |
| | REPS. | / / | / / | / / | / / | / / | / / | / / | / / | / / | / / | / / | / / | / / | / / | / / | / / |
| | WT. | | | | | | | | | | | | | | | | |
| | REPS. | / / | / / | / / | / / | / / | / / | / / | / / | / / | / / | / / | / / | / / | / / | / / | / / |
| | WT. | | | | | | | | | | | | | | | | |
| | REPS. | / / | / / | / / | / / | / / | / / | / / | / / | / / | / / | / / | / / | / / | / / | / / | / / |
| | WT. | | | | | | | | | | | | | | | | |
| | REPS. | / / | / / | / / | / / | / / | / / | / / | / / | / / | / / | / / | / / | / / | / / | / / | / / |
| | WT. | | | | | | | | | | | | | | | | |
| | REPS. | / / | / / | / / | / / | / / | / / | / / | / / | / / | / / | / / | / / | / / | / / | / / | / / |
| | WT. | | | | | | | | | | | | | | | | |
| | REPS. | / / | / / | / / | / / | / / | / / | / / | / / | / / | / / | / / | / / | / / | / / | / / | / / |
| | WT. | | | | | | | | | | | | | | | | |
| | REPS. | / / | / / | / / | / / | / / | / / | / / | / / | / / | / / | / / | / / | / / | / / | / / | / / |

## In-Season Weight Training

Strength improvement is the goal of the preseason weight training developmental program. Maintenance of the increased strength is accomplished by a scaled-down in-season weight training program that should begin about two weeks before the first game. If weight training is done only during the preseason period, the strength gains will gradually be lost as the season progresses. Research has shown that a weight training maintenance program of one to two workouts per week will prevent the reversal of strength gains. Performance will not be hampered by in-season weight training if three general rules are followed:

- Lifting should be limited to once or twice a week, with two to three days between weight training workouts.
- Do not schedule weight training workouts for the day before or the day of a game.
- Maintain the resistance at the last load level where 12 repetitions for all three sets could be done. Do not increase weight loads during in-season workouts. Use pre- and post-season periods for strength improvement with strength maintenance as the goal of the in-season workouts.

The workout program itself remains the same as in Phase 3 of the developmental program. The same series of exercises is followed, with 8 to 12 repetitions per exercise, for a total of three sets. As long as the athlete lifts at least once every four days and does not increase the weight load, there should be no muscle soreness or undue fatigue that will interfere with performance during games.

## Post-Season Weight Training

Once the competitive season is over, players can again focus on achievement of higher strength levels. A post-season break from training of at least two weeks can be followed by a return to the program outlined in Phase 3 of the preseason developmental program (see Table 24-2s). Three-set workouts, three times per week, can be continued throughout the off-season months. The "Weight Training Program Checklist" can be used to determine when weight loads should be increased. After the first year in which players build up gradually through the one-set and two-set phases during the preseason developmental program, Phase 1 and 2 should not be needed.

## YEAR-ROUND CONDITIONING PROGRAM

The year-round conditioning program contains two components. They are: (a) an interval training program for conditioning the aerobic and anaerobic energy-production systems, and (b) a weight training program for conditioning the muscular system (see Tables 24-8s through 24-10s). These components are integrated into a year-round conditioning program (see Table 24-11s).

**Table 24-7s.** Pre-season developmental weight training program.

| Phase | Duration | Reps | Sets | Days/Week | Comments |
|-------|----------|------|------|-----------|----------|
| 1 | 2 weeks | 8-12 | 1 | 3 | Maintain starting resistance level. |
| 2 | 2 weeks | 8-12 | 2 | 3 | Maintain starting resistance level. |
| 3 | 8 or more weeks | 8-12 | 3 | 3 | Increase resistance levels as strength gains are made. |

**Table 24-8s.** Year-Round Conditioning Checklist.

Name _____

(Mark the date of each completed workout in the box.)

## PRE-SEASON

| | AEROBIC/ANAEROBIC TRANSITION PROGRAM AND WEIGHT TRAINING PROGRAM (Phases 1 and 2 or 3) | | | | | |
|---|---|---|---|---|---|---|
| WEEK | TRANSITION WORKOUT | WEIGHT TRAINING | TRANSITION WORKOUT | WEIGHT TRAINING | TRANSITION WORKOUT | WEIGHT TRAINING |
| 1 | | | | | | |
| 2 | | | | | | |
| 3 | | | | | | |
| 4 | | | | | | |

## PRE-SEASON

| | DEVELOPMENTAL INTERVAL TRAINING PROGRAM AND WEIGHT TRAINING PROGRAM (Phase 3) | | | | | |
|---|---|---|---|---|---|---|
| WEEK | INTERVAL TRAINING | WEIGHT TRAINING | INTERVAL TRAINING | WEIGHT TRAINING | INTERVAL TRAINING | WEIGHT TRAINING |
| 5 | | | | | | |
| 6 | | | | | | |
| 7 | | | | | | |
| 8 | | | | | | |
| 9 | | | | | | |
| 10 | | | | | | |
| 11 | | | | | | |
| 12 | | | | | | |

(After 12th week, begin **in-season maintenance programs** (intervals once per week, weights one to two times per week)

**Table 24-9s.** Year-Round Conditioning Checklist.

Name _____

## IN-SEASON MAINTENANCE PROGRAMS

Place a check in the box corresponding to the month and week for each time you complete the interval and weight workout.

### WEEK

| MONTH | 1 | | 2 | | 3 | | 4 | | 5 | |
|-------|------|----------|------|----------|------|----------|------|----------|------|----------|
| | Wts. | Interval | Wts. | Interval | Wts. | Interval | Wts. | Interval | Wts. | Interval |
| 1 | | | | | | | | | | |
| 2 | | | | | | | | | | |
| 3 | | | | | | | | | | |
| 4 | | | | | | | | | | |
| 5 | | | | | | | | | | |
| 6 | | | | | | | | | | |

**Table 24-10s.** Post-Season Conditioning Checklist.

Name _____

Mark the date of each workout in the corresponding box. For aerobic workouts, record the distance covered and the total time of the workout.

| WEEK | Aerobic | Weights | Aerobic | Weights | Aerobic | Weights | Anaerobic Maintenance |
|------|---------|---------|---------|---------|---------|---------|-----------------------|
| 1 | | | | | | | |
| 2 | | | | | | | |
| 3 | | | | | | | |
| 4 | | | | | | | |
| 5 | | | | | | | |
| 6 | | | | | | | |

Table 24-10s (continued)

## POST-SEASON CONDITIONING CHECKLIST

| WEEK | Aerobic | Weights | Aerobic | Weights | Aerobic | Weights | Anaerobic Maintenance |
|------|---------|---------|---------|---------|---------|---------|-----------------------|
| 7 | | | | | | | |
| 8 | | | | | | | |
| 9 | | | | | | | |
| 10 | | | | | | | |
| 11 | | | | | | | |
| 12 | | | | | | | |
| 13 | | | | | | | |
| 14 | | | | | | | |
| 15 | | | | | | | |
| 16 | | | | | | | |
| 17 | | | | | | | |
| 18 | | | | | | | |
| 19 | | | | | | | |
| 20 | | | | | | | |
| 21 | | | | | | | |
| 22 | | | | | | | |
| 23 | | | | | | | |
| 24 | | | | | | | |
| 25 | | | | | | | |
| 26 | | | | | | | |
| 27 | | | | | | | |
| 28 | | | | | | | |
| 29 | | | | | | | |
| 30 | | | | | | | |

**Table 24-11s.** Overview of year-round conditioning program.

| Time | Interval Training Activity for Conditioning the Energy Production System* | Weight Training Activity for Conditioning the Muscular System** |
|---|---|---|
| **Pre-season** (start 14 weeks prior to first game) | Complete the Pre-season Aerobic/Anaerobic Transition program (four weeks). | New lifters complete the Pre-season Weight Training Program by beginning with four weeks of introductory weight training (Phase 1 and 2) and then starting the Post-Season Weight Training Program (Phase 3). |
| | Complete the Pre-season Anaerobic Developmental Interval Training Program (eight weeks). | Continuing lifters complete the Post-Season Weight Training Program. |
| **In-Season** (two weeks prior to first game until last game) | Participate in interval training as part of regularly scheduled practices. Complete the In-Season Anaerobic Maintenance Program. | Complete the In-Season Weight Training Maintenance Program. |
| **Post-Season** (two to four weeks after last game until 14 weeks before first game of next season) | Complete three days/week of aerobic activity (swimming, jogging and running, or bicycling). Complete the Post-Season Anaerobic Maintenance Program. | Complete the Post-Season Weight Training Program. |

*Note that all conditioning sessions should be preceded by warm-up and stretching and followed by cool-down and stretching (see Supplement 24-1).

**Descriptions of these activities are included in this supplement.

**Supplement 24-3.**

# Circuit Training Program

## Introduction

This supplement contains an example of a softball training circuit and recording form (see Table 24-12s). These forms can be photocopied and duplicated on the front and back of a 5 x 8 card. Also included in this supplement is a blank form (see Table 24-13s) upon which you can write your own training circuit to meet the specific needs of your players.

## Using A Training Circuit

A training circuit can be implemented one to three times per week during the season. The number of times per week you have your players engage in a training circuit should vary according to the number of games scheduled for a given week, the physical demands of an in-season interval training and weight training program, and other activities included in your practice. You should not have your players perform a circuit the day before or the day of a game.

The requirements for performance and scoring each station need to be thoroughly explained to the players. Players need to be informed that the correct performance of each station is as important as the number of repetitions. After all the players understand each of the items in the complete circuit, you may have them perform a partial circuit of four or five stations and then increase the number of stations by one on subsequent days until all stations of the training circuit are performed.

The prescribed time for exercise and for the rest interval, during which the players write their scores on their recording forms and rotate from one station to the next, should be controlled to create an exercise overload. The first day the team performs the entire circuit, 30 seconds of exercise and 20 seconds rest between each station might be appropriate. This results in an eight-station circuit that can be completed in 6 minutes and 20 seconds. Gradually the exercise interval should increase and the rest interval should decrease. You will need to judge what is the appropriate exercise/rest interval ratio for your players.

**Table 24-12s.** Example of a ten-station basketball training circuit and recording form on two sides of a 5 x 8″ card.

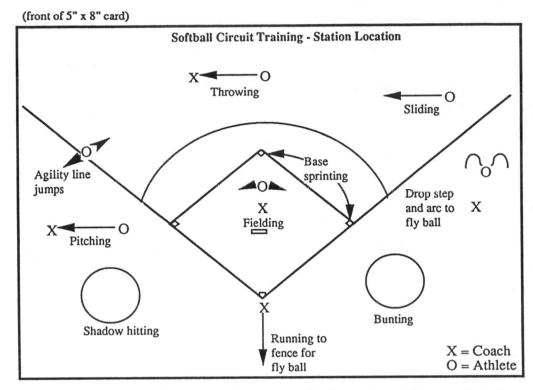

(front of 5″ x 8″ card)

Softball Circuit Training - Station Location

10 Stations

1. Shadow hitting
2. Pitching
3. Agility line jumps
4. Throwing
5. Sliding
6. Drop step and arc to fly ball
7. Base sprinting
8. Fielding
9. Bunting
10. Running to fence for fly ball

(back of 5″ x 8″ card)

Softball Circuit Training - Recording Form

| Name: | | | | | | | | | | | |
|---|---|---|---|---|---|---|---|---|---|---|---|
| Date (mo./day) | | | | | | | | | | | |
| Exercise/Rest interval (seconds) | | | | | | | | | | | |
| STATIONS | Performance Scores | | | | | | | | | | |
| Shadow hitting | | | | | | | | | | | |
| Pitching | | | | | | | | | | | |
| Agility line jumps | | | | | | | | | | | |
| Throwing | | | | | | | | | | | |
| Sliding | | | | | | | | | | | |
| Drop step and arc to fly ball | | | | | | | | | | | |
| Base sprinting | | | | | | | | | | | |
| Fielding | | | | | | | | | | | |
| Bunting | | | | | | | | | | | |
| Running to fence for fly ball | | | | | | | | | | | |

**Table 24-12s.** (continued)

| Station | Description | Equipment |
|---|---|---|
| Shadow hitting | See drill | 1 bat |
| Pitching | Player works on underhand pitching technique with slingshot or windmill windup. Coach serves as catcher. Stress concentration and proper mechanics. | 1 ball, portable plate |
| Agility line jumping | Player begins with both feet on one side of the foul line. The player jumps rapidly and continuously from one side of the line to the other. Stress quick footwork. | foul line |
| Throwing | Player throws bigger ball to coach. Distance thrown is varied by the coach depending on arm strength of player. Stress proper mechanics.<br>*Variation:* speed throwing | one 12 in. or 16 in. softball |
| Sliding | Player starts in foul territory, runs toward base, and slides when 8 to 12 ft. from base. Stress proper technique.<br>*Variation:* slide to inside and outside of bag; head first slide | 1 movable base 15 ft. from foul line |
| Drop step and arc to fly ball | Player is positioned 40 to 60 ft. from coach who throws fly balls to right and left of player. Stress drop step and arc to get proper position for catching a fly ball. | 1 softball |
| Base sprinting | Start at first base and sprint to second. Start at second and sprint to first. Stress quick start with imaginary pitch and rounding second. Stress proper running mechanics. Time each sprint. | 2 movable bases |
| Fielding | Player faces coach who is 10 ft. away. Coach rolls balls directly to player, to player's right, to player's left. Stress proper mechanics and footwork. Continue as quickly as possible. | 1 ball |
| Bunting | Player starts in hitting position and moves to bunt position, executes bunt, drops bat, and takes crossover step and two additional steps to first base. Repeat as many times as possible in allotted time. Stress proper mechanics. | 1 bat |
| Running to fence for fly ball | Player starts at home plate and visualizes a fly ball going to the fence. Player drop steps and runs to fence feeling for fence while keeping eye on ball. Repeat as many times as possible in allotted time. | portable plate |

**Table 24-13s.** Recording form to photocopy and complete.

(front of 5" x 8" card)

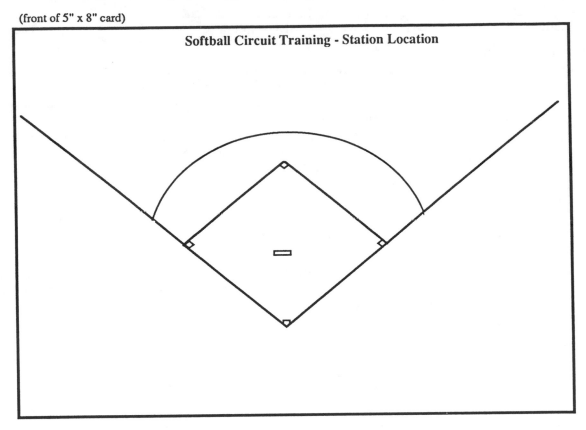

(back of 5" x 8" card)

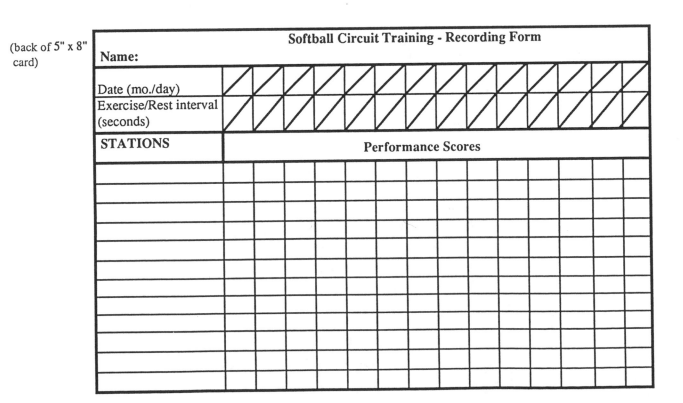

# 25
# Nutrition for Successful Performance

*Elaina Jurecki, Ph.D.*
*Glenna DeJong, M.S., M.A.*

---

### QUESTIONS TO CONSIDER

- What is a proper diet for young softball players?
- Do young athletes need protein, vitamin, and mineral supplements?
- Should there by any restriction on the amount of water consumed before, during, and after games and practices?
- Should salt tablets be provided for the players during practices and games?
- Are ergogenic aids important in improving softball performance?
- When should a pre-game meal be eaten and what should it contain?

---

## INTRODUCTION

All children have the same nutritional needs, but young athletes use more energy and, therefore, usually need to consume more calories. Good performance does not just happen; it requires training sessions to improve techniques, increase endurance, and develop game strategies. Good nutrition is another important factor that affects an athlete's performance, but it is less frequently understood and practiced. Studies have shown that good overall eating habits are more beneficial to the athlete than taking vitamin or protein supplements or eating special foods at a pre-competition meal.

Food consists of all the solid or liquid materials we ingest by mouth, except drugs. Breads, meats, vegetables, and fruits, as well as beverages—even water—are considered food, because they contain essential nutrients for the body. These nutrients include energy (calories from fat, protein, and carbohydrates), carbohydrates, protein (amino acids), fat, vitamins, salts (electrolytes), minerals, trace elements, and water. Water constitutes more than half the body's weight and provides the medium within which other nutrients are delivered to different body parts to perform their important functions.

What impact could you have on your athletes' diets? How can you influence what your athletes eat when you do not cook their meals? When you meet with the team's parents during an orientation meeting, explain to them how good nutrition can aid their children's performance. This information can be reinforced by giving your athletes similar nutritional advice. Frequently, your athletes will listen more closely to your advice than that of their parents and use the tips you suggest on improving their diets because they believe these tips will also improve their performance.

## PROPER DIET

A good diet is one that provides adequate energy (calories), proteins, carbohydrates, fats, vitamins, minerals, and water in the amounts needed by the body in order to perform its normal daily functions. A variety of foods needs to be eaten to provide the 40 plus nutrients essential for good health. This can be achieved by eating the specified number of servings from each of the four food groups (see Table 25-1).

### Calories

Calories are the energy content of food used to satisfy the needs of the energy body so it can properly function. Energy obtained from food is temporarily stored as glycogen in the liver and muscle, as fat in various deposit sites, and as protein in muscle and other places although protein is used as an energy source only during extreme situations. Foods vary in calorie and nutrient content. Foods to avoid are those that are high in calories and low in nutrient content. Foods that are high in sugar (candy, cakes, soda pop, cookies) or fat (fried foods, chips, salad dressings, pastries, butter) supply "empty calories," meaning they do not contribute to the essential nutrients discussed earlier but do contribute many calories. These foods should be used with discretion.

The energy cost of physical activity, or amount of calories burned, depends upon: (a) the intensity of the physical activity, and (b) the length of time of exertion. A young softball player, about 120 pounds in body weight, burns approximately 120 to 200 calories per hour of practice. (A softball pitcher, however, may burn up to 450 calories per hour.) During a game or training session, ranging from 45 to 90 minutes, your players burn up to 25 percent more energy than they do on a day in which they don't practice. Hence, heavy training may require an additional 175 to 250 calories per day intake to compensate for the calories burned during the activity.

An average adolescent burns differing amounts of calories during the various activities listed in Table 25-2.

When your players reach exhaustion, most of their bodies' energy stores are depleted and their blood sugar decreases, causing fatigue. This situation is remedied with appropriate rest and calorie ingestion—preferably from carbohydrate sources since these foods can replenish energy stores more efficiently.

### Carbohydrates

Carbohydrates are a group of chemical substances which includes sugars and starches. They are widely distributed in many foods. As stated previously, carbohydrates can be stored as liver and muscle glycogen or can be found in the blood as glucose. During moderate to high intensity exercise, carbohydrates supply the majority of the energy needed in the body (see "Energy Production Systems" in Chapter 24). However, the carbohydrate storage capacity of the body is limited and can be greatly decreased by skipping meals or with exercise. Since car-

**Table 25-1.** Recommended daily intake of each of the four food groups.

| | | |
|---|---|---|
| Dairy Products | 3-4 servings (milk, cheese, yogurt) to provide calcium, phosphorus, vitamin D, protein, and energy. | 1 serving = 1 cup of milk or 2 oz. of cheese |
| Protein Products | 2 servings (meat, fish, poultry, or vegetable protein foods such as beans and whole grains) to provide amino acids, B vitamins, iron, essential fatty acids, energy, and more. | 1 serving = 2 to 3 oz. of meat |
| Fruits and Vegetables | 4 servings (oranges, apples, pears, broccoli, carrots, green beans) to provide vitamin A and C, and electrolytes. | 1 serving = 1/2 cup of vegetables or fruit |
| Grain Products | 4 servings (bread, cereal, pasta, rice) to provide B vitamins and protein. | 1 serving = 1 slice bread or 1 cup of cereal, pasta, or rice. |

**Table 25-2.** Caloric expenditure during various activities.

| Activity | Calories/ minute* | Activity | Calories/ minute |
|---|---|---|---|
| Sleeping | 0.9 | Basketball | 5-7 |
| Sitting, normally | 1.0 | Calisthenics | 4 |
| Standing, normally | 1.2 | Skipping rope | 8-12 |
| Class work, lecture | 1.4 | Running (10 mph) | 16 |
| (listen to) | | Softball | 3-4 |
| Walking indoors | 2.5 | Soccer (game) | 6-8 |

*Based on an average adolescent, 120 lbs. Add 10 percent for each 15 lbs. over 120, subtract 10 percent for each 15 lbs. under 120.

bohydrates can be digested easily and quickly, they are the most readily available sources of food energy for storage energy replacement.

A diet high in carbohydrate (55-60 percent of total caloric intake) helps maintain adequate stores in the body. Most of the dietary carbohydrates should come from complex carbohydrate sources such as pasta, rice, fruits, and kidney beans. Refined sugars found in candy, cookies, and syrup should be avoided.

*Carbohydrates are easily digested and are the most readily available source of food energy.*

## Fat

Fat is the most concentrated source of energy. It contains twice as much energy (calories) per unit weight as either carbohydrate or protein. Fats have many important functions in the body including carrying vitamins A, D, E, and K to perform their necessary functions, building blood vessels and body linings, and providing a concentrated store of energy (calories).

During mild to moderate exercise, fats are an important energy source along with carbohydrates (see "Energy Production Systems" in Chapter 24). The storage capacity for fat is much greater than that for carbohydrate and only in extreme cases are fat stores depleted. Therefore, dietary intake of fat should be 30 percent or less of total caloric intake since replenishment isn't normally necessary. In fact, high levels of fat in the diet have been implicated in diseases such as coronary artery disease and cancer.

Foods high in fat content are digested at a slower rate than foods high in carbohydrates or protein. If players have high fat meals (ham-

burger, fries, pizza, etc.) before their game, chances are good that such meals will not empty completely from their stomachs for three to five hours, and this may adversely affect their play. Foods having a high concentration of fat include butter, margarine, vegetable oils, peanut butter, mayonnaise, nuts, chocolate, fried foods, chips, and cream products.

Figure 25-1 lists the percent of fat from a variety of food sources.

## Protein

Proteins are important as structural components of all body tissues (e.g. muscle, skin, brain, etc.), regulators of metabolism (e.g. hormones and enzymes), and as an energy source during starvation and exercise although its contribution is minor as compared to fats and carbohydrates (see "Energy Production Systems" in Chapter 24). Amino acids are the "building blocks" which comprise all proteins. Of the 20 amino acids necessary for protein synthesis in the body, 11 can be manufactured in the body and are considered nonessential amino acids. The other nine are considered essential amino acids as they must be supplied in the diet. In a balanced diet, 12-15 percent of the total caloric intake should come from protein.

Foods from animal sources (e.g., meat, fish, poultry, eggs, milk, and cheese) provide the body with all of the essential amino acids. Vegetable foods (dried peas, beans, nuts, cereals, breads, and pastas) are also important sources of protein, but most vegetables are lacking in certain essential amino acids. Therefore, a combination of foods from animal and vegetable sources assures meeting the body's requirement for essential amino acids, as well as other nutrients.

Because of an increased rate of muscular growth, athletes have a *slightly* larger protein requirement than non-athletes. Studies on the dietary habits of athletes show that this increased requirement can be easily met by the athlete's normal diet; no protein supplement is necessary. During training, at most, an additional nine grams of protein (which can be provided by one cup of milk or two ounces of meat or cheese) is sufficient to meet increased demands. In fact, too much protein can place undo stress on the body.

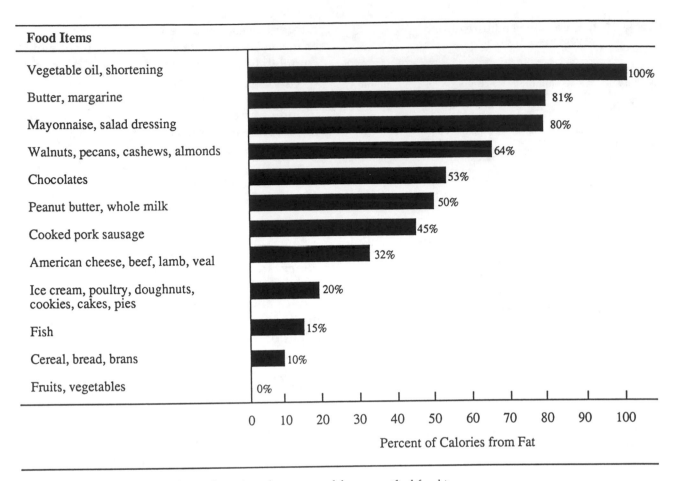

**Food Items**

| Food Items | Percent of Calories from Fat |
|---|---|
| Vegetable oil, shortening | 100% |
| Butter, margarine | 81% |
| Mayonnaise, salad dressing | 80% |
| Walnuts, pecans, cashews, almonds | 64% |
| Chocolates | 53% |
| Peanut butter, whole milk | 50% |
| Cooked pork sausage | 45% |
| American cheese, beef, lamb, veal | 32% |
| Ice cream, poultry, doughnuts, cookies, cakes, pies | 20% |
| Fish | 15% |
| Cereal, bread, brans | 10% |
| Fruits, vegetables | 0% |

Percent of Calories from Fat

**Figure 25-1.** Percentage of calories from fat when ingested from specified food items.

*Eating a high-protein diet could lead to dehydration of the body, which could actually decrease athletic performance.*

Excessive amounts of ingested protein—greater than the body's needs—are converted into body fat. The waste products from this conversion must be excreted by the kidneys, placing a greater strain on these organs. Water also is excreted with the protein-waste products in the urine. Thus, eating a high-protein diet could lead to dehydration of the body, which could actually decrease athletic performance.

It is a myth that building muscle requires a high-protein diet featuring large quantities of meat. Another myth is that a steak dinner eaten before an athletic event will help team members improve their performance. This type of meal may actually work against them if consumed less than three or four hours before playing time. These meals, as well as any high protein meal, are also usually high in fat. Players can-

not digest this type of meal as easily as a high-carbohydrate meal and may suffer from cramps and/or feel weighted down and sluggish.

## Vitamins and Minerals

Vitamins and minerals are found in varying quantities in many different kinds of foods, from a slice of bread to a piece of liver. Vitamins and minerals are nutrients required by the body in very small amounts for a larger number of body functions. They do not contain calories or give the body energy. When an athlete feels "run down," *this is usually not caused by a vitamin deficiency.*

We need vitamins and minerals in only minute quantities. Requirements of most vitamins and minerals are in milligram (1/1000 gram) amounts. These substances taken in excess of the body's need will either be stored in the body or excreted in the urine. The extra amounts will not provide more energy or enhance performance; however, they can be toxic or interfere with normal metabolism.

Vitamin and mineral supplementation is not necessary for the athlete who consumes a balanced diet. However, in certain sports such as wrestling, bodybuilding, and ballet, where weight loss through starvation is achieved, the athlete may not be obtaining adequate amounts solely due to the diminished caloric intake. Therefore, in situations where the athlete's diet is not balanced or caloric intake is low, supplementation may be advised. A much better approach, however, would be to encourage proper eating habits.

*Vitamins and minerals do not supply energy; high levels of vitamins and minerals can hinder the athlete's performance.*

Some vitamin and mineral supplements contain 10 or more times the Recommended Daily Allowance (RDA), which is sometimes just below the level of toxicity. If vitamin and mineral supplements are used, a single daily multi-vitamin/mineral tablet that provides 100 percent of the RDA or less for each nutrient is preferable to therapeutic level supplements providing greater than 100 percent of the RDA. The RDAs of vitamins and minerals are listed in Table 25-3.

## Water

Water plays a vital role in the health and performance of an athlete. Your softball players may lose more than two percent of their body weight due to dehydration from playing a fast-moving game or during a long workout. A player's performance significantly deteriorates after dehydration of more than 2 percent of his/her body weight. Drinking plenty of water is necessary for basketball players who are physically active in hot, humid weather (see Figure 25-2).

Physical exercise increases the amount of heat produced in the body. If sufficient water is not available for cooling of the body through perspiration, the body temperature may exceed safe limits. The individual will become tired more rapidly and in severe cases, heat exhaustion and heat stroke may result (see Chapter 27). A temperature/humidity guide for fluid and practice time is included in Table 25-4.

*Maintenance of adequate body water levels is necessary to help prevent heat illness.*

Feeling thirsty is not an adequate indication that the body needs water. In fact, by the time athletes feel thirsty, they already may have reached a dangerous level of body water depletion. It takes several hours to regain water balance once water loss has occurred. There is no physiological reason for restricting water intake before, during, or after athletic contests and practices. Players should drink eight to 16 ounces of water 30 minutes before the game and eight ounces every 20 minutes during the game.

*Athletes should be encouraged to drink water before, during, and after each game and practice session.*

**Table 25-3.** Recommended daily dietary allowances.*

| Age (Years) | Children 7-10 | Males 11-14 | Females 11-14 |
|---|---|---|---|
| Weight (pounds) | 62 | 99 | 101 |
| Height (inches) | 52 | 62 | 62 |
| Energy (calories) | 2,400 | 2,700 | 2,200 |
| range of calories | 1,650-3,300 | 2,000-3,700 | 1,500-3,000 |
| Protein (grams) | 34 | 45 | 46 |
| Vitamin A (mg RE) | 700 | 1,000 | 1,000 |
| Vitamin C (mg) | 45 | 50 | 50 |
| Calcium (mg) | 800 | 1,200 | 1,200 |
| Iron (mg) | 10 | 18 | 18 |

*Adapted from Food and Nutrition Board, National Academy of Sciences—National Research Council, Revised, 1980.

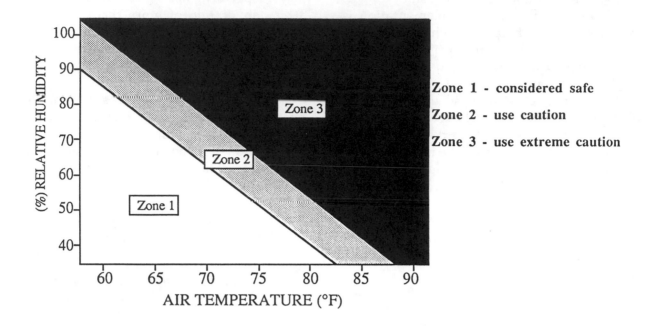

**Figure 25-2.** Guide for preventing heat illnesses associated with participation in physical activities under various conditions of temperatures and humidity.

## Salts and Electrolytes

Another common myth is that salt (sodium) tablets and electrolyte solutions (solutions containing the elements sodium, potassium, and chloride are needed by the athlete. These are not only unnecessary but can be harmful.

Salt tablets are irritating to the stomach and intestine and can increase the danger of dehydration by causing diarrhea when taken before a practice or game. Although the body needs to replace both water and sodium, the need for water is more critical.

Some coaches provide 0.2 percent salt solutions (drinking water containing small amounts of salt) during an athletic event, but research has shown that plain water is just as effective. The body needs water immediately to replace the water lost during a game or practice, but any sodium lost can easily be replaced by eating salted foods after the event. Most Americans get more sodium than they need from salt already in their diet; therefore, excessive salting of food is unnecessary and not recommended.

*The best replacement fluid is water.*

## ERGOGENIC AIDS

Ergogenic is derived from the Greek words ergon meaning work and gennan meaning to produce. In sports, ergogenic aids are agents thought to increase potential for work output. Various mechanical, psychological, physiological, nutritional, and pharmacological aids exist which purportedly improve performance. This discussion will focus on nutritional and pharmacological aids.

### Nutritional Aids

Ergogenic foods are those substances that claim to "give you more energy," "improve your performance," and/or "enhance your endurance." There is no scientific evidence supporting any of these claims. Most of these foods and dietary practices are harmless to the athlete. The only danger these foods pose occurs when they replace necessary foods that the athlete needs for normal bodily functions. Some

**Table 25-4.** Temperature/humidity guide for taking precautionary action during softball practices and games.

| Temperature | Precautions to Take |
|---|---|
| Under 60° (F) | No precaution is necessary. |
| 61-65° (F) | Encourage all players to take fluids. Make sure water is available at all times. |
| 66-70° (F) | Take water breaks every 30-45 minutes of playing or practice time. |
| 71-75° (F) | Provide rest periods with water breaks every 30-45 minutes of playing time—depending on the intensity of exercise. Substitute players during the game, so all may receive appropriate rest and fluids. |
| 76° (F) and up | Practice during coolest part of the day. Schedule frequent rest breaks. Force water intake. |
| | Tell players to wear light, loose clothing that allows free circulation of air. Remove outer clothing when it gets wet because wet clothing reduces evaporation, thus hindering one of the body's cooling mechanisms. |
| | Move to the shade if possible. |
| | Drink water before, during, and after practice sessions and competition. |
| Relative humidity greater than 90% | Similar precautions should be taken as those listed for 76° (F) and up. |

examples of these foods are bee pollen, pangamic acid, honey, lecithin, wheat germ oil, phosphates, alkaline salts (e.g., sodium bicarbonate, tomato juice, or organic juice), and gelatin.

Inform your athletes that these substances do not improve performance contrary to advertiser's claims. Encourage them to eat healthy diets and explain that this is the key to improving their performance.

## Pharmacological Aids

### • Steroids

Anabolic steroids (Dianabol, Anavar, Winstrol, etc.) have structures similar to the male sex hormone, testosterone. They are referred to as anabolic because, under certain circumstances, they promote tissue-building via increases in muscle mass and decreases in muscle breakdown. This effect is most evident in males when great increases in muscle mass and strength are seen at puberty. A 20-fold magnification in circulating testosterone levels accompanies these increases at this time. However, muscle mass and/or strength gains following steroid administration on already sexually mature subjects are questionable or at best show only moderate improvements.

In addition to their anabolic effects, steroids used in athletics also have androgenic or masculinizing effects. Males and females both may experience increased facial and body hair, baldness, voice deepening, and aggressiveness while using these drugs. Anabolic steroids also produce many reversible and irreversible side effects that are of great concern to the medical community as described in Table 25-5.

Steroid abuse is a major problem in athletics today even at the junior high and high school levels despite cases of well-known athletes who have been negatively affected by such abuse. In the 1983 Pan American games, 7 of the 19 athletes tested were disqualified for steroid use and many more withdrew from competition to prevent detection. Ben Johnson, the great Canadian sprinter, had his gold medal rescinded at the 1988 Olympic games following discovery of steroid abuse. Not only is steroid use unethical, it is dangerous. Your athletes should be informed of the dangerous and potentially fatal effects of steroid usage. The risk of infertility, liver damage, immune dysfunction, and aggressive behavior far outweighs any possible advantages of taking steroids.

### • Amphetamines

The use of pep pills or amphetamines is on the rise in athletics. These drug compounds cause reactions similar to adrenaline in that they increase heart rate, blood pressure, metabolism, breathing rate, and blood sugar levels. They may also cause headaches, dizziness, confusion, and sometimes insomnia, all of which could actually be detrimental to good physical performance. In fact, research suggests that amphetamines have little or no positive effect on exercise performance. Urge your athletes to stay clear of amphetamines as evidence for their potential detriment far exceeds any known benefits.

*The best prescription for increased strength and improved performance is hard practice, plenty of rest, a good diet, healthy eating habits, and plenty of fluids.*

**Table 25-5.** Harmful effects of anabolic steroids.*

| Body System | Reversible Effects | Irreversible Effects |
|---|---|---|
| Cardiovascular (heart/blood vessels) | High blood pressure, changes in blood fats, predisposing to heart disease, sticky platelets | Abnormal heart muscle, heart disease, stroke, heart attack |
| Skeletal | Minor changes in height | Early closure of the growth plates, making you shorter than you would be otherwise |
| Muscular | Increased water in muscle | Abnormal muscle cells, tendon rupture |
| Reproductive—male | Shrunken testicles, decreased sperm production, breast development, increased size of the prostate gland | Cancer of the prostate, increased breast development, abnormal testicles |
| Reproductive—of female | Decreased breast size, increased body hair (facial also), menstrual problems | Increased size of clitoris, deepening voice, baldness, use during pregnancy may cause fetal deformity or death |
| Liver | Increased leakage of liver enzymes, abnormal growth of liver cells, turning "yellow" from backup of bile in liver | Cancer of liver, blood-filled sacs in liver |
| Endocrine (hormones) | Too much insulin secreted, decreased thyroxine, decreases hormone secretion from pituitary gland in brain | Do not know which effects are permanent |
| Skin | Acne, increased facial hair | Severe acne, baldness |
| Mental Attitude | Irritability, aggressiveness, mood swings, problems getting along with people, change in sex drive | Relationships with people damaged, possible personality changes |
| Immune | Decreased functioning of the immune cells and antibody formation | Serious infections, cancer |

*This table comes from a paper entitled "What the High School Athletes, Coaches and Parents Should Know About Anabolic-Androgenic Steroids." This paper is available upon request from the Michigan State University Sports Medicine Clinic, Clinical Center, East Lansing, MI 48824.

### • Caffeine

A stimulant commonly found in coffee, tea, cola, and chocolate is caffeine. Its ingestion has been found to improve physical performance in such long duration events as cycling and running. Therefore, its use may be warranted in endurance events and if used should be consumed one hour prior to the event. However, caffeine may cause headache, insomnia, and/or irritability in persons who normally avoid this drug. These people should avoid caffeine as these symptoms may be detrimental to performance. Don't rely on caffeine as a miracle performance drug, as it is not! Sensible training and proper diet are the best prescriptions that can't be beat for improving performance.

## MEAL PATTERNS

Preadolescents and adolescents should eat at least three meals daily. Nutritional snacks may be added to the regular breakfast-lunch-dinner pattern if extra calories are needed. Most active athletes tend to skip meals, grab quick-fix meals, or depend on fast food restaurants and vending machines for meals on the run. This practice could lead to diets low in vitamins and minerals and high in fat and sodium. For example, a meal consisting of a hamburger, fries, and soda would provide 571 calories or approximately one-fourth of the energy requirement of a 15- to 18-year-old athlete, but less than one-tenth of the other nutritional requirements. Nutritional foods with good ratios of nutrients to calories are listed in Table 25-6. To maximize performance during periods of intense daily training, an athlete should consume approximately 500 grams (2000 Kcal) of carbohydrates per day.

## Pre-Game Meal

One of the biggest concerns of athletes and coaches is what the team members should eat for the pre-game meal. Unfortunately, there are no foods that contain any special, magical

**Table 25-6.** Contributions of nutritional snacks.

| Food | Amount | Calories | Vit A | Vit C | Calcium | Iron |
|---|---|---|---|---|---|---|
| | | | | % Recommended Daily Allowance | | |
| Fresh orange | 1 med. size | 65 | 8 | 150 | 7 | 5 |
| Orange juice | 1 cup | 110 | 14 | 200 | 3 | 5 |
| Peanut butter | 1 tablespoon | 95 | — | — | 0.5 | 3 |
| 2% Milk | 1 cup | 120 | 14 | 4 | 37 | 1 |
| Cheese and crackers | 1 oz. cheese, 4 crackers | 175 | 9 | — | 27 | 7 |
| Carrot sticks | 8 or 1 carrot | 30 | 70 | 13 | 3 | 5 |
| Ice cream | 1 cup | 270 | 15 | 2 | 22 | 1 |
| Fruit-flavored yogurt | 1 cup | 230 | 14 | 2 | 43 | 2 |
| Raisins | 1/4 cup pressed | 120 | — | — | 56 | 15 |
| Applesauce | 1/2 cup | 115 | 1 | 3 | — | 7 |
| Banana | 1 med. | 100 | 6 | 27 | — | 7 |
| Ready-to-eat cereal | 1 ounce | 110 | 29 | 27 | — | 36 |

properties that can improve your softball players' performances if eaten before the game. Performance during an event or workout is dependent more on food consumed hours, days, or even weeks before the event. The most important consideration should be to select foods that can be digested easily, tolerated well, and liked by the players.

Pre-game stress causes an athlete's stomach and intestine to be less active. Minor food intake is recommended before vigorous exercise to delay exhaustion, but should be eaten two or three hours before the competition to give the stomach and intestines sufficient time to empty. Meals eaten before a practice session should be given the same general consideration as the pre-game meal, except there is no need to compensate for nervous stress.

Carbohydrates leave the stomach earlier and are digested more readily than either fats or protein. Foods that are easily digested include cereals, bread, spaghetti, macaroni, rice, potatoes (baked, not fried), and fruits. Examples of high-fat foods which should be avoided include cake, peanut butter, nuts, luncheon-type meats, gravy, yellow cheese, butter, and ice cream. Gas-forming foods (e.g., cabbage, cucumbers, cauliflower, and beans) and foods high in fiber and roughage (e.g., whole wheat bread, bran cereal, and raw vegetables) may cause discomfort to the player if eaten the day of competition.

Those athletes who have difficulty digesting solid foods before competition may prefer a liquid meal. These products should not be confused with instant powdered meals or "instant breakfasts," which have too much fat, protein, and electrolytes to be eaten before athletic contests. Liquid meals have the following advantages: (a) they leave the intestine rapidly, (b) they provide substantial calories, and (c) they are more convenient than preparing a solid meal. However, liquid meals do not provide any greater benefits for improving performances than do easily digested, well-tolerated meals.

Lunch should be eaten about three hours prior to afternoon practices or games. Possible choices for lunch include: spaghetti with tomato sauce; sandwich of white bread with a thin spread; chicken noodle or vegetable soup; low-fat yogurt or cottage cheese; fresh or canned fruits and fruit juices; crackers with white cheese or cheese spread; low-fat milk; baked potato sprinkled with white cheese and bacon bits (not real bacon but the soybean-flavored brand); or pizza—heavy on the tomato sauce and light on the cheese. If the team has an early morning practice or game, (8:00 A.M.) athletes should eat breakfast about 5:00 A.M. to ensure plenty of time to digest their meal before playing time. If they do not wish to eat breakfast that early, they could eat a lighter meal (e.g., liquid meals or juice and a piece of white toast with jelly—no butter or margarine) an hour before playing time. However, eating the larger meal two or three hours before playing time would delay feelings of fatigue and hunger and would be recommended when the team has to play a softball tournament lasting more than four hours. Possible selections for breakfast would include: cereal with low fat milk, pancakes, French toast, fruit juice, oatmeal or cream of wheat, white toast with jelly or cinnamon sugar, soft- or hard-boiled eggs, and fresh or canned fruit.

*Pre-game meal:*
- *Eat carbohydrate-rich foods*
- *Avoid fatty foods*
- *Avoid gas-forming and high-fiber foods*
- *Eat three or four hours before the game*
- *Drink plenty of fluids hourly*
- *Avoid concentrated sweets*

Candy bars are not a good source of quick energy and will not help your players perform better. A candy bar eaten right before the game may give your athletes a sudden burst of energy, but this energy boost is only temporary. The body over-compensates for the increase in blood sugar that results from eating a simple sugar (such as candy), causing feelings of tiredness and hunger. Your athletes will be full of energy for only a short time, then they will become sluggish and weak. Therefore, candies and anything high in sugar should be avoided especially just prior to activity.

## Nutritional Support During Competition

Intense prolonged activities such as softball doubleheaders and distance running require significant fluid and energy replacement during the event. Water is the most important replacement, but performance and endurance may be enhanced with proper carbohydrate replacement.

In a study of elite soccer players (Williams 1983), muscle glycogen (carbohydrate) stores were assessed after a 90-minute soccer match. The groups of players that drank one liter of a 7 percent sugar solution during the game had 63 percent more glycogen in their muscles than the group that drank plain water. In other words, the group that drank the sugar solution had much more "reserve" energy stores.

A 7 percent carbohydrate solution easily can be made by dissolving 70 grams (4.5 tablespoons) of glucose (sugar) in one quart (32 ounces) of water. Athletes should drink about 8 ounces of this mixture every 20 minutes during a match to maintain normal blood glucose levels. Many commercial carbohydrate replace-ment "sport drinks" are available with similar concentrations.

## WEIGHT CONTROL

Each of your softball players is different in height and build and, therefore, they have different ideal body weights. Rather than suggesting that your players weigh a specific number of pounds, you should work at improving their skill and physical fitness.

### Weight Loss

Athletes who have too much fat will tend to be slower and tire more easily. For those individuals, some weight loss could improve their performance. In order to lose weight, energy output must exceed energy intake. Because of this, the more active athletes have an easier time losing weight than their less active peers.

One pound of fat has the energy equivalent of approximately 3,500 calories. Reducing food intake by 500 calories per day will result in a loss of about 1 pound per week. Increasing the athlete's activity or training may also result in extra weight loss. Because fat cannot be lost at a rate faster than one or two pounds per week, weight loss greater than this amount could result in loss of body protein and not body fat. Hence, crash diets are not recommended because loss of valuable body protein (muscle mass) can occur.

Sauna baths, cathartics, and diuretics are methods used to lose weight by dehydration. These methods are not recommended because body fluids, not body fat, are lost, which reduces strength and endurance. The key to losing weight is to begin months before the season starts, follow a healthy diet, avoid high-calorie foods, eat three balanced meals, and increase activity level.

*Important points to consider when attempting to lose weight:*
- *Start early*
- *Lose at a slow pace*
- *Lose fat, not fluid or muscle*
- *Avoid excessive weight loss, especially during growing periods*
- *Avoid use of saunas, diuretics, or cathartics*

## Weight Gain

The goal for athletes trying to gain weight is to add more muscle, rather than fat. Eating an extra 500 calories per day should result in gaining one pound of muscle per week. This increase in caloric intake must be accompanied with intensive exercise, at a level that is slightly less than full exertion. A good way to add those extra calories is by adding a daily snack such as dried fruit, nuts, peanut butter sandwich, juice, milk shake, or oatmeal-raisin cookies. Trying to gain weight at a faster rate will result only in more body fat in the wrong places, rather than muscle in the right places.

*Important points to consider when attempting to gain weight:*

- *Start early*
- *Gain at a slow pace*
- *Eat nutritious foods, and not foods high in fat content*

As a coach, you can give your players some tips on how to gain or lose weight properly—eating the right foods and gaining/losing weight at the proper pace. Encourage your players to eat a healthy diet because they should naturally achieve their ideal body weight by eating balanced meals and snacks and exercising. Most of your athletes will still be growing and will require additional calories to meet the demands of their growing bodies.

If you have athletes who are excessively over- or underweight, you may tactfully approach their parents and suggest that they seek medical attention for their child.

*At the ideal body weight, the athlete performs best.*

Many teenagers eat a lot of junk foods—high in calories and low in nutrients—but the motivated athletes would prefer foods high in nutrients if they realized that these foods could help them in performing their best.

## SUMMARY

Your group of softball players is a motivated group of individuals who want to improve their performances to become a successful team. As their coach, you can provide them with the necessary information on how they can play their best. Providing your team with the nutritional advice presented in this chapter will assist them in obtaining maximum performance through eating a healthy diet and avoiding unsafe habits.

### REFERENCES

Ivy, J.L. (1988). Muscle glycogen storage after different amounts of carbohydrate ingestion. *Journal of Applied Physiology, 65,* 2018-2023.

Ivy, J.L. (1988). Muscle glycogen synthesis after exercise: Effect of time on carbohydrate ingestion. *Journal of Applied Physiology, 64,* 1480-1485.

Mathews, D., & Fox, E. (1976). The physiological bases of physical education and athletics. Philadelphia: W.B. Saunders.

Williams, M.H. (1983). *Ergogenic aids in sports.* Champaign, IL: Human Kinetics.

### SUGGESTED READINGS

American College of Sports Medicine. (1987). Position stand on the use of anabolic-androgenic steroids in sports. *Medicine and Science in Sports and Exercise, 19*(5), 534-539.

Clark, N. (1981). *The athlete's kitchen: A nutrition guide and cookbook.* Boston: CBI Publishing.

Darden, E. (1976) *Nutrition and athletic performance.* Pasadena, CA: The Athletic Press.

*Food and Nutrition Board: Recommended dietary allowances.* Rev. Ed., 1980. Washington, D.C.: National Academy of Sciences.

Higdon, H. (1978). *The complete diet guide for runners and other athletes.* Mountain View, CA: World Publications.

Katch, F.I., & McArdle, W.D. (1977). *Nutrition, weight control, and exercise.* Boston: Houghton Mifflin.

National Association for Sport and Physical Education. (1984). *Nutrition for sport success.* Reston, VA: American Alliance for Health, Physical Education, Recreation and Dance.

Smith, N.J. (1976) *Food for sport.* Palo Alto, CA: Bull Publishing.

Williams, E.R., & Caliendo, M.A. (1984) *Nutrition, principle issues, and application.* New York, NY: McGraw-Hill.

Williams, M.H. (1983) *Nutrition for fitness and sport.* Dubuque, Iowa: Wm. C. Brown.

# 26
# Prevention of Common Softball Injuries

*Rich Kimball, M.A.*
*Eugene W. Brown, Ph.D.*
*Wade Lillegard, M.D.*
*Cathy Lirgg, A.T.C.*

---

## QUESTIONS TO CONSIDER

- What role does equipment and apparel play in the prevention of softball related injuries?
- How can the facilities be made safer for softball?
- What effect can warm-ups, cool-downs, and conditioning have on preventing injuries?
- What role does teaching players safety, appropriate softball techniques, and proper drills have in injury prevention?
- What injury prevention techniques can be implemented over the course of a season?

---

## INTRODUCTION

Softball involves the application of large muscular forces and physical contact at all levels of the game. In spite of rules designed to decrease body contact, collisions with fences, the ground, and other players are inevitable. Each collision presents an opportunity for an injury to occur. All of the muscular force and physical contact cannot be eliminated from softball. However, if you follow several steps aimed at preventing injuries, you can make softball a safer game.

*As a youth softball coach, you are responsible for doing everything reasonable to provide participants the opportunity to compete in an environment that is healthy and safe.*

## INJURY PREVENTION TECHNIQUES
### Equipment and Apparel

Although little equipment is necessary to protect against injury, a properly equipped and attired softball player is less likely to be injured. Because most softball injuries involve being hit with a ball or bat, it is essential that batters and catchers wear protective equipment (batting helmet, face mask, chest protector) that fit properly. Time should be taken to fit each player with a batting helmet and to fit all catchers with masks and chest protectors. Uniforms should be loose enough to allow freedom of movement but not so sloppy that players are preoccupied with pushing up sleeves or pulling up shorts. If a player must wear glasses, safety lenses or glass guards should also be required.

Parents should be informed during a pre-season parents' orientation meeting about appropriate equipment and apparel for their children. They should be made aware that: (a) if eyeglasses are essential for their child to play, they should be safety glasses worn with a safety strap; (b) their child's shoes and glove should fit properly; (c) jewelry is not appropriate at practices or games; and (d) gum chewing is prohibited.

At the start of the first practice, you should reinforce what you told the parents about appropriate equipment and apparel and determine if:

- all players are properly attired
- equipment (e.g., eyeglasses, gloves, batting helmet) properly fits

This type of inspection should be carried out regularly.

## Facilities

Inspection of a practice or game field for safety hazards is the responsibility of the adults in charge. For practices, the coach is responsible for the safety of all fields. For games, both the officials and coaches are responsible. Therefore, you or your assistant must inspect the fields before permitting your players to participate in practices and games. Whoever is responsible for inspecting the facilities should arrive approximately 10 minutes before the players to carry out the inspection.

*If a safety hazard is present, it must be avoided by either relocating, rescheduling, restricting the activity, or removing the hazard.*

There are three categories of safety hazards associated with facilities. These are field conditions, structural hazards, and environmental hazards. Safety hazards that are not easily rectified must be reported to the league and/or program administrators. If corrections are not made quickly, you should resubmit your con-

cerns in writing. Do not play on fields that you consider hazardous to your athletes!

- **Field Conditions**

Some playing fields may have rocks and holes which are dangers as well as detracting from the skill of playing the game. Other fields that have playable conditions can quickly change from one that is safe to one that is dangerous. These changing conditions are usually associated with an excessive buildup of water and mud from rain, broken glass, and holes in the fence.

- **Structural Hazards**

The softball field should be free of obstacles near boundary lines (e.g., bleachers, light poles) and free of extraneous objects or debris on the field that might threaten the safety of the participants. In cases where light poles are very close to the playing fields, the poles should be well-padded. The playing area itself should be smooth with all holes around home plate, first base, and the outfield filled before play or practice is allowed. Fences should be checked frequently to assure that wires are not protruding in a way to be dangerous to either players or spectators.

- **Environmental Hazards**

Lightning is an environmental condition that can be extremely hazardous. No matter how important a practice or game may seem to be, it is not worth the risk of an injury or a fatality due to environmental hazards. Other extreme weather conditions such as high winds, hail, high temperatures, humidity, cold, and rain need to be cautiously evaluated as potential safety hazards. Insufficient light is another environmental condition that could be hazardous.

*Activity should not be permitted to continue under the threat of lightning or any other environmental hazard.*

## Management of Practices and Games

Every physical activity that occurs during practices and games has some potential to result in an injury. Fortunately, in softball, most practice and game activities have only a rare chance in resulting in an injury. Injuries that do occur are the result of interactions between the situation in which the activity occurs and the physical status of the player. In addition to having an influence over the equipment, apparel, and fields in reducing the risk of injuries, you have a major influence over the physical activities of your players during practices and games. There are several steps you can take to properly manage the physical activities to reduce the rate and severity of injuries. These steps include:

- ## Teaching Safety to Players

Whenever appropriate, inform your players about the potential risks of injury associated with performing certain softball activities and methods for avoiding injury. For example, teach correct throwing and catching techniques so that injuries are not sustained by hard throws that are made when players are close together, or by incorrectly placing the hands when receiving the ball.

*The key to teaching safety to your players is to prudently interject safety tips in your instruction whenever appropriate.*

- ## Warming Up

A warm-up at the beginning of your team's practices and before games provides several important benefits. If the field is not immediately available for your team's use, warm-ups (i.e., stretching exercises) can start in a grassy area outside the field. Specific warm-up suggestions are included in Chapter 24 under "Warm-Up, Cool-Down" and "Stretching Activities for Softball." When warm-ups and stretching are completed, the skill-oriented drills on your practice plan or the formal drills before the game may begin. A warm-up period:

- increases the breathing rate, heart rate, and muscle temperature to exercise levels
- reduces the risks of muscle pulls and strains
- increases the shock-absorbing capabilities of the joints
- prepares players mentally for practices and games

- ## Teaching Appropriate Techniques

The instructions you provide during practices on how to execute the skills of softball have an influence on the risks of injuries to your players as well as to their opponents. Teach your players the proper ways to perform softball techniques, and avoid any temptation to teach how to intentionally foul opponents.

First, an improper technique often results in a greater chance of injury to the performer than does the correct execution. Acceptable techniques in sports usually evolve with safety as a concern.

Second, techniques involving intentional actions to hurt an opponent (e.g., throwing at a batter) should never be taught or condoned. Coaches who promote an atmosphere in which intentional violent actions are acceptable should be eliminated from the youth softball program. You should promote fair and safe play in practices and games with strict enforcement of the rules. Encourage skill as the primary factor in determining the outcome of the game.

- ## Selecting Proper Drills

Drills that you select or design for your practices and the ways in which they are carried out have an influence on the risks of injuries for your players. Drills should be selected and designed with safety as a primary feature. Before implementing a new drill into your practice, several safety questions should be considered.

- Is the drill appropriate for the level of maturation of the players?
- Are the players sufficiently skilled to comply with the requirements of the drill?
- Are the players sufficiently conditioned to handle the stress of participation in the drill?
- Are other, less risky drills available to achieve the same practice results?
- Can the drill be modified to make it less risky and yet achieve the desired training result?

- ## Conditioning

High intensity work is part of the game of softball. How well your players can handle fatigue determines how well they perform during the latter part of a contest. Is there, however, any relationship between fatigue and injury? The following sequence of events (see Figure 26-1) draws an association linking fatigue with an increased potential for injury.

In addition to improving performance, ev-

**Athlete becomes fatigued**

↓

**Skilled performance is reduced**

↓

**Concentration becomes difficult**

↓

**Reactions slow down**

↓

**Judgment becomes impaired**

↓

**Faulty decisions are made**

↓

**Injuries may result**

**Figure 26-1.** How fatigue is linked to an increased potential for injuries.

ery conditioning program should be designed to minimize fatigue and the potential for injury. Being "in shape" can postpone fatigue and its detrimental effects. By progressively intensifying your practices throughout the season, you can produce a conditioning effect that can be an important deterrent to injury (see Chapter 24.)

Coaches must also be aware that older players who engage in intense, frequent practices and games may need time off as the season wears on. It is possible to overtrain, and predispose to, rather than prevent, injuries. Injuries caused by overtraining have grown to represent an increased portion of reported sports injuries. Some telltale signs of overtraining include:

- elevated resting heart rate
- poor performance
- loss of enthusiasm
- depression
- higher incidence of injury
- longer time to recover from injury

Antidotes to overtraining include time off from practice, shorter practices, alternating intense practices with lighter workouts, or any combination of these suggestions. Overtraining is not usually a problem when players are practicing two or three times a week, unless they

are also: (a) playing two or more games per week, (b) playing on more than one softball team, or (c) playing on a different sport team during the same season.

- **Avoiding Contraindicated Exercises**

Over the past several years, researchers and physicians have identified a list of exercises that are commonly used by coaches but are potentially harmful to the body. These are called contraindicated exercises. This information has been slow in reaching coaches and their players. Table 26-1 contains a list of these exercises and how contraindicated exercises can be modified to eliminate their undesirable characteristics. Also included in Table 26-1 are substitute softball exercises that accomplish the same purpose in a safer manner.

- **Cooling Down**

There are few feelings more uncomfortable than finishing a vigorous workout, sitting down for a while, then trying to walk. Muscles in the body tighten during periods of inactivity following hard work.

To minimize the stiffness that usually follows a workout, and the soreness the following day, take time to adequately cool down at the end of practice. A gradual reduction of activity (the reverse of the warm-up procedure) facilitates the dissipation of waste products associated with muscular activity. Letting the body cool off gradually may not prevent injuries, but the players may experience less discomfort and be better able to function at high levels during the next workout (see Chapter 24, "Warm-up, Cool Down" and "Stretching Activities for Softball.")

## SUMMARY

This chapter has focused on three areas in which you can exert an influence to reduce the potential number and severity of injuries in softball. The first area involves your insistence that your players wear appropriate apparel and, when necessary, protective equipment. Avoiding safety hazards associated with the fields (field conditions, structural hazards, and envi-

**Table 26-1.** Contraindicated exercises and alternatives.

This table contains an outline of information on contraindicated exercises associated with the knee and spine. Safer alternative exercises that achieve the same objectives as the sample contraindicated exercises are provided.

### I. PROBLEM AREA: KNEE JOINT

#### A. Problem Activity—Hyperflexion (over flexion)

| Contraindicated Activities | Intended Purposes of Activities | Safer Alternatives |
| --- | --- | --- |
| 1. Hurdler's stretch<br> | Stretch the hamstring (back of thigh) | Seated straight leg stretch<br>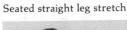<br><br>Standing bent knee thigh pull<br><br><br>Lying hamstring stretch<br> |
| 2. Deep knee bend<br> | To develop quadriceps (front of thigh), hamstrings, gluteal (buttocks), and back muscles | Half squat or half knee bend<br> |

# I. PROBLEM AREA: KNEE JOINT (continued)

## A. Problem Activity—Hyperflexion (over flexion)

| Contraindicated Activities | Intended Purposes of Activities | Safer Alternatives |
| --- | --- | --- |

3. Lunge

Wall sit

4. Landing from jumps

5. Deep squat lift

6. Squat thrust

## I. PROBLEM AREA: KNEE JOINT (continued)

### A. Problem Activity—Hyperflexion (over flexion)

| Contraindicated Activities | Intended Purposes of Activities | Safer Alternatives |
| --- | --- | --- |
| 7. Lying quad stretch (back lying position from hurdler's stretch)  | Stretch quadricep muscles | Kneeling thigh stretch  |
| 8. Double leg lying quad stretch  | | |
| 9. Standing one leg quad stretch  | | |

### B. Problem Activity—Hyperextension (over extension)

| Contraindicated Activities | Intended Purposes of Activities | Safer Alternatives |
| --- | --- | --- |
| 10. Standing toe touch  | Stretch the hamstring muscles | Seated straight leg stretch  |

## I. PROBLEM AREA: KNEE JOINT (continued)

### B. Problem Activity—Hyperextension (over extension)

| Contraindicated Activities | Intended Purposes of Activities | Safer Alternatives |
| --- | --- | --- |

11. One leg standing hamstring stretch

Standing bent knee thigh pull

Lying hamstring stretch

### C. Problem Activity—Twisting or forcing knee joint into unnatural position

| Contraindicated Activities | Intended Purposes of Activities | Safer Alternatives |
| --- | --- | --- |

12. Hurdler's stretch—see Contraindicated Activity 1.

13. Standing one leg quad stretch

Stretch quadricep muscles

Seated straight leg stretch

# I. PROBLEM AREA: KNEE JOINT (continued)

## C. Problem Activity—Twisting or forcing knee joint into unnatural position

| Contraindicated Activities | Intended Purposes of Activities | Safer Alternatives |
| --- | --- | --- |

14. Hero

Standing bent knee thigh pull

Lying hamstring stretch

15. Standing straddle groin stretch

Stretch inner thigh (groin) muscles

Seated straddle groin stretch

Butterfly

Lying groin stretch

Elevated legs straddle groin stretch

## II. PROBLEM AREA: SPINE

### A. Problem Activity—Forceful hyperflexion of cervical (neck) region

| Contraindicated Activities | Intended Purposes of Activities | Safer Alternatives |
| --- | --- | --- |
| 16. Yoga plough  | Stretch back and neck muscles | Standing bent knee thigh pull  |
| 17. Shoulder stand  | | Alternate yoga plough (Note that when lifting legs from the floor to assume this position, the knees should initially be bent.)  |
| | | Supine tuck  |
| | | Half neck circle    |

## II. PROBLEM AREA: SPINE (continued)

### B. Problem Activity—Hyperextension of the spine

| Contraindicated Activities | Intended Purposes of Activities | Safer Alternatives |
|---|---|---|
| 18. Wrestler's bridge | Stretch neck muscles | Half neck circle |

19. Full neck circle

20. Partner neck stretch

| | | |
|---|---|---|
| 21. Donkey kick | Stretch abdominal muscles | Kneeling thigh stretch |

22. Full waist circle

Reduced waist circle

## II. PROBLEM AREA: SPINE (continued)

### B. Problem Activity—Hyperextension of the spine

| Contraindicated Activities | Intended Purposes of Activities | Safer Alternatives |
| --- | --- | --- |
| 23. Back bend  | | |
| 24. Back arching abdominal stretch  | | |
| 25. Donkey kick (see Contraindicated Activity 21) | Strengthen gluteal muscles | Half squat or half knee bend  |

### C. Problem Activity—Excessive lumbar curve or hyperextension of the low back

| Contraindicated Activities | Intended Purposes of Activities | Safer Alternatives |
| --- | --- | --- |
| 26. Straight leg sit-ups  | Strengthen abdominal muscles | Bent knee sit-up  |
| 27. Double leg lifts  | | Reversed sit-up  |

ronmental hazards) is the second area. Management of practices and games is the third area. Proper management includes teaching your players safety, appropriate softball techniques, and proper drills; and conducting practices that include warming up, conditioning, and cooling-down exercises but exclude known contraindicated exercises. Safety and injury prevention should be a primary factor to consider in whatever plans you make for your softball team. You will be more than compensated for the extra time and effort required to implement the suggestions found in this chapter by the comfort of knowing that you have done as much as you can to assure that your players will have a safe season.

## REFERENCES

Rutherford, G., Miles, R., Brown, V., & MacDonald, B. (1981). *Overview of sports related injuries to persons 5-14 years of age.* Washington, DC: U.S.Consumer Product Safety Commission.
Seidel, B.L., Biles, F.R., Figley, G.E., &l Neuman, B.J. (1980). *Sport skills.* Dubuque, IA: W.C. Brown.

## SUGGESTED READINGS

American College of Sports Medicine, American Orthopaedic Society for Sports Medicine & Sports Medicine Committee of the United States Tennis Association (1982). *Sports injuries—an aid to prevention and treatment.* Coventry, CT: Bristol-Myers Co.
Jackson, D., & Pescar, S. (1981). *The young athletes health handbook.* Everest House.
Lane, S. (1990). Severe ankle sprains. *The Physician and Sportsmedicine,* 18, 43-51.
Micheli, L.J. (1985). Preventing youth sports injuries. *Journal of Health, Physical Education, Recreation and Dance,* 76(6), 52-54.
Mirkin, G., & Marshall, H. (1978). *The sportsmedicine book.* Little, Brown, & Co.

# 27
# Care of Common Softball Injuries

*Eugene W. Brown, Ph.D.*
*Rich Kimball, M.A.*
*Wade Lillegard, M.D.*

---

### QUESTIONS TO CONSIDER

- What are the steps to take in an emergency medical situation?
- What items belong in a well-stocked first aid kit?
- What procedures should you follow when a minor injury occurs?
- What information should you have about your players in case they become injured?

---

## INTRODUCTION

Chris is at the plate. The pitcher—a tall, strong player—winds up and delivers a fast pitch inside striking Chris in the chest. Chris lies motionless on the field. The umpire, sensing the likelihood of an injury, immediately signals Chris's coach onto the field to tend to the injured player.

Watching from the bench, the first, and normal, reaction of a coach is to be frightened by the possible outcome of Chris being hit. The sinking feeling in the stomach and the "Oh, no!" message sent out by the brain when Chris went down have been felt by most coaches at some point in their careers.

If this, or some similar situation confronted you, what would you do? Are you prepared to act appropriately? As a coach of a youth softball team, it is your obligation to be able to deal with such an emergency. Before your first practice, you should:

- obtain medical information on your players
- establish emergency procedures
- prepare to provide first aid

*You must not rely on the likelihood that a serious injury will not occur to the players on your team as an excuse for not being prepared to handle an emergency situation!*

## ESSENTIAL MEDICAL FORMS

Prior to the first practice, completed Athlete's Medical Information forms (see Figure 27-1) and Medical Release forms (see Figure 27-2) for all athletes must be in the possession of the coach. The Athlete's Medical Information form provides essential information about

**Figure 27-1.**

# Athlete's Medical Information

(to be completed by parents/guardians and athlete)

Athlete's Name: _____ Athlete's Birthdate: _____

Parents' Names: _____ Date: _____

Address: _____

Phone No's.: (____)_____ (____)_____ (____)_____
           (Home)                (Work)               (Other)

**Who to contact in case of emergency (if parents cannot be immediately contacted):**

Name: _____ Relationship: _____

Home Phone No.: (____)_____ Work Phone No.: (____)_____

Name: _____ Relationship: _____

Home Phone No.: (____)_____ Work Phone No.: (____)_____

Hospital preference: _____ Emergency Phone No.: (____)_____

Doctor preference: _____ Office Phone No.: (____)_____

## MEDICAL HISTORY

**Part I.  Complete the following:**

| | Date | Doctor | Doctor's Phone No. |
|---|---|---|---|
| 1. Last tetanus shot? | _____ | | |
| 2. Last dental examination? | _____ | _____ | _____ |
| 3. Last eye examination? | _____ | _____ | _____ |

**Part II.  Has your child or did your child have any of the following?**

| General Conditions: | Circle one | | Circle one or both | | Injuries: | Circle one | | Circle one or both | |
|---|---|---|---|---|---|---|---|---|---|
| 1. Fainting spells/dizziness | Yes | No | Past | Present | 1. Toes | Yes | No | Past | Present |
| 2. Headaches | Yes | No | Past | Present | 2. Feet | Yes | No | Past | Present |
| 3. Convulsions/epilepsy | Yes | No | Past | Present | 3. Ankles | Yes | No | Past | Present |
| 4. Asthma | Yes | No | Past | Present | 4. Lower legs | Yes | No | Past | Present |
| 5. High blood pressure | Yes | No | Past | Present | 5. Knees | Yes | No | Past | Present |
| 6. Kidney problems | Yes | No | Past | Present | 6. Thighs | Yes | No | Past | Present |
| 7. Intestinal disorder | Yes | No | Past | Present | 7. Hips | Yes | No | Past | Present |
| 8. Hernia | Yes | No | Past | Present | 8. Lower back | Yes | No | Past | Present |
| 9. Diabetes | Yes | No | Past | Present | 9. Upper back | Yes | No | Past | Present |
| 10. Heart disease/disorder | Yes | No | Past | Present | 10. Ribs | Yes | No | Past | Present |
| 11. Dental plate | Yes | No | Past | Present | 11. Abdomen | Yes | No | Past | Present |
| 12. Poor vision | Yes | No | Past | Present | 12. Chest | Yes | No | Past | Present |
| 13. Poor hearing | Yes | No | Past | Present | 13. Neck | Yes | No | Past | Present |
| 14. Skin disorder | Yes | No | Past | Present | 14. Fingers | Yes | No | Past | Present |
| 15. Allergies | Yes | No | | | 15. Hands | Yes | No | Past | Present |
| Specify:_____ | | | Past | Present | 16. Wrists | Yes | No | Past | Present |
| _____ | | | Past | Present | 17. Forearms | Yes | No | Past | Present |
| 16. Joint dislocation or | | | | | 18. Elbows | Yes | No | Past | Present |
| separations | Yes | No | | | 19. Upper arms | Yes | No | Past | Present |
| Specify:_____ | | | Past | Present | 20. Shoulders | Yes | No | Past | Present |
| _____ | | | Past | Present | 21. Head | Yes | No | Past | Present |
| 17. Serious or significant ill- | | | | | 22. Serious or significant in- | | | | |
| nesses not included above | Yes | No | | | juries not included above | Yes | No | | |
| Specify:_____ | | | Past | Present | Specify: _____ | | | Past | Present |
| _____ | | | Past | Present | _____ | | | Past | Present |
| 18. Others:_____ | | | Past | Present | 23. Others: _____ | | | Past | Present |
| _____ | | | Past | Present | _____ | | | Past | Present |

Figure 27-1 (continued)

**Part III.** Circle appropriate response to each question. For each "Yes" response, provide additional information.

|  | | Circle one | Additional information |
|---|---|---|---|

1. Is you child currently taking any medication? If yes, describe medication, amount, and reason for taking.　　Yes　No　_____

2. Does your child have any allergic reactions to medication, bee stings, food, etc.? If yes, describe agents that cause adverse reactions and describe these reactions.　Yes　No　_____

3. Does your child wear any appliances (e.g., glasses, contact lenses, hearing aid, false teeth, braces, etc.)? If yes, describe appliances.　Yes　No　_____

4. Has your child had any surgical operations? If yes, indicate site, explain the reason for the surgery, and describe the level of success.　Yes　No　_____

5. Has a physician placed any restrictions on your child's present activities? If yes, describe restrictions.　Yes　No　_____

6. Does your child have any existing and/or past medical or emotional conditions that require special concern and attention by a sports coach? If yes, explain.　Yes　No　_____

7. Does your child have any deformities (e.g., abnormal curvature of the spine, heart problems, one kidney, blindness in one eye, one testicle, etc.)? If yes, describe.　Yes　No　_____

8. Is there a history of serious family illnesses (e.g., diabetes, bleeding disorders, heart attack before age 50, etc.)? If yes, describe illnesses.　Yes　No　_____

9. Has your child lost consciousness or sustained a concussion?　Yes　No　_____

10. Has your child experienced fainting spells or dizziness while exercising?　Yes　No　_____

**Part IV.** Has your child or did your child have any of the following personal habits?

| Personal Habit | Circle one | | Circle one or both | | Indicate extent or amount |
|---|---|---|---|---|---|
| 1. Smoking | Yes | No | Past | Present | _____ |
| 2. Smokeless tobacco | Yes | No | Past | Present | _____ |
| 3. Alcohol | Yes | No | Past | Present | _____ |
| 4. Recreational drugs (e.g., marijuana, cocain, etc.) | Yes | No | Past | Present | _____ |
| 5. Steroids | Yes | No | Past | Present | _____ |
| 6. Others Specify: _____ | Yes | No | Past | Present | _____ |
| _____ | Yes | No | Past | Present | _____ |
| _____ | Yes | No | Past | Present | _____ |

**Part V.** Please explain, below, any "Yes" responses in Parts II, III, and IV or any other concerns that have present implications for my coaching your child. Also, describe special first aid requirements, if appropriate. An additional sheet may be attached if necessary.

_____

_____

_____

_____

_____

_____

_____

**Figure 27-2.**

# Medical Release Form

I hereby give permission for any and all medical attention necessary to be administered to my child in the event of an accident, injury, sickness, etc., under the direction of the people listed below until such time as I may be contacted.  My child's name is _____.
This release is effective for the time during which my child is participating in the _____
_____ softball program and any tournaments for the 19___/19___
season, including traveling to or from such tournaments.  I also hereby assume the responsibility for payment of any such treatment.

PARENTS' OR GUARDIANS' NAMES: _____

HOME ADDRESS: _____

                  Street              City         State      Zip

                                       (____)_____(W)

HOME PHONE: (____)_____ (____)_____(W)

INSURANCE COMPANY: _____

POLICY NUMBER: _____

FAMILY PHYSICIAN: _____

PHYSICIAN'S ADDRESS: _____ PHONE NO. (____)_____

In case I cannot be reached, either of the following people is designated:

COACH'S NAME: _____ PHONE NO. (____)_____

ASS'T. COACH OR OTHER: _____ PHONE NO. (____)_____

SIGNATURE OF PARENT OR GUARDIAN _____

SUBSCRIBED AND SWORN BEFORE ME THIS _____ OF _____, 19 ____

SIGNATURE OF NOTARY PUBLIC _____

whom to contact during the emergency as well as a comprehensive overview of past and current medical conditions that may have implications for coaching and/or emergency care. The Medical Release form is a mechanism by which parents and guardians can give permission to the coach and/or someone else to seek medical attention for their child. If the parents or guardians of an injured athlete cannot be contacted, this signed and notarized form is an essential element in the process of providing emergency medical attention.

Note that for most athletes their responses will be negative to a high proportion of the questions on their medical information forms. Therefore, an Athlete's Medical Information Summary form (see Figure 27-3) that parallels the Athlete's Medical Information form has been developed for transcribing any essential information. This summary, as well as the Medical Release, can be printed on the front and back sides of a 5 x 8-in. card. One completed card for each athlete must be present at all team events.

Another essential medical form is the On-Site Injury Report form (see Figure 27-4). This information may be helpful to provide some guidance for medical care and may be very important if any legal problems develop in connection with the injury.

The final form that the coach must have is the Emergency Plan form (see Figure 27-5). This form provides guidance for handling an emergency and is discussed in the next section.

## EMERGENCY PLAN FORM

The Emergency Plan form provides directions to a number of people in helping them to carry out their assigned responsibilities in an emergency. One completed form is needed for each of these individuals. The form also contains space for inserting site-specific emergency information. The following paragraphs describe the procedures associated with the Emergency Plan form.

Before the first practice, a number of responsible individuals must be assigned roles to carry out in an emergency. These roles are: attending to an injured athlete, attending to the uninjured athletes, calling for emergency medi-

cal assistance, and flagging down the emergency vehicle. Note that when a medical emergency occurs, all assignments must be simultaneously activated.

For most agency sponsored and for many school sponsored sports, a physician or athletic trainer are not present to assist the coach in handling the medical aspects of an emergency. Thus, after taking charge of the situation and alerting individuals with assigned tasks, the coach is likely to be the person to attend to the injured athlete. The steps in attending to the injured athlete are presented in Figure 27-5 under section B. In order to provide emergency care, knowledge, and skill in cardiopulmonary resuscitation (CPR), controlling bleeding, attending to heat stroke, attending to shock, and use of an allergic reaction kit are essential. This knowledge and skill should be obtained through Red Cross courses offered in most communities. When emergency medical personnel arrive, responsibility for the injured athlete should be transferred to these professionals. The 5 x 8-in. card that includes the Medical Release should be presented to the emergency medical personnel. If the parents or guardians are not available, the person designated on the Medical Release form (usually the coach) must accompany the injured athlete to the medical center.

If the coach is attending the injured athlete, the uninjured athletes should be directed to a safe area within voice and vision of the coach. The responsibilities assigned to the person in charge of the uninjured athletes is presented in Figure 27-5 under section C. A "rainy day" practice plan could have been prepared and available for an emergency or an accepted procedure for dismissing the uninjured athletes could be used.

Under section D of Figure 27-5 the responsibilities of the individual assigned to call for emergency medical assistance are presented. This section also includes space for entering site-specific information for the location of the nearest telephone, emergency telephone number, directions to the injured athlete, and the location of the flag person. If known, the person calling for assistance should report the nature of the injury to the receptionist. After completing the call for assistance, this individual

Figure 27-3.

# Athlete's Medical Information Summary
(important medical information to be transcribed by the coach or designee
from the Athlete's Medical Information form)

Athlete's Name: _____ Athlete's Birthdate: _____

Parents' Names: _____ Date: _____

Address: _____

Phone No's.: (____)_____  (____)_____  (____)_____
              (Home)              (Work)              (Other)

**Who to contact in case of emergency (if parents cannot be immediately contacted):**

Name: _____  Relationship: _____

Home Phone No.: (____)_____  Work Phone No.: (____)_____

Name: _____  Relationship: _____

Home Phone No.: (____)_____  Work Phone No.: (____)_____

Hospital preference: _____  Emergency Phone No.: (____)_____

Doctor preference: _____  Office Phone No.: (____)_____

## MEDICAL HISTORY

**Part I.  Transcribe Part I.**

| | Date | Doctor | Doctor's phone no. |
|---|---|---|---|
| 1.  Last tetanus shot? | _____ | | |
| 2.  Last dental examination? | _____ | _____ | _____ |
| 3.  Last eye examination? | _____ | _____ | _____ |

**Part II.  This athlete has or has had the following:**

| A. General Conditions: | Circle one or both | | B. Injuries: | Circle one or both | |
|---|---|---|---|---|---|
| _____ | Past | Present | _____ | Past | Present |
| _____ | Past | Present | _____ | Past | Present |
| _____ | Past | Present | _____ | Past | Present |
| _____ | Past | Present | _____ | Past | Present |
| _____ | Past | Present | _____ | Past | Present |
| _____ | Past | Present | _____ | Past | Present |

**Part III.  Summary of Part III responses that have present implications:** _____
_____
_____
_____
_____

**Part IV.  This athlete has or has had the following personal habits:**

| Personal Habit | Circle one or both | | Indicate extent or amount |
|---|---|---|---|
| _____ | Past | Present | _____ |
| _____ | Past | Present | _____ |
| _____ | Past | Present | _____ |

**Part V.  Responses in Parts II, III, and IV or any other concerns that have present implications for my coaching.  Also describe special first aid requirements, if appropriate.** _____
_____
_____
_____
_____
_____
_____

**Figure 27-4.**

## On-Site Injury Report Form

Name _____ Date of injury ____ / ____ / ____
         (Injured Player)                                         mo   day   yr

Address _____
       (Street)                         (City, State)                    (Zip)

Telephone _____
         (Home)                      (Other)

Nature and extent of injury: _____

_____

How did the injury occur? _____

_____

Describe first aid given, including name(s) of attendee(s): _____

_____

Disposition:        to hospital         to home         to physician

Other _____

_____

Was protective equipment worn?     _____ Yes     _____ No

Explanation: _____

_____

Condition of the playing surface _____

_____

Names and addresses of witnesses:

| Name | Street | City | State | Tel. |
|------|--------|------|-------|------|
| Name | Street | City | State | Tel. |
| Name | Street | City | State | Tel. |

Other comments: _____

_____

_____    _____    _____
     Signed                       Date                     Title-Position

# Emergency Plan Form*

Figure 27-5.

Essential Items:

1. Well-stocked first aid kit
2. Medical forms for each athlete (Athlete's Medical Information, Athlete's Medical Information Summary, and Medical Release)
3. On-Site Injury Report form

PROCEDURES

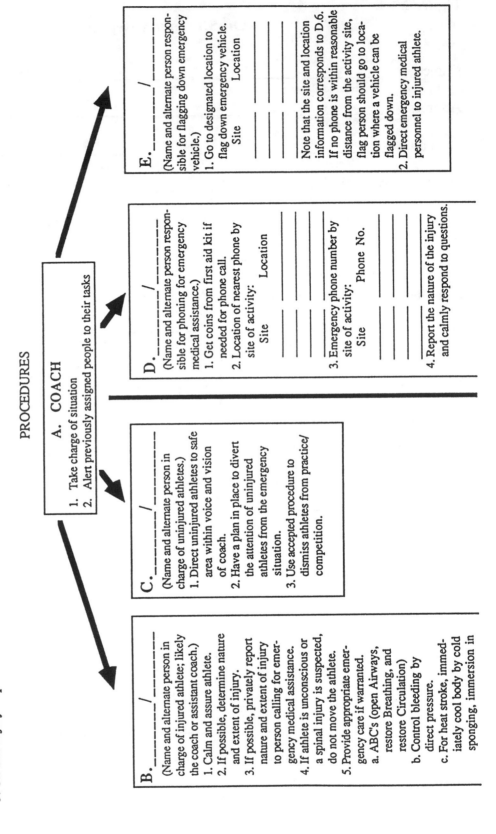

**A. COACH**

1. Take charge of situation
2. Alert previously assigned people to their tasks

**B. _____ / _____**

(Name and alternate person in charge of injured athlete; likely the coach or assistant coach.)

1. Calm and assure athlete.
2. If possible, determine nature and extent of injury.
3. If possible, privately report nature and extent of injury to person calling for emergency medical assistance.
4. If athlete is unconscious or a spinal injury is suspected, do not move the athlete.
5. Provide appropriate emergency care if warranted.
   a. ABC's (open Airways, restore Breathing, and restore Circulation)
   b. Control bleeding by direct pressure.
   c. For heat stroke, immediately cool body by cold sponging, immersion in

**C. _____ / _____**

(Name and alternate person in charge of uninjured athletes.)

1. Direct uninjured athletes to safe area within voice and vision of coach.
2. Have a plan in place to divert the attention of uninjured athletes from the emergency situation.
3. Use accepted procedure to dismiss athletes from practice/competition.

**D. _____ / _____**

(Name and alternate person responsible for phoning for emergency medical assistance.)

1. Get coins from first aid kit if needed for phone call.
2. Location of nearest phone by site of activity:
   Site        Location
   _____       _____
   _____       _____
   _____       _____
3. Emergency phone number by site of activity:
   Site        Phone No.
   _____       _____
   _____       _____
   _____       _____
4. Report the nature of the injury and calmly respond to questions.

**E. _____ / _____**

(Name and alternate person responsible for flagging down emergency vehicle.)

1. Go to designated location to flag down emergency vehicle.
   Site        Location
   _____       _____
   _____       _____
   _____       _____

   Note that the site and location information corresponds to D.6. If no phone is within reasonable distance from the activity site, flag person should go to location where a vehicle can be flagged down.
2. Direct emergency medical personnel to injured athlete.

Figure 27-5 (continued)

cold water, and cold packs.
d. For shock, have athlete lie down, calm athlete, elevate feet unless head injury, control athlete's temperature, loosen tight fitting clothing, and control pain or bleeding if necessary.
e. For allergic reaction, use ana-kit if available.
6. Transfer care to emergency medical personnel. (Note that the Medical Release Form and one individual whose name appears on the form must accompany athletes to medical center unless parents or guardians are available.)
7. Provide Athlete's Medical Information Summary to emergency medical personnel.

5. Directions to sites:

| Site | Directions |
| --- | --- |
| _____ | _____ |
| _____ | _____ |
| _____ | _____ |

6. Location of flag person by site:

| Site | Location |
| --- | --- |
| _____ | _____ |
| _____ | _____ |
| _____ | _____ |

7. Remain on the phone until the other person hangs up.
8. Return to person attending to injured athlete and privately report status of emergency medical assistance.

A. COACH, cont.

3. Use the information on the Roster Summary of Contacts in an Emergency to phone the injured athlete's parents (guardians) or their designees.
4. Complete the On-Site Injury Report form.

*A minimum of 4 completed copies of this form is needed; one for each of the individuals with assigned tasks. Make sure that information is included on all practice and competition sites.

should privately report the status of emergency medical assistance to the person attending the injured athlete.

Whether or not someone is needed to flag down and direct the emergency vehicle will depend on the site of the team's activities. The procedures for the flag person are described in Figure 27-5 under section E. In rare situations, where there is no telephone near the site of the injury, the flag person will be responsible for securing emergency medical assistance.

After the injured player is released to emergency medical personnel, the coach should complete the On-Site Injury Report form. Also, if the injured athlete's parents or guardians are unaware of the emergency situation, information on either the Athlete's Medical Information form or its Summary should be used to contact them.

## PROVIDE FIRST AID

### Aids for Proper Care

If the injury is less serious and does not require assistance from trained medical personnel, you may be able to move the player from the field to the bench area and begin appropriate care. Two important aids to properly care for an injured player include a first aid kit and ice.

#### • First Aid Kit

A well-stocked first aid kit does not have to be large but it should contain the basic items that may be needed for appropriate care. This checklist provides a guide for including commonly used supplies. You may wish to add and subtract from the kit on the basis of your experience and/or local policies or guidelines.

A good rule of thumb for coaches is, "If you can't treat the problems by using the supplies in a well-stocked first aid kit, then it is too big a problem for you to handle." You should be able to handle bruises, small cuts, strains, and sprains. When fractures, dislocations, back, or neck injuries occur, call for professional medical assistance.

#### • Ice

Having access to ice is unique to every local setting. Thus, every coach may have to ar-

___ white athletic tape

___ sterile gauze pads

___ Telfa no-stick pads

___ elastic bandages

___ Band-aids, assorted sizes

___ foam rubber/moleskin

___ tweezers

___ disinfectant

___ plastic bags for ice

___ coins for pay telephone

___ emergency care phone numbers

___ persons to contact in an emergency

___ scissors/knife

___ safety pins

___ soap

range for its provision in a different way. Ice, however, is very important to proper, immediate care of many minor injuries and should, therefore, be readily available.

### Care of Minor Injuries

#### • R.I.C.E.

Unless you are also a physician, you should not attempt to care for anything except minor injuries (e.g., bruises, bumps, sprains). Many minor injuries can be cared for by using the R.I.C.E. formula:

R = Rest: Keep the player out of action.

I = Ice: Apply ice to the injured area.

C = Compression: Wrap an elastic bandage around the injured area and the ice bag to hold the bag in place. The bandage should not be so tight as to cut off blood flow to the injured area.

E = Elevation: Let gravity drain the excess fluid.

*Most minor injuries can benefit from using the R.I.C.E. formula for care.*

When following the R.I.C.E. formula, ice should be kept on the injured area for 15 minutes and taken off for 20 minutes. Repeat this procedure three to four times. Icing should continue three times per day for the first 72 hours following the injury. After three days, extended care is necessary if the injury has not healed. At this time, options for care include:

• stretching and strengthening exercises
• contrast treatments
• visiting a doctor for further diagnosis

- **Contrast Treatments**

   If the injured area is much less swollen after 72 hours, but the pain is subsiding, contrast treatments will help. Use the following procedure:

1. Place the injured area in an ice bath or cover with an ice bag for one minute.
2. After using the ice, place the injured area in warm water (100° - 110°) for three minutes.
3. Continue this rotation for five to seven bouts of ice and four to six bouts of heat.
4. Always end with the ice treatment.

   Contrast treatments should be followed for the next three to five days. If swelling or pain still persists after several days of contrast treatments, the player should be sent to a physician for further tests. Chapter 28 deals with the rehabilitation of injuries. Read it carefully, because proper care is actually a form of rehabilitation.

## COMMON MEDICAL PROBLEMS IN SOFTBALL

   Information about 24 common medical conditions that may occur in softball is presented in this section. The information about each condition includes: (1) a definition, (2) common symptoms, (3) immediate on-field treatment, and (4) guidelines for returning the player to action.

## Abrasion

### Definition:

- superficial skin wound caused by scraping

### Symptoms:

- minor bleeding
- redness
- burning sensation

### Care:

- Cleanse the area with soap and water.
- Control the bleeding.
- Cover the area with sterile dressing.
- Monitor over several days for signs of infection.

### Return to Action:

- after providing immediate care

## Back or Neck Injury

### Definition:

- any injury to the back or neck area that causes the player to become immobile or unconscious

### Symptoms:

- pain and tenderness over the spine
- numbness
- weakness or heaviness in limbs
- tingling feeling in extremities

### Care:

- Make sure the player is breathing.
- Call for medical assistance.
- Do not move the neck or back.

### Return to Action:

- with permission of a physician

## Blisters

### Definition:

- localized collection of fluid in the outer portion of the skin

### Symptoms:

- redness
- inflammation
- oozing of fluid
- discomfort

### Care:

- Put disinfectant on the area.
- Cut a hole in a stack of several gauze pads to be used as a doughnut surrounding the blister.
- Cover the area with a Band-aid.
- Alter the cause of the problem when possible (e.g., proper size and/or shape of the softball shoes).

### Return to Action:

- immediately, unless pain is severe

## Contusion

### Definition:

- a bruise; an injury in which the skin is not broken

**Symptoms:**

- tenderness around the injury
- swelling
- localized pain

**Care:**

- Apply the R.I.C.E. formula for first 3 days.
- Use contrast treatments for days 4-8.
- Restrict activity.
- Provide padding when returning the player to activity.

**Return to Action:**

- when there is complete absence of pain and full range of motion is restored

## Cramps

**Definition:**

- involuntary and forceful contraction of a muscle; muscle spasm

**Symptoms:**

- localized pain in contracting muscle

**Care:**

- Slowly stretch the muscle.
- Massage the muscle.

**Return to Action:**

- when pain is gone and full range of motion is restored

## Dental Injury

**Definition:**

- any injury to mouth or teeth

**Symptoms:**

- pain
- bleeding
- loss of tooth (partial or total)

**Care:**

- Clear the airway where necessary.
- Stop the bleeding with direct pressure.
- Make sure excess blood does not clog the airway.
- Save any teeth that were knocked free; store them in the player's own mouth or a moist, sterile cloth.
- Do not rub or clean tooth that has been knocked out.

- Transport player to a hospital or dentist.

**Return to Action:**

- when the pain is gone (usually within two to three days)
- with permission of a dentist or physician

## Dislocation

**Definition:**

- loss of normal anatomical alignment of a joint

**Symptoms:**

- complaints of joint slipping in and out (sub-luxation)
- joint out of line
- pain at the joint

**Care:**

- mild
  —Treat as a sprain (i.e., R.I.C.E.).
  —Obtain medical care.
- severe
  —Immobilize before moving.
  —Must be treated by a physician.
  —Obtain medical care. Do not attempt to put joint back into place.
  —R.I.C.E.

**Return to Action:**

- with permission of a physician

## Eye Injury—Contusion

**Definition:**

- direct blow to the eye and region surrounding the eye by a blunt object

**Symptoms:**

- pain
- redness of eye
- watery eye

**Care:**

- Have the player lie down with his/her eyes closed.
- Place a folded cloth, soaked in cold water, gently on the eye.
- Seek medical attention if injury is assessed as severe.

## Return to Action:

- for minor injury, player may return to action after symptoms clear
- for severe injury, with permission of a physician

## Eye Injury—Foreign Object

### Definition:

- object between eyelid and eyeball

### Symptoms:

- pain
- redness of eye
- watery eye
- inability to keep eye open

### Care:

- Do not rub the eye.
- Allow tears to form in eye.
- Carefully try to remove loose object with sterile cotton swab.
- If object is embedded in the eye, have the player close both eyes, loosely cover both eyes with sterile dressing, and bring the player to an emergency room or ophthalmologist.

### Return to Action:

- with permission from a physician

## Fainting

### Definition:

- dizziness and loss of consciousness that may be caused by an injury, exhaustion, heat illness, emotional stress, or lack of oxygen

### Symptoms:

- dizziness
- cold, clammy skin
- pale
- seeing "spots" before one's eyes
- weak, rapid pulse

### Care:

- Have the player lie down and elevate his/her feet or have the player sit with his/her head between the knees.

### Return to Action:

- with permission of a physician

## Fracture

### Definition:

- a crack or complete break in a bone [A simple fracture is a broken bone, but with unbroken skin. An open fracture is a broken bone that also breaks the skin.]

### Symptoms:

- pain at fracture site
- tenderness, swelling
- deformity or unnatural position
- loss of function in injured area
- open wound, bleeding (open fracture)

[Note that a simple fracture may not be evident immediately. If localized pain persists, obtain medical assistance.]

### Care:

- Stabilize injured bone by using splints, slings, or bandages.
- Do not attempt to straighten an injured part when immobilizing it.
- If skin is broken (open fracture), keep the open wound clean by covering it with the cleanest available cloth.
- Check for shock and treat if necessary.

### Return to Action:

- with permission of a physician

## Head Injury—Conscious

### Definition:

- any injury that causes the player to be unable to respond in a coherent fashion to known facts (name, date, etc.)

### Symptoms:

- dizziness
- pupils unequal in size and/or non-responsive to light and dark
- disoriented
- unsure of name, date, or activity
- unsteady movement of eyeballs when trying to follow a finger moving in front of eyes
- same symptoms as noted for back or neck injury may be present

### Care:

- If above symptoms are present, player may be moved carefully when dizziness disappears. Players with head injuries should be

removed from further practice or competition that day and should be carefully observed for a minimum of 24 hours.
- Obtain medical assistance.

**Return to Action:**
- with permission of a physician

## Head Injury—Unconscious

**Definition:**
- any injury in which the player is unable to respond to external stimuli by verbal or visual means

**Symptoms:**
- player is unconscious
- cuts or bruises around the head may be evident

**Care:**
- ANY TIME A PLAYER IS UNCONSCIOUS, ASSUME AN INJURY TO THE SPINAL CORD OR BRAIN.
- If necessary, clear the airway keeping the player's neck straight.
- Do not move the player.
- Call for medical assistance.

**Return to Action:**
- with permission of a physician

## Heat Exhaustion

**Definition:**
- heat disorder that may lead to heat stroke

**Symptoms:**
- fatigue
- profuse sweating
- chills
- throbbing pressure in the head
- nausea
- normal body temperature
- pale and clammy skin
- muscle cramps

**Care:**
- Remove the player from heat and sun.
- Provide plenty of water.
- Rest the player in a supine position with feet elevated about 12 inches.
- Loosen or remove the player's clothing.

- Fan athlete.
- Drape wet towels over athlete.

**Return to Action:**
- next day if symptoms are no longer present

## Heat Stroke

**Definition:**
- heat disorder that is life-threatening

**Symptoms:**
- extremely high body temperature
- hot, red, and dry skin
- rapid and strong pulse
- confusion
- fainting
- convulsions

**Care:**
- Immediately call for medical assistance.
- Immediately cool body by cold sponging, immersion in cool water, and cold packs.

**Return to Action:**
- with permission of a physician

## Lacerations

**Definition:**
- a tearing or cutting of the skin

**Symptoms:**
- bleeding
- swelling

**Care:**
- Elevate area.
- Direct pressure with gauze (if available) to the wound for four or five minutes usually will stop bleeding.
- Continue to add gauze if blood soaks through.
- Clean the wound with disinfectant.
- Use the R.I.C.E. formula.
- If stitches are required, send to a doctor within six hours.

**Return to Action:**
- as soon as pain is gone, if the wound can be protected from further injury
- with permission of a physician, if stitches are required

## Loss of Wind

**Definition:**

- a forceful blow to mid-abdomen area that causes inability to breathe

**Symptoms:**

- rapid, shallow breathing
- gasping for breath

**Care:**

- Check player to determine if other injuries exist.
- Place player in a supine position.
- Calm the player in order to foster slower breathing.

**Return to Action:**

- after five minutes of rest to regain composure and breathing has returned to normal rate

## Nose Bleed

**Definition:**

- bleeding from the nose

**Symptoms:**

- bleeding
- swelling
- pain
- deformity of nose

**Care:**

- Calm the athlete.
- Get the athlete into a sitting position.
- Pinch the nostrils together with fingers while the athlete breathes through the mouth.
- If bleeding cannot be controlled, call for medical assistance.

**Return to Action:**

- minor nosebleed—if no deformity and no impairment to breathing, pack nose with gauze before athlete continues competition—when bleeding has stopped for several minutes
- serious nosebleed—no more competition that day; doctor's permission if a fracture has occurred

## Plantar Fasciitis

**Definition:**

- inflammation of the connective tissue (fascia) that runs from the heel to the toes

**Symptoms:**

- arch and heel pain
- sharp pain ("stone bruise") near heel
- gradual onset of pain, that may be tolerated for weeks
- morning pain may be more severe
- pain may decrease throughout day

**Care:**

- Rest the foot.
- Stretch the Achilles tendon before exercise.
- Use shoes with firm heel counter, good heel cushion, and arch support.
- Use of a heel lift may reduce shock to the foot and decrease the pain.
- Use adhesive strapping to support the arch.

**Return to Action:**

- when pain is gone

## Puncture Wound

**Definition:**

- any hole made by the piercing of a pointed instrument

**Symptoms:**

- breakage of the skin
- minor bleeding, possibly none
- tender around wound

**Care:**

- Cleanse the area with soap and water.
- Control the bleeding.
- Cover the area with sterile dressing.
- Consult physician about the need for a tetanus shot.
- Monitor over several days for signs of infection.

**Return to Action:**

- with permission of a physician

## Shin Splints

**Definition:**

- pain in the anterior-lateral (front-side) region

of the shin associated with running activities that may be caused by a tearing of the muscle (tibialis anterior) away from the tibia (shin), overuse of the muscle, fallen arches or excessive and repeated pronation (turning inward) of the ankle

## Symptoms:

- generalized pain in the anterior-lateral region of the shin
- usually night and morning pain
- pain may subside with activity

## Care:

- R.I.C.E.
- Have athlete engage in ankle flexibility exercises if pain free.
- If severe pain, see physician.

## Return to Action:

- when athlete no longer experiences pain
- when running no longer produces post activity pain

*[Note that mild pain may be tolerated. However, if post activity pain is pronounced, the athlete should continue the R.I.C.E. process and refrain from running types of activity.]*

## Shock

### Definition:

- adverse reaction of the body to physical or psychological trauma

### Symptoms:

- pale
- cold, clammy skin
- dizziness
- nausea
- faint feeling

### Care:

- Have the athlete lie down.
- Calm the athlete.
- Elevate the feet, unless it is a head injury.
- Send for emergency help.
- Control the player's temperature.
- Loosen tight-fitting clothing.
- Control the pain or bleeding if necessary.

### Return to Action:

- with permission of a physician

## Sprain

### Definition:

- a stretching or a partial or complete tear of the ligaments surrounding a joint

### Symptoms:

- pain at the joint
- pain aggravated by motion at the joint
- tenderness and swelling
- looseness at the joint

### Care:

- Immobilize at time of injury if pain is severe.
- Use the R.I.C.E. formula.
- Send the player to a physician.

### Return to Action:

- when pain and swelling are gone
- when full range of motion is reestablished
- when strength and stability are within 95 percent of the non-injured limb throughout range of motion
- when light formal activity is possible with no favoring of the injury
- when formal activity can be resumed with moderate to full intensity with no favoring of the injury

## Strain

### Definition:

- stretching or tearing of the muscle or tendons that attach the muscle to the bone (commonly referred to as a "muscle pull")

### Symptoms:

- localized pain brought on by stretching or contracting the muscle in question
- unequal strength between limbs

### Care:

- Use the R.I.C.E. formula.
- Use contrast treatments for days 4-8.

### Return to Action:

- when the player can stretch the injured segment as far as the non-injured segment
- when strength is equal to opposite segment
- when the athlete can perform basic softball tasks without favoring the injury

*[Note that, depending on the severity of the strain, it may take from one day to more than two weeks for an athlete to return to action.]*

## MAINTAINING APPROPRIATE RECORDS

The immediate care you provide to an injured player is important to limit the extent of the injury and to set the stage for appropriate rehabilitation. However, immediate care is not the end of prudent action when an injury occurs. Two additional brief but valuable tasks should be completed. The first of these is to fill out an On-Site Injury Report form (see Supplement 27-1) and the second is to log the injury on the Summary of Season Injuries form (see Supplement 27-2).

### On-Site Injury Report Form

It is important for you to maintain a record of the injuries that occur to your players. This information may be helpful to guide delayed care or medical treatment and may be very important if any legal problems develop in connection with the injury. Supplement 27-1 includes a standard form that will help guide the recording of pertinent information relative to each injury. These records should be kept for several years following an injury. You should check on legal requirements in your state to determine how long these records should be kept.

### Summary of Season Injuries Form

Supplement 27-2 lists each of the common medical conditions that occur in softball and also provides a space for you to record when each type of injury occurred. At the end of the season, you should total the incidences of each injury type to see if there is any trend to the kind of injuries your team has suffered. If a trend exists, evaluate your training methods in all areas of practices and games. Try to alter drills or circumstances that may be causing injuries. Review Chapter 26 for techniques that may help you prevent injuries. Perhaps your practice routine ignores or overemphasizes some area of stretching or conditioning. Decide on a course of action that may be implemented for next season, and write your thoughts in the space provided or note the appropriate changes you wish to make on your season or practice plans.

## SUMMARY

This chapter attempts to acquaint you with various injuries associated with softball and how you should be prepared to deal with these injuries. If you have prepared your first aid kit, brought along the medical records, and familiarized yourself with the different types of injuries, you should be able to handle whatever situation arises. Follow the steps that are outlined for you, and remember—you are not a doctor. If you are in doubt about how to proceed, use the coins in your first aid kit and call for professional medical help. Do not make decisions about treatments if you are not qualified to make them.

Remember, react quickly and with confidence. Most injuries will be minor and the injured players will need only a little reassurance before they can be moved to the bench area. Injuries cannot be completely avoided in softball. Therefore, you must prepare yourself to deal with whatever happens in a calm, responsible manner.

### REFERENCES

American Red Cross. (1981). *Cardiopulmonary resuscitation.* Washington, D.C.: American Red Cross.

Tanner, S.M., & Harvey, J.S. (1988). How we manage plantar fasciitis. *The Physician and Sportsmedicine,* 16(8), 39-40, 42, 44, 47.

Whitesel, J., & Newell, S.G. (1980). Modified low-dye strapping. *The Physician and Sportsmedicine,* 8(9), 129-131.

### SUGGESTED READINGS

American College of Sports Medicine, American Orthopaedic Society for Sports Medicine & Sports Medicine Committee of the United States Tennis Association. (1982). *Sports injuries—An aid to prevention and treatment.* Coventry, CT: Bristol-Myers Co.

Hackworth, C., Jacobs, K., & O'Neill, C. (1982). *Prevention, recognition, and care of common sports injuries.* Kalamazoo, MI: SWM Systems, Inc.

Jackson, D., & Pescar, S. (1981). *The young athlete's health handbook.* New York, NY: Everest House.

Rosenberg, S.N. (1985). *The Johnson & Johnson first aid book.* New York: Warner Books, Inc.

# On-Site Injury Report Form

Name _____ Date of injury ____/____/____
      (Injured Player)                                        mo   day   yr

Address _____
        (Street)                    (City, State)              (Zip)

Telephone _____
          (Home)                    (Other)

Nature and extent of injury: _____

_____

How did the injury occur? _____

_____

Describe first aid given, including name(s) of attendee(s): _____

_____

Disposition:          to hospital          to home          to physician

Other _____

_____

Was protective equipment worn?          _____ Yes          _____ No

Explanation: _____

_____

Condition of the playing surface _____

_____

Names and addresses of witnesses:

| Name | Street | City | State | Tel. |
|------|--------|------|-------|------|
| Name | Street | City | State | Tel. |
| Name | Street | City | State | Tel. |

Other comments: _____

_____

_____     _____     _____
      Signed                      Date                Title-Position

# Summary of Season Injuries Form

| Injury Type | First 4 Weeks | Middle Weeks | Last 4 Weeks | Total |
|---|---|---|---|---|
| 1. Abrasion | | | | |
| 2. Back or Neck Injury | | | | |
| 3. Blisters | | | | |
| 4. Contusion | | | | |
| 5. Cramps | | | | |
| 6. Dental Injury | | | | |
| 7. Dislocation | | | | |
| 8. Eye Injury—Cintusion | | | | |
| 9. Eye Injury—Foreign Object | | | | |
| 10. Fainting | | | | |
| 11. Fracture | | | | |
| 12. Head Injury Conscious | | | | |
| 13. Head Injury Unconscious | | | | |
| 14. Heat Exhaustion | | | | |
| 15. Heat Stroke | | | | |
| 16. Lacerations | | | | |
| 17. Loss of Wind | | | | |
| 18. Nose Bleed | | | | |
| 19. Plantar Fascitis | | | | |
| 20. Puncture Wound | | | | |
| 21. Shin Splints | | | | |
| 22. Shock | | | | |
| 23. Sprain | | | | |
| 24. Strain | | | | |
| 25. Others: | | | | |

Do you see a trend?        YES            NO

Steps to take to reduce injuries next season:

(1) _____

(2) _____

(3) _____

## SUMMARY OF SEASON INJURIES

(4) _____

(5) _____

(6) _____

(7) _____

(8) _____

(9) _____

(10) _____

(11) _____

(12) _____

(13) _____

(14) _____

(15) _____

(16) _____

(17) _____

(18) _____

(19) _____

(20) _____

(21) _____

(22) _____

(23) _____

(24) _____

(25) _____

(26) _____

(27) _____

(28) _____

(29) _____

(30) _____

(31) _____

(32) _____

(33) _____

(34) _____

# 28
# Rehabilitation of Common Softball Injuries

*Rich Kimball, M.A.*
*Eugene W. Brown, Ph.D.*
*Wade Lillegard, M.D.*

---

### QUESTIONS TO CONSIDER

- What are the important components of a rehabilitation program?
- How can a coach tell when athletes are trying to "come back" too fast?
- Is it necessary to obtain permission from parents and a physician before returning an injured athlete to competition?
- Following an injury, what determines if an activity is too stressful?

---

## INTRODUCTION

Decisions about the rehabilitation of injuries and re-entry into competition must be made according to a flexible set of guidelines; not hard and fast rules. Every individual on your team and each injury is unique. Therefore, rehabilitation techniques and re-entry criteria will differ for each injured player.

## GENERAL PROCEDURES

Most injuries suffered by your athletes will not be treated by a physician. Therefore, you, the athlete, and the athlete's parents will determine when the athlete returns to action.

Athletes, coaches, and parents realize that missing practices will reduce the athlete's ability to help the team. Pressure is often exerted on the coach to return injured athletes to action before they are fully recovered, especially

if they are the stars of the team. If an athlete has been treated by a physician for an injury, written clearance by both the physician and the parents should be obtained before permitting the athlete to return to practices and games. Also, clarification as to any limitations on participation should be obtained from the physician.

Chances of an injury recurring are greatly increased if an athlete returns too soon. The following five criteria should be met, in order, before allowing an injured athlete back into full physical activity:

1. absence of pain
2. full range of motion at the injured area
3. normal strength and size at the injured area
4. normal speed and agility
5. normal level of fitness

If a physician is not overseeing an injured

athlete's rehabilitation, the task of rehabilitation will probably fall upon the coach. Stretching activities, calisthenics, and possibly weight training exercises should form the basis of a rehabilitation program. Start with simple stretches. Presence of pain during movement is the key to determining if the activity is too stressful. The onset of pain means too much is being attempted too soon. When athletes can handle the stretching, then calisthenics and possibly weight training can be added to the program. The principles of training included in Chapter 24 should guide all phases of the rehabilitation program.

## Absence of Pain

Most injuries are accompanied by pain, although the pain is not always evident immediately when the injury occurs. Usually, the pain disappears quickly if the injury is a bruise, a strain, or a minor sprain. For more serious injuries such as dislocations or fractures, the pain may remain for days or weeks. Once the pain is gone, the athlete can start the stretching portion of a rehabilitation program.

The main goal of a rehabilitation program is to re-establish range of motion, strength, power, and muscular endurance at the site of the injury. As long as athletes remain free of pain, they should proceed with their program. If pain recurs, they should eliminate pain-producing movements until they are pain-free again. The athletes should be in close contact with their physicians during any rehabilitations from injury.

*The chance of an injury recurring is greatly increased if an athlete returns to action too soon.*

## Full Range of Motion

Injuries generally reduce the range of motion around a joint. The more severe the injury, the greater the reduction in range of motion, particularly when the injured area has been immobilized. As soon as they are able to move an injured area without pain, athletes should be encouraged to progressively increase the range of movement until a normal range is achievable. For example, if the athlete has strained a groin muscle, a fairly common injury

early in the season, the muscle should be stretched as much as possible without causing pain. Initially, the movement may be slight if the injury was severe. With stretching, the full range of motion will eventually return. The athlete's physicians must be involved at this stage of rehabilitation. Physicians often prescribe specific exercises to safely increase range of motion. When the athlete can move the injured joint through its normal range, strengthening exercises should begin.

## Normal Strength and Size

After a body part has been immobilized (by cast, splint wrap, or disuse), muscles become smaller and weaker than they were before the injury. Just because a cast is removed and the injuries have "healed" does not mean that athletes are ready to practice or play at full speed. Loss of muscle mass means a loss of strength. Letting athletes resume a normal practice schedule before their strength has returned to pre-injury levels could lead to re-injury. Strengthening the injured area should be done conservatively and under a physician's direction. If weights are used, start with light weights and perform the exercise through the entire range of motion. If the exercise causes pain, then lighter weights should be used. To determine when full strength and size has been regained, compare the injured area to the non-injured area on the opposite side of the body. When both areas are of equal size and strength, then the athletes may progress to the next phase of recovery.

*Your goal is to have the athletes regain full strength through the entire range of motion before allowing them to return to competition.*

## Normal Speed and Agility

When a physician gives written clearance for an athlete to return to practice, incorporate progressively greater levels of intensity of activity. You should be careful to gradually challenge the previously injured body part. In your observation of injured athletes, try to detect any favoring of an injured part or inability to smoothly perform a skill at increasing intensities. When athletes can move at pre-injury speed and agility, they are almost ready to play. However, they must still establish their pre-injury level of fitness.

*The main goal of a rehabilitation program is to re-establish range of motion, strength, power, and muscular endurance to the injured area.*

## Normal Level of Fitness

Every extended layoff reduces the level of muscular fitness. While recovering, the athlete may be able to exercise other body parts without affecting the injured area. For example, someone with a sprained ankle may not be able to run and field the ball, but he/she may be able to swim. Someone with a broken wrist may be able to do a variety of lower body activities such as jog, play defense, or walk through plays. Cautiously encourage this type of activity, because it helps to maintain portions of the athlete's pre-injury levels of fitness. Athletes who have missed long periods of time due to an injury should practice for several days after meeting the previous criteria before being allowed to play in a game. Their cardiovascular system and the endurance of the injured musculature need time to adjust to the demands of the game. The longer the layoff, the more conditioning work the athlete will need.

## SUMMARY

When the pain is gone, and the range of motion, strength, agility, and conditioning are back to normal, your athlete is ready to re-enter practice and competition. The entire process may have taken two days for a bruise to 12 or more weeks and assistance from physicians for a fracture. In either case, if you have followed the general guidelines of this chapter, you know you have acted in the best long-term interest of the athlete. Participation is important, but only if participation is achieved with a healthy body. Resist the pressure and the temptation to rush athletes into a game before they are ready. Your patience will be rewarded in the games to come.

# Appendix A

## DEFENSIVE AND OFFENSIVE DRILLS

The following pages contain: (1) a drill matrix indicating which drills are appropriate for a variety of skill levels and various positions within those skill levels; and (2) a description and illustration of each drill.

## SOFTBALL DRILL MATRIX

KEY: P-pitcher, C-catcher, 1-first base, 2-second base, 3-third base, S-shortstop, O-outfield, H-hitting, B-bunting, BR-baserunning

| | SKILL LEVEL | | |
|---|---|---|---|
| **DEFENSIVE DRILLS** | **Beginning** 6-10 yrs. | **Intermediate** 11-13 yrs. | **Advanced** 14 and over |
| *Catching, Throwing Infield Drills* | | | |
| Taped ball throwing | P C 1 2 3 S O | P C 1 2 3 S O | P C 1 2 3 S O |
| Long toss drill | P C 1 2 3 S O | P C 1 2 3 S O | P C 1 2 3 S O |
| Hot potato drill | P C 1 2 3 S O | P C 1 2 3 S O | P C 1 2 3 S O |
| Pickup drill | P C 1 2 3 S | P C 1 2 3 S | P C 1 2 3 S |
| Short hop drill | P C 1 2 3 S O | P C 1 2 3 S O | P C 1 2 3 S O |
| Diamond drill | 1 2 3 S | 1 2 3 S | 1 2 3 S |
| *Outfield Drills* | | | |
| Fly ball fielders' tennis drill | P C 1 2 3 S O | P C 1 2 3 S O | P C 1 2 3 S O |
| Quarterback drill | | P C 1 2 3 S O | P C 1 2 3 S O |
| Outfielder drop step/crossover drill | | O | O |
| Outfielder's pickup drill | O | O | O |
| Outfield fence drill | | O | O |
| Shoestring catch drill | | P C 1 2 3 S O | P C 1 2 3 S O |
| Sun fly ball drill | | P C 1 2 3 S O | P C 1 2 3 S O |
| Outfielders' game-saver drill | | O | O |
| *Position Drills* | | | |
| Pitcher's fielding drill | P | P | P |
| Pitcher covering home plate drill | P | P | P |
| Pitcher's quick throw | | | P |
| Catcher's bunt fielding drill | C | C | C |
| Catcher's pop-up drill | C | C | C |

## SOFTBALL DRILL MATRIX (continued)

KEY: P-pitcher, C-catcher, 1-first base, 2-second base, 3-third base, S-shortstop, O-outfield, H-hitting, B-bunting, BR-baserunning

| | | SKILL LEVEL | |
|---|---|---|---|
| **DEFENSIVE DRILLS** | **Beginning** 6-10 yrs. | **Intermediate** 11-13 yrs. | **Advanced** 14 and over |
| Catcher's down–up drill | C | C | C |
| Catcher's no-mitt block drill | C | C | C |
| Catcher's PB/WP 3 in 1 drill | P C | P C | P C |
| First baseperson's one-handed drill | | 1 | 1 |
| First baseperson's scoop drill | | 1 | 1 |
| Unassisted force out double play drill | P C 1 2 3 S O | P C 1 2 3 S O | P C 1 2 3 S O |
| SS-2B double play drill | 2 S | 2 S | 2 S |
| Third baseperson's slow roller drill | | 3 | 3 |
| Infield priority drill | P C 1 2 3 S | P C 1 2 3 S | P C 1 2 3 S |
| Infield–Outfield priority drill | P C 1 2 3 S O | P C 1 2 3 S O | P C 1 2 3 S O |
| Outfield priority drill | O | O | O |
| Relay drill | P C 1 2 3 S O | P C 1 2 3 S O | P C 1 2 3 S O |
| Basic relay drill | P C 1 2 3 S O | P C 1 2 3 S O | P C 1 2 3 S O |

## OFFENSIVE DRILLS

### Hitting

| | Beginning | Intermediate | Advanced |
|---|---|---|---|
| Shadow drill | H | H | H |
| Hip rotation drill | H | H | H |
| Batting tee drill | H | H | H |
| Soft toss hitting drill | H | H | H |
| Power swing drill | | H | H |
| Pepper game drill | | H P C 1 2 3 S O | H P C 1 2 3 S O |

### Bunting

| | Beginning | Intermediate | Advanced |
|---|---|---|---|
| Soft toss bunting drill | B | B | B |
| Target bunting drill | | B | B |
| Bunt and slap drill | | B | B |

### Baserunning

| | Beginning | Intermediate | Advanced |
|---|---|---|---|
| General baserunning drill | BR | BR | BR |
| Rounding first base drill | BR | BR | BR |
| Leadoff drill | BR | BR | BR |
| Leadoff/get a jump at first base drill | BR | BR | BR |
| Tag up drill | BR | BR | BR |
| Finding your sliding leg drill | BR | BR | BR |
| Sliding progression | BR | BR | BR |
| Rundown drill | BR P C 1 2 3 S O | BR P C 1 2 3 S O | BR P C 1 2 3 S O |

# SOFTBALL DRILLS

## Catching, Throwing Infield Drills

**Name:** Taped Ball Throwing Drill (see Figure A-1)

**Objective:** To practice throwing with proper spin on the ball

**Suggested for:** All skill levels

**Description:** This drill emphasizes correct grip and ball rotation for the overhand throw. A single strip of black electrical tape is applied around and across the wide seams of the ball. When the ball is thrown in a correct overhand fashion, a solid stripe appears on the ball. The stripe provides visual feedback to the thrower and indicates whether the ball is spinning correctly. To execute the drill, players form two parallel lines and throw the ball back and forth to each other emphasizing proper grip and rotation (see Figure A-1).

### Key Elements:

- This drill may be used as a throwing warm-up.

- The ball should be gripped with 2-4 fingers across the wide seams so that the black strip of tape is between the fingers. The thumb is opposite the fingers.
- The force production phase of the throw should not be sacrificed for spin. The two should occur together.
- The absence of the solid stripe on the ball in flight is an indication of a mechanical flaw in the throwing motion.

### Common Errors:

- Gripping the ball improperly.
- Throwing sidearm or three-quarter arm rather than overhand.

### Modifications:

- More experienced players can perform this drill hot potato fashion.
- Proper spin can be achieved initially by moving players close together and using the wrist only.

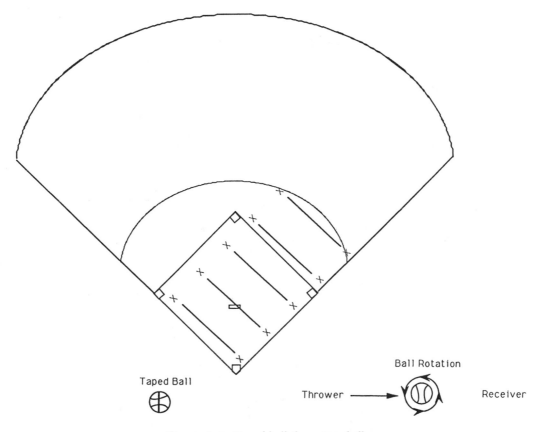

**Figure A-1.** Taped ball throwing drill.

**Name:** Long Toss Drill (see Figure A-2)

**Objective:** To strengthen and improve the accuracy of player's throwing arms

**Suggested for:** Players of all skill levels

**Description:** Partners play catch at a routine distance and gradually increase the distance of the throw. The final distance is determined by the skill level. The throws should be challenging but not unrealistic. Players continue to play catch for about 10 successful throws and catches (see Figure A-2).

**Key Elements:**
- Players should be thoroughly stretched before throwing long.
- Players must concentrate on throwing with correct form.
- All throws should reach the target in the air or on one bounce.

**Common Errors:**
- Throwing three-quarter arm or sidearm rather than overhand.
- Incomplete joint sequence (i.e. arm-only throws) which may be indicated by little or no follow-through.
- Excessive arc on the ball in an attempt to increase distance. Throws should be low and hard.

**Modifications:**
- The drill can be done individually by throwing down a foul line to home plate. The player gradually moves back on successive days. The player goes down the foul line with a bag of balls and uses home plate as a throwing target.

**Name:** Hot Potato Drill (see Figure A-3)

**Objective:** To practice receiving and throwing a ball quickly and accurately

**Suggested for:** All players proficient in catching and throwing

**Description:** Players are in pairs, 50-60 ft. apart. The drill begins on a command from the coach and each pair tries to make as many successful

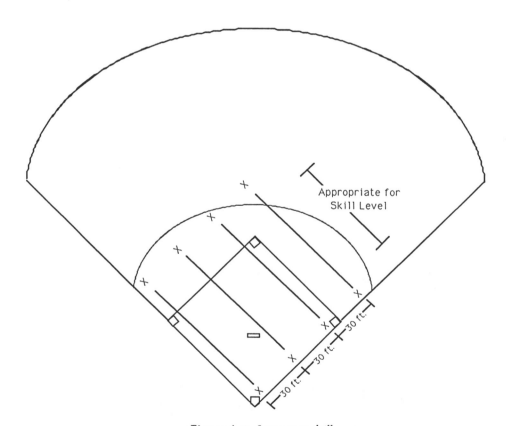

**Figure A-2.** Long toss drill.

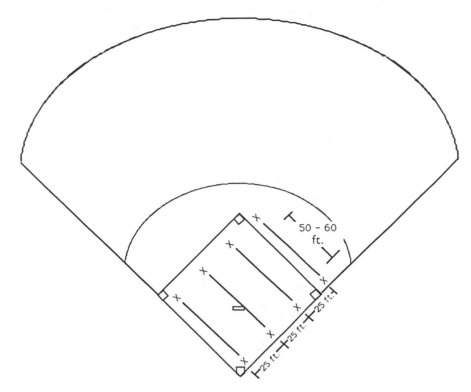

**Figure A-3.** Hot potato drill.

catches and throws as possible in a given period of time. Every time this drill is repeated, the pair should try to beat their previous total. Players can progress up to 1½ minutes of continuous catching and throwing (see Figure A-3).

### Key Elements:

- Throws should be chest high.
- The receiver should raise both hands as a target for the thrower.
- To catch throws that are off target, players should move their feet while the ball is in flight in order to be correctly positioned for an efficient return.
- Wild or missed throws should be chased promptly with the chaser returning to the original position before returning the ball.

### Common Errors:

- Lack of concentration.
- Catching the ball one-handed, slowing down the ball transfer to the throwing hand.
- Reaching for an inaccurate throw rather than moving the feet, slowing the return efficiency.
- Not moving back to the starting position after the throw.

### Modifications:

- Move less-skilled players closer together and eliminate the time element. Focus on correct technique.
- Using tennis balls, without gloves, will reinforce the use of two hands.
- More advanced players move further apart in order to build arm strength.

**Name:** Pickup Drill (see Figure A-4)

**Objective:** To improve endurance and to practice staying low when fielding ground balls

**Suggested for:** All skill levels

**Description:** Players are in pairs, about 6 ft. apart. Player A has a ball and Player B assumes a fielding position, with or without a glove. Player A rolls the ball about 5 ft. to one side of Player B who shuffles into position, fields the ball, and tosses it back. The ball is then rolled 5 ft. to the other side of Player B. This continues until Player B has 20-25 rollers. The players then switch roles (see Figure A-4).

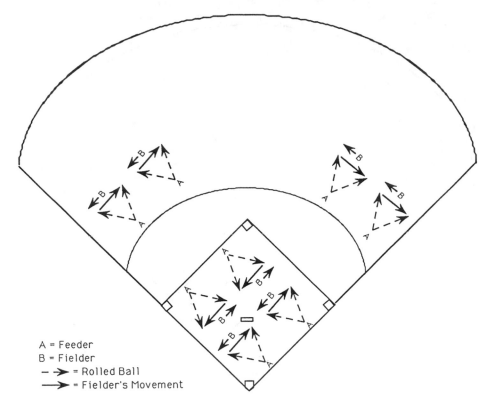

A = Feeder
B = Fielder
- ➤ = Rolled Ball
➤ = Fielder's Movement

**Figure A-4.** Pickup drill.

## Key Elements:
- Each pair should be given enough space so he/she does not interfere with other pairs.
- The fielder receives the ball with two hands, out in front of the body, watching the ball all of the way into the glove.
- Throughout the drill, the fielder must stay low. Form should not be sacrificed in order to increase the speed of performance.
- Adjust the pace of the drill in order to challenge the fielder.

## Common Errors:
- The feeder bounces the ball rather than rolling it.
- The feeder rolls the ball too slow, too fast, or too wide. This causes the drill to break down.
- The feeder does not challenge the fielder.
- The fielder does not work to get in front of the ball.

## Modifications:
- The drill can be done with two balls to quicken the pace.
- As players become more proficient, the number of repetitions can be increased.

**Name:** Short Hop Drill (see Figure A-5)

**Objective:** To practice fielding balls that bounce sharply in front of the fielder

**Suggested for:** Players of all skill levels

**Description:** Players are in pairs, 15-20 ft. apart. Player A bounces the ball about 2 ft. in front of Player B. The short hop is fielded by absorbing the ball with both hands and drawing it toward the body. The ball is then bounced back to Player A who fields the ball in the same fashion. The drill continues until a specific number of short hops are successfully fielded (see Figure A-5).

## Key Elements:
- Fielders must begin with the hands low and the feet apart.
- Fielders must execute the drill with game intensity.
- Fielders must absorb the ball with both hands.

## Common Errors:
- Fielders raise the glove up before moving it back down to attempt the catch.

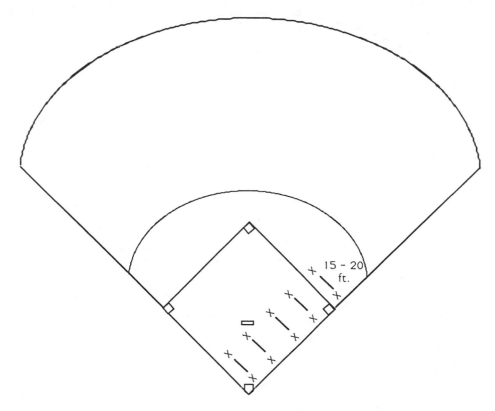

**Figure A-5.** Short hop drill.

- Fielders raise their heads and lose sight of the ball.
- The ball is bounced too far away or too close to the fielder and does not result in a short hop.

**Modifications:**

- Short hop throws may be made to the backhand and forehand sides.
- The location of the short hop can be random.
- Tennis balls or rag balls can be used to ensure safety.
- The distance between fielders can be decreased in order to sharpen reflexes.

**Name:** Diamond Drill (see Figure A-6)

**Objective:** To provide players with more ground ball fielding opportunities in a given period of time

**Suggested for:** Infielders of all skill levels

**Description:** Infielders are stationed at each infield position (1B, 2B, 3B, SS). Two players from each group hit ground balls and catch return throws. Players at each position field a ball that is hit to them and return to the end of the line. All four groups work simultaneously. After 10 ground balls per group, a different player hits, the hitter becomes the catcher, and the catcher returns to the field.

**Key Elements:**

- Fielders must use correct fielding technique and move quickly to field the ball.
- Activity in this drill must be constant!
- For safety reasons, all ground balls should be hit to a specific location (i.e., right, left, straight on) to eliminate the chance of two fielders colliding.

**Common Errors:**

- The ball is hit outside of the fielding area and the activity is stopped until the ball is retrieved.
- The hitters do not control the direction of the hit.

**Modifications:**

- If players are not skilled fungo hitters, ground balls can be thrown or rolled.

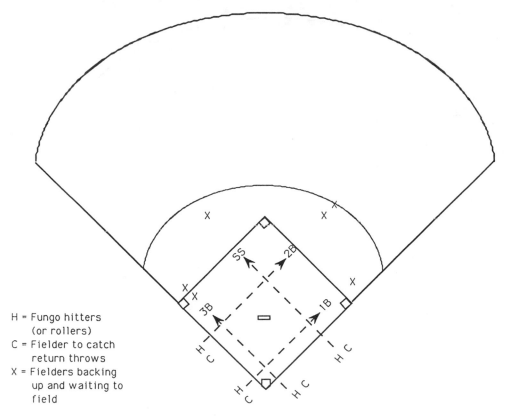

H = Fungo hitters
(or rollers)
C = Fielder to catch
return throws
X = Fielders backing
up and waiting to
field

**Figure A-6.** Diamond drill.

## Outfield Drills

**Name:** Fly Ball Fielders' Tennis Drill (see Figure A-7)

**Objective:** Practice judging fly balls without fear or risk of injury

**Suggested for:** All skill levels

**Description:** Using a tennis racket and a tennis ball, the coach hits a fly ball to a fielder. The fielder correctly catches the ball, makes a return throw to the coach and moves to the end of the line. The height of the fly ball and the distance between the fielder and the coach should be based on the skill of the fielder.

### Key Elements:

- Be sure the fielder assumes the correct ready position before hitting the ball.
- Keep lines small in order to reduce waiting time
- Keep the lines moving in order to decrease opportunities for distraction.

### Common Errors:

- Lines are: (1) too close to the fielder, result-

ing in a dangerous situation; (2) too long; and (3) too slow, resulting in a loss of interest.

- The height and distance of the flyball is not proportional to the skill of the fielder, and the fielder: (1) cannot make the catch, or (2) is not challenged by the fly ball and loses interest in the drill.

### Modifications:

- Because tennis balls are being used, fielders can do this with or without gloves. Both ways are recommended; without a glove reinforces two hands and eye contact and with a glove teaches glove control.
- Fielders form two lines 30-60 ft. apart. One fielder calls for the ball (i.e., "mine") and the other fielder moves into a back-up position.
- Fielders practice catching fly balls on the run, focusing on running on the balls of their feet in order to maintain a steady focus on the ball.
- Fielders may be set up in regular defensive positions and fly balls can be hit between infielders and outfielders. The fielders must

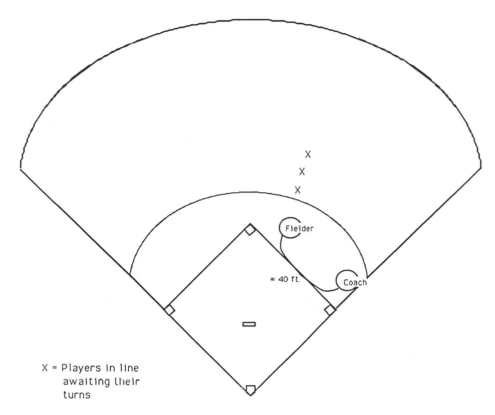

**Figure A-7.** Fly Ball Fielders tennis drill.

work on fielding technique as well as communication.

**Name:** Quarterback Drill (see Figure A-8)

**Objective:** To enhance conditioning and agility and to practice catching fly balls on the run

**Suggested for:** Intermediate and advanced players

**Description:** Players line up on the right-field foul line, about 10 ft. beyond the infield dirt. The coach stands about 20 ft. behind second base, facing the players. The first player in line runs toward the coach. As the player nears the coach he/she tosses the coach a ball. The player continues to run past the coach, sprinting toward the left-field foul line. When the player is half the distance to the foul line, the coach yells "RIGHT" or "LEFT." The player cuts in the designated direction, the coach throws the ball to lead the player, and the player catches the ball. When the ball is thrown, the next player in line runs toward the coach. When each player has had a turn, the drill is repeated in the opposite direction.

**Key Elements:**
- Before doing this drill, it is important the players are stretched and warmed up.
- The coach's throw should be challenging but realistic.
- Players must sprint on the balls of the feet.

**Common Errors:**
- The player fails to sprint for the ball or gives up too early.
- The player does not run on the balls of the feet and the ball is not clearly seen.

**Modifications:**
- The number of repetitions may be increased or decreased depending on the physical condition of the players.
- The coach can roll ground balls as the player passes. The player must get to the ball before it stops rolling.

**Name:** Outfielder Drop Step/Crossover Drill

**Objective:** To have outfielders practice getting an efficient jump on deep fly balls

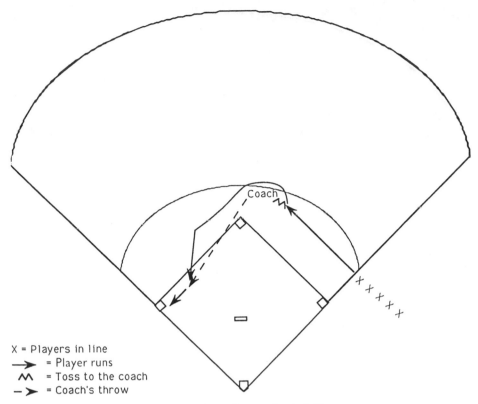

X = Players in line
→ = Player runs
Λ‍Λ = Toss to the coach
– ➤ = Coach's throw

**Figure A-8.** Quarterback drill.

**Suggested for:** Intermediate and advanced outfielders

**Description:** Outfielders are spread about 5 yds. apart. The coach faces the group and on command, the outfielders demonstrate the drop step/ crossover step in the direction of the command (i.e., "deep right," "deep left," "straight back"). Once the players consistently execute the correct form, a ball is used and the players perform one at a time. The first player assumes the ready position, the coach gives a command, and the player executes the drop step/crossover and moves in the direction of the ball. The coach leads the player with a long fly ball.

**Key Elements:**
- From the ready position, the outfielder uses an initial drop step/crossover and sprints to the ball.
- Whenever possible, the outfielder should move behind the ball and catch it with two hands on the throwing side of the body, so that the body's momentum is moving toward the coach.
- The fielders should run to the ball on the balls of the feet.

**Common Errors:**
- Starting in an incorrect ready position trying to anticipate the direction of movement.
- Misjudging the ball.
- Incorrect footwork.

**Modifications:**
- Coaches stress moving behind the ball with more advanced players.
- As skill improves, coaches can hit challenging fly balls.
- Infielders can use this drill to practice moving back on pop-ups.

**Name:** Outfielder's Pickup Drill (see Figure A-9)

**Objective:** To increase the conditioning level and the range of outfielders

**Suggested for:** All skill levels

**Description:** Minimum requirements include a hitter, a catcher, and an outfielder. The hitter hits a ground ball about 60-90 ft. to one side of the outfielder. The outfielder sprints and correctly fields the ball and throws it to the catcher.

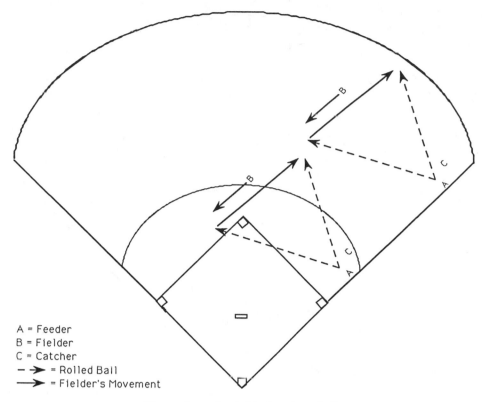

A = Feeder
B = Fielder
C = Catcher
- ➤ = Rolled Ball
──➤ = Fielder's Movement

**Figure A-9.** Outfielder's pickup drill.

The outfielder runs back to the initial position and the hitter hits a ground ball 60-90 ft. to the other side. After three ground balls to each side, the fielders change roles.

### Key Elements:

- The fielder must take a proper angle to the ball and the ball should be fielded along the midline of the body. Forehand or backhand is used as a last resort!
- The ground ball should challenge the outfielder.
- Extra balls should be available to the hitter in the event of a ball being overthrown or missed.
- The catcher may move toward the fielder or a relay person may be used to eliminate long throws.

### Common Errors:

- Not enough time is given between ground balls, and the outfielder sacrifices technique for speed. This results in missed ground balls and poor throws.
- The fielder jogs rather than sprints to field the ball.

- The fielder attempts to make the throw off balance, increasing the strain on the throwing arm.

### Modifications:

- As the players become more conditioned, the number of repetitions can be increased.
- Ground balls can be mixed with fly balls for more advanced players.
- The outfielder fields the ball and attempts to knock a ball off of a batting tee placed at least 30 ft. in front of the catcher.

**Name:** Outfield Fence Drill (see Figure A-10)

**Objective:** To practice moving to and catching fly balls in front of an outfield fence

**Suggested for:** Intermediate and advanced outfielders

**Description:** Outfielders form a line about 15 ft. in front of an outfield fence. The coach hits or throws a fly ball that lands a few feet in front of the fence. The outfielder runs back, finds the fence by extending the throwing arm,

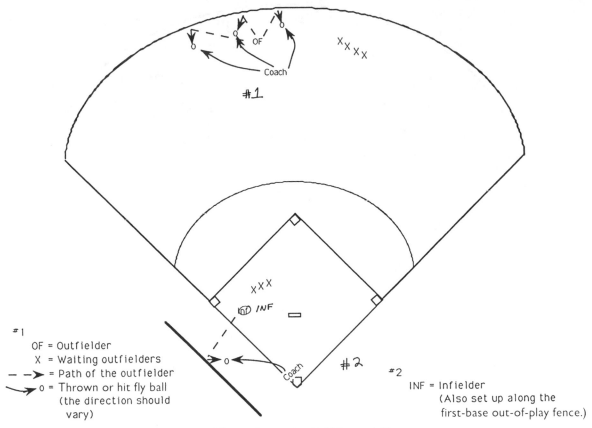

#1
OF = Outfielder
X = Waiting outfielders
- -> = Path of the outfielder
o = Thrown or hit fly ball
(the direction should vary)

#2
INF = Infielder
(Also set up along the first-base out-of-play fence.)

**Figure A-10.** Outfield fence drill.

and moves to the ball in order to make the catch. The fielder uses the throwing arm on the fence to facilitate jumping on balls hit over the fence.

### Key Elements:
- The outfielder uses an initial drop step with the ball-side foot and crosses over with the other foot.
- The outfielder catches the ball with two hands, moving away from the fence.
- The outfielder must be aware of the distance to the fence prior to the "hit."

### Common Errors:
- Back pedaling instead of sprinting.
- Being unaware of the distance to the fence.

### Modifications:
- As a lead-up drill, execute the correct technique without a ball. Move back, find the fence, and "make the catch."
- Skilled players may attempt to catch balls thrown closer to the fence in order to practice making difficult catches.

- Infielders can practice catching fly balls next to the out-of-play fences.

**Name:** Shoestring Catch Drill (see Figure A-11)

**Objective:** To practice catching sinking line drives or short fly balls and to help condition the players

**Suggested for:** Intermediate and advanced players

**Description:** Players are divided into groups of six to eight. Half of the players in each group are tossers and the other half are catchers. The groups begin 90 ft. apart and face each other. The first catcher sprints toward the first tosser. When the catcher is about halfway to the tosser, the tosser throws a short fly ball and the catcher attempts a catch on the shoestrings. Once the toss is made, the tosser sprints to the end of the catching line. Once the catch is made, the catcher continues to sprint toward the tossing line, hands the ball to the next tosser, just off the ground and moves to the end of the tossing

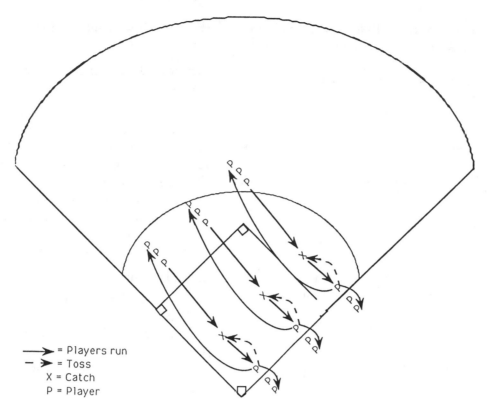

= Players run
= Toss
X = Catch
P = Player

**Figure A-11.** Shoestring catch drill.

line. Players continue until each one has been the catcher 5-10 times.

### Key Elements:

- The toss is the key to this drill. It must be challenging but realistic.
- If the ball cannot be caught in the air, the fielder must field it on the short hop and keep it in front of the body. The ball should not get past the fielder.
- Players in both groups must sprint hard. Any missed ball must be recovered quickly.
- Players must move to opposite lines without interfering with the catchers/tossers.

### Common Errors:

- Lack of intensity and concentration.
- Jogging rather than sprinting.
- Sprinting heel to toe causing a "jarred" perception of the ball.
- Raising the head on a possible short hop.

### Modifications:

- Decreasing the number of players per group will increase the conditioning benefits.
- Low line drives can be tossed as an alternative to short fly balls. The ball can also be tossed to either side.
- The players can form a line and the coach can fungo hit or toss the ball. The players charge the ball, throw to the catcher, and move to the end of the line.

**Name:** Sun Fly Ball Drill

**Objective:** To practice fielding fly balls in the sun

**Suggested for:** Intermediate and advanced players

**Description:** Players work in groups of three or four. One player is the thrower and stands with the sun behind his/her back. The other fielders stand 30-40 ft. from the thrower and face the sun. The thrower launches a fly ball and the fielders use their gloves to shade their eyes. The fielder in the best position calls for the ball and makes the catch.

### Key Elements:

- Using the glove to shield the sun.

- As the ball nears the fielder, the throwing hand is raised in order to make a two-handed catch.
- The fielders must call for the ball in order to make the catch.

**Common Errors:**

- Failing to correctly shade the eyes with the glove.
- Attempting to make the catch after losing sight of the ball in the sun.

**Modifications:**

- Tennis balls can be used in order to ensure safety.
- More advanced players may have fly balls thrown at all angles and depths in order to simulate game conditions.

**Name:** Outfielders' Game-Saver Drill (see Figure A-12)

**Objective:** Outfielders practice fielding and throwing with the winning run in scoring position

**Suggested for:** Intermediate and advanced players

**Description:** Baserunners take a normal lead at second base, and the coach hits a hard ground ball to an outfielder. On the hit, the runner attempts to score while the outfielder charges the ball and attempts to throw the runner out at home plate. The catcher calls for the throw, receives the ball, and tags the non-sliding runner. The coach hits another ball to another outfielder, and the drill continues.

**Key Elements:**

- The outfielder must charge the ball.
- The ball is fielded on the glove side of the body as the glove-side foot hits the ground.
- The outfielder must throw overhand and throw through the cutoff person.

**Common Errors:**

- Failure to charge the ball.

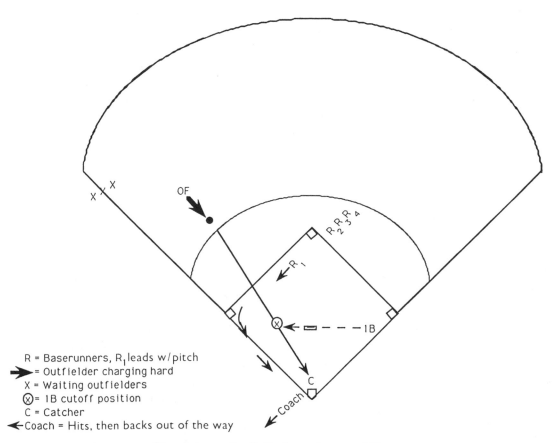

R = Baserunners, R$_1$ leads w/pitch
→ = Outfielder charging hard
X = Waiting outfielders
⊗ = 1B cutoff position
C = Catcher
←Coach = Hits, then backs out of the way

**Figure A-12.** Outfielder's game-saver drill.

- Taking too many steps to throw after fielding the ball.
- Raising the head before the ball is secured.

**Modifications:**

- Initially, outfielders may execute this drill without baserunners in order to focus on proper technique.

## Position Drills

**Name:** Pitcher's Fielding Drill (see Figure A-13)

**Objective:** To improve pitcher's fielding ability and to teach throwing locations for various situations.

**Suggested for:** All skill levels

**Description:** A pitcher throws a ball to a catcher. The coach hits or rolls another ball on the ground to the pitcher. First, the pitcher fields a ground ball and throws to first base. Second, the pitcher fields a bunt and throws to first base. The process is repeated with the pitcher throwing, going to 2B, 3B, and to home plate. When the series is completed, a new pitcher repeats the drill.

**Key Elements:**

- The pitcher must be sure the ball is secured before making the throw.
- The pitcher must sprint to the ball.
- The ball must be fielded with two hands.
- After the ball has been fielded, the pitcher must step toward the target and throw to the target.

**Common Errors:**

- Letting the anticipation of a ground ball detract from the pitching motion.
- Attempting to throw to a base off balance; moving away from the target as the ball is thrown, or throwing off of the wrong foot.
- Raising the head before the ball has been fielded.

**Modifications:**

- The coach calls the situation prior to the pitch

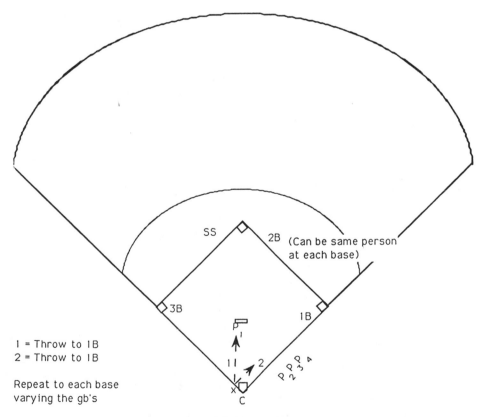

**Figure A-13.** Pitcher's fielding drill.

(i.e., R1, less than two outs). The pitcher must throw to the correct base.

- An entire infield can be used; the ball is hit or bunted after the pitch; P,C,1B,3B must call for the ball and react to the catcher's call.
- Baserunners can be added, and the catcher must make the correct call. The fielders call for the ball, field the ball, then react to the catcher's call.
- Two pitchers can practice throwing to 1B or 3B simultaneously by using another catcher at second base and using third base as a first base.

**Name:** Pitcher Covering Home Plate Drill (see Figure A-14)

**Objective:** To practice covering home plate on a wild pitch or passed ball, with a runner on third base

**Suggested for:** All skill levels

**Description:** A catcher is placed at various lo-cations along the backstop. A pitcher charges the plate after executing a pitching motion. The catcher tosses a ball to the pitcher, who then applies a tag to an imaginary runner.

**Key Elements:**

- The pitcher must sprint to home plate, hold-ing the glove high in order to give the catcher a target.
- The pitcher should expect a bad throw from the catcher in order to increase reaction time.
- The pitcher must practice making the correct tag on throws from all areas of the backstop.
- After the tag, the pitcher should look for plays at other bases.

**Common Errors:**

- The pitcher jogs to the plate.
- The pitcher tries to tag the runner before catching the ball.
- The pitcher sets up in the runner's path.

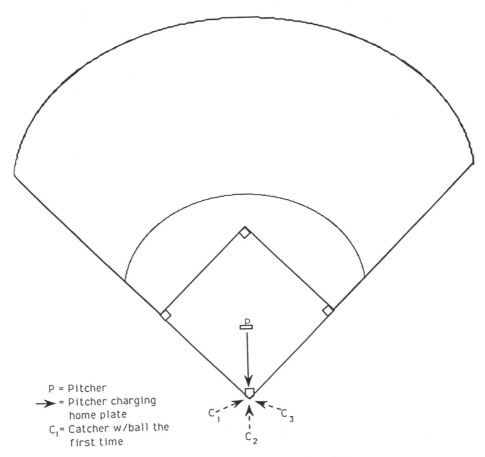

P = Pitcher
→ = Pitcher charging home plate
$C_1$= Catcher w/ball the first time

**Figure A-14.** Pitcher covering home plate drill.

**Modifications:**

- Baserunners can be added to the drill to create game-like situations.
- See the "Catcher's PB/WP 3 in 1 Drill."

**Name:** Pitcher's Quick Throw Drill (see Figure A-15)

**Objective:** To enhance the pitching motion and to increase pitching endurance

**Suggested for:** Advanced pitchers only

**Description:** Two pitchers pitch to each other at regulation distance. Pitcher A assumes the normal pitching position on the pitcher's plate and Pitcher B gives a target. Pitcher A pitches the ball to Pitcher B's target. Pitcher B repeats the process. The ball is pitched as many times as possible within a given time limit, up to 1 minute.

**Key Elements:**

- The pitchers must be completely warmed up prior to beginning this drill.

- Correct pitching form is essential with each pitch.
- Pitchers should throw hard with each pitch.
- For safety reasons, the area behind the pitchers should be kept clear.

**Common Errors:**

- Pitchers tense up in an attempt to increase speed.
- Pitchers do not concentrate on the target.
- Pitchers do not moveback to the pitcher's plate following the pitch.
- Pitchers do not take time to adequately set and deliver the pitch.

**Modifications:**

- Pitchers can set goals such as the number of strikes per minute
- Each pitcher can throw to a catcher who immediately returns the ball to the pitcher.
- Younger pitchers can throw successive pitches with quality (mechanical) goals rather than quantity goals.

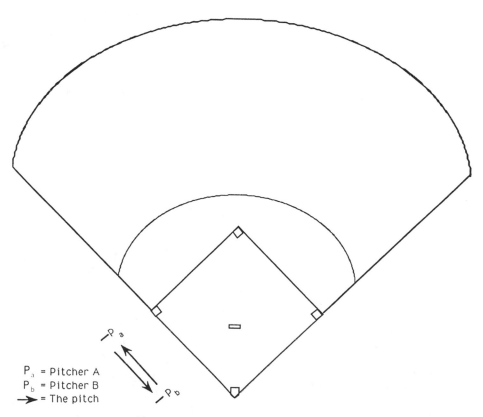

P$_a$ = Pitcher A
P$_b$ = Pitcher B
→ = The pitch

**Figure A-15.** Pitcher's quick throw drill.

**Name:** Catcher's Bunt Fielding Drill (see Figure A-16)

**Objective:** To practice staying low while fielding bunts, and to facilitate throwing to the correct base

**Suggested for:** Catchers of all skill levels

**Description:** A catcher charges a ball that is rolled 5-10 ft. in front of him/her, fields the ball, and pretends to throw to a base. The catcher rolls the ball again in another direction and repeats the process. All catchers repeat the drill down the first-base line and back.

**Key Elements:**

- Catchers must stay low when charging the ball.
- The ball is fielded with two hands.
- Crow hop and shift the weight into the throw.

**Common Errors:**

- Picking up the ball with the bare hand only or scooping the ball with the glove only.
- Standing up and moving to field the ball.

- Throwing the ball with the glove-side foot pointing away from the target.

**Modifications:**

- Can be done in the gym or on the perimeter of the infield for conditioning purposes.
- The coach can stand next to the catcher and roll a "bunt."
- Baserunners can be added that the catcher must "throw out."
- The coach can mix in pop-ups. The catcher can practice catching the pop-up and throwing to a base in order to execute a double play.

**Name:** Catcher's Pop-up Drill (see Figure A-17)

**Objective:** To practice reacting to and catching the infield drift of pop-ups

**Suggested for:** All skill levels

**Description:** The catcher assumes the crouch position behind the plate. The coach hits or throws a pop-up in the home plate area. The

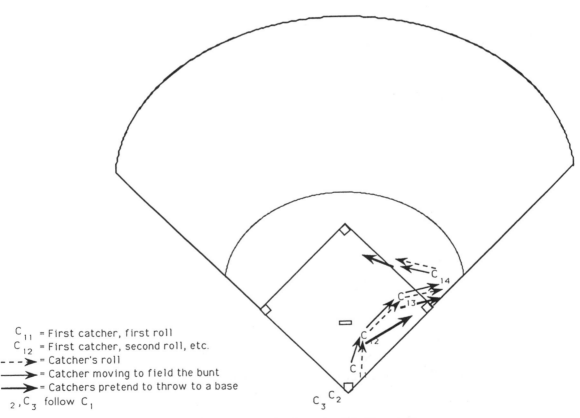

$C_{11}$ = First catcher, first roll
$C_{12}$ = First catcher, second roll, etc.
- - -> = Catcher's roll
——> = Catcher moving to field the bunt
——> = Catchers pretend to throw to a base
$_2$, $C_3$ follow $C_1$

**Figure A-16.** Catcher's bunt fielding drill.

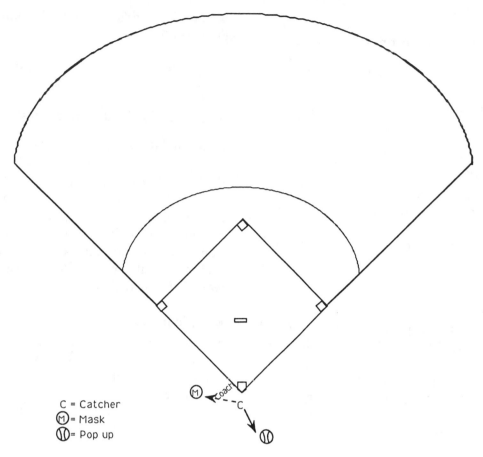

**Figure A-17.** Catcher's pop-up drill.

catcher must locate the ball, call for it, discard his/her mask away from the area of the descending ball, and make the catch.

### Key Elements:

- The catcher's back is to the infield when catching most pop-ups.
- In judging the pop-up, the catcher must take into account the wind's strength, direction, and the height of the pop-up.
- The catcher must wait until the flight of the ball is determined before discarding the mask.

### Common Errors:

- Discarding the mask too soon, before the catcher finds the ball.
- Catching the ball with the hands low.
- Facing the infield, the ball may tail away from the catcher forcing low hands to make the catch.

### Modifications:

- The height of the pop-ups can be varied. As the catcher becomes more skilled, the pop-ups can be hit higher.
- The coach can hit the pop-ups with a tennis racket for better control.
- The catcher can keep his/her head down, then look up after the ball is hit, locate the ball, and move to make the catch.

**Name:** Catcher's Down–Up Drill

**Objective:** To get the catcher from the recieving position to the two-knee blocking position and back to his/her feet as quickly as possible

**Suggested for:** Catchers of all skill levels

**Description:** Catchers in full equipment assume the correct recieving position. On a command from the coach, the catcher(s) drop to both knees as if blocking a pitch in the dirt then hop back to the recieving position in "one motion". The drill is repeated in sequences of four every ten seconds.

**Key Elements:**

- Proper position and technique must be executed.
- Equipment should be used, especially shin guards.
- Catchers should do each "down-up" as quickly as possible.

**Common Errors:**

- Sacrificing correct technique for speed.
- Losing balance when the knees are not dropped simultaneously.
- Failure to fully return to the recieving position.

**Modifications:**

- Repetitions can be progressively increased (i.e., 20-25 in 30 seconds for conditioning purposes).
- The coach or another player can throw the ball in the dirt for the catcher to block.
- The catcher can scramble after the blocked ball, field it, and "fake" a throw.

**Name:** Catcher's No-Mitt Blocking Drill (see Figure A-18)

**Objective:** To practice moving the entire body in front of pitches in the dirt

**Suggested for:** Catchers of all skill levels

**Description:** In full gear, the catcher assumes the receiving position, with both hands behind the back. The coach or another catcher throws balls in the dirt in front of and to the sides of the catcher. The catcher concentrates on quickly dropping to the knees and getting into a position to block the ball. For safety reasons, the catcher should move blocked balls out of the way of the next throw.

**Key Elements:**

- The focus is on correct technique with EVERY repetition: (1) the catcher must quickly shift and drop to the knees in order to get the body in front of the ball, (2) the catcher must roll the shoulders forward in order to keep the ball in front of the body.

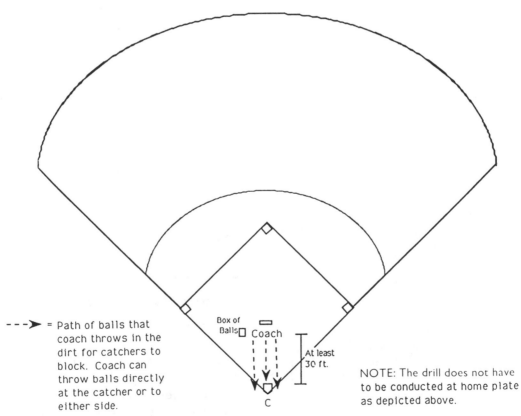

- - -> = Path of balls that coach throws in the dirt for catchers to block. Coach can throw balls directly at the catcher or to either side.

Box of Balls

Coach

At least 30 ft.

NOTE: The drill does not have to be conducted at home plate as depicted above.

C

**Figure A-18.** Catcher's no-mitt blocking drill.

**Common Errors:**

- Pitching the ball before the catcher is ready.
- Using improper technique due to fatigue.

**Modifications:**

- Using tennis balls instead of softballs to eliminate any fear of injury.
- For advanced catchers, different pitches may be thrown in order to learn adjustments for bounces with different spins.
- Allow the catcher to block with his/her mitt, recover quickly, and retrieve to throw.
- The pitcher may vary the speed and placement of the pitch.
- Many correct repetitions will also build endurance.

**Name:** Catcher's Passed Ball/Wild Pitch 3 in 1 Drill (see Figure A-19)

**Objective:** This drill is designed to develop: (1) communication between pitchers and catchers on passed balls or wild pitches with runners on base; (2) catchers' technique in retrieving the ball; and (3) pitchers' technique covering the plate

**Suggested for:** Intermediate and advanced players

**Description:** The pitcher executes an imaginary pitch and the coach rolls a ball to a variety of locations behind the catcher. The pitcher points to the ball and verbalizes the direction in which it is rolling (i.e., "1," "3," or "back" tells the catcher first base side, third base side, or straight behind). The catcher correctly fields and throws the ball to the pitcher. The pitcher correctly receives the ball and tags an imaginary runner.

**Key Elements:**

- The pitcher must yell the direction of the ball, as well as point to the ball.
- The catcher may remove the mask and must quickly move to the ball, and the pitcher must immediately cover home plate.
- The throw to the pitcher should be made with a compact snap throw.

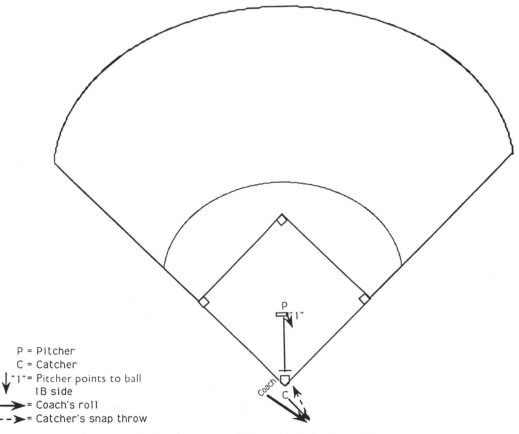

P = Pitcher
C = Catcher
↓"I" = Pitcher points to ball
    1B side
——➤ = Coach's roll
- -➤ = Catcher's snap throw

**Figure A-19.** Catcher's Passed Ball/wild pitch 3 in 1 drill.

- The pitcher must provide a target on the first-base side of the plate, catch the throw, and make the tag.

**Common Errors:**

- The pitcher and catcher move slowly.
- The catcher does not field the ball with the throwing side to the backstop.
- The catcher does not show the ball; rather he/she hides it in the mitt or with the body prior to the throw.
- The pitcher tries to tag the runner before the ball has been caught.

**Modifications:**

- Another player may roll the ball behind the catcher.
- Each drill may be done separately.
- The pitcher may pitch the ball in the dirt.
- Baserunners may be added to the drill (but are not encouraged to slide).

**Name:** First Baseperson's One-handed Drill (see Figure A-20)

**Objective:** To help the first baseperson gain confidence and competence in using one hand to stretch for the ball

**Suggested for:** Intermediate and advanced players

**Description:** Players work in groups of two; players within each group are spaced 60 to 90 ft. apart. Players stretch with the glove hand to receive a thrown ball while keeping the throwing hand in their back pocket. Throws should vary from side to side, and from high to low.

**Key Elements:**

- The first baseperson should always stretch to the ball.
- When catching the ball, the glove-side arm should be slightly flexed in order to absorb the force of the ball.
- The first baseperson should not jump in order to catch the ball unless absolutely necessary. If a jump is necessary, the first baseperson should propel the body upward with the glove-side leg and land on the throwing-side foot.

**Common Errors:**

- Failing to stretch for the ball.

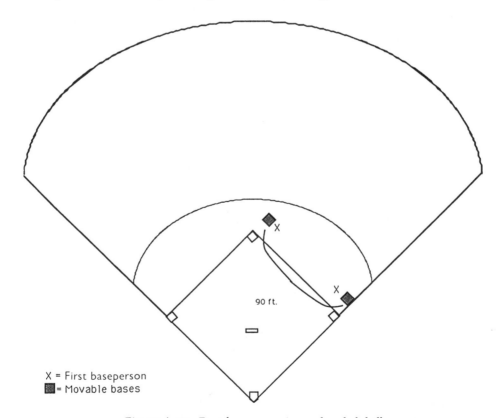

X = First baseperson
▓ = Movable bases

**Figure A-20.** First baseperson's one-handed drill.

- Stretching too soon, before the throw is made.
- Incorrectly positioning the foot on the base as the ball is caught.

**Modifications:**

- As players become adept at the drill, they can keep their hand out of the pocket but still catch the ball one-handed.
- The coach may also throw balls to the first baseperson.

**Name:** First Baseperson's Scoop Drill (see Figure A-21)

**Objective:** To facilitate fielding throws in the dirt

**Suggested for:** Intermediate and advanced players

**Description:** Players throw a softball back and forth so that all throws bounce in the dirt. Players should practice stretching to the ball and fielding it on the short hop.

**Key Elements:**

- The glove should be open and low to the ground. The arm and hands should absorb the force of the throw
- The eyes follow the ball into the glove.

**Common Errors:**

- Raising the head and losing sight of the ball.
- Stretching before the throw has been made.
- Standing upright with the glove well above the ground.

**Modifications:**

- Infielders can throw the ball in the dirt to the first baseperson during regular infield practice.
- Other infielders involved in force plays can also participate in the drill.
- Dressing the first baseperson in a catcher's mask and shin guards to eliminate the fear of fielding balls in the dirt.
- Using tennis balls for less-skilled players.

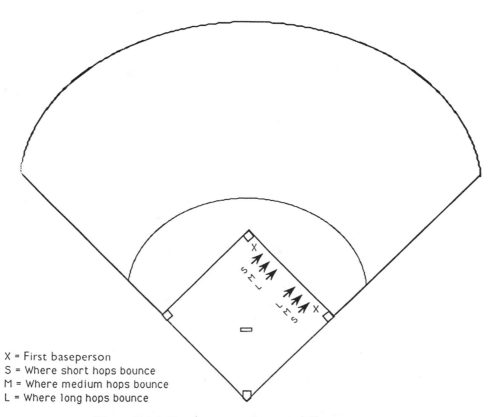

X = First baseperson
S = Where short hops bounce
M = Where medium hops bounce
L = Where long hops bounce

**Figure A-21.** First baseperson's scoop drill.

**Name:** Unassisted Force Out Double Play Drill (see Figure A-22)

**Objective:** To learn to recognize a potential unassisted force out double play opportunity and to practice the skills necessary to execute the play

**Suggested for:** All skill levels

**Description:** Standing at home plate the coach indicates the situation and hits a ground ball to an infielder. The infielder must field the ball, tag the base, and throw to 1B. For example: the coach says "runners on 1 and 2, less than two outs." The coach then hits a ground ball to third base. The third baseperson fields the ball, tags third base, and throws to first base.

**Key Elements:**

- The fielder must first concentrate on fielding the ball.
- The fielder must be aware of her/his position in relation to the base and take the shortest path to the base.
- The base should be touched with the throwing-side foot, in order to execute an immediate throw to first base.
- The fielder must understand and recognize the situation.

**Common Errors:**

- The thrower moves away from the first-base target after tagging the base, resulting in an off balance throw.
- The fielder does not communicate to the other fielders that he/she will make the play unassisted.
- The fielder is distracted by the baserunner and does not watch the ball all the way into the glove.

**Modifications:**

- Baserunners can be added in order to make the situation more realistic.
- For intermediate and advanced players, pop-ups and line drives may be mixed in with ground balls in order to make the situations more complex.

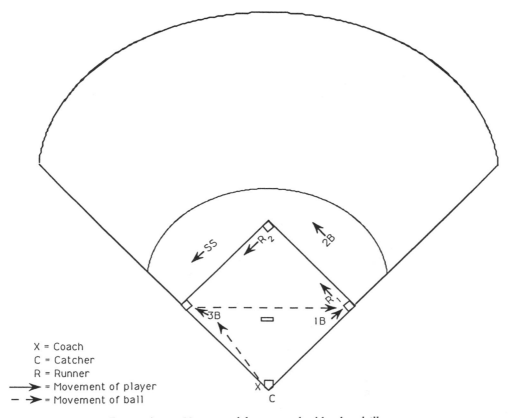

**Figure A-22.** Unassisted force out double play drill.

**Name:** SS–2B Double Play Drill (see Figure A-23)

**Objective:** To practice and enhance the 6-4-3 and 4-6-3 double play

**Suggested for:** All skill levels

**Description:** A "roller" rolls a ground ball to the SS or 2B person. The player not receiving the ground ball covers second base, receives the throw from the fielder, and completes the double play by throwing the ball to first base.

**Key Elements:**
- The ball should be rolled so the SS and 2B can practice receiving throws from different areas of the infield.
- The ball must be fielded cleanly and thrown chest high to the person covering the base.
- The fielders must ensure that they complete the force out at 2B before throwing the ball to 1B.
- The fielders should concentrate on receiving and throwing the ball correctly.

**Common Errors:**
- The SS or 2B tries to throw the ball before making the catch.
- The SS or 2B moves into the runner's path in order to make the throw to 1B.
- 1B does not stretch to make the catch.

**Modifications:**
- This drill can be set up on the infield with two groups of infielders performing simultaneously. One group is stationed at second base, throwing to first base, while the other group is stationed at home plate and throwing to third base. The rollers are positioned at the front and back of the pitcher's circle.
- The fielders can position themselves at their regular infield positions while the coach fungo hits ground balls.
- Baserunners may be added in order to provide an understanding of the time required to complete a double play.
- The coach may time the double play execution, with the goal of decreasing the time of execution.

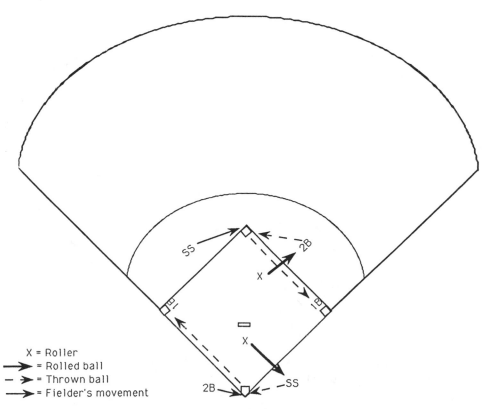

X = Roller
→ = Rolled ball
- > = Thrown ball
→ = Fielder's movement

**Figure A-23.** SS–2B double play drill (two groups at a time).

**Name:** Third Baseperson's Slow Roller Drill (see Figure A-24)

**Objective:** To practice charging and fielding slow rolling ground balls

**Suggested for:** Advanced level third basepersons

**Description:** The coach or another player rolls a slow grounder toward third base. The 3B person charges the ball and fields it. In a continuous motion, he/she throws the ball to 1B.

**Key Elements:**

- The player must use two hands.
- The fielder must charge the ball hard
- Ideally, fielding and throwing the ball should occur in one smooth continuous motion—with or without a crow hop.

**Common Errors:**

- The player does not charge the ball as quickly as possible.
- The head raises up before the ball is fielded.
- Players attempt to throw off balance.

**Modifications:**

- Players performing this drill for the first time may run through the play in slow motion, focusing on each component individually.
- Balls may be lined up from the third-base line out toward the pitcher's plate, and one at a time, players charge, field, and throw the stationary ball.

**Name:** Infield Priority Drill (see Figure A-25)

**Objective:** To learn, reinforce and promote communication among infielders

**Suggested for:** All skill levels

**Description:** The coach hits or throws pop-ups to the infield. When the ball is in the air, the player who thinks he/she has the best chance to catch it yells "Mine!" If two or more players call for the ball, the player with priority will make the catch. After several attempts, players alternate and/or switch positions.

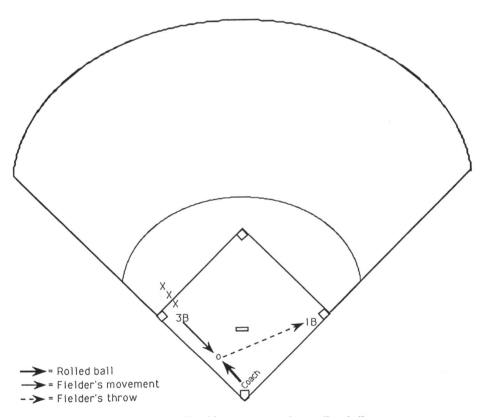

**Figure A-24.** Third baseperson's slow roller drill.

**Key Elements:**

- Players should call for the ball loudly!
- The player with priority should repeat the call several times in order to ensure being heard.
- Priority players should call off another player only if he/she has an equal or better chance of making the catch (i.e., the SS would not call anyone off on a pop-up near the first-base line).
- The coach should give appropriate feedback.

**Common Errors:**

- Failure to call for a ball before attempting to catch it.
- Calling for the ball too late. Other players may not have time to react and yield.
- Two players call for the ball simultaneously and one does not give way to the infielder with priority.

**Modifications:**

- Tennis balls may be used with less-skilled players.

- The coach may vary the difficulty of the pop-ups according to skill level.
- Instead of hitting or throwing a pop-up, the coach throws a flat object on the ground (i.e., frisbee) and the infielders move and call to stand on the object according to position priority.

**Name:** Infield-Outfield Priority Drill (see Figure A-26)

**Objective:** To learn, promote and reinforce communication between infielders and outfielders

**Suggested for:** Intermediate and advanced skill levels

**Description:** The coach hits or throws pop-ups between the infield and outfield. The fielder who thinks he/she has a chance to catch the ball yells "Mine!" If an infielder and outfielder call for the ball at the same time, the outfielder has priority to make the catch and the infielder moves out of the way.

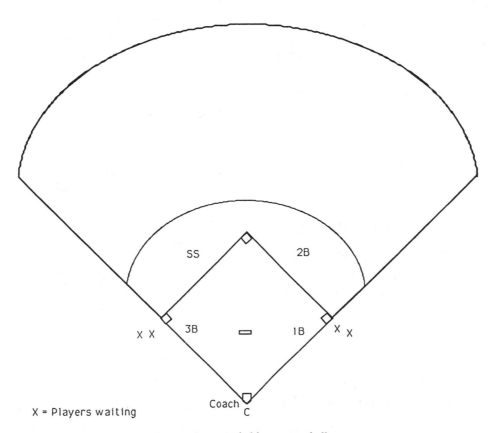

X = Players waiting

**Figure A-25.** Infield priority drill.

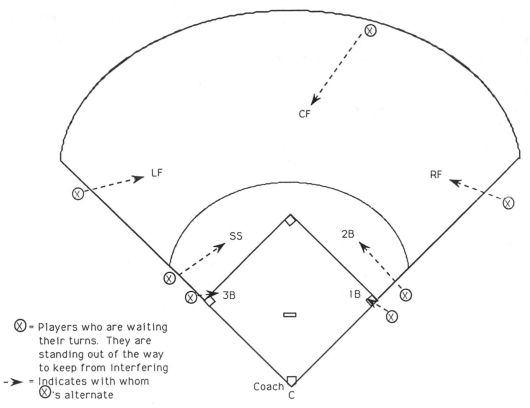

**Figure A-26.** Infield-outfield priority drill.

**Key Elements:**

- All players involved must be assertive.
- Balls should be called for loudly and repeatedly.
- If called off by an outfielder, the infielder must yield to him/her. The outfielder has priority over infielders and the CF has priority over all fielders.

**Common Errors:**

- Poor/no communication.
- Expecting someone else to catch the ball.

**Modifications:**

- Tennis balls may be used for less-skilled players. The primary emphasis is on calling for the ball and priorities. Catching skills should be stressed in more specific drills.
- For more advanced players, the coach can increase the difficulty of the pop-ups.

**Name:** Outfield Priority Drill (see Figure A-27)

**Objective:** To promote and facilitate communication and back-up skills among outfielders

**Suggested for:** Intermediate and advanced players

**Description:** The coach hits or throws a ground ball between two outfielders. The outfielder with the best position yells "Mine!" and fields the ball while the other outfielder backs up the play. If both fielders call for the ball, the CF has priority.

**Key Elements:**

- The outfielder must call for the ball loudly!
- CF has priority over the other two outfielders.
- Outfielders must assume their roles quickly.
- The non-fielding outfielder backs up the play.

**Common Errors:**

- Failure to yield to the center fielder when both fielders call for the ball.
- Failure to back up the play.
- Fielders do not "take charge" and immediately call for the ball, especially the CF.

**Modifications:**

- The drill can also be done with two lines of outfielders, one line being the designated CF.
- For less-experienced players, the coach may make the ball easier to field, so the outfielders may focus on priorities, calling for the ball and backing up the play.

**418   YOUTH SOFTBALL: A COMPLETE HANDBOOK**

**Name:** Relay Drill (see Figure A-28)

**Objective:** To help players learn, practice, and improve relay throws

**Suggested for:** Intermediate and advanced skill levels

**Description:** This drill is a race to see which row of players can most quickly get the ball from one end of the row to the other, and back again. A ball is placed on the same end of each of the rows. The coach says "Go," and the first player in each row throws the ball to the next player, and so on until the ball travels to the end of the row and back again. The first row to finish is the "winner."

**Key Elements:**

- The receiver keeps the arms up, makes the catch, and turns to throw.
- Throws should be chest high.

**Common Errors:**

- The player receiving the ball does not hold his/her arms up as a target.
- The player catching the ball does not step toward the target as the ball is caught.
- The thrower overthrows the target.

**Name:** Basic Relay Drill (see Figure A-29)

**Objective:** To introduce the basic relay and provide practice for enhancing relay throws

**Suggested for:** All skill levels

**Description:** *Balls are placed an equal distance beyond each outfielder. On the coach's signal, the outfielders sprint to the ball. A fielder lines up the relay players in order to maintain a straight line between all the players involved in the play. The relay person correctly receives the outfielder's throw and throws it to the appropriate fielder to complete the play.

**Modifications:**

- For more advanced players, the distance between the players in each row may be increased.
- As players become more proficient at this drill, each row may be rearranged so that players are staggered to the left and right of each other.
- For lower-skilled players, each group may be timed, with the goal of decreasing the time needed to complete the drill.

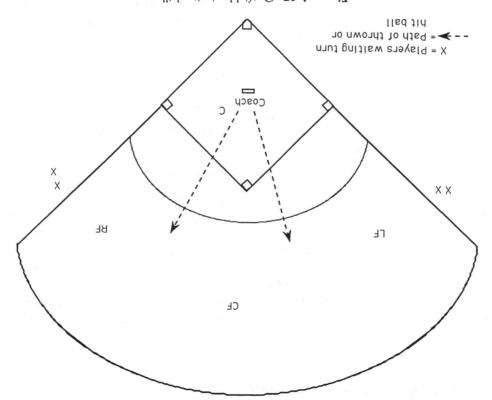

**Figure A-27.** Outfield priority drill.

X = Players waiting turn
- - = Path of thrown or hit ball

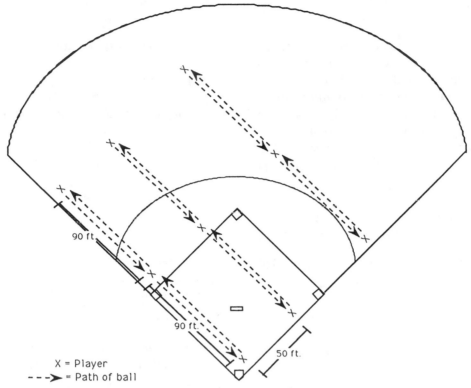

90 ft.

90 ft.

50 ft.

X = Player
- - -➤ = Path of ball

**Figure A-28.** Relay drill.

**Key Elements:**

- The fielder must provide loud, verbal commands.
- The relay person keeps the arms up and provides instruction to the outfielder (i.e., "hit me").
- The relay person turns to the glove side to relay the throw.
- The relay person should move to catch all throws in the air. A ball that bounces is harder to field.

**Common Errors:**

- The relay person looks to throw the ball before it is caught.
- The outfielder overthrows the relay person.
- The relay person makes a poor throw.
- Players fail to communicate.

**Modifications:**

- The distance between players may be increased or decreased according to the strength and accuracy of the fielders' throwing arms.
- Highly skilled players may compete with other groups. The first line to complete the relay is the "winner."

- The ball may be relayed from one end of the line to the other, and back again.

*Players are divided into equal groups of three or more. Players are arranged in lines across the field with about 60 ft. between each line. Players within a line are spaced 60 to 80 ft. apart with outfielders at the outfield end of the line and 2B and SS next in line.

**Hitting**

**Name:** Shadow Drill

**Objective:** To reinforce correct weight transfer when swinging a bat

**Suggested for:** Players of all skill levels

**Description:** The hitter assumes the hitting ready position with the sun or a bright light at his/her back. Another player places a ball on the shadow cast by the hitter's head. The batter swings the bat, holds the follow through and checks the shadow. If the ball is still on the head shadow, no weight transfer took place. If the ball is not on the head shadow, the other

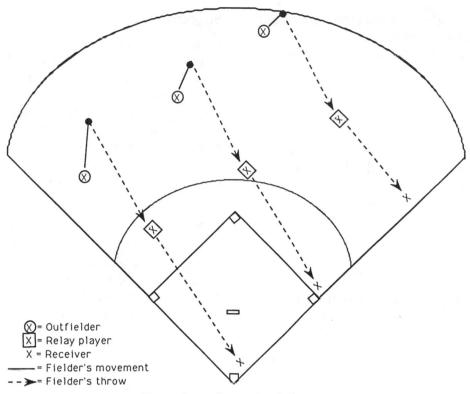

= Outfielder
= Relay player
X = Receiver
——— = Fielder's movement
- - ➤ = Fielder's throw

**Figure A-29.** Basic relay drill.

player places another ball on the new shadow in order to show how much the head moved forward and subsequently, how much weight transfer occurred.

**Key Elements:**

- The shadow must be clear!
- The batter's swing must be as if hitting a pitch.
- The weight shifts against the front foot rather than over the front foot.

**Common Errors:**

- Moving the weight over the front foot, thus moving the head.
- Swinging "easy" in order to keep the head still.
- Overstriding, causing the head to lower.

**Modifications:**

- If the hitter cannot keep the weight from shifting forward, a heavy rubber cord around the waist can be used to keep the midline steady. The hitter should focus on the difference between moving forward and moving against.

**Name:** Hip Rotation Drill

**Objective:** To promote correct stride and hip rotation for hitting (this drill can also be used as a warm-up technique in the on-deck circle)

**Suggested for:** All skill levels

**Description:** A bat is placed behind the player's back and is held parallel to the ground by the elbow joints of each arm. The hitter assumes the hitting ready position and strides with the front foot. The weight shifts against the front foot as the hips quickly rotate forward.

**Key Elements:**

- The stride is about 6-8 in., and the front foot is pointed about 45 degrees on a line from the pitcher to home plate.
- The weight shifts against the front leg and the front leg pushes forcefully against the ground in order to rotate the hips forward.
- At the end of the movement, the belt buckle should point toward the pitcher.

**Common Errors:**

- Overstriding.

- Shifting the weight over the front foot rather than against the front foot.
- Rotating forward by leading with the shoulders. This increases the friction between the bat and the arms and the arms may become sore.

**Modifications:**

- Advanced players can kneel on the back knee in order to execute the drill. This will reduce the effect of front knee extension but will help the player keep the weight from moving over the front leg.

**Name:** Batting Tee Drill (see Figure A-30)

**Objective:** To supplement the regular batting practice and to work on hitting mechanics

**Suggested for:** All skill levels

**Description:** The batting tee is positioned 6-8 ft. from a fence or net and away from any rigid support poles. Batters attempt to hit line drives into the fence. Batters can: (1) work individually and focus on specific hitting mechanics, one item at a time, or (2) work in pairs and focus on reinforcing a correct swing by doing a specific number of repetitions. When working in pairs, the non-hitter places balls on the tee until all balls have been hit.

**Key Elements:**

- Any type of ball can be used to hit off the tee. Used softballs, baseballs, or flat tennis balls are good to use for this drill.
- Each tee station should have balls equal to the number of balls to hit.

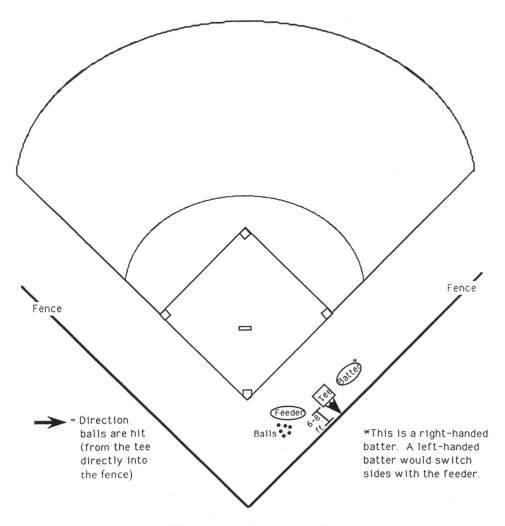

**Figure A-30.** Batting tee drill.

- When working in pairs, the player placing the ball on the tee must remain clear of the batter.

**Common Errors:**

- Hitters are too close to the tee and cannot fully extend their arms at contact.
- Players are even with the tee and cannot properly rotate their hips prior to contact.
- Practicing an incorrect swing reinforces that incorrect swing. It is important that the batter have a correct swing before practicing it on the tee.

**Modifications:**

- Less-skilled players may execute this drill using a larger ball. The larger ball will provide a greater chance of success.
- Highly skilled players can adjust the height and location of the tee in order to practice the swing required to hit pitches in various locations.
- The tee can be placed at home plate with the batter hitting to a defense. The batter practices hitting while the defense practices situation play.

**Name:** Soft Toss Hitting Drill (see Figure A-31)

**Objective:** To isolate and enhance components of the swing—also provides variety for batting practice

**Suggested for:** All skill levels

**Description:** Players work in groups of two, one being the hitter the other being the "feeder." The feeder kneels opposite the hitting side of home plate with a bucket of balls and tosses the ball underhand in the strike zone. The hitter

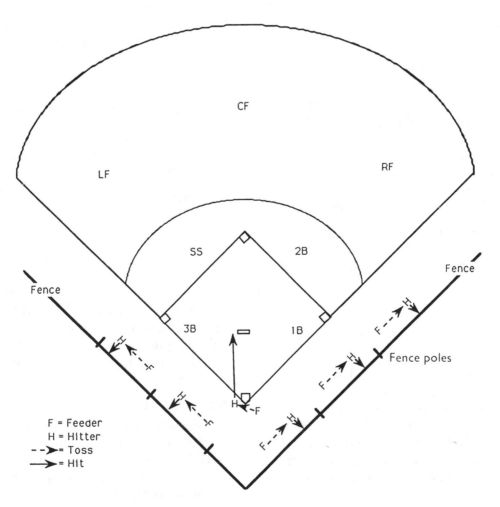

**Figure A-31.** Soft toss hitting drill.

attempts to hit line drives. Balls can be hit into an open field or into a net or fence. For safety reasons, groups must be spread out and clear of hitting into rigid fence poles.

**Key Elements:**

- The feeder must toss the ball in front of the hitter.
- The feeder should limit the arc and speed of the toss.
- The hitter should concentrate on a specific component of hitting or on hitting hard line drives.
- The hitter should focus on hitting one toss at a time.

**Common Errors:**

- The tosses are unhittable (i.e., at the hitter).
- Timing of the toss is too slow or too fast.
- The hitter shifts the weight over the front foot.
- The hitter drops his/her hands and swings up at the ball.

**Modifications:**

- The toss can be placed in a variety of locations for more experienced players.
- The hitter can hit to a defense so that batted balls are used as fielding practice for the fielders.
- The type and size of ball can vary—tennis balls, baseballs, plastic golf balls, etc.
- The hitting implement can vary—dowel rod, broomstick handle, tee-ball bat, etc.

**Name:** Power Swing Drill

**Objective:** To increase hitting power and strength

**Suggested for:** Intermediate and advanced hitters

**Description:** Starting in a correct batting stance, the batter takes a full swing with a weighted bat. After completing the follow-through phase, the batter returns the bat to the original position and repeats the swing. Initially, the batter may do one set of 10 repetitions. The number of sets may gradually increase as strength increases (i.e., three sets of 10).

**Key Elements:**

- Focus on feeling and maintaining a correct swing. If the swing cannot be repeated 10 times correctly, reduce the number of repetitions or the weight on the bat.
- The eyes should focus on a fixed object throughout the swing in order to promote correct head position.
- Execute the swing at full speed.

**Common Errors:**

- The batter begins to return the bat for the next swing before completing the follow-through.
- The bat is too heavy and the batter cannot execute a correct swing
- The batter does not concentrate, resulting in "lazy," incorrect repetitions.

**Modifications:**

- Younger batters should execute this drill with their regular bat.
- **\*** This drill can be executed in shoulder-deep water with a regular bat in order to obtain constant resistance.

**Name:** Pepper Game Drill (see Figure A-32)

**Objective:** To enhance hand-eye coordination and agility necessary to perform fielding and batting drills

**Suggested for:** Intermediate and advanced skill levels

**Description:** Players work in groups of three or four. One player is the batter and the other players are fielders. A fielder throws a ball to the batter and the batter hits the ball on the ground to any of the fielders in the group, using a half-swing. The fielder fields the ground ball and quickly lobs it back to the batter. After 10-15 swings, the batter and one fielder trade positions.

**Key Elements:**

- The batter takes a half-swing.
- The batter should attempt to hit the ball to each fielder.
- Fielders must work on quickly fielding and throwing the ball.

- Extra balls should be kept nearby in order to replace missed balls.

**Common Errors:**

- Lack of intensity and concentration.
- The batter swings too hard, endangering the fielders.
- Fielders shift their weight to their heels when fielding ground balls.

**Modifications:**

- For more advanced players, decrease the number of players in each group and/or move the fielders closer to the batter.
- For lower-skilled players, rag balls or Incrediballs may be used to ensure safety.
- More advanced players can be moved to "the end of the line" with a bad throw or a fielding error.
- Introduce competition between groups by counting the number of hits in a given time.

**Bunting**

**Name:** Soft Toss Bunting Drill

**Objective:** To practice giving with both arms while executing a sacrifice bunt

**Suggested for:** Beginning, intermediate, and advanced bunters

**Description:** Players work in groups of two—one player is the bunter, the other player is the tosser. The tosser stands about 10 ft. in front of the bunter and tosses the ball to the bunter. The bunter, already squared to the tosser, absorbs the force of the toss by giving equally with both arms. Because of the slow speed of the toss, if executed correctly, the ball will drop directly to the ground. After 7-10 bunts, the players switch roles.

**Key Elements:**

- The bat is held at the top of the strike zone with the arms extended.

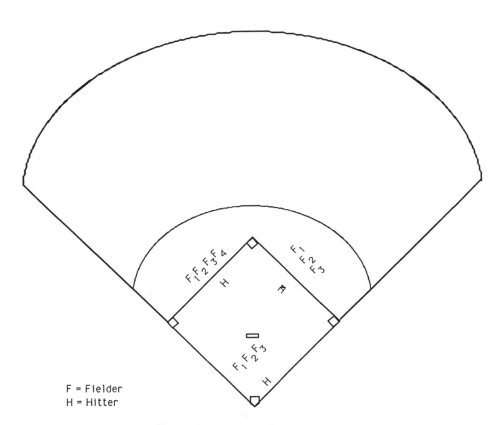

F = Fielder
H = Hitter

**Figure A-32.** Pepper game drill.

- The eyes follow the center of the ball to the center of the bat.
- Both arms give equally to absorb the force of the toss and drop the ball directly to the ground.

### Common Errors:
- The bunter gives with one arm only, usually the arm near the top of the bat.
- The bunter attempts to bunt tosses that are not in the strike zone. If the bat is held at the top of the strike zone, anything above the bat is a ball.
- The bunter starts with the arms flexed, then extends the arms to the ball and pushes it back to the tosser.

### Modifications:
- The batter starts in the hitting ready position then squares around or pivots to the bunting position. Once in the bunting position, the tosser tosses the ball.
- The tosser moves to 20 ft. in front of the bunter and the bunter practices the bunt for a hit.

**Name:** Target Bunting Drill (see Figure A-33)

**Objective:** To improve bunting accuracy and consistency

**Suggested for:** Intermediate and advanced bunters

**Description:** A target is placed on each baseline, approximately 10 ft. from the plate and 3 ft. inside the baseline. Wearing a helmet, a bunter squares or pivots and attempts to bunt the pitch as close to the target as possible.

### Key Elements:
- Strikes should consistently be thrown.
- The bunter should be selective and bunt only strikes.
- The bunter should work on timing the square or pivot.
- Proper bunting technique should be used.

### Common Errors:
- Bunting pitches that are not strikes.
- Dropping the bat away from the eyes.
- Pushing the ball rather than catching the ball with the bat.

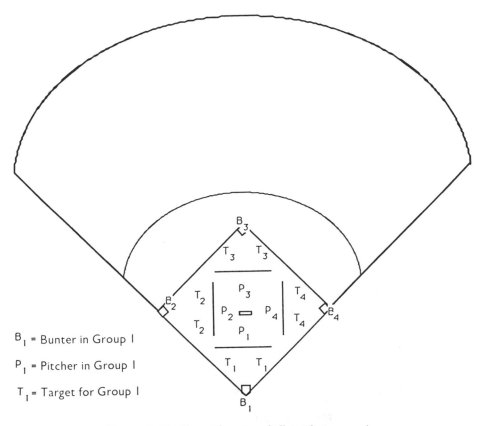

$B_1$ = Bunter in Group I

$P_1$ = Pitcher in Group I

$T_1$ = Target for Group I

**Figure A-33.** Target bunting drill (with 4 groups).

**Modifications:**

- More experienced players can alternate sacrifice bunts and bunts for hits.
- Players can be placed into groups (i.e., infielders versus outfielders) and groups can compete for accuracy points.

**Name:** Bunt and Slap Drill (see Figure A-34)

**Objective:** To practice the various types of bunts and the slap against a live defense—also, to practice defensive reactions to bunt situations

**Suggested for:** Intermediate and advanced skill levels

**Description:** A batter decides before entering the batter's box whether he/she will execute: (1) a bunt, or (2) a slap. As a pitcher prepares to pitch, the batter squares around to bunt. If the pitch is in the strike zone, the batter executes the play.

**Key Elements:**

- Pitchers should throw strikes consistently.
- Players must duplicate the intensity and concentration of a game situation.
- The batter can wait for the ball to approach the plate and bunt for a hit.

**Common Errors:**

- The batter attempts to bunt pitches that are not strikes.
- The batter does not decide before entering the batter's box which bunt to execute.

**Modifications:**

- For more advanced players, pitchers can throw a variety of pitches (i.e., drop ball, change-up).
- The coach can give signs to the batter, simulating a game situation.
- The coach can act as the pitcher.
- Advanced players may use pickoff plays in order to keep the base runners "honest."

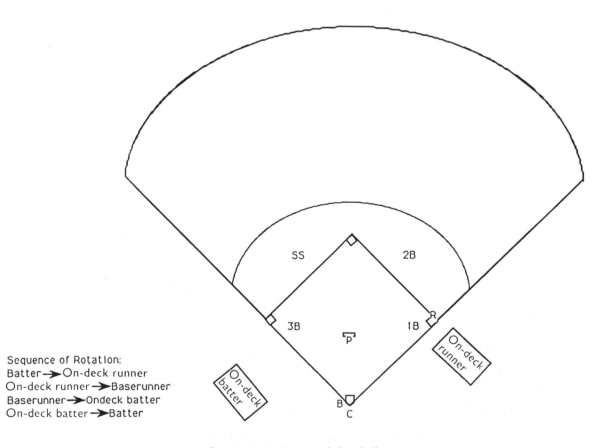

**Figure A-34.** Bunt and slap drill.

## Baserunning

**Name:** General Baserunning Drill (see Figures A-35 to A-39)

**Objective:** Players correctly practice touching and rounding bases (can also be used to condition players)

**Suggested for:** All skill levels

**Description:** Players line up behind home plate. The first player in line assumes the hitting ready position in the batter's box and pretends to swing and hit a pitch. The player runs hard to first base as if trying to beat out an infield ground ball. As the first player touches first base, the next player swings and runs, and so on. After passing first base, the runners slow down, turn toward the foul line and walk back to the end of the line. The next time through, each player will react as if hitting a single to the outfield. In successive rounds, each runner will "hit" a double, a triple, and an inside-the-park home run.

**Key Elements:**

- The run to first base is in foul territory.
- The bases are touched with the left foot, without slowing down.
- The runners should slow down gradually and return to the line without interfering with other runners.
- Baserunners must use correct technique and simulate game speed!

**Common Errors:**

- Not allowing enough time between runners; the faster runners have to slow down or pass the slower runners.
- Slowing as the base is approached or taking small steps in order to touch the base with the left foot.

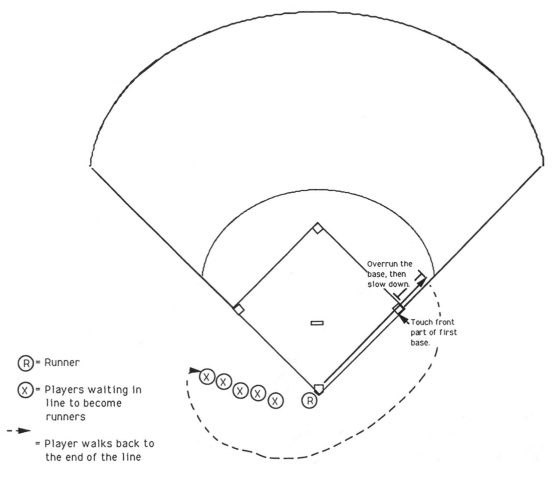

**Figure A-35.** General baserunning drill: Running out an infield grounder.

- Not running at full speed and/or running with the head down.
- Not concentrating on making changes when technique is incorrect.

**Modifications:**

- For less experienced players, the coach can walk the players through each step of the drill to familiarize them with the proper steps.
- More advanced players can do several repetitions for conditioning purposes.
- Traffic cones can be used as markers to direct the players where to look, when to arc, and what path to take.

**Name:** Rounding First Base Drill (see Figure A-40)

**Objective:** This drill is designed to teach players the proper techniques for round first base—this drill also emphasizes taking the extra base whenever possible

**Suggested for:** Players of all skill levels

**Description:** This drill requires players at 1B, 2B, 3B, SS, one OF, and runners lined up behind home plate. The first runner assumes the hitting ready position in the batter's box. The coach hits a hard ground ball to the outfielder, who either fields the ball or purposely misplays it. When the ball is hit, the runner runs to first base and rounds the base. As the base is rounded, the runner locates the ball and reacts accordingly. The runner should always expect an error! Second base and SS should work on the relay in the event the outfielder misses the ball.

**Key Elements:**

- The initial step to first base is a crossover step.
- On the third step, the runner looks to locate the ball and begins an arc in order to round the base.
- Upon rounding the base, the runner must focus on the fielding action of the outfielder, always anticipating an error.

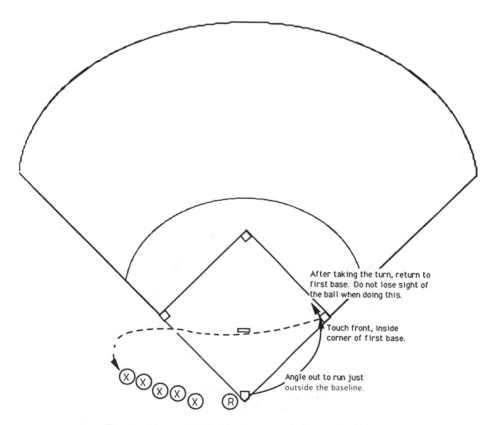

After taking the turn, return to first base. Do not lose sight of the ball when doing this.

Touch front, inside corner of first base.

Angle out to run just outside the baseline.

**Figure A-36.** General baserunning drill: Running out a single to the outfield.

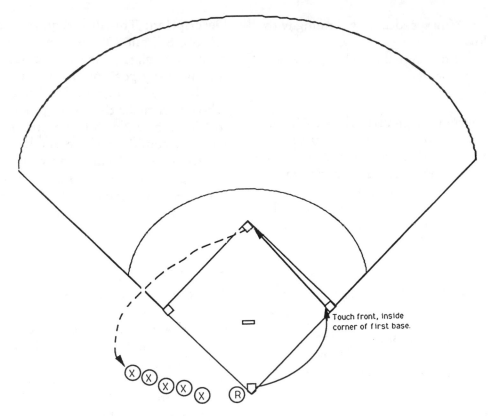

**Figure A-37.** General baserunning drill: Running out a double.

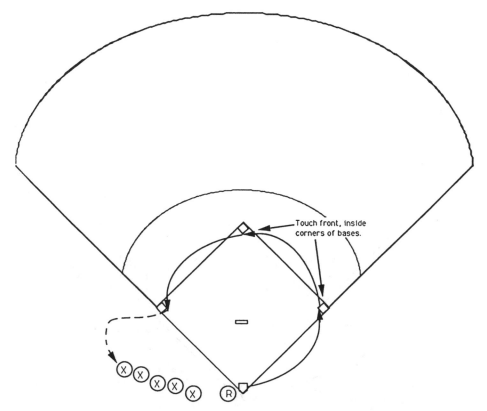

**Figure A-38.** General baserunning drill: Running out a triple.

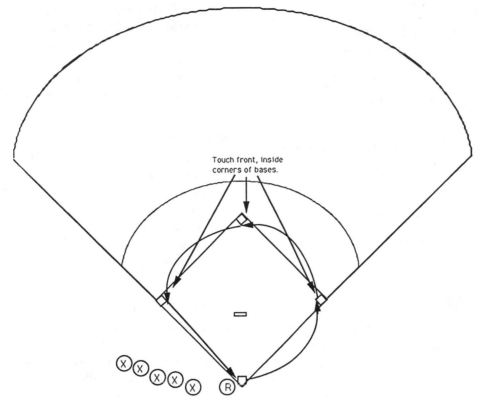

**Figure A-39.** General baserunning drill: Running out a home run.

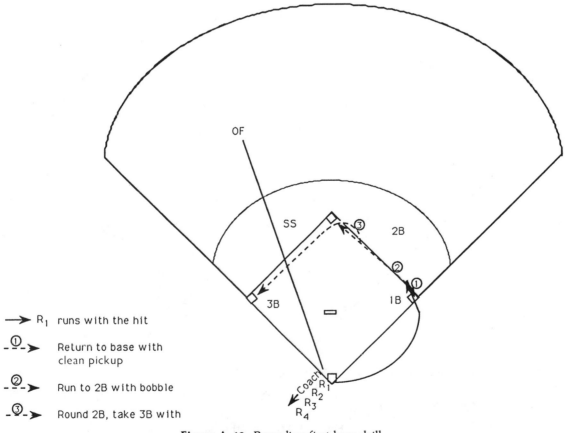

**Figure A-40.** Rounding first base drill.

**Common Errors:**

- Running with the head down.
- Turning too wide after first base has been touched.
- Assuming the fielder will field the ball and not advancing on a misplayed ball.

**Modifications:**

- A full team can be put on the field to simulate game conditions.

**Name:** Leadoff Drill (see Figure A-41)

**Objective:** To practice taking a proper lead and react assertively to a batted ball or to a catcher's action

**Suggested for:** All players

**Description:** This drill requires a pitcher, a catcher, a hitter, and baserunners at first base. Baserunners line up at three first bases, spaced 10 ft. apart behind the legal base. The pitcher throws the ball, the runners take a lead and watch the batter. The batter may: (1) swing at the ball (half-swing); (2) take the pitch; or (3) swing and miss. The baserunners break assertively for second base on batted balls that strike the ground or on pitched balls that are in the dirt. Runners return quickly to first base if the batter takes the pitch or swings and misses.

**Key Elements:**

- Runners must focus on the ball and react assertively!
- The runner should anticipate running to second base on every pitch.
- The runner should use the drill to recognize his/her own ability and ensure a correct reaction in a game.

**Common Errors:**

- Runners go through the motions and don't concentrate.
- Not enough variety of action—ground balls, pop-ups, passed balls, and blocked balls.
- Runners lose sight of the ball as they return to first base.

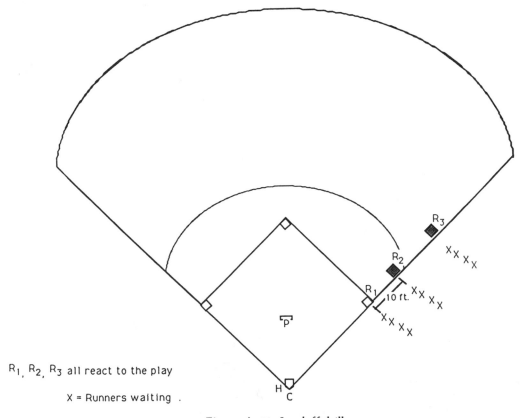

R$_1$, R$_2$, R$_3$ all react to the play

X = Runners waiting .

**Figure A-41.** Leadoff drill.

**Modifications:**
- Tennis or rag balls can be used indoors.
- If the runner on first base breaks for second base, the catcher can practice throwing him/her out.
- A first and second baseperson can be added and pickoffs can be practiced.

**Name:** Leading Off/Getting a Jump at First Base Drill (see Figure A-42)

**Objective:** Players practice taking leads, reading situations, and getting a jump in order to steal second base

**Suggested for:** All skill levels

**Description:** This drill requires a pitcher, catcher, 1B, and runners with helmets. The baserunners form a line in foul ground behind first base. One at a time, runners practice "getting a jump" as the pitcher throws a ball. If the runner attempts to steal on the pitch, he/she immediately sprints to second base as the pitch is thrown. Otherwise, the runner quickly returns to the base in order to avoid a pickoff. If the catcher mishandles the ball, the runner breaks to steal second base. After the runner steals he/she goes to the end of the line, and the next person in line becomes the baserunner.

**Key Elements:**
- The runner must concentrate on the pitcher's delivery.
- On a straight steal, the runner must sprint immediately with the pitch.
- If not stealing, the runner must react and move quickly.

**Common Errors:**
- Lack of concentration and intensity.
- Failure to react quickly.
- Failure to get a good jump off of the base.

**Modifications:**
- For experienced players, leads may be lengthened and players may work on diving back to the base.
- Leads from other bases should be practiced.

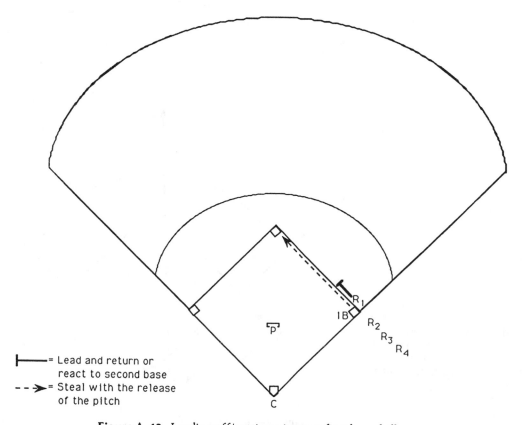

= Lead and return or react to second base

= Steal with the release of the pitch

**Figure A-42.** Leading off/getting a jump at first base drill.

**Name:** Tag Up Drill (see Figure A-43)

**Objective:** To teach runners at third base to take a proper lead, return to the base on a fly ball, and break for home plate when the ball is caught in the outfield

**Suggested for:** All skill levels

**Description:** Two additional third bases are placed in foul territory in line with the original base. Three runners take their leads toward home plate as the pitcher throws to a catcher. The coach hits a fly ball to the outfield. The runners tag up, watch the catch, and break for home.

**Key Elements:**
- Leadoff should be in foul territory.
- Players should watch the catch, usually with the left foot on the base.
- Runners must run at full speed.

**Common Errors:**
- Runners do not concentrate.
- Runners do not react at full speed.

- Runners lead off in fair territory, resulting in an out if hit by a batted ball.
- Runners leave the base too soon.

**Modifications:**
- Can be done during batting practice with the runner reacting to a real batter.
- Indoor drill can be done with tennis balls, with the coach throwing the fly balls.
- Outfielder can practice catching a fly ball and throwing it in one motion. The catcher can practice catching the outfield throw and tagging a runner.

**Name:** Finding Your Sliding Leg (see Figure A-44)

**Objective:** To teach and reinforce correct sliding technique

**Suggested for:** All skill levels

**Description:** Players spread out in the practice area and support their body with their hands and feet, belly facing skyward. On a command

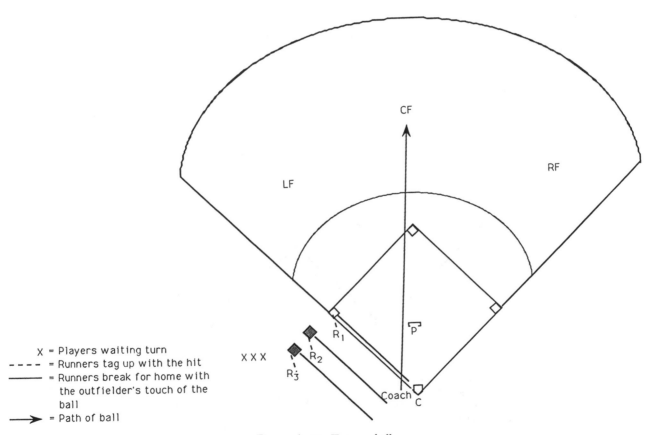

X = Players waiting turn
---- = Runners tag up with the hit
——— = Runners break for home with the outfielder's touch of the ball
——▶ = Path of ball

**Figure A-43.** Tag up drill.

from the coach, the players tuck one leg and settle to the ground. The leg that instinctively bends is generally the leg that bends when sliding. If either leg is comfortable, a bent left leg should be reinforced.

**Key Elements:**
- Inverted crab position should have chest parallel to the ground.
- The straight leg extends to the base.

**Common Errors:**
- Not snapping the bent leg under and kicking the straight leg out.
- Moving up to a sitting position as the leg tucks. Players should keep their head and shoulders back.

**Modifications:**
- Everyone sits on the ground with the legs extended. The players bend one leg under, then the other. The position that feels most comfortable should be used for sliding.

**Name:** Sliding Progression Drill (see Figure A-45)

**Objective:** To understand and learn the "Figure 4" straight-in slide

**Suggested for:** All skill levels

**Description:** When players know their sliding leg, they line up in a sliding area. The first player takes three steps and drops onto a sliding mat, bending the takeoff leg and extending the other leg. The chin stays down and the hands move up. As the player progresses, more steps are added prior to the takeoff. Eventually the players run the regulation distance to the base at full speed and slide on a sliding surface (i.e., cardboard).

**Key Elements:**
- The hands are in the air versus on the ground.
- The chin is on the chest.
- The runner should lean back on contact with the ground.

**Common Errors:**
- Taking too many steps too soon.
- Sitting up in the slide and jamming the knee into the ground.

(a)

(b)

**Figure A-44.** Finding your sliding leg drill.

**Figure A-45.** Sliding progression drill.

**Modifications:**
- The runners can slide on a plastic sheet with water or on wet grass.
- The runners can wear football pants for added protection during the learning process.

**Name:** Rundown Drill (see Figure A-46)

**Objective:** To introduce and reinforce the fundamentals of a rundown situation

**Suggested for:** Intermediate and advanced players

**Description:** Players work in groups of five on a pair of regulation bases. Two players are primary fielders, two players are back-up fielders, and one player is the runner. Primary Player A starts with the ball held high and visible, calls the side of the baseline, and chases the runner toward the opposite base. If the runner cannot be tagged, primary Player B, who is in front of the other base, yells "NOW!" in a timely manner. Player A snaps the ball to Player B who

moves to the throw and immediately tags the runner. If the runner cannot be immediately tagged, Player B chases the runner back, Player A moves to become a back-up player, and back-up Player 1 becomes a primary player.

**Key Elements:**
- The runner must wear a helmet.
- The action should take place at full speed with the runner trying to prolong the rundown by avoiding the tag.
- The fielders must be positioned on the same side of the baseline; the chaser must make the ball visible to the receiver.
- The receiver calls for the ball and moves into the throw.

**Common Errors:**
- Too many throws; the receiver calls for the ball too soon giving the runner time to change direction.
- The fielders are on opposite sides of the baseline causing the throw to cross the runner's path.

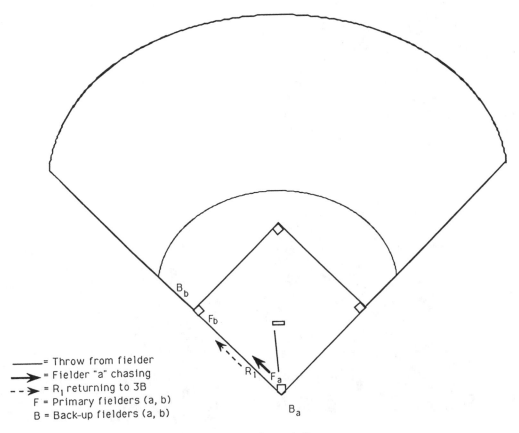

= Throw from fielder
= Fielder "a" chasing
= $R_1$ returning to 3B
F = Primary fielders (a, b)
B = Back-up fielders (a, b)

**Figure A-46.** Rundown drill.

- The chaser hides the ball in the glove. This makes it harder for the receiver to see it and also requires valuable time to move the ball into the throwing position.

**Modifications:**
- Tennis balls can be used for less-experienced players.

- A full infield and a runner at third can be used. The coach hits a ground ball, the runner on third breaks for home, and the batter runs to first base. The defense has to rundown the runner breaking from third and prevent the batter from reaching second base.
- Less-experienced players can initially be walked through the rundown.

# Index